Cognitive Motivation

Motivation and cognition were treated as separate concepts throughout most twentieth-century psychology. However, in recent years researchers have begun viewing the two as inextricably intertwined: not only does what we want affect how we think, but how we think affects what we want. In this innovative study, Beswick presents a new general theory of cognitive motivation, synthesising decades of existing research in social, cognitive and personality psychology. New basic concepts are applied to a wide range of purposive behaviour. Part I of the volume reviews different forms of cognitive motivation, such as curiosity, cognitive dissonance, achievement motivation and the search for purpose and meaning, while Part II examines the basic processes that underlie it, such as working memory, attention and emotion. The central concept is the incomplete gestalt, in which motivation is generated by a universal striving to integrate information and make sense at all levels of cognitive organization.

David Beswick is Professor Emeritus and Principal Fellow at the Centre for Positive Psychology, Melbourne Graduate School of Education, the University of Melbourne. He is a Life Member of the Australian Psychological Society, a Fellow of the Australian College of Educators and a minister in the Uniting Church in Australia. He was formerly director of the Melbourne Centre for the Study of Higher Education, before which he researched and taught in psychology and educational research at the Australian National University. He held visiting appointments at Berkeley, London and Uppsala, and has published more than 100 articles and monographs.

Cognitive Motivation

From Curiosity to Identity, Purpose and Meaning

David Beswick
The University of Melbourne

CAMBRIDGE
UNIVERSITY PRESS

CAMBRIDGE
UNIVERSITY PRESS

University Printing House, Cambridge CB2 8BS, United Kingdom

One Liberty Plaza, 20th Floor, New York, NY 10006, USA

477 Williamstown Road, Port Melbourne, VIC 3207, Australia

4843/24, 2nd Floor, Ansari Road, Daryaganj, Delhi – 110002, India

79 Anson Road, #06-04/06, Singapore 079906

Cambridge University Press is part of the University of Cambridge.

It furthers the University's mission by disseminating knowledge in the pursuit of education, learning, and research at the highest international levels of excellence.

www.cambridge.org
Information on this title: www.cambridge.org/9781107177666
DOI: 10.1017/9781316822920

First published 2017

Printed in the United Kingdom by Clays, St Ives plc

A catalogue record for this publication is available from the British Library.

ISBN 978-1-107-17766-6 Hardback

To Joan and Hazel

Contents

Preface

Beginning with the study of curiosity, this book presents a new general theory of motivation in which a few basic concepts are applied to a wide range of cognitive motivation. It is the result of two sustained bursts of research and writing separated by a decades-long career in academia and ministry. I first explored the subject of psychogenic motivation in the late 1950s and early 1960s in my doctoral work at Harvard. Although I did not know it at the time, I was working in the midst of a movement in psychology that became known later as the cognitive revolution. The founders of that movement combined an exalted academic style with a commitment to new principles that promised to reshape the way human thought, feeling and behaviour were understood. 'That revolution was intended to bring "mind" back into the human sciences after a long cold winter of objectivism,' some of the leaders aiming 'to establish meaning as the central concept of psychology – not stimuli and responses' (Bruner 1990, pp. 1–2). As a PhD student, my contribution was a cognitive process theory of curiosity in which I explained curiosity as a result of conceptual conflict. Reflecting on this work some 40 years later I found that I was dissatisfied with the narrowness of my explanatory dynamic – in particular, its failure to give a greater motivational role to emotion. I began to explore the many lines of research that spanned the intervening years, and I soon encountered George Loewenstein's review of the subject (Loewenstein 1994), in which he propounded a general principle that curiosity is motivated by gaps in knowledge. Could we explain this kind of motivation by reference to gaps rather than conflicts? I found this interesting but thought focussing on gaps was too negative, based as it was on a desire to escape unfavourable conditions created by a perceived deficiency.

At around that time (2001) I was contacted by a PhD student at Buffalo, Todd Kashdan, who has since published a significant book on curiosity (Kashdan 2009) and become a leader in the developing field of positive psychology. He favoured Lowenstein's gap theory, and in his later work he rejected my conceptual conflict model. Interestingly, he had the same objection to my model as I had to the gap theory: he thought it too negative. I agreed that curiosity should have a positive motivation, so we needed something other than gaps and conflicts that could nevertheless accommodate those two ideas. Reflecting on this, it occurred to me that there is an overarching concept that can account for both the gap theory and the conceptual conflict theory. I hit upon the idea of completing incomplete images, resolving both gaps and conflicts, and more – reaching for a new whole image or gestalt. Whether Gordon Allport had planted that idea in my mind at Harvard all those years ago, I cannot say, I probably had the rudiments of it from my studies at Melbourne, but I recalled his proposition from an earlier time: 'Motives are always a kind of striving for some form of completion' (Allport 1937b, p. 154). He was one who still found relevance in gestalt concepts, as did his once junior colleague Jerome Bruner. The idea of an incomplete gestalt offered itself to me as a general model of cognitive and affective processes that could provide for the filling of gaps in knowledge and the resolution of conceptual conflicts, and do so in such a way as to lead to a new creation. Gestalt theory was no longer at the forefront of cognitive psychology, but this idea pointed to the possibility of a general theory that extended the explanation of curiosity through the field of intrinsic motivation and beyond, to the full range of cognitive motivation. That was what I aimed to explore – the application of a few very basic ideas in a general theory to explain a wide range of related motivational phenomena.

Except as part of some applied work on education in later years, I had only been able to do a little more empirical work on curiosity myself around 1970. It was represented by my paper at the Toronto conference on intrinsic motivation in that year (Beswick 1971), and then the publication of my Intrinsic Motivation scale (Beswick 1974) while I was at the Australian National University (ANU) in Canberra, and in my article with Kast Tallmadge (Beswick and Tallmadge 1971) on aptitude-treatment interactions in reference to inductive reasoning in complex learning tasks when I was with him at American Institutes for Research in the Behaviorial Sciences (AIR) in Palo Alto, California. Then there was the work with Judy Boreham, in the Education Research Unit at ANU and in the Centre for the Study of Higher Education at the University of Melbourne, on the development of scientific interests and competence. That was in a longitudinal study of career development among students proceeding from secondary to higher education and entering the professions. We observed some interesting effects of intrinsic and extrinsic reward seeking among students in different kinds of courses (Beswick and Boreham 1986). At that time my thinking was also stimulated in a joint project with Paul Ramsden concerned with 'Curiosity and Learning with Understanding' (Ramsden, Beswick and Bowden 1986; Beswick and Ramsden 1987) in reference to deep and surface approaches to learning that had been described by Ference Marton in Sweden, who was in Melbourne briefly and who I visited at Gothenberg in 1986. I was encouraged to believe that not only were there useful practical implications of research on curiosity, but that field studies could yield some vital insights of theoretical significance which should have wide application in a general cognitive motivation theory.

I had, of course, been aware from an early stage of continuing work on curiosity over many years by researchers in the period after Berlyne's original foundation studies in the 1950s, such as that of Mary Ainley, Carol Sansone and Judith Harackiewicz, up to the 2000s. Especially, I kept in mind the provocative research on the suppressing effects of extrinsic rewards on intrinsic motivation by Edward Deci and others from 1971. However, I felt that Deci and his colleagues did not go far enough in breaking away from the old need or drive models of motivation. I had been persuaded of the necessity for a radical break by my original work on curiosity that had been reinforced particularly by my thesis adviser Robert White in his since much cited paper 'Motivation reconsidered: The concept of competence' (White 1959). I had been inducted by David McClelland into the study of what Henry Murray called psychogenic motives. I could see some overlap of his achievement motivation theory with my cognitive process theory of curiosity – hence the later prospect of a general theory that would apply not only to achievement motivation and curiosity but also to such motives as power and affiliation, as well as the theories of cognitive dissonance, attribution theory and self-efficacy. So I set about looking for the basic processes that underlie these different forms of cognitive motivation and I found at least some of them in studies of working memory and in the signalling function of emotions in motivation. I was then driven back to understand in greater depth the early gestalt theories of von Ehrenfels, Wertheimer, Köhler, Koffka and later Lewin.

The culture of the original group that worked on need for achievement had a pervasive influence. It was something I received from McClelland, especially his approach to assessment and the combination of creative insights with quantitative empirical methods in the field of personality research – a combination I had already learned to appreciate from the influence of Sam Hammond at Melbourne. The subsequent development of my understanding reflected other influences from those days: provision for the unique individual, even to the point of allowing for the possibility of a singularity in every person, is something that was inspired by Gordon Allport, together with a willingness to include contrary indications and hidden prospects I saw in Henry Murray; while on emotion and cognition I was influenced in different ways, both then directly and later from their publications, by three other of my teachers at Harvard: George Mandler, Walter Mischel and Jerome Bruner. Another was Elliot Aronson, but I learned much more from his later writings than from him at that time. The evaluation of 'non-intellectual factors' in learning mathematics for the School Mathematics Study Group (SMSG) at Yale led at Harvard by Richard Alpert supported some of my early survey research on curiosity.

Fellow graduate students Ralph Metzner, George Litwin and Merrill Carlsmith also contributed to my thinking. Metzner was working with Mischel on delay of gratification and shared with me in the curiosity and delay of gratification project reported in Chapter 2. Litwin, with whom I shared research assistance work for McClelland on achievement motivation, published a paper on risk taking and achievement motivation at this time with John W. Atkinson, with whom he had worked at Michigan. It was one of the foundations of expectancy-value theory discussed in Chapter 5. At this time also Carlsmith was co-author with Leon Festinger in their recently completed work at Stanford, their now classic study of cognitive dissonance from forced compliance, which I discuss in Chapter 4 – 'the single most important study ever undertaken in social psychology,' according to Aronson (1999, p. 106)

In regard to the theory of cognitive dissonance, I should confess that when I developed the cognitive process theory of curiosity (see Chapter 2) around 1960, shortly after Festinger's theory appeared, I avoided much discussion of cognitive dissonance. Dissonance was too close to what I wanted to say about the central role of conceptual conflict in motivation with which it might have been confused, and I wanted to make a completely different emphasis. The main difference, which became more apparent as the field developed, was that dissonance is an aversive state, but in cognitive motivation theory derived from the work on curiosity I am concerned more with positively attractive arousal in which the aim is not avoidance of an unpleasant state, but the prospect of satisfaction in developing whole new forms. I did not accept Festinger's aversive theory of arousal, although in retrospect it is obvious that I might have learned a good deal from his writing and from Aronson had I paid more attention to developments in the study of cognitive dissonance in the following years. I owe more to them than I was prepared to acknowledge at the time, although, of course, I still prefer positive alternatives to the aversive model.

These historical reflections are relevant to the treatment I have given many of the topics in this book. Although I have not aimed to write a book that is concerned primarily with the history of psychology, I hope that it might make a contribution to the history of this branch of psychological theory. I have traced many of the central ideas over a period of a hundred years or so. The historical treatment I have given to basic concepts in the general theory of cognitive motivation will contribute to the understanding of those concepts in depth and to the history of the various lines of research in which they were developed. At the same time I hope that the wide range of literature I have reviewed in its historical context will be a rich resource for new researchers in this field and for established scholars who might not be able to spare the time to search widely for the background of a topic of current interest.

The breadth and depth with which I have treated the main topics and the amount of information I have included raise a question about the best way to read this book. Relevant disciplines range from cognitive and affective neuroscience to personality and social psychology, including contemporary and historical accounts of cognition and motivation. Some sections are quite technical and others discursive, bridging into tangentially related fields like philosophy and literature. Although there is a logical sequence in the topics, which should be apparent in the chapter summaries, not every reader will want to read the whole work from beginning to end like a novel. It is intended to hold together as both a rich resource and a coherent account of the field rather than serve as a reference work on discreet subjects. I recommend taking the topics in the order in which they appear, but selective attention to topics of interest is likely, nevertheless, to be productive. For each chapter, there is a list of section and subsection headings in the Table of Contents and a summary appears at the end of the chapter. There are numerous cross-references between chapters that are designed to enable the reader to pursue related topics of interest, find further substantiation of the arguments being made and explore further implications. Particular sections may contain more detail than is useful to a particular reader. Except perhaps for the orientation given to the whole work in the Introduction, it should be possible to begin almost anywhere, skip on from part way through a chapter to a section of interest in another chapter and still construct a satisfying sequence.

I am indebted to the Melbourne Graduate School of Education in the University of Melbourne for providing me with an academic home and general support while I worked on this book after retirement, and especially its Centre for Positive Psychology in the later stages of the work. My previous position as director of the Centre for the Study of Higher Education at Melbourne was a base for much relevant background in applied research and basic theory, as was the Department of

Psychology and the Education Research Unit of the Research School of Social Sciences at the Australian National University. I should also acknowledge with real appreciation the time out from regular ministry, and their tolerance of my testing combination of interests in theology and psychology, that was extended to me over many years by the Victoria and Tasmania Synod of the Uniting Church in Australia and the former Victoria and Tasmania Conference of the Methodist Church of Australasia.

Many thanks are due to several scholars in Australia and overseas for comments on drafts of chapters at various stages of the work: I think particularly of Mary Ainley, Alan Baddeley, Roy Baumeister, David Beckett, Bruce Beswick, Reijo Byman, Norman Feather, Erica Frydenberg, Todd Kashdan, Jordan Litman, Ference Marton, Lindsey Oades, Jean Russell, Christine Siokou, Gavin Slemp, and Lea Waters. They are not, of course, responsible for any defects that remain. The contribution of my son Bruce has been significant both in his assistance with editing and through many hours of discussion that helped to clarify theoretical concepts.

It is with warm appreciation that I acknowledge the love and support of my wife Hazel while I worked on this book at a time when she might have expected more time together in retirement. It was time that my first wife Joan did not live to enjoy for long enough, but she too had shared gladly with much understanding my diverse and sometimes conflicting professional commitments.

Introduction: The Incomplete Gestalt

> Motives are always a kind of striving for some form of completion
> – Allport 1937

How we think affects what we want. It is usually put the other way around – what we want affects how we think – but it works both ways. Cognitive processes can have motivational effects, as well as being affected by motivation. It is well established in psychological research that there is a kind of motivation with many interesting properties that is cognitive in origin and explains some of the most basic and the most highly developed aspects of human behaviour and experience. This work explores a theory of cognitive motivation that brings together motivation and cognition in a way that explains a range of such motivation.

A prime example of cognitive motivation is curiosity in which attention to perceived novelty gives rise to conceptual conflict and awareness of gaps in knowledge. People then seek additional information, review their thinking and strive to overcome inconsistencies and gaps in their view of the world and themselves. Other examples of cognitive motivation include cognitive dissonance, achievement motivation, attribution theory, self-efficacy, competence for its own sake and various types of intrinsic motivation, in all of which there is some initial sense of incompleteness in one's conception of the world and oneself. Awareness of incompleteness motivates people to seek new information and reorganize present knowledge to form a new understanding of themselves and the world in which they live. That search for a new understanding defines a goal for purposive behaviour. Motivated behaviour is purposive by definition.

It is a common psychological conception that motivation both gives direction and impels action, and so it is with cognitive motivation. When behaviour is directed towards a goal, we assume that there are information-processing conditions within the individual that direct and energize behaviour for the attainment of that goal. As with all kinds of motivation, cognitive motivation is goal oriented, but its goals are often intrinsic to the motivated behaviour itself. It is not dependent upon the satisfaction of physiological needs, but on forms of information processing. In order to provide a theoretically useful basis for understanding behaviour with a purpose, however, the internal processes which constitute a particular type of motivation need to be explicated. It is not enough simply to name a motive or ascribe a need for whatever is defined as a goal. To advance psychological understanding we need to know how it works.

In the theory of cognitive motivation that I propose in this work, the internal conditions that we infer are not static, but dynamic: that is, we look for a *process* of motivation, not simply a motive state or disposition. The process of arousal and direction defined in this theory is called *cognitive* motivation because it is cognitive in origin and in its contents, as distinct from motivation that has physiological or other pre-programmed biological sources. But while cognitive in its processes, it is derived from both thoughts *and* feelings. In a theory of cognitive motivation we are concerned with processes that include cognitive elements representing emotions with physiological components which help to initiate and guide behaviour towards a goal.

It was common in 20th-century psychology to separate cognition from motivation, so that the term 'cognitive motivation' might not have appeared initially to make sense in the prevailing theoretical framework. In a fairly typical statement in the development of this field Gordon Allport said '[N]o theory of cognition, however dynamic, would give us the required foundation for a full-blooded psychology of personality. We need also a doctrine of motivation to explain the facilitating, inhibiting, selecting, and vivifying of our cognitive and behavioural systems' (Allport 1955, p. 15). The theory of cognitive motivation combines the two, cognition and motivation, in a single process. It does so by incorporating emotions as signs in cognitive functions.

Curiosity is the prime example of cognitive motivation. A cognitive process theory of curiosity (Beswick 1964, 1971) is presented in Chapter 2 as a model of the underlying processes of *intrinsic* motivation, which are then generalized to a broader concept of *cognitive* motivation. Curiosity is the prototypical example of intrinsic motivation in which motivation is inherent in the motivated activity itself, that is, in something done for its own sake rather than being a means to some other end (see Chapter 3). Intrinsic motivation falls within the scope of cognitive motivation, but not all cognitive motivation is strictly intrinsic. Some of the goals of other forms of cognitive motivation may be separable from the motivated behaviour which serves as a means to those ends. On the one hand, cognitive motivation includes competence for its own sake or 'effectance motivation' that is intrinsically rewarding (White 1959), while on the other, cognitive dissonance is an example in which extrinsic feedback from social interaction may be important in reconciling dissonant cognitions (Festinger 1957). In another example, achievement motivation can be rewarded either intrinsically or extrinsically – compare the satisfaction that an inventor receives in his or her own mind from a unique accomplishment with the accolades received from others by the winner of an Olympic race (McClelland, Atkinson, Clark and Lowell 1953). Attribution theory (Weiner 1986), self-efficacy (Bandura 1997) and personal searches for identity, purpose and meaning depend upon higher levels of cognitive organization that, while intrinsically rewarding in processes of self-understanding, incorporate feedback from external sources in social and personal developmental experiences (see Chapters 3, 6 and 12). There are different theories for each of these types of cognitive motivation. This work is an inquiry into the possibility that a general theory of cognitive motivation can be applied to all its forms.

The Incomplete Gestalt

The basic idea I suggest we explore is that cognitive processes have motivational effects as people strive for completion of incomplete images of the world, including themselves and their place in it. In the theory of cognitive motivation, as in other general cognitive theories, the images we have of the world and ourselves are organized in a cognitive map with dynamic properties which owe their effects to a general principle of striving for meaningful organization. This map is not only a simplified summary of past experience but a coherent meaningful representation which extends into images of the future. Cognitive processes have motivational effects when attention is focused on some point at which the organization of a cognitive map is incomplete, and purposive imagination conceives of possibilities for its completion. We form images of the future and compare them with the present state of affairs. We both see and feel the difference. Feelings guide us toward the fulfilment of our aspirations as we move conceptually from a present state to an imagined future state: '[T]he difference between a desired state and a current state drives the organism toward reducing that difference' (Austin and Vancouver 1996, p. 340). It is a basic principle of the theory of cognitive motivation, however, that we never arrive exactly at a previously imagined position. New forms emerge and a new order is established as new information is processed in the resolution of what I call an *incomplete gestalt*, the key concept in this theory. The aim of the resolution is not simply to overcome deficiencies, but to achieve growth of organization and meaning (Hebb 1949; Bruner 1990) so as to make sense of what is happening and equip the person to cope more effectively with future challenges. There is a similar set of assumptions in the recently developed meaning maintenance model (Heine, Proulx and Vohs 2006) which I discuss in Chapter 1 and at other points.

Many theorists in the early and mid-20th century, such as Woodworth, Allport, Hebb, Bruner, Hunt, McReynolds and the Gestalt psychologists, suggested directly or indirectly that there is an inherent tendency in the way the brain processes information for the level of organization to be increased. In this view it is to be expected that there is a tendency for an incomplete image to be transformed into a more nearly complete form, or gestalt, that stands out from a background. This is a basic hypothesis in the cognitive motivation theory. Recent developments in biological and physical sciences have described 'self-organizing systems' similar to those suggested by the early Gestalt psychologists, Köhler in particular (see Chapter 9). In this theory it is assumed that self-organizing systems in the brain produce new forms of order, so that identifiable gestalts[1] appear. As a new order develops, at a point of transition between chaos and cosmos, people strive for 'some form of completion,' to use Allport's term for the goal of all kinds of motivation (Allport 1937b, p. 154; see also Allport 1937a). In the process that I describe, an incomplete gestalt is the engine which drives cognitive motivation: it is a motivating force that gives direction to goal-oriented activity and energizes behaviour for that purpose. Its varying effects in different types of cognitive motivation depend upon the specific contents of an image or schema, the different ways in which it can be incomplete and the various strategies that may be adopted for its completion.

Cognitive approaches to motivation have been developed over the past half-century or so, but no general theory of cognitive motivation has been put forward. What was known previously as a cognitive 'approach' may be seen as a step towards a cognitive theory of motivation. A cognitive view of motivation in general is represented in Kagan's definition of a motive as 'a cognitive representation of a future goal state that is desired' (Kagan 1972, p. 54). That definition could have a very wide application, but I propose a theory of cognitive motivation which applies to only certain types of motivation. That is, I do not aim

[1] I am using the Anglicized forms of the German word *gestalt* and its plural *gestalten*, but I intend the term to have the meaning given to it by the Gestalt theory pioneers: von Ehrenfels, Wertheimer, Köhler and Koffka. As in the original Gestalt theory, by 'gestalt' I mean a form, image or whole unit of perception or conception that coheres as a single entity and is different from the sum of its parts (see Chapter 9).

to give a general account of all motivation, but only motivation that falls within the wide range of cognitive motivation. There are signs, however, of a general theory of all kinds of motivation being developed in the foreseeable future.

In a recent paper which appeared too late to be taken fully into account for this book, Baumeister has suggested some steps 'Towards a general theory of motivation' (Baumeister 2016). His purpose was to look ahead to 'a broad understanding of motivation that would apply across multiple domains of desire and motivated behaviour' (p. 1). He too refers to the last half-century as a time in which emphasis has shifted to cognitive processes, and to the present as a time when motivation has generated renewed interest, and he argues, as I do, that a full understanding must encompass both cognition and motivation in a new conceptual paradigm. I agree with him on the basic function of emotion acting with cognition in the service of motivation, and on the emergence of new forms of motivation like the search for meaning. He has some very interesting suggestions on the nature of possible long-term change in the base level to which motivational arousal returns in an equilibrium type of motivation. I differentiate cognitive motivation from the equilibrium model, but his idea of adaptation could fit quite well with my argument for the resolution of an incomplete gestalt never returning the system to a previous state. He concludes with a hope 'that moving toward a general theory of motivation will help psychology as a whole acknowledge and embrace the fundamental importance of motivation in the grand scheme of integrative psychological theory' (p. 9). I do not aim to offer a general theory of motivation, but a theory applicable to the limited range of *cognitive* motivation which I define in Chapter 1. However, it would be consistent with my general theory of cognitive motivation if, 'in the grand scheme of integrative psychological theory' (p. 9), a general theory of all motivation was built upon the principles of cognitive, personal and social *integration*.

Cognitive motivation occurs in a variety of forms, including cognitive dissonance (Chapter 4), achievement motivation (Chapter 5), attribution and self-efficacy (Chapter 6), as well as curiosity (Chapter 2), competence and intrinsic motivation in general (Chapter 3). I will attempt to identify the cognitive processes that underlie these examples and help to explain cognitive motivation in general. Among the underlying processes with explanatory power are those of conscious cognitive integration which take place in working memory (Chapter 7), the function of emotions as signals for the changing relationship of a person to a goal in the course of purposive activity (Chapter 8) and the processes of meaningful organization that guide the pursuit of goals and intentions (Chapters 9 and 10). Some of the examples, like curiosity, achievement motivation and self-efficacy, will be discussed in detail in Part I of the book, and the more general underlying cognitive processes in working memory, consciousness, emotions, goals and intentions will be discussed in Part II, which concludes with applications of the general theory to identity, purpose and meaning in Chapters 11 and 12.

Summary

There is a kind of motivation with many interesting properties that is cognitive in origin. A prime example of cognitive motivation is curiosity (Chapter 2). Others include cognitive dissonance (Chapter 4), achievement motivation (Chapter 5), attribution theory and self-efficacy (Chapter 6), competence for its own sake, various types of intrinsic motivation (Chapter 3) and the search for meaning and purpose in life (Chapter 12), in all of which there is some initial sense of incompleteness in one's conception of the world and oneself. Awareness of incompleteness motivates people to seek new information and reorganize present knowledge to form a new understanding of themselves and the world in which they live. A key concept in this theory is the idea of an *incomplete gestalt*. We look for a *process*, not simply a state of motivation. It is a process that tends to complete new whole images that stand out from a background.

While cognitive in its processes, cognitive motivation is derived from both thoughts *and* feelings. A cognitive process theory of curiosity is presented as a model of the underlying processes of *intrinsic* motivation, which are then generalized to a broader concept of *cognitive* motivation. Among the underlying processes with explanatory power are those of conscious cognitive integration which take place in working memory (Chapter 7), the function of emotions as signals for the changing relationship of a person to a goal in the course of purposive activity (Chapter 8) and the role of goals and intentions (Chapters 9 and 10). Some of the examples, such as curiosity, achievement motivation and self-efficacy, are discussed in detail in Part I of the book, and the more general underlying cognitive processes in working memory, consciousness, emotions, intentions, purpose and meaning are discussed in Part II. The same basic processes found at the micro level in curiosity can be applied at the macro level of personal identity, purpose and meaning (Chapters 11 and 12).

Part I

Forms of Cognitive Motivation

1 Towards a General Theory of Cognitive Motivation

> In cognitively generated motivation, people motivate themselves and guide their actions anticipatorily by exercising forethought.
>
> – Bandura 1991

Introduction

A general theory is prefigured in the idea that cognitive processes such as those generating expectancies, attribution of causes, evaluations and beliefs about one's capacity to produce an effect are common processes that have motivating properties. This work is concerned with a general theory of cognitive motivation with the aim of giving an account of how these processes work, and which applies to all levels cognitive organisation. The basic processes are seen in curiosity in which people make an approach response to a novel object, review their cognitive map of the world and themselves and seek additional information to resolve conceptual conflicts or gaps in knowledge. We will explore the application of the same model from the micro level of perceptual responses to complex behaviour at the macro level of the whole person acting with purpose and meaning in a social context.

While a 'cognitive approach' is not the same thing as a theory of cognitive motivation, it is a step along the way to a general theory. A range of cognitive approaches to motivation has been illustrated in textbooks and collected works such as Weiner (1974b), Dalgleish and Power (1999) and Petri and Govern (2004). In the volume edited by Weiner, Bolles reviewed the historic trend in a number of cognitive views of human motivation (Bolles 1974). Emphasis on rationality in the basic explanation of behaviour from Plato on made the original psychology in Western culture necessarily cognitive, but then came Watson's behaviourism (Watson 1913) and the trial-and-error reinforcement theory of Thorndike (1911, 1913, 1935); and, of course, Freud appealed to the irrational at that time. Bolles emphasised also the later historic importance of the systematic observation of the phenomena of motivation which began in the Gestalt tradition in Berlin (Lewin, Heider and Heider 1936). It was followed by related developments in the United States with Tolman (1932/1949), from which came the idea of purposive behaviour guided by a cognitive map (Tolman 1948). Tolman's cognitive approach combined a motivational matrix embodying constructs like the value of a goal object with a second matrix which contained primarily the construct of expectancy, a cognitive concept. Moving closer to the present day, in his understanding of motivation and reinforcement as at least dependent in part on cognition, Bolles took note of the cognitive approach to emotions by Lazarus, which was then being developed (Lazarus 1974). This provided a basis for the incorporation of affective components into a cognitive theory of motivation.

Developing Ideas of Cognitive Motivation

The term 'cognitive motivation' has appeared previously in reference to a loosely defined type of motivation which has various forms, but without a theory of the common basic processes of cognition that provide motivation in those different forms. It was used by Paul McReynolds when he began to develop an account of its underlying processes. In his historical review of early research on intrinsic motivation McReynolds described '[t]he three faces of cognitive motivation' with optimization principles for the assimilation of novel inputs, innovation in the category system, and completion of cognitive commitments (McReynolds 1971, p. 33). In the relatively few instances where the term 'cognitive motivation' has been used for a general class of motivation, however, different theories have been put forward to account for different examples of it. So, for example, when Bandura used related terms he said, 'One can distinguish three forms of cognitive motivators around which different theories have been built. These include *causal attributions*, *outcome expectancies*, and *cognized goals*. The corresponding theories are attribution theory, expectancy-value theory, and goal theory' (Bandura 1991, p. 71). Apart from its use in reference to a class of motivation, the term has also been employed with a specific operational definition of individual differences in 'need for cognition' as 'dispositional differences in cognitive motivation' (Cacioppo, Petty and Kao 1984; Cacioppo, Petty, Feinstein and Jarvis 1996).

In his social cognitive theory (see Chapter 6) Bandura distinguishes three broad classes of motivation: 'One class of motivators is biologically based and includes biological conditions arising from cellular deficits and external aversive events' (Bandura 1991, p. 69); '[t]he second class of motivators operates through social incentives' (p. 70); and '[t]he third major source of motivators is cognitively based. In cognitively generated motivation, people motivate themselves and guide their actions anticipatorily by exercising forethought. They anticipate likely outcomes of prospective actions, they set goals for themselves, and they plan courses of action designed to realize valued futures.' Bandura referred to 'the capability for self-motivation and purposive action' as being 'rooted in cognitive activity' (p. 71). That cognitive activity on which cognitive motivation is based is the subject of much of this book in which I propose a general theory for the various types of cognitive motivation.

As with most other psychological concepts, there were forerunners of the idea of cognitive motivation in the work of William James. It is seen, for example, in his remarks on curiosity and 'the philosophical brain' which 'responds to an inconsistency or a gap in knowledge' (James 1890, Vol. 2, pp. 429–430). Similarly, without the same terminology, there are examples from early 20th-century experimental psychology in the writings of R. S. Woodworth (1918, 1921). Woodworth referred particularly to the intrinsically rewarding character of such motivation as a kind of drive or instinct that was 'less concerned with the struggle for existence than with the joy of living' (Woodworth 1921, p. 139) (see Chapter 3). In personality theory a little later Gordon Allport advanced a theory of the functional autonomy of motives which was cognitive in its basic conception (Allport 1937b). At about the same time, Henry Murray made an early differentiation of psychogenic from physiological needs (Murray 1936, 1938). Lewin, Tolman, Hebb and Harlow developed somewhat similar conceptions of psychogenic needs and neurogenic needs which were not dependent on tissue deficits (see Chapters 2 and 3). Until the 1950s these were still minority positions.

By the mid-20th century, however, a basic change was developing. Harlow introduced explicitly the concept of intrinsic motivation (Harlow 1950) which had been implicit in the work of Woodworth and Allport. It has since been highly developed by Deci and others (Deci 1975; Ryan and Deci 2000c; Sansone and Harackiewicz 2000a). At the time of the cognitive revolution in psychology in the late 1950s (Baars 1986), Robert White wrote a seminal paper, 'Motivation reconsidered: The concept of competence' (White 1959), which marked a decisive shift away from reactive drive reduction models of motivation towards self-generated forward-looking cognitive formulations. The implications of that paper were still being worked through in recent years (Deci and Moller 2005; Elliot and Dweck 2005b; Seligman 2011). Intrinsic motivation theory, which is discussed in Chapter 3, covers part, but by no means all, of the same field as cognitive motivation. However, at least in the formulation by Deci and his colleagues, intrinsic motivation theory starts with a given quality of motivation and does not explicate the underlying cognitive processes which I propose can and should be done, as I and others, including McReynolds, began to do in the 1960s (Beswick 1964, 1971, 1974).

The Scope of Cognitive Motivation

Although the term 'cognitive motivation' has not been widely used in psychological literature, it is generally recognised, and, as we have noted, some authors such as McReynolds, Bandura and Cacioppo have given it explicit treatment. Appley recognised its fundamental qualities in processes of meaningful integration in his review of equilibrium theories (Appley 1991). He referred to Kagan (1972), whose theory of personality and development shares with 'many other examples of cognitive motivation theories' a basic idea of seeking personal consistency (Appley 1991, p. 14). Appley related this central theme of cognitive motivation theories to others such as the 'Self-concept discrepancy theory of Higgins, Klein and Strauman (1985).' These ideas were significantly extended by Higgins from 'a theory relating self and affect' to 'learning about what matters in the social world.' Kagan related development of a person's identity to uncertainty, but it is quite a distance from processing uncertainty to the development of an identity. That is a journey that takes us through curiosity and intrinsic motivation, to the basic processes of cognitive motivation described in later chapters that lead to the discussion of identity, purpose and meaning in Chapters 11 and 12. The scope of relevant theories is quite wide.

Petri and Govern's well-established general textbook *Motivation: Theory, Research and Applications* (Petri and Govern 2004, 2013) maintained Petri's unusually extensive treatment in previous editions of 'Cognitive Approaches to Motivation.' Chapters under this heading cover Expectancy-Value Approaches, Social Motivation and Consistency, Attribution Approaches, and Competence and Control. Those chapters include forms of cognitive motivation such as cognitive dissonance, achievement motivation, attribution theory, self-efficacy and competence that I discuss in detail in the following chapters; but other forms of cognitive motivation, especially curiosity, which is central to my theory, are treated separately by Petri as instances of hedonism and incentive motivation. The general heading 'cognitive approaches' harks back to an earlier period represented by Bolles's historical review of cognitive approaches to motivation (Bolles 1974) and the papers associated with it (Weiner 1974b; see also Bolles 1975).

The scope of cognitive motivation is also indicated in Feather's list of conditions required for foresight and planning. He noted a number of emerging new perspectives that are discussed at various points in this work. They include the following: the need to recognise longitudinal effects that carry over from the past and are extended in anticipations of the future; the distinction between instigating and inhibitory forces and their resultant tendencies; the various determinants of expectations and valences; attributional concepts and their role in motivation; the influence on behaviour of self-related motivation, attitudes and values; and the information value of success and failure (Feather 1982b). Woodworth's early statements on different kinds of instincts (Woodworth 1918) and the conditions for intrinsic motivation in general discussed in Chapter 3 help to spell out further the scope of cognitive motivation.

In their extensive work on intrinsic motivation, Deci and Ryan developed 'self-determination theory,' in which they proposed that people strive to satisfy three basic needs: autonomy, competence and relatedness (Deci and Ryan 1985, 2002b). The significant contribution of their work is discussed in Chapter 3 and elsewhere. My proposal is that the basic needs proposed by Deci and Ryan are like the learned psychogenic needs of Murray, McClelland and others in that they all depend upon a common basic process for integration of diverse elements into meaningful whole figures, forms or gestalts. Depending upon their specific contents, I would characterize some purposive combinations of cognitive elements as expressing a concern with autonomy, others with competence, still others with social acceptance, etc. That is the same process as concerns achievement, affiliation, power and the like as examples of psychogenic motivation. I suggest that the contents are different due to past experience and present context, but the process of integration is the same. That process is simple, basic and innate while the particular forms of motivation developed from it, and by it, are diverse and largely learned. The tendency to form gestalts is innate, but there is no basis for innate specificity of goals in cognitive motivation. Goals may be specified for other motives by reference to reinforcing stimuli which are innate to a large extent in physiologically defined motives. Rolls, for example, has suggested that there is genetic determination of reinforcing stimuli that is characteristic of a species (Rolls 2005, 2008); but, of course, in cognitive motivation, preference for stimuli which are relevant to the attainment of goals for psychogenic motives is learned.

There is a similar distinction in the work of Walter Mischel and his colleagues in a cognitive-affective theory in which 'hot' and 'cool' images of rewards are compared (Kross and Mischel 2010). It corresponds fairly well but not exactly to the distinction between cognitive and other forms of motivation. 'Hot' images tend to fall outside the range of cognitive motivation, but not in all cases. The hot system responds automatically to trigger events and elicits aversive, fight-or-flight reactions as well as appetitive and sexual approach reactions. The cool system is a controlled system attuned to informational, cognitive and spatial stimuli. Nodes of the cool system are elaborately connected to each other. 'Whereas the hot system is conceptualized as the basis of emotionality, the cool system is thought to be the basis of self-regulation and self-control' (Mischel and Ayduk 2010, p. 10).

Mischel and Shoda (1995) have employed related concepts in their cognitive-affective processing systems (CAPS) theory. In the CAPS theory, cognitive-affective units (CAUs) mediate between a representation of the interpersonal situation and the responses generated. Mischel and colleagues claim that the two systems continually interact with each other so that 'hot' representations can be evoked by the activation of corresponding 'cool' representations. In the general theory of cognitive motivation, cognitive processes evoke emotions that guide goal directed behaviour, but there is not the same distinction between the basis for emotionality and the basis for self-regulation as Mischel and colleagues make. There is a kind of 'hot' emotional arousal that Mischel describes as automatically evoked which belongs to the 'big four' equilibrium type of motives (hunger, thirst, sex and fear), but in the cognitive motivation theory the same cognitive processes that control self-regulation can sometimes evoke quite 'hot' motivation from purely cognitive sources. I discuss the CAPS theory further in Chapter 6, and types of emotional arousal in Chapter 8.

A distinction such as that made by Weiner between viscerogenic needs which fall beyond the range of theories engendered by attribution processes is commonly made between cognitive motivation and what some, such as Hull, have called the big four – hunger, thirst, sex and pain (Hull 1943a). Weiner's attribution theory is considered as an example of cognitive motivation in Chapter 6. While it is recognised that cognitive processes such as expectations do enter into the operation of the 'big four,' Weiner made a sharp differentiation of his understanding of motivation (that I would call cognitive motivation) in comparison with Hull's 'viscerogenic' needs. A similar claim could be made for Bandura's theory of self-efficacy also discussed in Chapter 6. These theories, like much else, are among the indirect outcomes of the cognitive revolution of the late 1950s that I discuss at the beginning of Chapter 2, with further background in the introduction of the next two chapters. Other theories of different types of cognitive motivation stemming from that time of revolution in psychological theory are presented in Chapters 3 to 5. The scope of cognitive motivation is also indicated in Chapters 7 to 12 by the range of relevant basic processes and their applications: that is, the processes of consciousness and integration in working memory; the function of emotion in cognitive motivation; goals and intentions; and applications of the basic processes to identity, purpose and meaning.

Need Reduction and Historic Points of Contention

Before the cognitive revolution, attainment of a goal was commonly understood to restore equilibrium by satisfying a need (Miller and Dollard 1941; Hull 1943a; Dollard and Miller 1950; Hull 1951/1964; Miller 1951). There were alternative views in McDougall's instinct theory (McDougall 1908, 1920, 1923, 1945) and the cognitive theories of Lewin (Lewin 1935; Lewin et al. 1936; Lewin 1951) and Tolman (Tolman 1925, 1932/1949, 1948). On the history of this difference, see also Pervin (1989). Models of the need reduction kind were applied subsequently to acquired social or psychogenic needs like need for achievement or need for affiliation which were learned in a social context. Atkinson's expectancy value theory (Atkinson 1958b; Atkinson and Feather 1966a) was developed in the same period in the 1950s as other cognitive theories, such as Festinger's theory of cognitive dissonance (Festinger 1957, 1964), which were presented in more explicitly cognitive terms describing internal motivating conditions. These theories nevertheless retained some of the qualities of need reduction.

A further step away from seeing motivation in terms of physiological homeostatic needs was taken when aspects of intrinsic motivation came under study: for example, in Robert White's paper on the concept of competence (White 1959), or Harlow's study of curiosity in monkeys (Harlow 1953a) which, as Marvine Levine said, 'broke completely out of the Hullian drive-reduction mold' (Baars 1986, p. 226). However, Berlyne's pioneering account of curiosity originally retained a version of tension reduction theory in the Hullian tradition (Berlyne 1960) before it was modified to allow more adequately for approach behaviour (see Chapter 2). I argue in Chapter 8 that in later forms of drive reduction theory, for example in Damasio's reference back to homeostatic models, a sophisticated and subtle development of the concept of homeostasis can be interpreted in cognitive terms to be consistent with processes resolving an incomplete gestalt (Damasio 1994, 1999, 2010). Physiological and behaviouristic biases have persisted in parallel with the development of information-processing models which had begun to develop a cognitive approach to motivation before the more recent theories of cognitive neuropsychology (Weiner 1974b).

When cognitive accounts of purposive behaviour are offered, the question naturally arises of whether the term 'motive' will continue to be needed. Could not a description of cognitive processes simply replace it? When I had developed a cognitive theory of curiosity which was completely different from Berlyne's Hullian model, I did wonder whether, given an adequate understanding of relevant cognitive processes, we would continue to need the concept of motive (Beswick 1964, 1971). David McClelland wrote in response, 'I am not even shocked at the notion that we might not need the concept of "motive". To me it is simply a convenient term for affectively toned associative clusters of a given content' (McClelland, personal communication 1964; for a more detailed statement, see McClelland 1965a). It is important to note that a cognitive account of motivation does not exclude emotion. McClelland included a reference to emotion in *affectively* toned associative (cognitive) clusters. The inclusion of affective qualities in the understanding of motivation prevented a purely cognitive account from completely replacing motivation terminology.

Motives are like possums that invade the huts where Australian bush walkers rest; you chase them out the door and they come in the window. They can be chased out for ideological reasons, perhaps to avoid inferences about internal processes, or when a computational model is considered sufficient. However, the phenomena covered by the various examples and theories of cognitive motivation provide good reason why some provision for a dispositional property of motive is required even if a cognitive account is given of it, but then cognitive processes explain purposive behaviour only when emotions are taken into account. 'Motivation' is the process in which emotion gives direction to behaviour, and 'motive' refers to the disposition of readiness for it to happen. 'Motive' is a concept that has remained useful, provided that it is used in the context of a process of motivation in which dispositional properties form only one part, as Elliot, in particular, has argued in his hierarchical theory of achievement goals, making a distinction between motive as a dispositional property and motivation as a process (Elliot 2006).

There is another respect in which those developments in cognitive psychology which avoid or exclude reference to concepts like motivation or purpose depart from the original aims of the cognitive revolution. Bruner, one of its originators, wrote much later:

> Very early on, for example, emphasis began shifting from 'meaning' to 'information', from the *construction* of meaning to the *processing* of information. (Bruner 1990, p. 4)

I take up the important question of how 'meaning' enters into cognitive motivation at the highest level of personality organisation in Chapter 12. In Bruner's view, cognitive psychology lost its way when computing became the model of the mind and computability replaced the concept of meaning:

> If one falls into the habit of thinking of those complex programs as 'virtual minds' (to borrow Daniel Dennett's phrase), then it takes only a small but crucial step to go the whole way to believing that 'real minds' and their processes, like 'virtual' ones and theirs, could be 'explained' in the same way (Bruner 1990, p. 6).

It will be helpful to retain the concept of motive in a cognitive approach as we apply a generalized form of the basic model developed in the study of curiosity to higher-level processes of meaning and purpose. The approach I take then to the higher-level processes is similar to that of Bruner in his discussion of meaning, but it agrees also with others such as Frankl (1959) at an early stage and Baumeister in more recent developments (Baumeister 1991, 2005; Baumeister, Masicampo and Vohs 2011).

Prospects for Theory Development

Bolles (1974), concluded his historical review of cognitive approaches to motivation, saying that there is going to be a rich diversity of hypothesized cognitive mechanisms (involved in the purposive determination of behaviour). He added, in a prophetic mode,

> I predict, too, that if anyone ever achieves closure and gives us a satisfactory, small set of cognitive mechanisms that have claim to broad generality for the human subject, he will be a very astute and perceptive theorist indeed. I will also predict that when this theorist arrives upon the scene, he will provide us with a system which contains just one matrix containing both motivational and structural mechanisms; I predict that both kinds of mechanisms will be cognitive; that he will assume man to be active rather than passive; and that he will support his theoretical position by systematically observing what people do in naturalistic settings (Bolles 1974, p. 19).

The anticipated diverse proliferation of hypothesized cognitive mechanisms has developed since. In this work I hope to show that we can now move to a basic theory of cognitive processes applicable across the field of cognitive motivation. There has been much development in this direction to which many minds have contributed in recent decades. Many have given some idea of the shape of a future synthesis. The kind of theoretical system Bolles anticipated is what I have to offer, but just as the theory applies basic principles from my earlier theory of curiosity, so does my attitude to it: we do not expect a perfect final resolution in a new complete system. It also follows from the theory and the necessary humility with which one must always approach observation and explanation of natural phenomena, especially in human beings, that any closure reached is necessarily 'for the time being.' It is in the nature of the cognitive processes that I propose that completion of an incomplete gestalt always results in new visions being opened up, inspired by creative conceptual closure, and those new visions will offer new challenges.

A cognitive process theory of curiosity is used in this work as an entry point to open the much bigger cognitive motivation box. Curiosity leads us first into intrinsic motivation that is a compartment within the bigger box. To illustrate the basic approach, instead of accepting intrinsic motivation as a given quality, we try to open it up to reveal its underlying properties and make explicit the cognitive processes which account for its operation. Then those basic processes which bring structure and motivation together in cognitive terms can also be applied to higher-order phenomena in the way that intrinsic motivation works in the more general model of cognitive motivation. The higher-order phenomena are those seen at the macro level of the whole person behaving purposively in a social context. They are illustrated in such well-established findings as the moderation of intrinsic motivation by extrinsic rewards for which a whole set of additional principles have been introduced, as Deci and Ryan proposed in self-determination theory (Deci 1980; Deci and Ryan 1985). These are principles which I regard as unnecessary and explicable in more basic terms. I argue, particularly in Chapter 3, that if those additional principles can themselves be accounted for or rendered unnecessary by the same basic processes as explain curiosity at the micro level, then we can see how the desired simpler basic set of ideas has a wide application.

A high degree of generality is being attempted here, but by no means is it intended to make an ambit claim to offer a general model of cognition and motivation, let alone a theory applicable to the broad range of learning, personality and social behaviour, even if such phenomena as personal integration, identity and meaning will lead us into those fields. The higher-order purposive phenomena of adult social and covert reflective behaviour in a personally meaningful life are what must be accounted for in the macro-level application of the theory (see Chapters 10, 11 and 12), and taking the title of Robert White's last book, it applies centrally to 'the enterprise of living' (White 1972).

The Motivational Consequences of an Incomplete Gestalt

Movement towards completion of incomplete forms is the basic mechanism of cognitive motivation. In particular, it accounts for intrinsic motivation in its various forms, and it lays foundations for understanding a wider range of examples of cognitive motivation. The imperative for completion of an incomplete gestalt provides the required dynamics.

Elements of the experience of incompleteness include inconsistency, gaps in knowledge, awareness of an imperfectly apprehended figure that stands out from a background, a quality of potential wholeness attributed to an imperfectly perceived or partially apprehended image or concept, some limited awareness of what is needed for completion, and the evocation of strategies for completion, while there is a feeling of something being not quite right, or something missing or conflicting or incomplete, often with a hopeful prospect of attainment. It will be obvious that while the idea of an incomplete gestalt is simple enough, there are complexities in the processes which are associated with the experience of it and its operation in purposive behaviour. The incomplete gestalt bridges over from cognition to motivation by incorporating emotions as signs in cognitive motivation. Robert Sears was probably right when he concluded a discussion of papers by several leading theorists, quite a few years ago, saying that 'Motivation cannot be understood in terms of drive alone, nor in terms of cognitive transformations alone' (Sears 1974, p. 90), but drive qualities and cognitive transformations are brought together in the role of emotions in cognitive motivation that I spell out particularly in Chapter 8.

Integration

In the general theory of cognitive motivation, it is assumed that a basic process of integration motivates purposive behaviour. We aim for goals that will overcome gaps and conflicts in how we see the world and ourselves. Or it can be put the other way around, that engagement in purposive behaviour facilitates personal integration. The mutually reinforcing interaction between purpose and meaning discussed in Chapter 12 suggests that both these statements are true, but there is some disagreement on whether there are 'universal natural or inherent principles that promote growth, integration, and the resolution of psychological inconsistencies and conflicts' (Ryan 1995, p. 397). Many influential theorists have assumed that there are: for example, Ryan took note of Freud's *synthetic function of the ego* (Freud 1923/1962), Jung's *individuation* (Jung 1951/1959), Maslow's and Rogers' *actualizing tendency* (Maslow 1954; Rogers 1963) and Piaget's *organisation* (Piaget 1971). This point is discussed in Chapter 3, in which I argue that Ryan's substitution of specific innate needs for a general tendency to integration is unhelpful. In addition, I argue in Chapter 7 for the importance of basic processes of integration in working memory facilitated by consciousness.

The general principle of striving for integration to achieve future wholeness in images of the world as well as images of the self was present quite early in classical gestalt theory (von Ehrenfels 1890/1988; Wertheimer 1912; Köhler 1920/1924; Wertheimer 1923; Köhler 1929/1947; Heider 1960) There was a similar concept in Freud's late solution to the problem of the instincts in which he postulated as basic instincts a general tendency towards integration and an opposing pressure for disintegration, i.e. *eros* and the death instinct (Freud 1936). Freud had earlier referred to integrating processes as the synthetic function of the ego (Freud 1923/1962), but he then brought the ego instincts within the general integrating pleasure functions of *eros*. Against the prevailing opinions in the behaviourist period, Allport maintained a different view from that of Freud, one which highlighted a motivating principle of integrative and directing properties at the heart of personality in his concept of a functionally autonomous motivational belief system and a purposive sense of self in his understanding of the *proprium* (Allport 1937a, 1937b, 1955, 1961b). As I will note elsewhere, similar concepts are found in more recent literature, for example, Antonovsky's sense of coherence (Antonovsky 1987, 1998), and similarly in Korotkov (1998) and Kruglanski's treatment of need for closure (Kruglanski 2004). Research on the need for closure is discussed in Chapter 2. General theories of 'making sense' and the integrative functions of consciousness are discussed in Chapters 7 and 9.

The meaning maintenance model (MMM) proposed by Heine, Proulx and Vohs is based on the same general cognitive structures and processes for 'making sense' across many domains in which the *structure of relations* gives meaning, intra-psychically, in relation to the external world and socially (Heine et al. 2006; see also Proulx and Heine 2006; Proulx and Heine 2010). Based on Kierkegaard's 'relational mode of being' and Camus's 'nostalgia for unity' with his reiteration of existential thought affirming a 'universal human need to relate all elements of perceived reality into a single, unified, cohesive framework of expected relationships,' they 'propose an overarching model that parsimoniously integrates the diverse literatures on meaning-making, as well as the literatures on self-esteem maintenance, uncertainty reduction, affiliative motives, and terror management theory' (p. 89). In some respects the MMM is a further development of the self-affirmation theory of cognitive dissonance (Steele and Liu 1983; Steele 1988; Heine and Lehman 1997) that is discussed in Chapter 4. The MMM is further applied in the conclusion to that chapter concerned with dissonance and general theories of the self. It is also relevant to my discussion of processes of integration in relation to supposed basic needs in Chapter 3, similarly to the development of meaningful cognitive structures in Chapters 9 and 11 in regard to goals and identity, and most directly it is significant for the discussion of meaning and purpose in Chapter 12.

Gestalt psychology prepared the ground for and later contributed key concepts to the cognitive revolution in many ways that were not recognised at the time (Ash 1995; Murray 1995). The central role of cognitive integration remained in the background but nevertheless influenced studies of perception, learning, memory and information processing as cognitive psychology developed. The development of psychotherapy as a field of professional practice tended also to encourage theories of integration, as seen, for example, in the approach to learning theory and psychiatry in the work of Mowrer and in the gestalt therapy movement (Perls 1951/1972; Mowrer 1960, 1961; Perls 1976; see also Henle 1955 on motivational processes in cognition).

Those were very general ideas about cognitive integration. More is now known about processes of integration from both behavioural and neurological research. In Chapter 7 I discuss how theories such as Baars's conscious access hypotheses (Baars 1997, 2002a, 2005a) have given an account of the role of consciousness in cognitive integration; how Baddeley's model of working memory (Baddeley and Hitch 1974, Baddeley 1986, Baddeley and Logie 1999, Baddeley 2007) provides a framework for understanding integration as a central executive function; and how studies of the neural correlates of consciousness support an information integration theory of consciousness (Koch 2004; Tononi 2004, 2005; Tononi and Koch 2008). Others have proposed various brain systems to account for conscious integration: for example, the supervisory attentional system (Shallice 1988), the anterior attention system (Posner 1994; Posner and Dehaene 1994) and the dynamic core (Tononi and Edelman 1998). In Chapter 11 I discuss the further development of similar theories in reference to Gazzaniga's hypothesis of a 'left hemisphere interpreter' which produces a narrative form of integration (Gazzaniga and Ledoux 1978; Gazzaniga 1995, 1997, 2000). While studies of the neural correlates of consciousness have helped to illuminate our understanding of processes of integration, much remains unknown about the details of the brain structures and processes, and I have discussed integration in much of this work in functional terms.

Curiosity and, to a lesser extent, other forms of intrinsic motivation provide us with a window into basic cognitive processes which arise from a sense of incompleteness. Contradictions, uncertainties and gaps in knowledge arouse people to search, inquire, manipulate, learn, construct and create new orders out of the old with new information input. Most important in this understanding of how intrinsic motivation functions is the idea that a process of restructuring cognitive elements into a new whole never restores a previous state of affairs. To close an incomplete circle, the brokenness of which has attracted attention, requires *new* elements to be integrated, even if they only represent newly conceived relations between other previously existing elements. When incompleteness is transformed by resolution of an incomplete gestalt, we have incorporated something new into our previous understanding, and our cognitive map of the world is different from what it has ever been before. In such an account as the cognitive process theory of curiosity, or the more general theory of cognitive motivation, we see the part played by a basic process of integration; however, that is not sufficient in itself. More than integration is required to account for goal-oriented behaviour.

Reaching for the Gestalt

Processes of integration explain purposive behaviour only when we know how a condition of incompleteness gives *both* energy *and* direction to a person's striving for completeness. It is not difficult to imagine that some elements of the experience of incompleteness energize activity. A person senses that something is missing, or some conflict needs to be resolved. Something needs to be done, and people do appear to get up and do things. But *what* to do; *where* to head? To know what points the direction in which a solution might be found requires something more than awareness of incompleteness. It certainly requires more than awareness of inconsistency or dissonance that can have motivating qualities (Festinger 1957, 1964). Such an experience gives reason for a person to move away from the present conditions, but it does not provide a basis for deciding the direction in which movement will occur. I suggest that an incomplete gestalt must be apprehended to direct behaviour. A sense of incompleteness gives direction only when some form or pattern is apprehended but not yet fully realized. We need to be able to imagine what we are looking for, and envisage some means of getting there.

Another gestalt quality that is required, in addition to the coherence implied by a sense of potential wholeness, is the way we tend to see and to seek a figure that stands out from a background. The figure-ground phenomenon is a basic property of gestalt perception. This is profoundly different from mere consistency, or the removal of conflicts, contradictions and discrepancies, which may be motivating qualities in stimulus objects that give rise to curiosity or cognitive dissonance. Those things alone do not fill gaps in meaning or complete incomplete figures, nor do conflicts in themselves indicate the form in which a newly integrated whole might be resolved or bring a sense of completion. Some notion of a whole figure with properties that not only cohere but make it distinct from the field in which it is perceived, or conceptually anticipated, is required. It is an entity that stands out as a figure in a field of many elements which might otherwise lack integration into a meaningful unit that possesses identity and integrity, so that one can name it and recognise it when one sees it again. No amount of effort in reconciling conflicting elements in a cognitive field can integrate elements into a new whole without the figure-ground quality of a gestalt.

There must be some idea of what the complete image/concept/schema/gestalt is or could be like for the incompleteness of what is currently apperceived to be experienced in a creative way. The Gestalt psychologists a hundred years ago suggested that there is a natural tendency in the brain to form unified whole images which stand out from a background. In Chapter 9 I canvass the possibility, anticipated by Köhler (Köhler 1920/1924; Arnheim 1998), that what have become known in recent years in the physical and biological sciences as self-organising systems may illustrate such processes in the brain. Such images have an identity and can be named even when they are imperfect forms not fully realized. Imagining their possible completion is a process of apperception rather than perception. One projects, as it were, the form of an integrated image without knowing exactly how it will appear when the process is completed. That is quite different from assuming that everything is potentially connected with everything else. It is the gestalt which is both anticipated and experienced as an identifiable and distinct object of attention which calls us forward into the future with a purpose. That image must be meaningful, even in its imperfection, to achieve its motivating effect.

In Chapter 2 I refer to Bruner's recollection of the cognitive revolution as an attempt to put meaning making back at the heart of psychology. An illustration of the motivating effect of the search for meaning is found in his account of the conditions antecedent to the construction of meaning when a child is motivated to master language (Bruner 1990, p. 78). Language is acquired as a functional necessity for a social being with a capacity for high-level adaptability and forward planning through the operation of more basic cognitive processes which preceded it. A classic case study, *Narratives from the crib* (Nelson and Bruner 2006), illustrated language acquisition in a young child in reference to these principles. The recent appearance of a capacity for discerning intentions and theory of mind, which is said to have preceded the development of language in human evolution, is discussed in Chapter 10. It is seen particularly in the comparative studies of primates by Tomasello and his colleagues (Tomasello and Call 1997; Tomasello 1999; Tomasello, Carpenter, Call,

Behne and Moll 2005). In our terms, it is those preceding operations invoking an intentional orientation to the future which give rise to cognitive motivation.

Bruner provides a different example of cognitive motivation in his account of the way that narrative integration gives meaning to exceptional events within a framework of canonical or commonly expected sequences of social behaviour. This is an illustration, at a complex level of human social experience, of the sequential form of an incomplete gestalt. Sequential forms are found in melodies and narratives, while visual forms and patterns of personality illustrate a different 'iconic' kind of gestalt. They are different ways of giving expression to the unity and identity of a person, group or culture. I describe the iconic and narrative forms of identity in Chapter 11. Bruner refers to a 'push' for language learning and to an 'innate' or primitive predisposition to narrative organisation which underlies its development (Bruner 1990, pp. 77–80; see also his later work on narratives making sense of the otherwise unexplained, Bruner 1996, 2003), and he postulates an 'early readiness to mark the unusual and to leave unmarked the usual' (Bruner 1990, p. 78). Curiosity theory as a model of the required cognitive processes seeking completeness or meaningful understanding after arousal by unusual stimuli addresses the same point. The general principles of integration to form meaningful units of cognition with motivational effects apply at all levels of cognitive organisation.

Emotion and Goal Seeking

Representation of feelings is an essential element in the information processing of cognitive motivation. Just as there are images of perceived physical objects or remembered actions which may be the content on which cognitive operations are performed, there are also images of feelings which constitute data for the processes which define cognitive motivation. Operations performed on representations or symbols of emotion can have consequences. That is, although I might once have seen things otherwise (Beswick 1964), emotion is not a subjective by-product of information processing outside the loop of causal explanation for motivation, but an active component, a necessary part of cognitive motivation.

In one of the more traditional theories of emotion and cognition proposed by Lazarus, emotion is understood to be a result of evaluation when a goal is compared with the present state of affairs (Lazarus 1974, 1994a, 1999). Evaluation is then a cognitive process out of which emotion becomes information guiding goal-oriented behaviour. There are competing theories of how this might work, and there have been disputes about which is prior – emotion or cognition – that we will consider in Chapter 8. An alternative which appears to give priority to emotion over cognition is Damasio's somewhat controversial 'somatic marker hypothesis' (Damasio 1994, 1999, 2000b). However, although his homeostatic model of motivation is inconsistent in some respects with the view I have taken, Damasio's purposive construction of the function of emotions illustrates very well the role emotion has in this cognitive theory (Damasio 2000b, 2010). In Chapter 8 I take this further to suggest, in company with several recent theorists (Swartz and Clore 1983; Frijda 1994; Gray, Schaeffer and Braver 2005; Baumeister, Vohs, DeWall and Zhang 2007; Forgas, Baumeister and Tice 2009) that the function of emotions in cognitive motivation is to act as signs of the current relationship of a person to desired goals. Alternative models of the function of emotion in cognitive motivation are given detailed attention in later chapters, but the basic hypothesis is that motivation includes the information value of emotion in both the initial conditions of arousal and the cognitive operations in which direction is given to goal seeking. Emotions are signs along the way from where we are now to the goal we aim to reach.

The Form of Cognitive Explanations

The mode of explanation that I adopt is to use basic concepts to explain higher-order processes, but I do not hold with reductionist explanations. Making sense of human behaviour and experience in the complex functioning of unique personalities, with attention to identity, purpose and meaning, is often more like drawing a picture or telling a story than it is like the logical application of mathematically expressed scientific laws in the physical sciences. I describe patterns and processes of cognitive organisation at a basic level that have parallel forms at higher levels. So, for example, I seek to show how understanding curiosity provides a model for explanation of personality integration. A basic starting point offers the potential of a simpler, more foundational and more widely applicable theory than does a theory that takes off at a higher level of cognitive organisation. An effective strategy in theory construction for phenomena like cognitive motivation is to unpack simple forms, learn how their underlying processes work, and then apply that understanding to more highly developed and complex cognitive and motivational processes, ranging from scientific curiosity to the intentional behaviour of a mature person in a social context where purposes are fulfilled in 'acts of meaning' (Frankl 1962; Bruner 1990; Baumeister 1991; Wong and Fry 1998; Baumeister 2005).

The cognitive process theory of curiosity at a basic level, and in particular the key concept of an incomplete gestalt, provides a model that can be applied across all forms of cognitive motivation. There are many common concepts. So, for example, expectancy-value theory in achievement motivation (Atkinson 1964; Atkinson and Birch 1974; Birch, Atkinson and Bongard 1974), especially when viewed in terms of attribution theory (Weiner 1974c, 1985a), combines well with the results of a meta-analysis of findings which demonstrate the effects of praise to illustrate this wider application (Henderlong and Lepper 2002). These results, discussed in Chapter 3, demonstrate that the intrinsic motivation of a person engaged in an interesting task is enhanced rather than depleted when, by such means as praise, attention is directed to those means of goal attainment that are under his or her control, just as in achievement motivation a person with high need for achievement prefers alternative strategies that provide feedback with high information value for the effectiveness of available achievement strategies. These are examples of high-level functions in which the same kind of feedback and developmental processes are found as at more basic levels of cognitive organisation.

Similar high-level functions can be described for the operation of systems defining personal identity. Systems of meaning which contribute to the development of personal identity, in what I have called its iconic and narrative forms, are discussed in Chapters 11 and 12, with reference to general principles of purpose and meaning at the highest level of personality organisation. The same basic processes which account for curiosity at the level of a specific perceptual or problem-solving task can also be applied at the higher level for making sense of personal identity, purpose and meaning.

Summary

This work is concerned with the potential for a general theory of cognitive motivation with the aim of giving an account of how basic processes of integration work and apply to all levels of cognitive organisation. McReynolds introduced the term 'cognitive motivation' when he described '[t]he three faces of cognitive motivation' in his review of early work on intrinsic motivation. When Bandura used related terms, he said, 'One can distinguish three forms of cognitive motivators around which different theories have been built. These include *causal attributions*, *outcome expectancies*, and *cognized goals*.' (Bandura 1991, p. 71). This work is an inquiry into the possibility that a general theory of cognitive motivation can be applied to all its forms.

William James remarked that 'the philosophical brain' 'responds to an inconsistency or a gap in knowledge' (James 1890, pp. 429–430), and in early 20th-century developments Woodworth and Allport referred to the intrinsically rewarding character of such motivation without giving it a distinctive name. By mid-20th century, Harlow introduced explicitly the concept of intrinsic motivation. In their later extensive work on intrinsic motivation, Deci and Ryan developed self-determination theory. (Deci 1980; Deci and Ryan 1985, 2002b). My proposal is that the basic needs for autonomy, competence and relatedness proposed by Deci and Ryan are like the learned psychogenic needs of Murray, McClelland and others in that they all depend upon a common basic process for integration of diverse elements into meaningful whole figures, forms or gestalts.

Cognitive processes explain purposive behaviour only when emotions are taken into account. As we reach for the gestalt, emotions are signs along the way from where we are now to the goal we aim to reach. Drive qualities and cognitive transformations are brought together in the role of emotions in cognitive motivation. The general principle of striving for integration to achieve future wholeness in images of the world as well as images of the self was present quite early in classical gestalt theory. Freud referred to integrating processes as the synthetic function of the ego, but he then brought the ego instincts within the general integrating pleasure functions of *eros*. At the heart of Allport's conception of the unique personality was his idea of a functionally autonomous motivational belief system and a purposive sense of self. The Meaning Maintenance Model (MMM) proposed by Heine, Proulx and Vohs (2006) is based on the same general cognitive structures and processes for 'making sense' across many domains in which the *structure of relations* gives meaning.

Studies of the neural correlates of consciousness have helped to illuminate our understanding of processes of integration, but processes of integration explain purposive behaviour only when we know how a condition of incompleteness gives *both* energy *and* direction to a person's striving for completeness. A sense of incompleteness gives direction only when some form or pattern is apprehended but not yet fully realized. There must be some idea of what the complete image/concept/schema/gestalt is or could be like for the incompleteness of what is currently apperceived to be experienced in a creative way.

Patterns and processes of cognitive organisation at a basic level have parallel forms at higher levels. The cognitive process theory of curiosity at a basic level, and in particular the key concept of an incomplete gestalt, suggests a model that can be applied across all forms of cognitive motivation.

2 Curiosity

Curiosity is in great and generous minds, the first passion and the last.
– Samuel Johnson 1751

Introduction

The psychology of curiosity occupies a pivotal point in the study of motivation and cognition. Its theoretical importance came to the fore in what Loewenstein in his general review of research on curiosity (Loewenstein 1994) called the first phase of increased research activity, in the 1950s and 1960s, which was characterised by attention to its underlying or internal processes. In this chapter I present a theory of those internal processes and empirical support for it. Initially, when it was first proposed in that formative period that became known as the cognitive revolution, it was called the cognitive process theory of curiosity, from which I later developed the general theory of cognitive motivation.

Curiosity was significant for general psychology because its intrinsically rewarding character attracted attention at a time when there was considerable debate about whether drive reduction models of motivation were any longer sustainable. Marvine Levine, for example, said of Harlow's work on curiosity, 'it broke completely out of the Hullian drive-reduction mold' (Baars 1986, p. 226). Harlow had said, 'A drive-reduction theory of learning, emphasising the internal physiological state, is untenable. Learning efficiency is far better related to "tensions in the brain than in the belly"' (Harlow 1953b, p. 26). His monkeys would learn to open doors to see bright and moving objects.

Curiosity is the prototypical example of intrinsic motivation from which basic principles of the broader concept of *cognitive* motivation have been generalised. The concept of intrinsic motivation had been explicitly introduced by Harlow in 1950 (Harlow 1950; White 1972). There is a deeper history of related concepts developed earlier by Woodworth and Allport, which is discussed in Chapter 3. Robert White and J. McV. Hunt argued that, in the study of intrinsic motivation, drive reduction models were indeed superseded. (White 1959; Hunt 1960, 1963, 1965; White 1972). Hebb at about this time, followed his earlier suggestion (Hebb 1949) of an inherent tendency of the central nervous system towards integration of new information so as to 'make sense' of it, and recommended 'the *immediate drive value of cognitive processes*, without intermediary' as 'one problem in particular that I would urge should not be forgotten' (Hebb 1955, p. 252). The hypothesis was being developed that cognitive processes themselves can have motivating properties.

Loewenstein identified a second phase of intense activity in the study of curiosity, in the 1970s and 1980s, which was concerned with the measurement of individual differences in curiosity as a trait or state. The measurement of curiosity was associated with discussion of its dimensionality. Is curiosity a unitary concept? William James had suggested at least two different kinds of curiosity (James 1890, Vol. 2, pp. 429–430). He first referred to curiosity and fear as 'antagonistic emotions' that may be aroused by attention to a novel object. In this he indicated the emotional ambivalence of curiosity that would have important theoretical implications. He commented that '[s]ome such susceptibility for being excited and irritated by the mere novelty, as such, of any moveable feature of the environment must form the instinctive basis of all human curiosity.' James then suggested that what he called 'scientific curiosity' and 'metaphysical wonder' probably has nothing to do with that instinctive root. I will make a case for the scientific or wonder aspects being built upon the former susceptibility to be excited by novel objects. In a passage in this context, that appears particularly prescient in foreshadowing later attention to conflicts and gaps which are central to cognitive theories, he said, 'The philosophical brain responds to an inconsistency or a gap in knowledge, just as the musical brain responds to a discord.' (James 1890, pp. 429–430). Gestalt principles, although not named and only just beginning to appear in the literature (von Ehrenfels 1890/1988), seem to be implied.

Did the 'antagonistic emotions' point to different biological bases and different kinds of curiosity? Similar questions arose during the first phase from experimental research, especially in the work of Berlyne (1954, 1960, 1971a). Were there many kinds of curiosity? If so, did they develop and function differently in theoretically significant ways? On the other hand, should we be dealing with curiosity as an instance of a more common general class of motivation? From the first phase right up to the present time there has been a continuing stream of theoretical publications not only on curiosity specifically but in the more general field of intrinsic motivation, openness to experience and related topics. The approach I wish to introduce began in Loewenstein's first stage in the late 1950s, but it was developed initially in a study of individual differences which was more characteristic of the second phase.

Origins of Curiosity Research in the Cognitive Revolution

That period in the late 1950s and early 1960s was a critically important historical turning point in psychology, known later as the cognitive revolution (Baars 1986). Many apparently unrelated initiatives in what became cognitive psychology were being taken then, especially in Cambridge, Massachusetts, at Harvard and MIT, with other important centres at Wisconsin under Harlow, a little earlier at McGill in Montreal with Hebb, and at Toronto where Berlyne had moved from Britain. There was another indirect starting point in Britain with studies of information theory and attention by Cherry and Broadbent (Cherry 1953; Broadbent 1954; Cherry 1956, 1957; Broadbent 1958). Chomsky at MIT published his famous critical review of Skinner's book on verbal behaviour (Skinner 1957; Chomsky 1959) followed by his foundational contribution, *Aspects of the Theory of Syntax*, bringing a new approach to cognitive studies through psycholinguistics (Chomsky 1959, 1965) and setting a pattern that remained influential up through recent debates on modularity. Those debates are relevant to the question of the generality of the cognitive processes that account for curiosity, and to their possible application to higher-order processes.

George Miller's signal article, 'The magic number seven, plus or minus two: Some limits on our capacity for processing information' (Miller 1956), was one of the initial points of departure for the development of information processing models of cognition, which were later elaborated in cybernetic models (Miller, Galanter and Pribram 1960). His book *Psychology: The Science of Mental Life* (Miller 1962) then reinforced the shift of emphasis from behaviour to internal cognitive processes.

The revolutionary attitudes of those involved was expressed strongly in Jerome Bruner's recollection, a generation later, of the early days of the Centre for Cognitive Studies at Harvard that he founded with Miller in 1959: 'That revolution was intended to bring "mind" back into the human sciences after a long cold winter of objectivism' (Bruner 1990, p. 1). He wrote of a more interpretative approach to 'meaning making' in which the original intention was 'to establish meaning as the central concept of psychology – not stimuli and responses, not overtly observable behaviour, not biological drives and their transformation, but meaning' (Bruner 1990, p. 2). According to Bruner, the cognitive revolution 'focused upon the symbolic activities that human beings employed in constructing and making sense not only of the world, but of themselves'. These symbolic activities are the basic points of reference for cognitive motivation.

In his book *The Cognitive Revolution in Psychology*, Baars says, 'The cognitive revolution may represent a living example of a "scientific revolution"' (Baars 1986, pp. 2–3), but the breadth and depth of the changes that were then taking place were not always apparent to those engaged in it. Mandler, in his history of experimental psychology, has referred to '[t]he major events of the miraculous five years between 1955 and 1960 [that] occurred in memory, language, and problem solving' (Mandler 2007, p. 173). He does not mention Bruner with whom he shared the teaching of a graduate course that I took in 1958. Bruner's contribution could have been seen at that time to be in a different field. Neither does Mandler mention personality research and social psychology as contributing fields, but McClelland's model of motivation (McClelland et al. 1953; McClelland 1958a, 1961) brought another perspective into cognition from personality research. Robert White was also in the same department as Bruner and McClelland, but even quite recently Elliot and Dweck (2005b) have pointed out the extraordinary lack of cross-reference between research on McClelland's theory of achievement motivation and White's 'concept of competence' (see my discussion of it in Chapter 6).

Others have said that the so-called revolution was a more gradual change of emphasis (Baars 1986; Appley 1991), and that is probably right, but the import of the changes was truly revolutionary. However broadly defined and with whatever degree of revolutionary zeal it was undertaken, a great change in psychology took place around a time that coincided with Loewenstein's first period in the intense study of curiosity with its attention to internal processes and the beginning of a more comprehensive concern with intrinsic motivation that was evident particularly in White's paper on 'effectance motivation' (White 1959) (see Chapter 7). The following year, however, the principal pioneer of research on curiosity in the early 1950s, Daniel Berlyne, came out with a substantial book which employed concepts from cognition, such as conflict and complexity, but based his explanations essentially on a model which was a sophisticated development of Hullian drive reduction theory (Berlyne 1960). That debate was to continue, but it would proceed on different terms

Common Language Concepts of Curiosity

There have always been various senses of curiosity as a word in common language. The likely possibility arising from the range of uses for terms like 'curiosity' and 'exploration' was that different usages could indicate different elements in a single complex model of the cognitive processes that account for it. The following conceptual definition, with five senses of the word 'curiosity', was developed from historical uses and taken as a starting point in the construction of a test of individual differences (Beswick 1964, 1971).

1. A desire (need, wish, want, etc.) or inclination to know or learn especially about novel or strange things.
2. A feeling of interest leading one to make inquiries or perform some acts in order to gain understanding.
3. The application of careful attention to a learning task, the outcome of which has no immediately obvious pragmatic value.
4. A scientific or artistic interest which is intrinsic to the person and oriented to understanding rather than to expression.
5. A desire to make trial or experience of anything novel; to see what will happen; to find out what it would be like; to see whether it would work.

Careful Attention

Historical uses include some senses of 'curiosity' that are now obsolete but indicate psychologically significant attributes. For example, 'curious' was used in the eighteenth century as a description of craftwork which might have been said to have been 'curiously wrought'. It points to a basic function of careful attention, and the word 'cure', which is preserved today in cognate words like 'accurate' and 'curate' as well as 'curiosity'. These words are derived from the same Latin root as the medieval English word of French origin 'cure,' meaning care. Its relationship to curiosity in an intellectual endeavour is illustrated in Chaucer's description of the 'Clerk of Oxenford' in his 'Prologue to the Canterbury Tales':

> A clerk ther was of Oxenford also
> That unto logik hadde longe ygo.
> ...
> But al be that he was a philosophre,
> Yet hadde he but litel gold in cofre,
> But al that he mighte of his friendes hente
> On bokes and lernynge he it spente,
> And bisily gan for the soules preye
> Of hem that yaf hym wherwith to scoleye.
> Of studye took he moost *cure* and moost hede.
> ...
> And gladly wolde he lerne and gladely teche.
> – (Chaucer 1387/1969, Skeat's edition, lines 287–310).

In the care with which the clerk regarded books and learning we have in its purest form what Berlyne (1960) called 'epistemic curiosity': *Of studye took he moost* **cure** *and moost hede ... And gladly wolde he lerne and gladely teche.*

While he might have sought payment, and was pleased to receive it, it was not the reason he undertook his work. Rather, the money enabled him to pursue his interest in study: ... *al that he mighte of his friendes hente/ On bokes and lernynge he it spente*. He would gladly learn and gladly teach because it was intrinsically rewarding. The notion of *cure* casts the net of meaning somewhat wider than curiosity as we use the word today and leads into the more general field of intrinsic motivation. There is theoretical significance in this ancient usage putting careful attention at the heart of epistemic curiosity.

The value of careful attention in scientific curiosity is seen nowhere more clearly than in the life of Charles Darwin. (See the various biographies of Darwin, especially Desmond and Moore 1991, 2010, and the introduction and afterword by Ekman to his work on the expression of emotions, Darwin, Ekman and Prodger 1998). Darwin himself confessed,

> I have no great quickness of apprehension or wit which is so remarkable in some clever men, for instance Huxley. My power to follow a long and purely abstract train of thought is very limited ... [but] I am superior to the common run of men in noticing things which easily escape attention, and in observing them carefully. (Darwin and Barlow 1958, pp 140–141; see also Darwin 1872/1998, Darwin 1876–1882)

Both care and attention are key concepts in the cognitive process theory of curiosity. Darwin referred to 'my love of natural science,' and 'the strongest desire to understand or explain whatever I observed, – that is, to group all facts under some general laws. These causes combined have given me the patience to reflect or ponder for any number of years over any unexplained problem.' (Darwin and Barlow 1958, p. 141). Einstein made a similar claim: 'I have no special talents. I am only passionately curious' (Mischel 1996, p. 7, cited by Kang et al. 2009). I will discuss shortly an example of Darwin's grappling with a problem over many years in reference to his observation of a platypus in 1836 and its relevance to his theory of evolution published more than 20 years later. First, some literary examples throw light on curiosity in a different perspective.

Literary Examples of Epistemic Hunger and Its Ambivalence

> Curiosity is one of those insatiable passions that grow by gratification
> – Sarah Scott, 1762

> The gratification of curiosity rather frees us from uneasiness than confers pleasure
> – Samuel Johnson, 1751

These contrasting appetitive and aversive tendencies in responses to novelty appear in English literature in the middle of the eighteenth century, at the beginning of what the biographer Richard Holmes has called *The Age of Wonder* (Holmes 2008) – an age that produced many great scientific and literary achievements. Sarah Scott employed the image of an appetitive kind in her utopian novel *A Description of Millenium Hall*, when she was describing the excitement that built up in a group of travellers passing through a richly varied environment appealing to their different senses:

> The eye is charmed with the remarkable verdure and neatness of the fields … that time steals away insensibly … a shepherd playing a flute … Our ears afforded us fresh attraction, and with quicker steps we proceeded … Curiosity now prompted us to walk on; the nearer we came to the house, the greater we found the profusion of flowers which ornamented every field … The mixture of perfumes … filled us with reflections on the infinite variety of nature … a number of children … their eyes sparkled … Curiosity is one of those insatiable passions that grow by gratification; it still prompted us to proceed, not unsatisfied with what we had seen, but desirous to see still more of this earthly paradise. (Scott and Kelly 1762/1995, pp. 56–58)

Samuel Johnson provided the contrast:

> The gratification of curiosity rather frees us from uneasiness than confers pleasure; we are more pained by ignorance than delighted by instruction. Curiosity is the thirst of the soul; it inflames and torments us, and makes us taste everything with joy, however otherwise insipid, by which it may be quenched. (Samuel Johnson, *The Rambler*, 12 March 1751)

The contrast of Scotts's joyful image of anticipation with the painful experience of Johnson's teasing ignorance points to a facet of curiosity – its affective ambivalence – that requires close examination. Johnson's pain-joy transition suggests the emotion of euphoric anticipation recently described by Panksepp as characteristic of the 'seeking system' in his affective neuroscience of basic emotions (Panksepp 1998, 2011a; Panksepp and Biven 2012). It was illustrated in the 'age of wonder' by the naturalist Gilbert White in his report of seeing one of the first balloon flights on 16 October 1784: 'I was wonderfully struck with the phenomenon, and, like Milton's "Belated Peasant," felt my heart rebound with joy and fear at the same time' (White, Greenoak and Mabey 1986; Holmes 2008, p. 136).[1] He was 'wonderfully struck.' What a wonder! That a man could fly! His feelings illustrate, with fear and joy, the ambivalent emotion characteristic of curiosity. It recalls William James's association of curiosity with fear of the unknown. Gilbert White said explicitly that it was an occasion for curiosity. In anticipation of the pioneering balloon

[1] The 'Belated Peasant' quote by Gilbert White is from Milton: Paradise Lost, Book I, lines 781–788.

flight by Blanchard passing his way, he 'exhorted all those who had any curiosity to look sharp from about one to three o'clock as they would stand a good chance of being entertained with a very extraordinary sight.'

The nobility of curiosity in Johnson's conception is seen in his attribution of it to 'great and generous minds' as 'the first passion and the last' in his reflection upon a passage from Seneca concerning the value of misfortune. Seneca seemed 'almost to allure us to it, by representing it as necessary to the pleasures of the mind' (Johnson 1751/1969, p. 34). He quotes Seneca in praise of struggle:

> 'He that never was acquainted with adversity,' says he, 'has seen the world but on one side, and is ignorant of half the scenes of nature.' He invites his pupil to calamity, as the Syrens allured the passenger to their coasts, by promising that he shall return *pleiona eidos*, with increase of knowledge, with enlarged views, and multiplied ideas.
>
> Curiosity is, in great and generous minds, the first passion and the last; and perhaps always predominates in proportion to the strength of the contemplative faculties. (Johnson 1751/1969, p. 32)

Johnson saw mental fitness to be strengthened by struggle in much the same way as physical and moral strength is increased in courageous contests with an adversity.

Curiosity and Cognitive Organisation in the Arts and Sciences

Young children show uninhibited curiosity where adults would be more circumspect. Rachel Carson, encouraging parents to take their children into wild places to strengthen an 'inborn sense of wonder,' wrote of the 'clear-eyed vision, that true instinct for what is beautiful and awe-inspiring,' with which she said children are born (Carson, Kelsh and Pratt 1998/1964). Robert White and other psychologists made a similar point about children and young animals generally in regard to their playful, testing and exploring behaviour as prime examples of intrinsic motivation (White 1959). These are Johnson's 'first passions'. The same might appear with a different reflective kind of wonder concerning the 'last passions' in old age.

Holmes in his celebration of such first and last passions in the second, 'romantic' age of European science in the modern era quotes Coleridge and Wordsworth, claiming the same cultural base and inspiration for the arts as for the sciences in that period. Humphry Davy, famed chemist and inventor of the miners' safety lamp, poet and friend of Coleridge, wrote of this commonality in 1807 in terms that would be echoed by both Coleridge and Keats:

> The perception of truth is almost as simple a feeling as the perception of beauty; and the genius of Newton, of Shakespeare, of Michael Angelo, and of Handel, are

not very remote in character from each other. Imagination, as well as the reason, is necessary to perfection in the philosophic mind. A rapidity of combination, a power of perceiving analogies, and of comparing them by facts, is the creative source of discovery. Discrimination and delicacy of sensation, so important in physical research, are other words for taste; and love of nature is the same passion, as the love of the magnificent, the sublime, and the beautiful. (Quoted by Holmes from Humphry Davy Works Vol 8 p. 308, Holmes 2008, p. 276)

Wonder

For Holmes, the scientific passion which, at least for a time, the poets also lauded was summed up 'in that childlike, but infinitely complex word, *wonder*'. Coleridge recalled Plato who 'argued that the notion of "wonder" was central to all philosophical thought: "In Wonder all Philosophy began: in Wonder it ends ... But the first Wonder is the Offspring of Ignorance; and the last is the Parent of Adoration."' (Holmes 2008, p. xx). Here Coleridge is giving his own version of Plato's argument (Coleridge 1825, p. 236).[2] A sense of wonder associated with adoration also appeared in the mid-18th century in Charles Wesley's hymn 'Love divine' which concludes with the pilgrim 'Lost in wonder, love and praise' (Wesley and Wesley 1747). These are the sentiments which Philip Fisher in his book *Wonder, the Rainbow and the Aesthetics of Rare Experiences* said spilled out of 'the jar of religion' in the romantic movement 'onto such parts of experience as our relation to landscape, the nearly religious importance of romantic love, and our worshipful interest in our own subjectivity, ... allowing the modern intellectual to hold onto covert religious feelings under an aesthetic disguise' (Fisher 1998, pp. 1–2).

The full romantic expression is found in Wordsworth. Holmes quotes Wordsworth's lyric *My heart leaps up when I behold A rainbow in the sky* with its passion of wonder at the beginning, middle and ending of life:

> My heart leaps up when I behold
> A rainbow in the sky;
> So was it when my life began;
> So is it now I am a man;
> So be it when I shall grow old,
> Or let me die! ... (Wordsworth 1977, p. 522;
> the poem dates from 1802)

[2] Plato in *Theaetetus*: **Socrates.** I see, my dear Theaetetus, that Theodorus had a true insight into your nature when he said that you were a philosopher, for wonder is the feeling of a philosopher, and philosophy begins in wonder. He was not a bad genealogist who said that Iris (the messenger of heaven) is the child of Thaumas (wonder).

There is a little more to be learned here from literature. Holmes does not include in his quote the remaining few lines of the poem:

> The child is father of the man;
> And I could wish my days to be
> Bound each to each in natural piety.

Piety in Wordsworth is typically inspired by 'nature', in a passion shared with scientists of the period as illustrated by Davy.

Wonder is the purest expression, the most intimate and direct experience, of intrinsic motivation. To be struck with a sense of awe and wonder is a common yet by no means ordinary human experience. To be fascinated, interested, puzzled or intrigued, by an unexpected, strange, unusual, novel, marvellous, wonderful, even conflicting or contradictory event, and hence to feel an urge to understand, discover or make sense of something, is one of the most basic and yet elevating experiences. In cognitive theory it tends towards unification in the resolution of an incomplete gestalt.

In his final solution to the problem of the instincts Freud defined *eros* in terms of a basic tendency to seek the unity of all things, in contrast to the 'death instinct' tending to disintegration (Freud 1936). Curiosity is concerned with seeking unity in the face of disunity and diversity. Something has happened to produce a sense of incompleteness in one's understanding. In psychoanalytic theory, the link with orderly control is at the point where sadomasochistic elements are supposed to become differentiated from the libidinal complex (Aronoff 1962). The suggestion is that we should look for two contrasting facets of curiosity. The desire to experience disorder and the desire to order experience are compounded in a cognitive style or strategy with tantalizing ambivalent affective properties.

The Cognitive Process Theory of Curiosity

The cognitive process theory of curiosity was initially inspired more by Hebb and Piaget (Hebb 1949; Piaget 1950; Piaget, Gattegno and Hodgson 1951; Piaget 1953; Hebb 1955, 1958) and by information theory (Cherry 1956; Berlyne 1957; Cherry 1957) than by Freud and Western literary traditions, but all these contributed together with insights from the history of mathematics, science and aesthetics. In my early research on the measurement of curiosity, individual differences in curiosity were construed as evidence of a preferred cognitive strategy for dealing with uncertainty that leads to conceptual conflict. In my original presentation, however, the process of curiosity arousal and resolution was mistakenly seen to depend exclusively upon the generation of conceptual conflict out of uncertainty (Beswick 1964, 1971). The revised version of the cognitive process theory of curiosity now includes attention to gaps in knowledge as well as conceptual conflict, and beyond that the function of incomplete gestalts.

Gaps in Knowledge, Uncertainty, Conflict and Good Form

Berlyne's understanding of curiosity was based primarily on the arousal value of conflict, as expounded in his book *Conflict, Arousal and Curiosity* (Berlyne 1960). However, he also acknowledged the role of gaps in knowledge in his earlier presentation of a theory of human curiosity (Berlyne 1954), and in his posthumously published unfinished work on curiosity and learning (Berlyne 1978). In his address at the conclusion of the Toronto conference on Intrinsic Motivation in 1970 he defined specific curiosity in terms of a need of the brain for specific information, while diversive exploration covers activities aimed at stimulation providing sufficient variety, regardless of content (Berlyne 1971a).

Berlyne followed this with a reference to conflict as a necessary condition for curiosity, and to diversive exploration as having nothing to do with curiosity:

> Specific exploration depends on uncertainty and on the conflict that results from uncertainty. This is the kind of motivational condition that I myself would call 'curiosity' (Berlyne 1960, 1963, 1965). As I have used the term, curiosity has nothing whatever to do with diversive exploration (Berlyne 1971a, p. 190).

As is evident in my paper given at the same conference, I had not then incorporated the idea of gaps in knowledge into the cognitive process theory, although I did agree with Berlyne on the distinction of specific *curiosity* from diversive *exploration* (Beswick 1971). But the inclusion of gaps was not sufficient. Although I later adopted Loewenstein's suggestion of a central role for gaps in knowledge (Loewenstein 1994), I became dissatisfied with it, even as an addition to the role of conceptual conflicts. The trouble is that a model dependent on gaps tends to suggest that a person might seek a predefined item of knowledge to fit a specific gap that might restore a previous order, whereas in fact combining new information with the old always produces a new order that cannot be foreseen. No new information fits exactly, and that requires some accommodation. Any degree of accommodation results in a new conceptual order. Most importantly, this new order is what a curious person is seeking.

In the general theory of cognitive motivation, both conceptual conflict resolution and the filling of knowledge gaps are aspects of a more general process of striving for the completion of an incomplete gestalt in which 'good form' is sought. That kind of resolution is postulated to be the result of a basic integrating characteristic of the brain enabling people to 'make sense' of the world, along the lines of what Hebb suggested (Hebb 1949) and Köhler and other early Gestalt psychologists proposed (Köhler 1938). The fact of seeing whole images is a starting point for theory construction. The idea of an incomplete gestalt moving towards completion is developed further in Chapter 7 in regard to processes of integration in working memory, in Chapters 9 and 10 when considering the nature of goals and intentions, and in Chapter 11 in regard to personal identity.

The Cognitive Map and the Coding Operation, Assimilation and Accommodation

In the cognitive process theory of curiosity, as it was originally conceived (Beswick 1964, 1971), we assume a category system or cognitive map, which is a simplified grouping of experiences that has been organised to make sense of the world, to which incoming information is referred and within which it is coded for meaning. Input may be an external stimulus or a covert event. Individual differences in curiosity are seen to be a function of category system characteristics and differences in the coding operation. The relevant differences in the coding operation are those which arise when there is some difficulty in coding (or decoding) a signal. Whenever any degree of difficulty of coding is present, the coding operation will involve a corresponding degree of one or both of two processes of modification: assimilation and accommodation in Piaget's terminology. Assimilation is modification of the signal; accommodation is the modification of the cognitive map (Piaget 1950).

At about the same time as this theory was originally developed McReynolds presented a similar model applied principally to perception. He assumed that

> higher animals develop a cognitive structure which represents for them the nature of the world ... When new experiences occur a certain amount of reorganization would be required ... It is postulated that animals have an inherent tendency to assimilate new input, i.e. to carry through such cognitive restructuring as necessary to 'fit' new percepts congruently into the over-all cognitive structure. (McReynolds 1962, pp. 312–313; see also McReynolds 1971)

There are many sources of individual differences in these processes of adjustment to unexpected changes. Some people experience coding difficulties of greater intensity and more frequently than others do. Difficulty of coding will also vary within a person from time to time. Some situations are more likely than others to be the source of uncertain signals and some people are more likely than others to be in such situations. In any particular situation different people will have different probabilities of coding difficulties. Category systems vary in their efficiency regarding a particular signal and also in the probability of their being inefficient given a different signal. For any given degree of difficulty there will be differences in the degree to which assimilation or accommodation takes place. In many such respects we can expect some consistency within people across a large number of situations. Such consistencies which differentiate one person from another may be called traits or motives, or perhaps we might think of them as highly general habits or cognitive styles or strategies. These individual differences derive from different probabilities of uncertainty, and different strategies for dealing with uncertainty.

Berlyne held that curiosity is not to be explained with reference to uncertainty alone, but to conflict which is a product of uncertainty and the absolute strength of competing responses (Berlyne 1960). In this he was following Hull's principles of behaviour (Hull 1943b). Instead of the Hullian idea of competing responses, in the cognitive process theory I refer to *conceptual* conflict and see it as a function of information processing. Instead of the absolute strength of competing responses, I refer to degrees of accommodation that would be required for the coding operation to be completed. Conceptual conflict is then a function of the uncertainty of the signal and the extent of accommodation that would be required for the signal to be coded without a degree of assimilation that results in loss of the uniqueness of the signal.

Having a well-developed capacity to reorder one's cognitive map with appropriate accommodation, a highly curious person is well able to deal creatively with conceptual conflict, or with any other form of incompleteness. But it might not be an easy process. How painful it is (remember, to be creative is to give birth) will depend upon the extent of accommodation required for a 'good' solution.

Let me illustrate this idea of degrees of accommodation. Suppose you are walking along a bush track and hear something move nearby. You might have that creepy feeling of apprehension illustrating William James's conjunction of curiosity with fear. You could be very uncertain whether it is a mammal, a bird or a reptile. If it is an animal you are familiar with, a brief investigation might satisfy your curiosity without much change in your cognitive map. But if you are a naturalist with an 18th-century view of the animal kingdom and you discover a platypus, which has fur like a cat, a bill like a duck, both lays eggs and suckles its young, and even has a poison gland like a snake, then accommodation will require a fundamental restructuring of your taxonomy to define a new order of mammals, the monotremes. Being the only mammals that lay eggs, and like birds and reptiles has only one opening for elimination, excretion and reproduction, monotremes (platypus and echidna species) are seen in some respects as intermediate in evolution between reptiles and mammals. The uniqueness of the platypus was celebrated by the Australian poet, A. B. 'Banjo' Paterson:

> In a style that is most elusive;
> With few relations and fewer friends,
> For Old Man Platypus descends
> From a family most exclusive ...
>
> As he goes on his journey lonely;
> For he's no relation to fish nor fowl,
> Nor to bird nor beast, nor to horned owl;
> In fact, he's the one and only!

As Stephen Jay Gould (1991, p. 270) put it, the platypus 'surely wins first prize in anybody's contest to identify the most curious mammal' because of 'its enigmatic mélange of reptilian (or birdlike), with obviously mammalian characters.' In the final year of his long voyage of exploration on the *Beagle*, Charles Darwin was fascinated by the platypus he found in a river, Cox's Creek near Bathurst, NSW, when the *Beagle* called at Sydney in 1836: 'Certainly it is a most extraordinary animal' (Darwin 1988, p. 402). The 'paradoxical' nature of the distinguishing characteristics of the animal, which he recorded as *ornithorhyncus paradoxicus*,[3] peaked his curiosity, as did many other strange phenomena, in the direction of the theory he published more than two decades later.[4] Darwin made a point of recognizing in his diary its specific name as he knew it, *paradoxicus*. The paradoxical combination of mammalian and reptilian features in one animal illustrated stimulus conditions for the arousal of conceptual conflict which would provide an incentive for re-ordering his cognitive map so radically in this case that, when combined with other observations, it led eventually to the theory of evolution.[5]

The greater the conflict, the more radical the revision required of the category system. The challenge for Darwin was enormous, such was the radical nature of the new ordering of species and their origins he

[3] In later systematics it is known as *Ornithorynchus anatinus.*

[4] Charles Darwin, *Beagle Diary*, January 19, 1836.

[5] That this observation was associated by Darwin with deep thought about the ordering of nature is revealed in his very next diary entry: 'Would any two workmen ever have hit upon so beautiful, so simple, and yet so artificial a contrivance? It cannot be thought so: one Hand has surely worked throughout the universe.' Darwin still held a traditional Christian understanding of nature at this time.

considered in reflection upon the rich data collected during his voyage on the *Beagle*. His recent biographers comment in reference to notes he made in May 1838: 'The speed with which Darwin adopted evolution hints at a gestation on the voyage' (Desmond and Moore 2010, p. 114). He recorded his musings about evolution in the years immediately after the return of the *Beagle* only in secret notebooks. These were times of struggle for Darwin, with many symptoms of stress noted by his biographers. Begun early, it was a long struggle commensurate with the amount of conceptual accommodation required by such paradoxes, illustrating Darwin's own recognition of his 'patience to reflect or ponder for any number of years over any unexplained problem' (Darwin and Barlow 1958, p. 141). Could the platypus represent a step in evolution from reptiles to mammals? Umberto Eco in his *Kant and the Platypus: Essays on Language and Cognition* used the example of the arrival of the platypus in Europe, followed by eighty years of debate on its classification, in his discussion of negotiated meanings. It is the same set of processes as those of cognitive accommodation in curiosity at the macro level of organisation (Beswick 1964, 1971; Eco 1999).

The Combination of Approach and Avoidance

Conflict is not the whole story. Most significantly it does not specify directly the importance of directed grow of organisation that Hebb had originally emphasised. More than conflict is required, but it is also a mistake to dismiss conflict theories entirely on the grounds that such theories attempt to explain curiosity as an aversive response. Kashdan and his colleagues have tended to take this view, although in more recent work they have seen it as part of a tension between mechanisms that might be resolved (Kashdan 2004; Peterson and Seligman 2004; Kashdan and Silvia 2009). In their discussion of curiosity and well-being as an aspect of positive psychology Kashdan and Silvia pick up the tension between what they regard as the old conflict model and new evidence on the value of curiosity as an experience of positive attraction:

> [T]here are a number of discrepancies that need to be resolved. For example, some research suggests that the pleasures of curiosity are derived from resolving ambiguity and uncertainty (Beswick 1971, Loewenstein 1994), whereas other work finds that the process of discovery and meaning making is intrinsically enjoyable (Feist 1994) and that positive emotions can be sustained by intentionally attending to the lingering uncertainty in a given situation (Wilson, Centerbar, Kermer, & Gilbert, 2005; Kashdan and Silvia 2009, p. 371)

Moving on from my early conflict model of curiosity towards a more general theory, intrinsically enjoyable processes of meaning making are the subject of much that I discuss in this book. Resolution of the difference Kashdan and Silvia identify is quite simple: We need to take into account the *whole process* of curiosity, from the input of ambiguous signals to the central processes in which they are coded for meaning. In that process an incomplete gestalt is resolved with positive anticipation.

An approach response to novelty is characteristic of curiosity, but there is a place for negative emotions in the power of conflict to set up conditions for future attraction. The attractive value of an aversive state of conflict is illustrated in the masochistic qualities in Freud's account of curiosity, and in the experimental conditions in which punishment has been found to increase the strength of punished responses (Church 1963). A response tendency has been found to be strengthened under certain conditions of punishment: i.e., when the punishment is mild so that the response continues to be emitted and the escape response is identical with the punished response, or when fear is the discriminative stimulus for the response, or a positive reward is used to maintain a response that is periodically punished. All those conditions can be present in the creation and resolution of conceptual conflicts.

When Loewenstein referred to relief from feelings of deprivation and he suggested a central role for attention to gaps in knowledge, he pointed explicitly to the relevance of Gestalt principles for completing whole images (Loewenstein 1994). These principles bring a positive orientation to the use of conflict for the development of good form in cognitive schemas. We will see this later in reference to several different dimensions in measures of curiosity, including the comparison of interest and deprivation types of curiosity and of 'liking' and 'wanting' types of arousal, in the work of Litman and his associates (Litman 2005, 2008, 2010).

There is ample evidence and argument that a simple bivalent hedonic view of the effect of feelings, in which pleasure signals approach and pain avoidance, is inadequate. Affects for approach and avoidance are both seen in curiosity, and they can be ambivalent and complex. A more differentiated view of the pleasure principle given by Tory Higgins (1997, 1998, 2001) is discussed briefly later in this chapter and in Chapter 8, in which I consider the general role of emotions in cognitive motivation. I refer there also to Panksepp's description of basic affective systems in which curiosity is represented in the SEEKING system, with its emotion of excited, euphoric anticipation that is 'is entirely different from the pleasurable release of consummation' (Panksepp and Biven 2012, p. 96). This finding from neuroscience refers to basic biological processes, while the excited ambivalent feelings associated with curiosity that Gilbert White described as 'joy and fear at the same time' are culturally developed and modified. In Chapter 12, in reference to 'needs for meaning',

I discuss a view of emotions with an infinite range of qualities associated with an infinite range of human needs. The dichotomy of pain or pleasure is oversimplified and misleading.

Within a general paradigm of self-regulation, Higgins has described variations in *regulatory focus*, 'a principle that underlies the hedonic principle but differs radically in its motivational consequences' (Higgins 1997, p. 1280). It has different effects from those attributed to the pleasure principle that was previously supposed to govern approach and avoidance: 'According to regulatory focus theory, goal pursuit takes place in two distinct motivational systems (Higgins 1997, 1998)' (Cornwell and Higgins 2016, p. 339). One strategy is preventive and aimed at security or defence of the status quo. The other, a promotion focus, seeks to exceed the status quo through the attainment of growth and accomplishments. The first is characterised by vigilance and the second by eagerness. Both are found in curiosity. In the cognitive process theory of curiosity the preventive or vigilance strategy is typically invoked at an early stage of perception when something strange appears; it might perhaps be combined at the early stage with anticipation of a new understanding, but that hope for growth of organisation is more likely to arise after some period of reflection when the second strategy of eagerness in seeking growth of organisation appears with strength. Growth of organisation is characteristic particularly of the last stage of the curiosity process when ambiguous signals are coded for meaning. Implications of the regulatory focus theory are explored further in Chapter 8 with reference to the different types of emotional experience that arise from different motivational conditions.

The general explanation of curiosity in cognitive theory is that awareness of conflicts and gaps in knowledge directs attention to an incomplete gestalt. This leads to the cognitive processes that result in growth or development of organisation in which conflicts are resolved and gaps filled as an incomplete gestalt moves towards completion. This is the general form of cognitive motivation theory of which the cognitive process theory of curiosity is a special case.

Delay of Gratification

Conflicts and gaps must be maintained while new information is gathered and incompleteness eventually resolved. The delay caused by this step is an important part of the process. Berlyne commented on the need for delay of gratification: 'Ultimately, the only effective way to deal with ambiguity is to procure additional information through exploratory and epistemic behaviour, but this means that the conflict must be borne for a while' (Berlyne 1960, p. 216).

For many people, it is counter-intuitive to see curiosity as in part a function of concern for order and willingness to delay gratification in order to achieve it, but these predicted correlations were confirmed (Beswick 1971). Curiosity is typically seen to be a response to novel events, and to be associated with an attitude of openness to varied experience, but novelty attracts attention when it is seen against an ordered background. A novel occurrence in a field of chaos is not noticed. People are attracted to novelty when it contrasts with order. They seek to reconcile the resulting conceptual conflicts and perceived gaps in knowledge. This takes time while they seek additional information and process it in relation to what is already in their cognitive systems. A person with little curiosity could make a quick and careless adjustment to account for new information, or they could reject it altogether; but a highly curious person will take time and maintain the tension while they work out a good resolution. To do that, they must be able to tolerate delay of gratification.

In the process of coding a signal, assimilation and accommodation are delayed by attention given to a unique signal and care taken not to disrupt the category system. The aim of a highly curious person is to order experience in a new way, even at the risk of placing his or her cognitive map in jeopardy. In contrast, a person with low curiosity has learned a risk avoidance strategy. The highly curious person has regard for both the unique qualities of the signal and the integrity of the category system. Resolution is thus delayed while a 'good' solution or gestalt is sought.

Empirical Support for the Cognitive Process Theory

In the early stages of renewed attention to curiosity and exploration in the 1950s, one of the principal points of reference for operational definitions was insight into the nature of curiosity from the experimental work of Daniel Berlyne (Berlyne 1954, 1957, 1960, 1966, 1971a). Berlyne's work continued to provide guidance for measurement of curiosity up to recent years (e.g. Collins, Litman and Spielberger 2004). I want to introduce two measures of curiosity that I employed in early work beginning in the late 1950s and extending into the 1970s. These measures provided evidence in favour of the cognitive process theory. One was a fantasy measure and the other a questionnaire type of scale. Both owe some important concepts to Berlyne, but this theory did not share all of Berlyne's assumptions: i.e. not the remnants of drive reduction theory.

The initial aim was to assess reliable individual differences in a predisposition to adopt a characteristic strategy for coping with novel stimuli. Previous experimental work had concentrated on the manipulation of stimulus conditions. In the simplest case it seemed reasonable to expect that an approach rather than an avoidance response to a novel stimulus would be related to learned strategies for coping with such situations in general. That would amount to a trait type of motive characterising a person and differing between people. Both the Curiosity TAT and the Test of Intrinsic Motivation were designed to assess that kind of variable.

Parallel Development of Theory and the Fantasy Measure

The Curiosity TAT (Beswick 1964, 1971) was a measure of individual differences in curiosity in the tradition of studying what McClelland and Atkinson, following Murray, called 'psychogenic' needs or motives, such as need for achievement (Murray 1938; McClelland et al. 1953; Atkinson 1958a). I began work on curiosity with their approach but soon developed a different theoretical orientation because I found that their need satisfaction model of motivation did not work with curiosity. The cognitive process theory of curiosity that was developed in parallel with the test required quite different concepts.

The method developed in fantasy measures standardized by McClelland and his colleagues used a modified version of Murray's Thematic Apperception Test (TAT) (Murray 1938, 1953; Atkinson 1958a). New sets of stimulus pictures for story telling were developed for the Curiosity TAT. Pictures that were selected in preliminary investigations had high ratings by judges of potential for curiosity arousal given the conceptual definition of curiosity, and later evidence of curiosity imagery in stories written in response to them. Subjects were asked to write imaginative stories about what was going on in the scenes depicted. The same kind of instructions were used in the Curiosity TAT as in the assessment of needs for achievement, affiliation and power (Atkinson 1958a). Curiosity-arousing conditions were employed in experimental groups in which junior high school students were shown pictures of strange animals and encouraged to ask questions about them. Their stories were compared with those produced in control groups. It was soon found that the means-ends relations of instrumental acts in the kind of goal directed sequences described by McClelland and colleagues were not evident in stories written in response to curiosity-arousing conditions, so that the need satisfaction model of motivation was abandoned and an information-processing model adopted in accordance the developing theory.

The nature of curiosity as it was being measured in the special purpose Curiosity TAT is illustrated by the scoring categories.[6] Five principal

[6] The Curiosity TAT scoring manual is available on line at www.beswick.info/psychres/curiosityTATscoringmanual.html.

categories of curiosity imagery were defined: wonder-interest (WI); perceptual investigatory acts (Pe); cognitive acts instrumental in problem solving (Co); exploratory role behaviour (Eb); and a cue-response sequence of two points in a sequence of interesting stimulus, intrapsychic excitement and overt information gathering (CR). There were also minor categories of imagery concerned with interesting stimuli (Si), an intrapsychic response of excitement (Ix) and overt seeking behaviour (Ov); and there were contrary indications (CI). Scoring criteria were specified in detail with example stories and a high degree of scoring reliability was obtained. A total score for each story was obtained by following certain rules to combine scoring categories, and an individual person score was the total across four stories.

Content analysis of fantasy material is no longer widely used in personality research, although a renewed presentation of such fantasy measures was produced in the 1990s (Smith 1992). It even included a measure similar my Curiosity TAT: a method of assessing individual differences in 'uncertainty orientation' (Sorrentino, Roney and Hanna 1992). Such measures lend themselves to the illustration of the basic processes of curiosity motivation evident in a narrative only when a cognitive rather than a need reduction approach has been adopted. Only the basic concepts of information theory were generally known at the time of the original studies, although Berlyne had already introduced information theory into the study of curiosity (Berlyne 1957). The concepts of information theory that I adopted came initially from Cherry (1956, 1957). Conceptualizing what was happening in this way led to the early formulation of a theory of curiosity in cognitive terms.

The content analysis method of assessment was preferred in the early years of this research on curiosity (Beswick 1964, 1971). For practical reasons of administration in large survey samples and a need for increased reliability, other theoretically related measures in questionnaire form were developed in later work (Beswick and Tallmadge 1971; Beswick 1974, 1983; Beswick and Boreham 1986). The most useful of these was the Test of Intrinsic Motivation that we will come to shortly, after considering some the correlates of curiosity as it was measured by the Curiosity TAT.

Orderliness, Openness, Delay of Gratification and Other Correlates

Among the correlates found in the construct validation of the Curiosity TAT were attitudinal preferences for both orderliness and novelty, and for delay of gratification, all important in confirmation of predictions made in the cognitive process theory. These correlates were found together with school achievement (in some situations), voluntary use of a school library, independent inquiries in religion and teachers' ratings of children with high curiosity scores as more intellectually inclined and more internally controlled (Beswick 1964, 1971). Evidence was also found for learning style effects, or aptitude treatment interactions, in the moderation of learning performance by curiosity under varying condition of curiosity arousal in instructional treatments (Beswick and Tallmadge 1971).

Both openness and orderliness are predicted to be positively correlated with curiosity, although they may be negatively correlated with each other. Such constructs appear on different factors, for example, in the five factor model of personality (Digman 1990, Goldberg 1990). Most people readily associate curiosity with openness. The relevance of orderliness is not as commonly recognized, although some theorists, such as Maddi at an early stage, independently arrived at the conclusion that curiosity is associated with orderliness (Maddi 1971). The importance of structure as well as openness in the functioning of curiosity in learning was recognized also in education (Corlis and Wiess 1973). A combination of openness with orderliness will dispose a person to generating conceptual conflicts, the resolution of which is facilitated by a capacity for delay of gratification.

Taking a cue from Freudian theory, a scale of orderliness was constructed[7] with items selected from a set of anal metaphors used by Couch and Keniston in their work on Agreement Response Set. It correlated positively with the Curiosity TAT for both girls and boys. Items in the orderliness scale that correlated best with curiosity were:

> I am a great one for picking things up and putting them where they belong.
> I always use the same system in studying.
> I do things more slowly and carefully than most people.
> I like to have everything in its proper place.

The openness variable was less well defined in the original study with less certain results, but when a stronger measure of openness was developed from Fitzgerald's Openness to Experience scale and used with university students, the correlation was positive for both sexes (Couch and Keniston 1960; Fitzgerald 1966; Beswick 1971).

Delay of gratification as a personality measure was predicted to correlate with curiosity. That was found to be the case in the same study as the original orderliness and openness findings, but only for girls,

[7] This study of curiosity and orderliness was a joint project with Ralph Metzner.

probably because of the effect of agreement response set for boys. The measure of delay of gratification was a simple behavioural test employed by Mischel and Metzner in which subjects were offered a choice between a small candy bar now and large candy bar later (Mischel and Metzner 1962). At the early stage of research on curiosity, inconsistencies were not uncommon or surprising. It was also at an early stage in Mischel's later much extended work on delay of gratification (Mischel 1974). The overall effect, however, of these and related findings was to confirm the approach taken in the development of the cognitive process theory and the TAT test of curiosity.

Other correlates of the curiosity TAT measure included positive attitudes to reading, as in the questionnaire attitude item 'I love to read a lot,' and a behavioural measure in the number of books secondary school students borrowed voluntarily from their school library (Beswick 1971). Given these correlations, it was to be expected that curiosity should be related to school achievement, and in these early investigations there was usually a stronger correlation with average school achievement than with intelligence, although the correlation with school achievement varied between schools and was very low in some. Some school cultures are more amenable to learning motivated by curiosity than are others. Kashdan and Silvia have concluded from a range of different studies that while 'In general students with greater curiosity have more academic success than less curious peers' (Schiefele, Krapp and Winteler 1992, Hidi and Berndorff 1998), 'there are crucial contextual matters that moderate whether curious students thrive academically' (Kashdan and Silvia 2009, p. 369). Although highly curious students initiate more questions, they are inhibited when teachers are perceived as threatening (Peters 1978). In Hong Kong, high grades were associated with an academically challenging school environment (Kashdan and Yuen 2007).

In my earlier Australian study, when high school teachers were asked to comment on high- and low-scoring groups on the Curiosity TAT, without knowing the basis of their classification, they tended to describe high scorers as more intellectually inclined, asking more good-quality questions, showing originality, reading more voluntarily, being more socially responsible and perhaps most interestingly, by one teacher, as 'lik[ing] to chew new material well before making a start, but then very quick.' Low scorers were described as more cheerful about work, more demanding of attention, more careless, unable to concentrate, noisy, lively, tending to complain and lacking internal controls (Beswick 1971).

In the same study, an intriguing and quite strong association with religious interests for high scorers on the curiosity test was found among high school students who had been identified in the community as making independent inquiries in religion but whose families were not connected with any religious institution (Beswick 1971). These finding all tend to confirm the validity of the Curiosity TAT, and to support the cognitive process theory of curiosity.

Specific Curiosity and Diversive Exploration

When we consider a range of different measures of curiosity, there are important questions about what is being measured. There has been a continuing concern with the possibility that we could be talking about a number of different things. 'Is curiosity a unitary construct?' was the title of an important early paper on the dimensionality of curiosity tests by Langevin (1971). Following a distinction made by Berlyne and Day, he found two general factors of theoretical importance separating specific curiosity from sensation seeking. While many studies are mentioned in later reviews as justifying some doubt about the unidimensionality of measures of curiosity (Loewenstein 1994; Spielberger and Starr 1994; Kashdan 2004; Peterson and Seligman 2004), two pieces of empirical research (Ainley 1987; Byman 2005), supported by a third (Starr 1992; Spielberger and Starr 1994), stand out as usefully demonstrating what Langevin had found: that there are two independent factors which appear to correspond to Berlyne's theoretical distinction between 'specific curiosity' and 'diversive exploration' (Berlyne 1960, 1963, 1966, Day 1968, 1969, 1971; Langevin 1971).

Ainley tested a two-factor theory after examining the pattern of correlations among a wide range of measures of curiosity, exploration and related constructs reported in the literature which suggested that 'they are not all assessing the same general behavioural function' (Ainley 1987, p. 55). She characterised these two groupings as representing (1) 'a breadth-of-interest curiosity style' and (2) 'a depth-of interest curiosity style'. These factors were generally known as specific curiosity and diversive curiosity or exploration. In Ainley's investigation, those scales and subscales with high loadings on Factor 1 were all scales which were classified as representing a depth-of-interest curiosity style. On the other hand, those scales which had a high loading on Factor 2 were all scales classified as being concerned with a breadth-of-interest curiosity style concerned primarily with seeking out new sensations and experiences (Ainley 1987). The scale with the highest loading on the depth factor was the Test of Intrinsic Motivation (IM) (Beswick 1974), the construction of which had been guided by the cognitive process theory of curiosity and which had been developed from items which correlated with the Curiosity TAT.

Support for the two-factor solutions of Langevin and Ainley is found in a similar study by Starr (1992) (see also Spielberger and Starr 1994). She found the same two factors: the first, she named Information Seeking, and the second Experience Seeking.

Berlyne's distinction between diversive *exploration* and specific *curiosity* – 'as I have used the term, curiosity has nothing whatever to do with diversive exploration' (Berlyne 1971a, p. 190) – is brought out in the introduction to Byman's more recent research:

> Curiosity has been seen (e.g., Beswick 1971, Deci and Ryan 1985) as a prototypical example of *intrinsic motivation*. Several researchers (e.g., Ainley 1987, Zuckerman 1994, Collins et al. 2004, Kashdan, Rose and Fincham 2004) have also included the concept of sensation seeking in the concept of curiosity. Specifically, they have argued that sensation seeking comes very close to *diversive curiosity* in the epistemic-diversive curiosity distinction first suggested by Day, (1968) (Zuckerman 1994, p. 27). (Byman 2005, p. 1366)

Seeking novelty and being prepared to take risks are part of curiosity, but these qualities are not sufficient to describe curiosity because we need to include also those central cognitive processes that give meaning to incoming information.

Byman's conclusions, which were similar to those of Ainley, came from a study with a different age group in a different cultural setting. Byman's subjects were fifth grade children in Finland, for whom he used a translation of the original tests from English into Finnish verified as appropriate to the age group, whereas Ainley had tested college students in Australia. The differences in age, language and nationality are helpful, because we assume that in curiosity we are dealing with universal human qualities. Separate analyses were conducted for girls and boys, and the same factors were found for both. He named his two factors 'Curiosity' and 'Sensation Seeking.' The Curiosity factor corresponds closely to Ainley's depth of interest curiosity factor and Sensation Seeking to her breadth of interest factor.

The Intrinsic Motivation Test

Significantly, the same test of Intrinsic Motivation (IM) (Beswick 1974) was the best predictor of the 'Curiosity' factor[8] in Byman's analysis as for the depth of interest curiosity factor in the Ainley study (Byman 2005). These findings tend to strengthen the claims of the cognitive process theory of curiosity which guided the development of the IM test.

[8] Factor loadings 0.81 for boys and 0.76 for girls in Byman's analysis, and 0.78 combined in the Ainley study.

It could have been called simply 'curiosity,' but it was curiosity broadly conceived. As Byman observed, curiosity was regarded as the prototypical example of intrinsic motivation. Several others had taken a similar view. Day developed the Ontario Test of *Intrinsic* Motivation (OTIM) which assessed specific and diversive *curiosity*. In the years leading up to the development of those measures, Bruner had said, 'Curiosity is almost the prototypical example of the intrinsic motive' (Bruner 1966, p. 114). 'What activates and satisfies curiosity is something inherent in the cycle of activity by which we express curiosity' (Bruner 1966, p. 115). (For definitions and an extended discussion of intrinsic motivation, see Chapter 3.)

Some of the items in the IM test have obvious face validity for a measure of 'curiosity':

> I visit a library to read material not directly related to my class work.
> I like to look at pictures which are puzzling in some way.
> If I come across something interesting, I drop everything and study it. It is never a waste of time.

Somewhat different qualities in a broad concept of curiosity found in intrinsic motivation generally are represented in other items: for example, in a person appreciating conceptual conflict, being able to give careful attention to an item of interest and having the capacity to envisage in response a newly created whole image or gestalt. Such other items in the IM test included:

> Some truths can only be expressed in paradoxical statements.
> At times I have focused on something so hard that I went into a kind of benumbed state of consciousness, or at other times into a state of extraordinary calm and serenity.
> I have had experiences which inspired me to write a poem or a story, or make up a humorous tale, or paint a picture.

The IM test was developed to correlate with a range of other tests of specific epistemic curiosity or intrinsic motivation, including the OTIM and ratings by peers and teachers. Items which correlated with the TAT scores in the early samples were found to be associated also with peers' and teachers' ratings and the other curiosity scales. The broad empirical base of the IM test was thus combined in its development with reference to the cognitive theory that had been developed jointly with the Curiosity TAT.

What is being measured by this test is the specific curiosity or the depth of interest factor defined in the two factor studies of Langevin,

Ainley, Starr and Byman. It also corresponds to Berlyne's theoretical definition of specific epistemic curiosity and both theoretically and empirically to the operational definition in Day's measure of specific curiosity in the OTIM and theoretically to Litman and Spielberger's measure of epistemic curiosity. The cognitive process theory applies to this depth type of specific curiosity and not to diversive exploration. It is concerned particularly with internal processing of new information for meaningful integration.

Components of Curiosity

Instead of a single test which sampled various aspects of the process defined by the theory, as in the CuriosityTAT and the Intrinsic Motivation test, we could have several different tests to sample different aspects of curiosity at different points in the process of encoding a difficult signal. In contrast with the single dimension of the broadly conceived IM test, Carbonneau, Vallerand and Lafreniere (2012) have recently published a test for a tripartite model of intrinsic motivation in which one factor appears to correspond closely with the specific epistemic curiosity that is measured by the IM test, another factor is concerned with what Berlyne and others have called diversive exploration, and a third is concerned primarily with achievement motivation. A recent impressive series of studies by Litman and his associates can be interpreted similarly, as sampling the information processing functions in a multidimensional view of curiosity with associated affective qualities that can be observed at different points in a basic set of related cognitive processes.

Multidimensional Direct Measurement of Components in the Curiosity Process

Litman reported these studies as defining different *kinds* of curiosity. These 'kinds' of curiosity were within the domain of specific curiosity as it was defined by Berlyne. I suggest that Litman and his colleagues' 'dimensions' or 'types' of curiosity are related aspects of the one set of basic curiosity processes. They developed tests of sensory (Litman, Collins and Spielberger 2005), perceptual (Collins et al. 2004) and epistemic curiosity (Litman and Spielberger 2003), and then of interest and deprivation, and 'liking' and 'wanting,' types of curiosity within the domain of specific curiosity (Litman and Jimerson 2004; Litman 2005; Litman and Silvia 2006; Litman 2008).

All of Litman's 'dimensions' of curiosity are correlated or oblique factors. The correlations between the seven curiosity scales in his paper on

'Interest' and 'Deprivation' factors (Litman 2008) are all clearly positive in each of three studies, ranging from 0.49 to 0.80.[9] These oblique factors are distinguished from one another in such a way as to point to what can be regarded as different but related mechanisms underlying curiosity at different points in one integrated system.

Sensory, Perceptual and Epistemic Curiosity

The perceptual and epistemic curiosity constructs were introduced by Berlyne as forms of specific curiosity motivating the search for specific kinds of information, as distinct from seeking diverse stimulation in general that might be the purpose of undirected exploration (Berlyne 1954, 1960, 1963, 1965, 1966, 1971a). Byman, when testing his two-factor model of curiosity and sensation seeking (leaving aside the method factor), found that he could have settled on a solution that defined latent variables of perceptual and epistemic curiosity instead of a single curiosity factor (Byman 2005). His report strengthens support for Berlyne's original definitions of epistemic and perceptual curiosity and for Litman and Spielberger's measurement of these variables. In the cognitive process theory perceptual curiosity is on the input side of epistemic curiosity which is more heavily dependent upon central processing. A further 'dimension of sensory curiosity' (Litman et al. 2005) samples information processing operations still closer to the input side than does perceptual curiosity.

Feelings of Deprivation and Interest

Litman's distinction between 'Interest' and 'Deprivation' factors (Litman 2005; Litman and Silvia 2006; Litman 2008) brings another perspective to curiosity that recalls some of the early discussion of its ambivalent nature. It is a distinction of *feelings*. 'Curiosity as a feeling of interest' was distinguished from 'Curiosity as a feeling of deprivation' (or I-type from D-type curiosity). When taken together with Litman's further distinction between 'Liking' and 'Wanting' types of curiosity, it points to the underlying affective processes which are responsible for the emotional ambivalence that is traditionally associated with curiosity. It refers to different mechanisms for emotional arousal that are invoked by different aspects of curiosity.

Treating interest and deprivation factors together keeps an emphasis on resolution of conflicts and gaps in knowledge as distinct from arousal

[9] Leaving aside the correlation of subscales with the total scale of which they were a part.

of interest. Intrinsic motivation certainly has appetitive qualities, while it retains elements of tension reduction in cognitive terms: 'But the nervous system, and in particular the brain, has its needs no less than other parts of the body, and intrinsic motivation is bound up with these ... At one time, in more dualistic and mentalistic days, people used to talk about the "needs of the mind" or of "the spirit"' (Berlyne 1971a, pp. 187–188).

Harlow had referred to 'tensions in the brain' (Harlow 1953b). When Litman drew attention to a feeling of deprivation in curiosity, it was to *cognitive* deprivation like a sense of missing something when gaps in knowledge are experienced (Loewenstein 1994). Similarly, for the other, I-type, of curiosity, the feeling of interest associated with seeking novelty is not indiscriminant stimulus seeking, but seeking information input that is likely to generate meaningful new cognitive developments. In the simplest cognitive model, the generation of interest by a novel stimulus is close to the input side. At later stages of incorporating this input, as the interest arousing information is processed in interaction with the existing cognitive map, it generates conflicts and a sense of incompleteness, which might be experienced as a feeling of deprivation. Litman's interest and deprivation factors thus describe individual differences at different stages in the process of seeking, receiving and processing new information.

Rather than defining different kinds of curiosity, interest or deprivation 'types' of curiosity are, then, better understood in the general theory of cognitive motivation to sample different aspects of curiosity as a sequential process. The feeling of deprivation that arises from giving attention to gaps in knowledge can be understood as the latter part of a process that includes, and may begin with, arousal of interest through attention being given to uncertain signals and concludes with the alleviation of a feeling of deprivation when the gap or conflict is resolved in the development of new understanding in a revised cognitive map.

Neural Bases for Liking and Wanting as Different Kinds of Arousal

Litman presented a 'Wanting and Liking model of information processing' in which a high level of 'Liking (Degree of pleasure)' is associated with both I-type (Interest) and D-type (Deprivation) curiosity, but 'Wanting (Intensity of appetite)' was associated only with D-type curiosity (Litman 2010). So there is 'liking' of stimulus input for both interest and deprivation aspects of curiosity, while 'wanting' input is characteristic only of the deprivation type or aspect.

It is part of this understanding that the interest and deprivation cognitive processes have different affective qualities. Litman wrote several subsequent papers further separating these two aspects of epistemic curiosity, characterising the feeling of interest as 'pleasure' associated with 'liking' the effects of stimuli that are of the interest arousing kind, and separately the 'pain' of 'wanting' input to satisfy conditions of deprivation associated with attention to gaps in knowledge (Litman 2005; Litman and Silvia 2006; Litman 2008, 2010). He and his colleagues suggested that the liking and wanting feelings which are associated with interest and deprivation factors in curiosity may be associated with different degrees of activation in two different neurological bases for the emotional components of motivation in sub-cortical processes:

> The terms *wanting* and *liking* refer to two subcortical neurobiological systems that appear to underlie appetitive motivation and subsequent experiences of pleasure (Berridge and Robinson 1998, Berridge 1999). Wanting involves mesolimbic dopamine activation, and is theorised to motivate approach behaviour and to attribute incentive value to stimuli associated with reward (Berridge 1996, Berridge and Robinson 1998, McClure, Daw and Montague 2003). Liking involves activity in the nucleus accumbens, and handles the evaluation of stimuli in terms of immediate or anticipated hedonic impact and corresponding affective value. (Litman 2005, pp. 802–803)

While there remains some room for debate among neuroscientists on these matters, it appears that dopamine is primarily associated with 'desire' for an incentive, a 'wanting' type of arousal. But even in the absence of much desire, certain attractive stimuli can still produce pleasure, the 'liking' type of arousal that is associated with opioid activity. Although they depend upon activity in independent pathways, the two kinds of arousal can act together, and it is suggested that a combination of the two can produce a very strong response when an interesting prospect is added to a strong desire.

The key point for a cognitive motivation theory is that a neural base for different affective functions has been identified for different aspects of curiosity. Initially, this was done with animal studies, but several direct relationships have now been reported in human subjects between subjective ratings or other evidence of curiosity and activity in various brain areas including those suggested by Litman (Kang et al. 2009; Gruber, Gelman and Ranganath 2014; Kidd and Hayden 2015). At this stage the evidence from neuroscience is suggestive of the relationships expected from psychological studies, although the findings are not entirely consistent.

Kang et al. (2009) contributed significantly to further work on brain functions in relation to curiosity by using functional magnetic resonance imaging (fMRI) to map brain activity during arousal of curiosity by trivia questions and found that 'the level of curiosity when reading questions was correlated with activity in caudate regions previously suggested to be involved in anticipated reward' (p. 963). They found no correlation with activity in the nucleus accumbens, which might have been expected, and which was found later by Gruber et al. (2014) with similar arousal conditions. We need a theoretically coherent explanation of the different findings.

Gruber et al. (2014) used fMRI to investigate how curiosity induced by trivia questions is related to activity in dopaminergic pathways and how it influences memory, with the expectation that people would learn better what they were curious to know. They found that states of high curiosity enhance learning not only of interesting information but also of incidental information. Learning with high curiosity was associated with activity in the relevant brain areas: 'Imaging results demonstrated that these learning benefits are related to anticipatory brain activity in the mesolimbic dopaminergic circuit including the hippocampus' (Gruber et al. 2014, p. 491). Although the level of arousal found in the hippocampus with high-curiosity conditions was relatively weak, 'curiosity had large and long-lasting effects on memory for interesting information' (Gruber et al. 2014, p. 493). As expected, activity in the midbrain (substantia nigra/ventral tegmental area complex SN/VTA) and the nucleus accumbens was enhanced during states of high curiosity, but there were differences between the two brain areas: 'Anticipatory activation in the nucleus accumbens predicted later memory performance only for high-curiosity trivia answers, whereas activation in the SN/VTA was related to memory for high- and low-curiosity trivia answers.' (Gruber et al. 2014, p. 492). Their suggestion that 'anticipatory activity in the nucleus accumbens may set the stage for encoding of upcoming information that is goal relevant' (p. 492) can be aligned with a conception of the interest aspect of curiosity arousal preceding the resolution of the deprivation aspect in a cognitive completion process.

In their review of recent research on the neural mechanisms of curiosity, Kidd and Hayden (2015) note evidence that dopamine neurons signal both primary reward and information value, and suggest that the dopamine response reflects an integration of multiple reward components to generate an abstract reward response. It is not clear whether this response is the same as Litman's proposal for dopamine activation of the wanting type of curiosity arousal, but they do note a proposal that the dopamine reward signal is constructed of input signals originating in the orbitofrontal cortex where input is received from basic sensory and association structures and which they see as a possible input to the evaluation system that should carry information about the reward value of curiosity. It may be inferred that the reward value of dopaminergic activity is associated with the 'deep processing' of information that is being integrated in a meaningful development of the cognitive map in the later stages of the cognitive processes that define curiosity.

Panksepp's affective neuroscience (Panksepp 2005, 2011a) gives a comprehensive neurological account of the basic affective systems that human beings share with other mammals. In Chapters 8 and 12 I discuss the account of basic human emotions in his book with Biven, *The Archaeology of Mind: Neuroevolutionary Origins of Human Emotions* (Panksepp and Biven 2012). The most pervasive of his basic systems is called the SEEKING system.

> *The SEEKING system*: Brain sources of eager anticipation, desire, euphoria, and the quest for everything. Arousal of this SEEKING system produces all kinds of approach behaviors, but it also feels good in a special way. It is not the kind of pleasure that we experience while eating a fine meal, or the satisfaction we feel afterwards. Rather it provides the kind of excited, euphoric anticipation that occurs when we look forward to eating that meal ... This positive feeling (euphoria) of anticipatory eagerness, this SEEKING urge, is entirely different from the pleasurable release of consummation. (Panksepp and Biven 2012, pp. 95–96)

They identify curiosity 'with the mere arousal of the SEEKING system' (p. 360). This 'eager anticipation' is a kind of excitement that is represented in the Curiosity TAT scoring manual as 'an intrapsychic response of excitement' and in several items in the Intrinsic Motivation Test. It is an approach type of excitement produced by attention to interesting stimuli, and in Litman's theory most powerfully represented in the dopamine enhanced 'wanting' type of arousal. Panksepp and Biven say that 'dopamine fuels the SEEKING system.' On the other hand, they also suggest a role for opioids in the relief of tension in the SEEKING system (p. 100).

If, as Panksepp proposes, there are basic mammalian neurological functions that differentially contribute to emotional responses evoked by novelty and these are expressed in the two different aspects of curiosity described by Litman as interest and deprivation factors, then a new account of curiosity could relate its subjective and behavioural manifestations to physiological bases for different feelings. Further studies by Litman and his colleagues have strengthened the empirical base for his distinction of interest and deprivation types of curiosity (Litman and Mussel 2013; Richards, Litman and H. 2013; Piotrowski, Litman and Valkenburg 2014; Lauriola, Litman, Mussel, De Santis, Crowson and Hoffman 2015). In the most recent of these there is an interesting relationship of these two types of curiosity to self-regulation. Briefly, they found that Interest (I) type EC [Epistemic Curiosity] involves optimism, taking risks and having fun while learning; while Deprivation (D) type EC involves caution and thoughtfulness in seeking knowledge. The findings in relation to self-regulation are consistent with the proposition that both openness and cognitive orderliness are factors in curiosity and that curiosity may be facilitated by delay of gratification.

Recently, Lauriola, Litman and their colleagues have commented in regard to their findings on curiosity and self-regulation that 'activation of D-type EC [epistemic curiosity] might not quite reflect "drive-like" experiences as previously hypothesized … but might be more precisely understood as prolonged, moderately intense emotional motivational states that underlie sustained intellectual activity and concentration' (Lauriola et al. 2015, p. 206). The moderately intense emotional states that underlie sustained intellectual activity are what should be expected from the cognitive process theory of curiosity when it is applied at the macro level of long-term interests, such as those in Darwin's reflections upon his own intellectual motivation noted earlier in this chapter and Einstein's report of his thought processes being guided by feelings in his discussions with Wertheimer reviewed in Chapter 9.

Metacognitive Processes

An interesting and theoretically significant aspect of metacognitive processes involving curiosity has been reported by Litman and colleagues in research on 'tip of the tongue' (TOT) experiences (Litman, Hutchins and Russon 2005). It arose from Loewenstein's observation that 'TOT' memory experiences were likely to be accompanied by intense curiosity (Loewenstein 1994).

This phenomenon was investigated by Litman and his associates in studies using the measures of interest and deprivation types of curiosity (Litman 2005; Litman et al. 2005; Litman 2008). The TOT experience was found to be associated with the most intense feelings of curiosity, especially for people with high scores on Epistemic Curiosity (EC). A knowledge gap was necessary, but the intensity of a state of epistemic curiosity increased as the solution was brought closer. When the excitement of the chase for relevant information is nearing its end, we have again the teasing, ambivalent character of the emotions typical of curiosity. For this interaction to produce positive results for curiosity requires delay of gratification, a degree of tolerance of ambiguity, the ability if not actually to accept then at least to bear unresolved conflicts and gaps while new information is sought. So Litman (2010) found a positive correlation of I-type curiosity with MacDonald's Ambiguity Tolerance (AT) scale which also had a predicted weaker negative correlation with D-type curiosity (MacDonald 1970). These findings fit with the cognitive process theory and early results found with the Curiosity TAT.

The theory predicts an association between curiosity and need for closure as movement towards completion of an incomplete gestalt is anticipated with curiosity, but Litman failed to find a correlation between his D-type curiosity and Kruglaski's Need for Closure (NFC) (Kruglanski 2004; Litman 2010). There is something to be learned from this. It was almost certainly due to the method of measuring need for closure that was employed in this study (Webster and Kruglanski 1994). In cognitive motivation theory, the kind of closure to be sought in curiosity is not aimed simply at getting rid of the problem: it is seeking closure with the aim of achieving a new development, completing a new 'form.' It is proactive and not a defensive reaction. In Webster and Kruglanski's scale, the items refer to quick and simple resolution without regard for the uniqueness of the signal or the quality of the resulting new cognitive structure. A defensive resolution shutting out or carelessly categorizing a novel signal is the antithesis of seeking creative solutions with a new gestalt, as a highly curious person tends to do.

As I have noted earlier in reference to curiosity and self-regulation, whether some kind of preference for order or need for closure is to be expected as an attribute of curiosity has been a question in other recent research:

> The cognitive flexibility inherent to curious people is best illustrated by their preference for growth over safety, complexity over simplicity, autonomy over obedience and rules, and openness over closure (Roberts and Robins 2000, Litman 2005, Vittersø, Søholt, Hetland, Thoresen and Røysamb 2010). Because of their preference for new information (Loewenstein 1994), curious people are less likely to prematurely commit to initial ideas and perspectives (Kruglanski and Webster 1996). In fact, there is evidence that the need for structure and cognitive closure are not only inversely related to curiosity (Litman 2010), but reside at the other end of the continuum (Mussel 2010). (Kashdan, Sherman, Yarbro and Funder 2013b, p. 143)

The problem is that there is more than one continuum. There are different kinds of cognitive closure. Some are related to seeking good-quality outcomes in understanding the world and oneself. The preference of highly curious people for complexity, autonomy and openness advanced by Kashdan and colleagues is well supported in much of the research I have cited in this chapter and in Chapter 3. Work with the Curiosity TAT and the IM test has supported the idea that 'curious people are less likely to prematurely commit to initial ideas and perspectives' (Kruglanski and Webster 1996; Kashdan, Sherman, Yarbro and Funder 2013b, p. 143). They give careful attention to interesting events and do not seek quick and easy closure. To achieve an effective accommodation of the cognitive map to new information, they are likely to keep the ball bouncing while they seek a good solution to an incomplete gestalt.

There are many other tests of curiosity and related constructs. There is a useful set of studies on 'Need for Cognition' (Cacioppo et al. 1996). The measure of curiosity in the recent work of Kashdan and colleagues on curiosity in social contexts (Kashdan et al. 2013b) has used a method of ratings by people who know the subjects well that is quite different from the questionnaire methods: it recalls some of the early work by Wallace and Ethel Maw that used teachers and peers ratings as well as self-ratings (Maw and Maw 1964, 1968; Maw 1971).

Two other recent scales of theoretical significance, apart from those developed by Litman, Spielberger and colleagues, have appeared in positive psychology research. Peterson and Seligman's Curiosity/Interest in the World scale forms part of their Values in Action Inventory of Strengths as a positive trait in *Character Strengths and Virtues*. Kashdan, who wrote the curiosity chapter in that handbook, has an important book on curiosity (Kashdan 2009). It will be treated mainly in Chapter 12 in regard to the role of curiosity in the discovery of meaning and purpose in life. Kashdan produced with Rose and Fincham another measure with an emphasis on curiosity as a facilitator of personal growth, titled *Curiosity and Exploration Inventory*. The cognitive process theory of curiosity (Beswick 1964, 1971) formed part of the theoretical base for the development of that measure (Kashdan et al. 2004). A second version was published later (Kashdan et al. 2009). These tests are relevant to the macro model of cognitive motivation in the purposeful integration of the whole person in a social context, somewhat along the lines of what we began to consider in an historical context in reference to Samuel Johnson's last passion and Williams James's philosophic brain.

Metacognitive processes in which people reflect upon their own thoughts and feelings are part of the reflexive nature of the self that is found in macro level expressions of curiosity concerned with meaning and purpose in life. It is fairly obvious for positive psychology in which mindfulness is an important consideration. It is represented in the new measures of curiosity that have been employed in positive psychology, such as those of Petersen and Seligman and of Kashdan and his colleagues. The fundamental processes of cognitive integration that are assumed in the general theory of cognitive motivation apply in considerations of curiosity and well-being and should be relevant also in the clinical uses of curiosity (Kashdan and Silvia 2009; Kashdan, McKnight, Fincham and Rose 2011; Kashdan, Dewal, Pond, Silvia, Lambert, Fincham, Savostyanova, and Keller 2013a; Kashdan et al. 2013b). Wholeness and healing and identity, purpose and meaning are themes I take up later in this work.

They are key concepts in the macro model of curiosity as it is generalised in the theory of cognitive motivation.

There are some challenging topics to follow before we come to purpose and meaning – not least agency and consciousness. As we proceed from curiosity towards identity, purpose and meaning, we take account of other forms of cognitive motivation such as cognitive dissonance, achievement motivation, attribution theory and self-efficacy in Chapters 4 to 6, and of intrinsic motivation in Chapter 3 where a sense of agency is found to be a critical factor. Discussion of several different examples of cognitive motivation leads us to a closer study of the underlying cognitive processes in working memory in Chapter 7. Equally important is the function of emotion in cognitive motivation discussed in Chapter 8, while the basic processes for goal definition and pursuit in Chapter 9 and the nature of intentions as an expression of human agency in Chapter 10 lead to a wide range of applications.

Summary

The psychology of curiosity occupies a pivotal point in the study of motivation and cognition. Its intrinsically rewarding character attracted attention at the time of the cognitive revolution in the 1950s and 1960s when there was considerable debate about whether drive reduction models of motivation were any longer sustainable. The hypothesis was being developed that cognitive processes themselves can have motivating properties. The historical background in literary uses of the word curiosity and cognate words illustrates the role of careful attention as well as the complex and ambivalent nature of epistemic hunger. These qualities are demonstrated in recent empirical studies.

The first phase of intensive research on curiosity was concerned with its underlying processes. These are explored in detail and a cognitive process theory of curiosity is presented. This theory deals with the arousal, maintenance and resolution of conceptual conflicts and gaps in knowledge. Openness to experience, orderliness and delay of gratification are predicted correlates. A second phase of intense activity in the study of curiosity, in the 1970s and 1980s, was concerned with the measurement of individual differences in curiosity as a trait or state. In this phase a key question was whether curiosity is a unitary concept, or whether several different things are called curiosity. The empirical basis is reviewed for distinguishing between a depth of interest type of curiosity and a breadth factor more concerned with stimulus seeking.

A fantasy measure in which a standardized method of content analysis was employed confirmed predictions from the cognitive process theory. A questionnaire measure of intrinsic motivation, constructed with reference to the fantasy measure, was found to be a strong representative of the depth type of curiosity. Recent work on the measurement of individual differences in curiosity is reviewed in which oblique factors for sensory, perceptual and epistemic curiosity, and scales of deprivation and interest types of curiosity, as well as wanting and liking, are treated as aspects of the general process of curiosity arousal and resolution. Other measures of curiosity are discussed briefly. I emphasise cognitive processes for the making of whole images. Curiosity at the micro level of a specific task is understood to model the same motivational processes that operate at a higher level of organisation in a macro form of cognitive motivation evident in the purposive strivings of a person seeking long-term fulfilment in a meaningful life.

3 Intrinsic Motivation

> ... less concerned with the struggle for existence than with the joy of living
>
> – Woodworth 1921

Introduction: The Nature of Intrinsic Motivation

Intrinsic motivation is the motivation to do something for its own sake: 'An intrinsic motive is one that does not depend upon reward that lies outside the activity it impels' (Bruner 1966, p. 114). It is a process of arousal and satisfaction that energizes and directs behaviour in which rewards come from the experience of carrying out an activity rather than from results of the activity that are experienced subsequently. Behaviour motivated in this way is purposive, but its goals are within the intrinsically motivated behaviour itself rather than being separable from it. In cognitive terms it is motivation inherent in information processing and action (Hunt 1971). The classic distinction of intrinsic from extrinsic motivation was restated by the principal authors in the field in the context of a general review of definitions of motivation, as follows:

> The most basic distinction is between *intrinsic motivation*, which refers to doing something because it is inherently interesting or enjoyable, and *extrinsic motivation*, which refers to doing something because it leads to a separable outcome. (Ryan and Deci 2000b, p. 55)

Curiosity is a typical example of intrinsic motivation. Bruner said it was 'almost a prototype' (Bruner 1966, p. 115). I referred to it as a prototypical example when I published a test of individual differences in intrinsic motivation which was closely related to specific curiosity (Beswick 1974; Ainley 1987; Byman 2005). 'The most outstanding characteristic of curiosity is that the means-ends relationships of instrumental behaviour do not apply. If the highly curious person is pragmatic at all the pay-off he [or she] seeks is intrinsic to the behaviour itself' (Beswick 1964, p. 55).

In the theory of cognitive motivation, when curiosity is aroused and an attempt is made to satisfy it, an incomplete gestalt is created, maintained and resolved in a renewed cognitive map, making sense of the world including the person concerned. A fundamental process of striving for completion is assumed. 'Motives are always a kind of striving for some form of completion' (Allport 1937b, p. 154). Striving for completion involves processes of incorporation and integration. Deci and Ryan have discussed intrinsic motivation in terms of integrative functions that I will discuss later in this chapter (Deci and Ryan 1991; Ryan 1995). I have extended the theory of intrinsic motivation to cognitive motivation in general.

The general theory of cognitive motivation was developed from the cognitive process theory of curiosity which was originally expounded in relation to individual differences in curiosity, and then to intrinsic motivation more generally: see Chapter 2 where reference is made to several different methods of measuring individual differences in curiosity and intrinsic motivation, in both single factor and multidimensional conceptions. Individual differences in intrinsic motivation are not discussed in this chapter.

Alternative Conceptions of Intrinsic Motivation

In addition to the 'traditional' idea of intrinsic motivation as motivation inherent in an activity that is satisfying in itself, the term 'intrinsic' has also been employed in reference to motives that are, in some sense, intrinsic to the person – that is, where rewards are found within the person as distinct from some external source. For example, Alfred Mele said in answer to the question *What Qualifies as Goal Pursuit:*

> There are two common errors people make that lead them to misclassify non-goal-pursuing behavior as goal-pursuing behavior. The first is that when an actor behaves *as if* pursuing a goal, people often mistakenly take this as an indication of intrinsically motivated goal pursuit. A heat-seeking missile is a good example of something that behaves as if pursuing a goal and may meet all the behavioral criteria for goal pursuit, but, of course, a missile has no mental life. Actual goal pursuit must be intrinsically motivated and not simply have the appearance of goal pursuit. (Mele 2010, p. 62)

Mele represents intrinsic motivation as a product of the mental life of a person who can have a genuine intention and not merely behave 'as if' he or she had an intention. The directing of behaviour is under the internal control of the person.

Deci and his colleagues did not use the term 'intrinsic motivation' in the broader sense of intrinsic to the person, but distinguished different kinds of *extrinsic* motivation, some of which were more self-determined than others (Deci and Ryan 1985, 2000). 'Although the quality of self-determination, characterized by psychological flexibility and the experience of choice, is inherent in intrinsically motivated behavior, it is also present in some extrinsically motivated behaviors' (Deci and Ryan 1985, p. 40). When Deci and his colleagues applied self-determination theory to certain kinds of extrinsic rewards, and described 'self-determined extrinsic motivation' (Deci and Moller 2005), they approached the alternative broader meaning of intrinsic motivation as motivation intrinsic to the person.

Maintaining consistency with the cognitive process theory of curiosity, I preferred Deci's original strict formulation of *intrinsic* motivation, but I came to see later that the broader view can be incorporated into the macro model of *cognitive* motivation. That macro model applies at the highest level of personality organisation in which people try to make sense of their lives as a whole. This view of curiosity is developed further in terms of personal meaning and purpose in Chapter 12, in which I refer to a broader view of curiosity in recent work by Kashdan (2009).

Intrinsic and extrinsic *goal contents* have been distinguished from intrinsic and extrinsic *motives*: 'While the former pertains to the type of goals people might focus on during their goal pursuits (the "what" of goal pursuit), the latter refers to the motives or reasons that are underlying people's goal pursuit (the "why" of goal pursuit)' (Vansteenkiste, Simons, Lens, Soenens, Matos and Lacan 2004, p. 756). This distinction is similar to that between the contents of achievement goals and the achievement motive made by Elliot who linked his analysis with intrinsic motivation (Elliot 1994, 2006). Vansteenkiste and colleagues argued that 'people can be intrinsically or extrinsically motivated to reach intrinsic or extrinsic goals, and both have been found to independently predict well-being' (Sheldon, Ryan, Deci and Kasser 2004). (See also Ryan, Sheldon, Kasser and Deci 1996 on 'All goals are not created equal', for an organismic perspective on the nature of goals.)

Seeking to explain purposive behaviour in terms of basic cognitive processes, including the information value of emotions, I have adopted a position which differs from theories such as that of Deci and Ryan. They are not concerned with the causes of intrinsic motivation but accept it as 'an evolved propensity' (Ryan and Deci 2000c, p. 70). I offer an explanation of intrinsic motivation in terms of deeper *underlying cognitive* processes with general application, whereas Ryan and Deci sought to explain cognitive representations of the self in terms of *underlying motivational* processes.

The Concept of Interest

Intrinsic motivation is shown when people do something out of *interest* in the activity itself, rather than doing it as a means to an end. But what is an interest? In many experimental studies of intrinsic motivation people are given tasks which they find 'interesting,' defined operationally as something people say is interesting or with which they are sufficiently engaged to persist and return to when interrupted. In the early studies of curiosity discussed in Chapter 2, questionnaire items concerned with interest and wonder were amongst those most highly correlated with the Curiosity TAT. Some of these items appeared in the Intrinsic Motivation (IM) test (Beswick 1964, 1974). Interest seems commonly to be experienced as a state of affective arousal, which might nevertheless be a reflective state, typically appearing when the subject is focussed on something novel or conceptually challenging. Ainley and colleagues say of interest: 'This psychological state is characterized by focused attention, increased cognitive and affective functioning, and persistent effort' (Ainley, Hidi and Berndorff 2002, p. 545).

There have been many parallel developments and related concepts relevant to the study of interests in fields of research that developed more or less independently in the period 1980–2000 (Hidi 2000). Hidi listed as related fields areas of goal orientation, self-efficacy, task value, intrinsic/extrinsic motivation and interest. These different approaches are all within the scope of research on cognitive motivation. They can all be understood as aspects of a single system in which interest studies address a significant part of the signalling function of emotion in cognitive motivation. 'In summary, interest as the immediate reaction to a new learning task is an affective state that involves feelings of arousal, alertness, attention and concentration and is a key variable in the motivation of learning' (Ainley 2006, p. 399). She also described interest as an effect of a long-term personal orientation or trait.

The distinction between interest as an immediate affective response and individual interest as a long term personal orientation was made particularly by Renninger (1992).

> As Renninger, Hidi and Krapp (1992) noted, interest has recently been studied as a habitual tendency, trait, a component of personality, and as being elicited by text characteristics. Most frequently, however, interest has been defined as a psychological state and/or as an individual disposition (e.g. Krapp, Hidi and Renninger 1992; Todt and Schreiber 1998). (Hidi 2000, p. 311)

A motive as a trait depends upon arousal conditions to make it effective. It is different from a habit type of trait in that respect. Hidi referred to the actualization of an individual interest, that is, to the process of evoking an active expression of a continuing predisposition to have such an interest. Ainley has expounded a model of interest as an affective state that involves broader questions concerning motivation and cognition. She claimed that there is a strong consensus that 'in the state of interest affect, motive and cognition function as a coordinated system' (Ainley 2006, p. 398). This conception of an interaction between affective and cognitive factors brings us back to the nature of cognitive motivation exemplified in curiosity as a process of arousal.

'The feeling of interest involves positive activation (affect), directed attention and impulses to action (motivation), and information processing (cognition)' (Ainley 2006, pp. 398–399). In cognitive motivation theory, affect provides signals that give information about the relationship of the person to a goal. Ainley, for example (p. 397), cited Panksepp, indicating this process in which 'events become imbued with special affective meanings that can guide actions' (Panksepp 2000, p. 254). Ainley described as a *gestalt* the new configuration which results from the integration of this set of affective, motivational and cognitive factors (Ainley 2006). In the general theory of cognitive motivation its production is the completion of an incomplete gestalt.

Origins of Intrinsic Motivation Theory

Woodworth can be credited with introducing the general idea of intrinsic motivation to modern empirical psychology, as motivation inherent in an activity, in his exposition of 'dynamic psychology' (Woodworth 1918, 1921). It was developed further in his behaviour primacy theory (Woodworth 1958). The term 'intrinsic', used explicitly in reference to a kind of motivation, seems to have appeared first in an article by Harlow (1950), 'Learning and satiation of response in intrinsically motivated complex puzzle performance by monkeys.'

Harlow referred to 'intrinsic rewards' and 'intrinsic motivational conditions.' He reported problem-solving behaviour of monkeys who were observed manipulating mechanical puzzles, in which manipulation behaviour persisted for many hours in the absence of extrinsic rewards such as food. Against a background of drive theory as the general model of motivation, Harlow and others from around that time studied, in addition to manipulation, a similarly postulated intrinsic motive for exploration as an independent primary drive (Harlow 1953a, 1953b, 1954; Butler 1957; Dember and Earl 1957; Butler 1958; Berlyne 1963; Fowler 1965). These proposed new primary drives were offered as additions to the 'big four' drives postulated by Hull (1943a): hunger, thirst, sex and pain, which were supposedly physiological and extrinsically satisfied.

The Search for a New Kind of Drive

Experimental studies in learning and motivation, especially those using animal subjects, tended to maintain the earlier conception of a number of independent primary drives that might be added to Hull's 'big four', and which gave attention to a new kind of drive of a stimulus seeking nature, such as manipulation or exploration. But in the 1960s 'intrinsic motivation' came to be discussed explicitly in cognitive theoretical terms, in particular by J. McV. Hunt and Paul McReynolds (Hunt 1960; McReynolds 1962; Hunt 1963, 1965; McReynolds 1971). In the first of those papers Hunt referred to 'reinforcement intrinsic to the organism's relations with its environment, intrinsic, if you will, to the organism's information-processing' (Hunt 1960, p. 293). McReynolds, taking up Tolman's idea of 'cognitive maps' (Tolman 1948), and influenced like Tolman also by Gestalt psychology, conceived of higher animals developing a cognitive structure which represents for them a simplified representation of the world in reference to which they have an inherent tendency to process new information. In the course of such information processing, which typically requires the input of addition information, it is proposed that people tend to display exploratory behaviour (McReynolds 1962, 1971). Berlyne had already presented an information theory approach to understanding curiosity. He suggested that people and animals might seek additional information to reduce uncertainty and moderate a less than optimal level of arousal (Berlyne 1957). An information-processing model of motivation was developed in the second of those papers by Hunt, 'Motivation inherent in information processing and action' (Hunt 1963, p. 35). He later used the same phrase to define 'intrinsic motivation' in his review of its history (Hunt 1971).

The concept of intrinsic motivation was implicit in Berlyne's early work on curiosity (Berlyne 1949, 1950, 1954, 1955, 1957, 1958, 1960) and it became explicit in his later discussions (e.g. Berlyne 1971a). In one of his last publications, 'Behaviourism? Cognitive theory? Humanistic psychology? – To Hull with them all,' he recognized the need for departure from drive reduction theory in the direction of the new cognitive theories with some reluctance and advocated a multi-level view of behaviour-controlling mechanisms of increasing complexity. This multilevel view employed Hull's conception of mediating 'symbolic or cognitive functions' which he said 'are found only at the highest levels' (Berlyne 1975, p. 79). Berlyne initially preferred a tension reduction model of motivation and Hullian drive theory (Hull 1943a), which was under serious challenge in 1960 when he wrote *Conflict, Arousal and Curiosity*. He claimed then that the study of curiosity might perversely confirm the tension reduction model, but this view was later modified (see Chapter 2 and further discussion of Berlyne's position later in this chapter).

The new theoretical perspective, which no longer limited purposive behaviour to the relationship of instrumental acts to extraneous goals, was brought into a central position in the study of motivation by White in his analysis of 'the concept of competence' which was opposed to tension reduction models (White 1959). The term 'intrinsic motivation' came into general use around 1970, exemplified by the papers presented at the Toronto conference 'Intrinsic motivation: A new direction in education' in that year (Day, Berlyne and Hunt 1971). Independently, several papers were published at about the same time which reported suppressing effects of extrinsic rewards on intrinsic motivation (Deci 1971; Kruglanski, Friedman and Zeevi 1971; Lepper, Greene and Nisbett 1973). These papers heightened interest in the nature of intrinsic motivation.

Bruner, some years earlier, had recommended a 'the shift from extrinsic to intrinsic rewards' to promote learning by discovery (Bruner 1962, p. 83). He took note of the reports of mathematicians, physicists and historians on their experience with new curricula, in which he noted 'repeatedly an expression of faith in the powerful effects that come from permitting the student to put things together for himself, to be his own discoverer' (Bruner 1962, p. 82). One such curriculum that was being evaluated at Harvard at about that time was the one developed by the School Mathematics Study Group (SMSG) at Yale in which an appeal to intrinsic motivation was noted:

> After making a content analysis of the SMSG textbooks one investigator remarked, 'The experimental book is trying to draw a child from life as he knows it to life as he doesn't know it. Motivation is here – the arousal of curiosity beyond the life area which he knows. It is trying to make mathematics into the psychological equivalent of reading an adventure or mystery story.' (Beswick 1964, pp. 162–163)

An appeal to intrinsic motivation, however, was vulnerable to undermining by extrinsic rewards. The original experiment by Deci led to many others showing that extrinsic rewards, like pay and status, when contingent upon the outcome of an interesting task, tend to suppress intrinsic motivation for that task (Deci 1971, 1972, 1975). Deci found that if people are paid to do something they would otherwise have done out of interest, they will be less likely to do it in the future without being paid. Similar findings were reported by Lepper and others. The suppressing effects of extrinsic rewards had already been proposed as a theoretical possibility in personality theories concerned with a sense of agency (Kelly 1967; deCharms 1968).

Play Types of Instinct and the Functional Autonomy of Motives

Roots of the idea of intrinsic motivation are found in Woodworth's theory of a drive that is inherent in an activity (Woodworth 1918, 1921) and in Allport's related theory of the functional autonomy of motives (Allport 1937a, 1937b). Woodworth described behaviours that were engaged in for reasons other than extraneous motives derived from biological needs or a desire to secure an extrinsic reward or to avoid punishment (Woodworth 1918, 1921; Deci and Ryan 1985; Sansone and Harackiewicz 2000b).

> As a general proposition, we may say that the drive that carries forward any activity, when it is running freely and effectively, is inherent in that activity. It is only when an activity is running by its own drive that it can thus run freely and effectively; for as long as it is being driven by some extrinsic motive, it is subject to the distraction of that motive. (Woodworth 1918, p. 70)

He observed that even in an activity that had been initiated by an extrinsic motive many people become absorbed in what they find of interest in that activity. It becomes an interest in itself. Such independence of intrinsically satisfying behaviour from any separate initial reasons for the action was later developed by Allport in his theory of the functional autonomy of motives (Allport 1937a, 1937b). People engage in these activities as ends in themselves, with motives which are associated with positive feelings of interest, enjoyment and satisfaction that Woodworth described as 'less concerned with the struggle for existence than with the joy of living' (Woodworth 1921, p.139).

Woodworth referred to three groups of 'instincts', saying that the first two aside, there was a third he characterized as 'random' or 'play.' 'Our classification then has three heads: 1. Responses to organic needs. 2. Responses to other persons. 3. Play responses' (Woodworth 1921, p. 139). These three kinds of instinct, organic, social and play types, have a much later parallel in Bandura's three types of motivators: biological, social and cognitive (Bandura 1991) described in Chapter 1, but there is a difference in regard to the 'random' nature of this third group. Woodworth's idea of a miscellaneous collection of random instincts of the third type corresponds to one way of conceiving of curiosity: 'But there can be a great variety of disorders in the cognitive map requiring a great variety of very specific signals for integration to take place. In this sense, curiosity is not to be regarded as another need to be added to hunger, thirst, sex, etc., but (if we must speak of needs) as a process which includes satisfaction of a great variety of uncommon needs' (Beswick 1964, p. 64).

Psychologists like Harlow and Hunt, from a generation later than Woodworth's original conceptions (Harlow 1950, 1953a, 1953b, 1954; Hunt 1960, 1963, 1965, 1971), would have been inclined to name as intrinsic motivation what Woodworth here described as an 'instinct' for playful activity. White described play as a prime example of what he called 'effectance motivation' (White 1959, 1960). Woodworth (1921, p. 155) went on to say, 'The stimulus that arouses this sort of behavior is something new and unfamiliar, or at least relatively so.' He discussed curiosity as one among 'a group of conscious impulses and emotions' that 'goes along with exploratory behaviour' and includes also 'surprise' and 'wonder'.

Whether referred to as a drive or an instinct, the early understanding of motive in experimental psychology held by Woodworth included two qualities that were deliberately set aside by the behaviourists: intention and consciousness. Both referred to internal conditions not directly observable by others, and each left open the possibility that directions could be chosen by the actor, that voluntary behaviour was possible. Far from being matters only of historical interest, intention and consciousness are issues that remain pertinent to the understanding of motivation up to the present day.

In Woodworth's early understanding, intrinsically motivated behaviour like curiosity was seen to be *consciously* purposive: 'A purpose is a set for a certain activity with foresight of the result of that activity.' 'Anticipation may be more or less definite – more or less conscious, but unless there is some *conscious anticipation* of the result we should hardly speak of purpose' (Woodworth 1932, p. 243; emphasis in the original.) He then recognized the challenge that is still with us:

> How can a conscious purpose have any effect on the brain and muscles anyway? Thus one of the old puzzles of philosophy is injected into our peaceful psychological study, muddling our heads and threatening to wreck our intellectual honesty. We cannot deal with this metaphysical question here. But we can object to any one who would frighten us away from the facts of human purpose for fear they would disturb some neat philosophical system. (Woodworth 1932, p. 244)

In his later work, Gordon Allport had much to say about the value of a consciously purposeful orientation to the future. At this point he put forward a theory of the functional autonomy of motives (Allport 1937a, 1937b). He took particular note of Woodworth's dynamic psychology and his intrinsic drive theory, according to which, '[a]ctivities and objects that earlier in the game were means to an end, now become ends in themselves' (Allport 1937b, p. 144). He quoted Woodworth: 'The fundamental drive towards a certain end may be hunger, sex, pugnacity or what not, but once the activity is started, the means to the end becomes an object of interest on its own account' (Woodworth 1918, p. 201 fn).

Allport drew inspiration from reports of research on interrupted tasks in Lewin's laboratory in Berlin, with what he called 'conative perseveration' giving evidence of functional autonomy:

> Many experiments show that incompleted tasks set up tensions that tend to keep the individual at work until they are resolved. No hypothesis of self-assertion,

rivalry, or any other basic need, is required. The completion of the task itself has become a quasi-need with dynamic force of its own. It has been shown, for example, that interrupted tasks are better remembered than completed tasks (Zeigarnik 1927), that an individual interrupted in a task will, even in the face of considerable opposition return to that task (Ovsiankina 1928), that even trivial tasks undertaken in a casual way become almost haunting in character until they are completed. (Allport 1937b, p. 147)

Allport claimed for his theory of functional autonomy that 'This theory embraces very easily the work of K. Lewin and his associates upon the nature of "quasi-needs"' (p. 154 fn). The intrinsically motivating power of never-quite-completing an incomplete image of the future, and its application to the nature of the self, are principles advanced by Allport, and they are basic principles in the general theory of cognitive motivation. In more recent years Wicklund and Gollwitzer have proposed 'symbolic self-completion theory' (Wicklund and Gollwitzer 1982). It illustrates Allport's idea that motivation is fundamentally about processes of completion. Their theory suggests, as I do, that it can be applied in the macro model of cognitive motivation at the level of the whole person in a social context. Gollwitzer and colleagues appealed to Ovsiankina's findings and Lewinian principles in their application of symbolic self-completion theory (Gollwitzer, Wicklund and Hilton 1982). These principles of completion by-pass, if they do not directly contradict, drive-reduction theory. This is not to say that the theory of the functional autonomy of motives has gone unchallenged. Neal Miller (1951), for example, argued that with generalization, higher order reinforcements, and the substitution of one reinforcer for another it was difficult to determine whether any 'habit' was in fact functionally autonomous.

Berlyne remarked in reference to Hull's drive reduction theory:

It would be ironical if, after all, the study of curiosity provided this type of theory with its firmest stronghold, and if the study of the role of curiosity in learning as a whole served to buttress its claim to far-ranging jurisdiction. There can, however, be little doubt that more satisfactory formulations will come to light before long and replace it. (Berlyne 1960, p. viii)

The cognitive process theory of curiosity and the cognitive motivation theories of Hunt and McReynolds which appeared in the next few years might have met the need for 'more satisfactory formulations' (McReynolds 1962; Hunt 1963; Beswick 1964; Hunt 1965; Beswick 1971; Hunt 1971; McReynolds 1971).[1]

[1] Indeed, these theories were presented at the same conference in Toronto in 1970 at which Berlyne referred to 'the old drive-reduction view of reward' as inadequate.

Personality Dynamics That Moderate the Effects of Rewards

At the centre of the debate about the effects of extrinsic rewards on intrinsic motivation is the question of *how* making an interesting task into a means to an end reduces motivation for that interesting task. Several related theories predict that when extrinsic rewards are used to harness work for a purpose that is not in harmony with the interests of a worker or student, it will be experienced as a loss of freedom (Deci and Ryan 1985; Deci and Flaste 1995; Deci, Koestner and Ryan 1999b). People will lose motivation especially for work that is creative (Amabile 1993, 1996, 1998). Power has moved from the person who undertakes the task to some other person or an impersonal agency which defines or controls the rewards. Concepts of *personal causation* (deCharms 1987, 1992), *responsibility* (Winter 1992b) and *self-determination* (Deci 1980; Deci and Ryan 1985, 2002b) have been applied in attempts to understand the process.

Personal Causation

Several theorists have addressed the problem of finding successful strategies for encouraging intrinsically motivated behaviour when extrinsic rewards are offered. It has been suggested they must include some means of integrating the rewarded behaviour with personal goals and developmental processes (Sansone and Harackiewicz 2000a; Beswick 2009). Deci and Ryan (1985) have written of this in terms of their theory of self-determination. They built their theory partly on deCharms's theory of *personal causation*. In his earlier work deCharmes had defined personal causation in these terms: '*Man's primary motivational propensity is to be effective in producing changes in his environment*' (deCharms 1968, p. 269, emphasis in the original). He later discarded the terminology of motivation theory. Associated with this tradition was the contribution of White (1959) on effectance motivation, which is acknowledged by almost all subsequent authors in this field. White's 'concept of competence' and the motivation to be effective in transactions with the environment was, in addition to Heider's 'locus of causality' (Heider 1958), a forerunner of deCharms's idea of personal causation. White drew attention to the fact that people typically gain pleasure from the sheer sense of being able to do something, to be effective at it.

In his later work, however, while still retaining the value of people feeling effective at what they do, deCharms dropped the motivational disposition quality from his definition of personal causation and saw it more simply: personal causation means doing something intentionally to produce a change'., (deCharms 1992, p. 325). He said, 'Personal causation is *not* the name of a motive, nor is it a personality disposition. Every human being "has" personal causation, that is experiences herself, as a cause' deCharms 1992, p. 325). It was described in subjective terms as a personal experience of having a sense of being the *origin* of one's own actions.

DeCharms reported that he had taken the idea of personal causation from Heider's concept of 'perceived internal locus of causality for behaviour' (Heider 1958). He acknowledged McClelland's theory of motivation and Kelley's attribution theory (Kelly 1967), while 'White's concept of competence was seminal' (deCharms 1992, p. 326). He later preferred 'personal' to 'internal' causation, to remove ambiguities in the loose term 'internal' and to differentiate this concept from Rotter's 'locus of control of reinforcements' (Rotter 1954) with its internal and external orientations. DeCharms made a distinction between Heider's phrase 'causality for behaviour' and Rotter's 'control of reinforcements' (deCharms 1992), and, following McClelland, he put emphasis directly on the actions of a person rather than the results of an action in a means-ends relationship. Rotter's measure of internal vs. external control is a self-report measure of perceived control over reinforcements that is uncorrelated with DeCharmes and Plimpton's *origin* scale (deCharms and Plimpton 1992). The distinction between deCharms's conception of causality and Rotter's construct of control was found to be important in later studies of intrinsic motivation. In the discussion of reward effects on intrinsic motivation, Deci and his colleagues replied to their critics that they had confused locus of control with locus of causality (Deci et al. 1999b).

The concept of origin is crucial to deCharms's understanding of personal causation. His reference to a sense of origin is to what a person *feels* regardless of any objective criterion of causation. DeCharms was *not* concerned with the question whether or not, or in what sense, a person may be independently responsible as a causal agent, i.e. actually free to act. He focussed attention on a person's own experience of being the origin of his or her actions. He sought to 'describe a *personal experience* that accompanies a behavioural episode of personal causation' (deCharms 1992, p. 326, italics in original).

Elements of this experience were used to provide an operational definition of personal causation in a scoring manual for the sense of *origin* in content analysis of fantasy material with reference to sequences of images for 'goal setting' and 'responsibility'(deCharms and Plimpton 1992). Evidence for goal setting was defined in a sequence which included at least some of the following: independent determination of one's goals; free choice of means to achieve the goals; realistic assessment of abilities and relationships with others and the environment; and self-confidence in one's ability to initiate successful behaviour leading to a positive conclusion. The same elements, combined with a responsibility sequence, were used to train children so as to increase their sense of being origins rather than pawns in a classroom situation. Effects that were evident some years later included improved achievement test results and increased rates of graduation from high school (Jackson 1976; deCharms 1992).

Responsibility

It was in the tradition of McClelland's and Atkinson's studies of individual differences in motives such as need for achievement and need for power that Winter developed his understanding of responsibility. Its operational definition included content analysis of imaginative verbal material for evidence of *self-control*, *awareness of the consequences of one's actions*, *'owning' one's behaviour* and *taking responsibility for others* (Winter 1992b). Responsibility, as he measured it, was conceived as a habit type of stable disposition, not as a motive which might energize and direct behaviour, but rather as a cluster of cognitions (beliefs and values) that act to shape the ways in which motives are expressed.

Winter developed his measure of responsibility as a result of having worked on ways of distinguishing 'good' expressions of the power motive in socially responsible leadership from 'bad' expressions termed 'profligate expansive impulsivity,' (McClelland and Boyatzis 1982; Winter 1992a, 1992b; see also Winter 1973). Results of the measurement studies indicated that responsibility has two components which differentiate between criterion groups in the same direction but consist of unrelated clusters. There is a self-critical 'must' cluster that refers to *moral standards, obligation* and *concern for others*, and an 'altruism' cluster that is oriented towards consequences for the future. Winter's measure of responsibility has been found in validation studies to act as a moderator variable in the effects of power motivation. So, for example, among men and women who scored high on the responsibility measure, power motivation predicted office holding, effective and 'conscientious' functioning and openness to experience, while for those low in responsibility power motivation predicted 'profligate' behaviours such as drinking, reading sex-oriented magazines and sexual possessiveness. Winter found in a project re-scoring earlier data from McClelland and Boyatzis that the combination of high responsibility with high power motivation predicted managerial success eight years later (Winter 1992b).

The way responsibility acts as a moderator of the effects of power motivation helps to explain the function of personal causation in the operation of intrinsic motivation. McClelland found an association of the deCharms origin scale (deCharms 1992) with power motivation, but only for children who were high in 'Activity Inhibition.' The moderator effect of activity inhibition is another illustration of the importance of self-regulation in cognitive motivation. The point of theoretical interest is that intrinsic motivation is expected to remain effective, not simply when a person is able to exercise personal power, but when power is exerted in a controlled manner within a social and personal context that is autonomously controlled and consciously purposeful. It suggests that behaviour in a means-ends sequence that is rewarded extrinsically will not be experienced as reducing the person to a pawn to the extent that, at the same time, it is rewarding within the person's own understanding of who they are and where they are heading as an effective responsible agent.

The findings and implications of research on personal causation and responsibility support a general theory of the operation of intrinsic motivation which draws a parallel between the micro level of engagement in an intrinsically rewarding task and the macro level of intrinsically satisfying behaviour that makes sense within a person's self-understanding and purposes. At both the macro and micro levels there are basic processes of integration and development which are intrinsically satisfying. At both levels there is the development of a new order, a new whole or gestalt, whether it be in that part of a person's map of the world that was affected by engagement in the task or in the broader concept of the self and one's place in the world. The value of people understanding who they are, and where they are heading as responsible agents, points to the need to understand further the function of a sense of identity and purposeful becoming. It has been suggested, for example, that intrinsic motivation occurs when the activity is central to the self (Hidi 2000; Hidi and Harackiewicz 2000; Sansone and Harackiewicz 2000c). This topic is taken up in Chapters 11 and 12.

Self-Determination and the Effects of Extrinsic Rewards

Deci and Ryan (1985) put forward three mini-theories as part of their self-determination theory. Among these, *Organismic Integration Theory* is an account of the development of intrinsic and extrinsic motivation from the function of needs for competence and self-determination (and, later, relatedness) that motivate the ongoing process of unifying the structure of the self through the continual integration of internal and external stimuli (Deci and Ryan 1985). From the point of view of Deci and Ryan, events which increase a sense of competence in self-determination will enhance intrinsic motivation, while rewards for taking part in or completing an activity that is *task-contingent* would reduce intrinsic interest by lessening self-determination. However, quality-dependent extrinsic rewards are said to increase rather than decrease feelings of competence and are thus less likely to suppress intrinsic interest. That contingent rewards commonly suppress intrinsic motivation, but not in all circumstances, was subject to much debate.

Challenging reviews from meta-analyses by Cameron and Pierce (1994) and Eisenberger and Cameron (1996) concluded that there was support from many studies for the view that tangible rewards such as money tend to suppress intrinsic motivation in so far as it is evident in the subsequent time spent on the task, but not in their view when it is measured by verbal expressions of attitude. They inferred from their classification of many investigations that the effect occurred when the reward was expected and independent of performance. They also found that tangible rewards had a small positive affect on attitude to the task if the reward was quality dependent, as well as that verbal rewards, praise and the like, tended to have a positively reinforcing effect, concluding that 'the decremental effects of reward occur under limited conditions that are easily avoided' (Eisenberger and Cameron 1996 p. 1164; see also Eisenberger and Selbst 1994).

Whether conditions which produce the negative effect are very limited or quite common is one of the points of several critical notes written in response to Eisenberger and Cameron (Hennessey and Amabile 1998; Lepper 1998; Sansone and Harackiewicz 1998). Hennessey and Amabile argued, for example, that suppression effects were quite common, and that research has shown that only in very specific conditions do extrinsic rewards have no impact or a positive impact on intrinsic motivation or creativity.

Deci and colleagues (Deci, Koestner and Ryan 1999a) published a later review directly contradicting the conclusion by Einsberger and Cameron that the suppressing effect of tangible rewards was limited to conditions in which rewards were independent of performance. Their conclusion was that all expected tangible rewards made contingent on task performance do reliably undermine intrinsic motivation.

Later they concluded that there was a universal suppression of intrinsic motivation by tangible rewards that were contingent upon task performance:

> To summarize the primary findings from the meta-analyses, when free-choice behavior was used as the dependent measure, all rewards, all tangible rewards, all expected rewards, engagement-contingent rewards, completion-contingent rewards, task-contingent rewards, and performance-contingent rewards significantly undermined intrinsic motivation. (Deci, Koestner and Ryan 2001, p. 13)

In a further general article on self-determination theory, Ryan and Deci (2000c) refocussed attention 'on the fundamental needs for competence and autonomy'. They saw *competence* and *autonomy* as distinct variables, having different but complementary effects. So feedback and communication rewards that induce feelings of competence during action can enhance intrinsic motivation for that action. But they believed that feelings of competence would not enhance intrinsic motivation unless accompanied by a sense of autonomy, that is, unless those feelings could be experienced as the result of an internal locus of causality (the sense of *origin* in deCharms' terms). In the wider context of what I would call the macro model of cognitive motivation, they suggested that social support or long-term personal development can also provide conditions for the maintenance of intrinsic motivation, as this effect of personal causality requires either immediate contextual support for autonomy or abiding inner resources that are typically the result of prior developmental supports. So in addition to competence and autonomy, *relatedness* was proposed as a further need contributing to the support of intrinsic motivation in interpersonal settings. Intrinsic motivation is then more likely to flourish where there is a sense of personal security in relationships with others.

Beyond Self-Determination Theory

The function of needs for competence, autonomy and relatedness was specified by Deci and Ryan in their organismic integration theory, a sub-theory of self-determination theory. 'The theory is based on the proposition that the needs for competence and self-determination motivate the ongoing process of elaborating the internal, unified structure of self through the continual integration of internal and external stimuli' (Deci and Ryan 1985, p. 9). But rather than these needs motivating integration, I suggest that inherent processes of integration lead to recognition of the value of competence, autonomy and relatedness in development of the self. They are necessary conditions for development of a whole, self-conscious, unique personality. That is, I will argue in what follows that basic processes of integration underlie the needs for competence, autonomy and relatedness, rather than vice versa, and that makes those needs psychogenic rather than innate. Deci and Ryan argue that 'organismic integration (or simply, the integrative) process' 'is itself intrinsically motivated' (Deci and Ryan 1985, p. 116), which is what the cognitive motivation theory would imply, but they do not infer that the process of integration accounts for autonomous functioning, as I suggest we should.

Organismic Integration and Cognitive Motivation

Ryan and Deci say that integration occurs when identified regulations for control of behaviour are fully assimilated to the self, having been evaluated and brought into congruence with one's other values and needs. The generalised form of the cognitive process theory of curiosity suggests that social conditions and tangible rewards will have a facilitating effect on intrinsic motivation when they enable further development of an integrated person through personally meaningful purposive behaviour. Both organismic integration theory and cognitive motivation theory recognize a basic tendency to integrate experiences, but in the cognitive motivation theory the starting point for explanations is moved back a step or two from Ryan and Deci's unanalysed acceptance of intrinsic motivation as a given quality. If we know how it works, starting with its underlying cognitive and affective processes, given a primitive tendency towards integration, it should be easier to specify conditions under which intrinsic motivation can be developed, protected, increased and made more effective.

In the generalised form of the cognitive motivation theory, the information value of affective feedback for intrinsically motivated behaviour plays an important part. It is illustrated by a review of studies on the effects of praise (Henderlong and Lepper 2002) that followed the reviews and debates on the effects of extrinsic rewards. Henderlong (Corpus) and Lepper argued against a purely behavioural definition of praise as verbal reinforcement and in favour of the view that praise may have a range of different motivational effects, depending upon how it is done. Praise can be a means of external control suppressing intrinsic motivation, but it can also enhance feelings of personal causation, or a sense of agency and self-determination. To have positive effects on intrinsic motivation, besides being sincere, praise needs to encourage performance being attributed to controllable causes, to promote autonomy, and enhance competence without over-reliance on social comparisons, and convey attainable standards and expectations.

In the cognitive motivation theory, I argue for an open-ended view of purposive behaviour with potential for unexpected yet satisfying outcomes, in preference to a strict notion of preconceived goal attainment which might be implied in the idea of self-determination. The symbolic effect of praise then should be to give insight into what works, rather than reinforcing a particular outcome. As Henderlong and Lepper saw it, causal inferences then guide behaviour and emotional reactions as ways of making praise effective. That is consistent with attribution theory and the way that emotions function as feedback information in the general theory of cognitive motivation. Henderlong and Lepper's review of the effects of praise suggests that the emotions arising from praise have information value. Affect is then effective in a cognitive motivational process. In Chapter 8 I discuss theories of the information value of emotions as feedback in goal-directed behaviour. The completion of a process of developing a new order in one's cognitive map should produce signals in which emotion is not so much controlled by an externally managed reward as it is a sign of what is effective in a process of internal integration. The self is active in this process. Autonomy and personal causation appear to be necessary conditions for effective integrative solutions which produce a new cognitive order including a positively appreciated self-concept.

A Cognitive-Affective Account of Basic Needs

Ryan has given a theoretical justification for the foundational role he and Deci gave to innate needs for autonomy, competence and relatedness. He questioned the historically important assumption that he saw in Freud's *synthetic function of the ego* (Freud 1923/1962), Jung's *individuation* (Jung 1951/1959), Maslow's and Rogers' *actualizing tendency* (Maslow 1954; Rogers 1963), Piaget's *organisation* (Piaget 1971) and Werner's *orthogenetic principle* (Werner 1948), that 'the psyche contains its own natural or inherent principles that promote growth, integration, and the resolution of psychological inconsistencies and conflicts' (Ryan 1995, p. 397). A similar assumption is made in the meaning maintenance model of Heine et al. (2006), as I also make in the general theory of cognitive motivation. On this assumption, basic processes of integration underlie the needs for competence, autonomy and relatedness.

Deci and Ryan took intrinsic motivation as a given quality, but I suggest that our understanding of it would be better if we could offer an account of the cognitive-affective processes that give rise to it. Deci and Ryan are not concerned with the causes of intrinsic motivation. They regard it as an evolved propensity (Ryan, Kuhl and Deci 1997). They are more concerned with 'the conditions that elicit and sustain, versus subdue and diminish, this innate propensity' (Ryan and Deci 2000c, p. 70).

An adequate account of intrinsic motivation must have the potential to explain its effects. In particular, we need to know how self-determination works – what makes the needs for competence, autonomy and relatedness effective. Can we go back behind these supposed innate needs to gain insight into the dynamics of their effects? I suggest that behind these proposed needs there is a basic process of integration which helps to explain their effects.

Reduction of intrinsic motivation that results from loss of autonomy is understandable if autonomy is indeed a basic need that must be satisfied as an absolute requirement; but why begin the explanation at the point of designating a need for autonomy as an innate property? There is very little agreement on lists of innate needs, or, if they exist, how they are constituted. A more productive step in theory construction might appear if we ask what it is about reduced autonomy that produces the suppressing effect on intrinsic motivation. The next step is to see that *autonomy is necessary for self-integration to form a gestalt of the self.* The same would apply for competence and relatedness as conditions required for self-integration.

In the macro model for completion of an incomplete gestalt of personal identity, the capacity to be true to oneself, to develop in one's own way, to make sense of diverse, even conflicting information about oneself, is limited if one's autonomy (or competence or relatedness) is limited. Effective integration of diverse elements of the self is likely to produce a less meaningful whole image of the self when autonomy is reduced and an attempt is made to integrate alien, extrinsically controlled elements. It is also easier to make sense of myself if I can distinguish clearly between me and not-me, and the gestalt of personal identity stands out from a background. (See the discussion of 'good form' and the figure-ground phenomenon in gestalt conceptions of identity in Chapter 11, and the gestalt properties of goals described in Chapter 9.)

If this model fits the facts, then the function of an incomplete gestalt is 'more basic' than the supposed 'basic' needs for autonomy, competence and relatedness. The processes of cognitive completion in a meaningful whole image provide the dynamics of that form of motivation. These dynamics are processes which include searching, incorporating and integrating new information to make sense of inputs in relation to what is already in the system. It is a learning process in which psychogenic needs may be developed.

It is quite a radical change from the organismic integration theory of Deci and Ryan, which also includes processes of searching, incorporating and integrating new information, to reverse the emphasis on basic needs to make autonomy, competence and relatedness dependent upon something 'more basic,' that is, upon a fundamental natural process of integration that is assumed by many theorists but which they reject. In the general theory of cognitive motivation, systemic integration is the fundamental basis for the development and operation of autonomy, competence and relatedness, that I suggest are simply psychogenic needs like many others. Yet acceptance of those needs as psychogenic changes very little of what Deci and Ryan say about them otherwise.

In reference to autonomy and the support for it, their conclusion still applies: '[T]hat autonomy support has generally been associated with more intrinsic motivation, greater interest, less pressure and tension, more creativity, more cognitive flexibility, better conceptual learning, a more positive emotional tone, higher self-esteem, more trust, greater persistence of behavior change, and better physical and psychological health than has control' (Deci and Ryan 1987, p. 1024). Their continuum from autonomy in self-regulation to external control remains highly relevant to questions of well-being. My alternative formulation is 'only' a matter of theoretical priority in the causes underlying motivational processes.

Ryan argues that the integrative tendencies of organismic integration are facilitated by conditions that satisfy, or provide nutriments for the three specified psychological needs. He refers to *conditions that provide* what is needed. He made his argument in reference to a definition of 'need' that refers to external conditions. It is not the definition commonly assumed in the psychology of motivation exemplified by Murray's conception of many needs, and followed by McClelland and others, that Ryan gave as 'any motivating force, including one's desires, goals, wants, or values – whether these are implicit or self-attributed' (Ryan 1995 p. 410, and see Murray 1936; McClelland, 1985; McClelland, Koestner and Weinberger 1989).

In Ryan's alternative definition, 'needs refer to the nutriments or *conditions that are essential to an entity's growth and integrity*' (Ryan 1995, p. 410, my emphasis). In this definition the processes of integration are dependent upon *context*: 'Contexts where psychological needs are neglected or frustrated promote fragmentation and alienation, rather than integration and congruence' (Ryan 1995, p. 399). He is quite right about context affecting integration, but as far as psychogenic needs such as autonomy are concerned, that is because the process of cognitive integration is fundamental in the development and operation of those needs.

I suggest that rather than their being innate needs, autonomy, competence and relatedness are conditions of interaction with the environment which affect integration. Ryan said that his formulation 'derives from the controversial idea that there may be some basic psychological needs essential to motivation and growth in any domain (Deci and Ryan 1985, Ryan 1993)' (Ryan 1995, p. 410), but he referred to environmental not intra-psychic conditions to define these needs. When he said that 'needs refer to the nutriments or conditions that are essential to an entity's growth and integrity', Ryan was not referring directly to conditions within the person, but to situational conditions. This reference to nutriments for growth has the same effect as my proposition that inherent processes of integration lead to recognition of the value of competence, autonomy and relatedness as *conditions or circumstances required for development of the self.* They are necessary conditions for development of a whole, self-conscious, unique personality by virtue of the requirements for integration, but they are not innate needs.

Ryan and Deci (2017) have recently published a new and very substantial book on *Self-Determination Theory* in which they revisit their definition of basic psychological needs as essential elements for wellness and flourishing. It appeared too late to be taken properly into account for this book, but while it reinforces their arguments for the positive effects of basic need satisfaction, which I would not dispute, it does not appear to deviate significantly from their previous position on the definition of (just three) basic psychological needs.

Conditions necessary for creativity give some further insight into the process. Open prospects, freedom to choose and personal control of effective means to reach a goal are components of creative endeavour that are shared with intrinsic motivation (Amabile 1983a, 1996; Amabile and Kramer 2010). Externally imposed, arbitrary limitations on the ways in which conceptual conflicts are resolved, gaps in knowledge filled or imagined possibilities realized will limit the operation of intrinsic motivation. Creativity requires these essential elements of intrinsic motivation. In addition, in a creative activity there must always be the possibility of unanticipated outcomes that will be valued by the creative person. As Deci and Ryan said in their organismic integration theory, 'Development is anything but preprogrammed' (Deci and Ryan 1985, p. 114). In cognitive motivation theory, resolution of an incomplete gestalt is a creative process that produces an unpredictable and sometimes perhaps a unique outcome. Such is not the case when a person is seeking a clearly defined extrinsic reward. The theory of cognitive motivation predicts that the resolution of an incomplete gestalt will always result in a condition which has not existed before: there will be no restoration of a previous state. New forms require a significant degree of freedom on the part of an independent agent for their achievement. There is no call for postulation of innate needs for autonomy, etc., because the effects attributed to them can be accounted for by the same process of integration. Autonomy, competence and relatedness are conditions which facilitate creative integration to complete incomplete images with integrity.

Summary

Intrinsic motivation is the motivation to do something for its own sake. It does not depend upon a reward that lies outside the activity it impels. It is distinguished from *extrinsic* motivation in which instrumental behaviour is rewarded by subsequent events that result from the motivated activity. Arousal of interest in an activity is a basic process of intrinsic motivation, and the psychology of interests is reviewed briefly indicating a set of affective, motivational and cognitive factors, which results in a new configuration.

The history of research on intrinsic motivation can be traced from the early 20th-century foundations of experimental psychology in which theories of 'dynamic psychology' were proposed. Play types of instinct, 'less concerned with the struggle for existence than with the joy of living' (Woodworth), were postulated, and a theory of the functional autonomy of motives was developed (Allport). A new kind of stimulus seeking drive was sought (Harlow). Examples of cognitive motivation illustrate aspects of intrinsic motivation, but frequently in combination with other cognitive processes which have motivational effects.

The personality dynamics that moderate intrinsic motivation include the effects of personal causation, responsibility and self-determination. Consciousness as a process of *integration* has a central role in these processes in which an incomplete gestalt is resolved. Deci and Ryan have offered explanations in terms of *organismic integration theory*, a subtheory within self-determination theory, in which basic *needs* for competence, autonomy and relatedness facilitate integration. I argue for a different conception in which such needs are seen not to be innate, but psychogenic developments reflecting conditions in which basic processes of integration account for the effects of those supposed needs.

4 Cognitive Dissonance

> Cognitive dissonance theory is essentially a theory about sense making.
> – Aronson 1999

Introduction

Leon Festinger's theory of cognitive dissonance (Festinger 1957, 1964) was a major influence on social psychology and personality research for several decades from the middle of the 20th century. It was one of a large number of cognitive consistency theories that appeared at about the same time – a time coinciding with the cognitive revolution (Baars 1986). In his introduction to the collected work, *Theories of Cognitive Consistency* (Abelson, Aronson, McGuire, Newcombe, Rosenberg and Tannenbaum 1968), Theodore Newcombe observed (1968b, p. xv):

> Often in the history of science, when the time is ripe, a large number of similar theories are put forward contemporaneously by researchers who have little if any direct contact with one another. So it was a decade or so ago when at least a half dozen of what we shall call "cognitive consistency" theories appeared more or less independently in the psychological literature.

Among theories that flourished between 1940 and 1960, Simon and colleagues grouped together Heider's balance theory, cognitive dissonance theory, congruity theory and a number of neobalbance theories and saw 'gestalian' principles (Wertheimer 1922/1938; Asch 1946b) at their heart (Simon, Snow and Read 2004, p. 815). Cognitive dissonance theory was more successful than any of the other consistency theories of that time. It attracted attention by generating predictions that were counterintuitive, and yet were confirmed by experimental and field research. It was cogently argued with many detailed propositions capable of empirical testing.

The first chapter in the 1968 collection of papers on consistency theories was Aronson's review of Festinger's theory of cognitive dissonance (Festinger 1957, 1964; Aronson 1968). Aronson was generally supportive of Festinger's approach, but he put forward a significant revision of the theory, known as self-consistency theory. It was one of many challenges to Festinger's original work and foreshadowed later developments concerning the role of the self. Cognitive dissonance theory was intensively studied from the time of its original publication; and it has gained renewed strength and inspired various revised versions and alternatives in more recent years (Zajonc 1990; Aronson 1992; Harmon-Jones 1999; Cooper 2010; Gonzales, Tarvis and Aronson 2010). I will discuss a selection of the main themes in the original work and its later offshoots to illustrate its contributions and its fruitfulness and to provide some links and contrasts with the general theory of cognitive motivation.

Some Gestalt Theory Origins

Festinger developed cognitive dissonance theory after working with Lewin, but he did not explicitly base his theory on Gestalt psychology or Lewin's work in particular. Cognitive dissonance, achievement motivation, attribution theories and self-efficacy theory are conceptually rich and highly developed fields of inquiry into human motivation, and each contains many original ideas not shared with Gestalt psychology. Nevertheless, there are roots of these theories in the classic studies of shifts in level of aspiration (Dembo 1931) and the recall of interrupted tasks (Zeigarnik 1927) that were undertaken in Berlin under Lewin and later in group dynamics research in the United States shortly before the new cognitive theories were developed (Festinger 1942; Lewin, Dembo, Festinger and Sears 1944). Basic ideas from Lewin's field theory appear at a number of points.

Continuity of the gestalt tradition and Lewin's influence in and through Festinger's work was recalled in the tribute paid by Thomas Pettigrew to one of Festinger's most esteemed intellectual descendants, Elliot Aronson, as 'The Ultimate Lewinian' (Gonzales et al. 2010). Festinger's theory was thus one of the principal means by which Lewin's concepts and gestalt principles, conceived early in the century, were carried forward to the new age of cognitive psychology that appeared in the middle and flourished towards the end of the 20th century. The new theories included modified versions and developments of Festinger's original theory.

Newcombe saw Heider's article, 'Social perception and phenomenal causality' (Heider 1944), followed by his later work (Heider 1946, 1958), as marking the beginning of this fertile development. Heider described conditions for balance between cognitive and affective elements in clusters called 'dyads' and 'triads'. The basic assumption was that an unbalanced cluster of cognitions is associated with 'tension' and a consequent tendency to seek its reduction. Newcombe noted that Heider had drawn upon Lewin's distinctions between *approach-approach, avoidance-avoidance*, and *approach-avoidance* conflicts, and on experimental studies of conflict in laboratory animals. He referred to 'cognitive personality organization' and the concept of 'intolerance of ambiguity' (Frenkel-Brunswick 1949), which had been studied in relation to *The Authoritarian Personality* (Adorno, Frenkel-Brunswick, Levinson and Sanford 1950). He also cited G. A. Miller's paper on 'The magic number seven' (Miller 1956), which I have cited in Chapter 2 as an inspiration for the development of cognitive studies. It was further evidence of the ripeness of the time for cognitive theories. Heider's review of the gestalt theory of motivation, especially Lewin's work in this area, is also a significant background factor (Heider 1960).

The tendency to seek consistency, however, is not sufficient in itself to provide motivation with both energizing and directing properties. I will argue that cognitive dissonance theory is deficient in this respect. It is one thing to be driven out of a condition of discomfort; it is another to know where to go. The way cognitive elements come together must not only relieve discomfort but make sense in a whole figure, or have meaning, or move towards a meaningful pattern, in order to both energize and direct purposive behaviour.

Cognitive Dissonance as a Theory of Motivation

Festinger's understanding of personal adjustment was that the individual strives for internal consistency; that his or her opinions and attitudes, for example, tend to exist in clusters that are internally consistent. He observed that exceptions occur, and that when they do, 'they capture our interest primarily because they stand out from a background of consistency' (Festinger 1957, p. 1). The idea that certain identifiable cognitive clusters stand out from a background is an example of the gestalt figure-ground phenomenon, while inconsistency challenges the other great gestalt principle that people tend to perceive whole figures. Festinger did not, however, identify a cluster of cognitive elements explicitly as a gestalt, nor did he see its inconsistency as making it an incomplete gestalt, with the implications for motivation that such phenomena suggest in a general theory of cognitive motivation.

Festinger's Basic Principles of Dissonance

Festinger wished his theory to address a wide range of personal experience and social behaviour in which feelings as well as thoughts played a part. He was not concerned only with the logical consistency of ideas and chose the term 'dissonance', in preference to 'inconsistency', to refer also to how people feel. The experience of dissonance is like hearing a discordant sound where harmony is expected. Feelings are evoked. Motivational arousal then comes not from logical inconsistency in rational thinking, but from the *psycho-logic* of thoughts and feelings taken together.

Dissonance theory began by postulating that elements of knowledge can be relevant or irrelevant to one another, and if relevant, they are either consonant or dissonant. Any pair of elements is dissonant if one element implies the opposite of the other. Just as people seek consistency among their attitudes and opinions, they also seek consistency between their beliefs and what they do. When attempts to achieve consistency fail, there is psychological discomfort in the presence of inconsistency; hence the concept of dissonance with its affective quality. The magnitude of the dissonance a person may experience in a particular instance is a function of the number and importance of dissonant elements in comparison with the number and importance of consonant elements – that is, dissonance is a function of what Festinger called the *dissonance ratio*.

Although cognitive dissonance was at first studied as a social psychological phenomenon, with attention to such behaviour as social agreement and self-justification, it is clear in the first of his basic hypotheses that Festinger intended his theory to be primarily a theory of motivation, referring to internal processes:

1. The existence of dissonance, being psychologically uncomfortable, will motivate the person to try to reduce the dissonance and achieve consonance. (Festinger 1957, p. 3)

He envisaged people working to restructure or re-evaluate the cognitive representations of their experience by seeking new information to reduce dissonance, but that they would also tend to avoid input of information that would have the opposite effect, so his second basic hypothesis was:

2. When dissonance is present, in addition to trying to reduce it, the person will actively avoid situations and information which would be likely to increase the dissonance. (Festinger 1957, p. 3)

Festinger summarized his theory as composed of eight sets of connected propositions (Festinger 1957, pp. 260–265). Examples of the many detailed propositions which have attracted research interest include the following:

> Dissonance almost always exists after a decision has been made between two or more alternatives.

The magnitude of post-decision dissonance is an increasing function of the general importance of the decision and of the relative attractiveness of the unchosen alternatives.

There are three major ways in which dissonance may be reduced: (a) by changing one or more of the elements involved in dissonant relations; (b) by adding new cognitive elements that are consonant with already existing cognition; (c) by decreasing the importance of the elements involved in the dissonant relations.

While most of the principles in Festinger's summary of his theory deal with internal processes that are cognitive and motivational, some refer to social behaviour or to personal adjustment in a social context. After he worked with Lewin at Iowa, and after Lewin died, Festinger continued to study aspects of his field theory at Michigan where he was program director in the group dynamics centre. Consistency theories had long been applied in the study of groups (Newcombe 1968b), and dissonance theory found an application there. For example, 'Dissonance introduced by disagreement expressed by other persons may be reduced by changing one's own opinion, by influencing the others to change their opinion, and by rejecting those who disagree' (Festinger 1957, p. 265). More typical, however, are the principles which have a social context but are predominantly matters of internal personality dynamics. For example, 'Dissonance may be reduced by changing private opinion to bring it into line with the overt behaviour or by magnifying the amount of reward or punishment involved' (Festinger 1957, p. 264). Festinger continued to represent his theory as a topic in social psychology, particularly in regard to attitude change, and it was in social psychology that his influence is most clearly marked.

One of the signs of cognitive dissonance studied by Festinger and his associates in the early stages of their research was the effort people would make to gather information justifying a decision already made, such as studying advertising material on *both* accepted and rejected options *after* having made the purchase (Ehrlich, Guttman, Schoenbach and Mills 1957). Post-decision dissonance is postulated to occur regularly, because, in making a choice, the attractive qualities of a rejected alternative and the negative features of the one chosen have been assimilated, and remain in memory, but are inconsistent with the choice. Adding cognitive elements to shift the balance more strongly in favour of the chosen alternative is postulated to reduce dissonance. Changes would then be made to the perceived desirability of the alternatives, widening the gap by making the chosen one appear more attractive and/or the rejected alternative less so (Brehm 1956, 1962).

Induced Compliance Effects

A principle of insufficient justification was derived from dissonance theory propositions, such as Proposition 4 (b) in Festinger's eight sets of propositions summarizing his theory (Festinger 1957, pp. 260–265): 'If forced compliance is elicited, the magnitude of the dissonance *decreases* as the magnitude of the reward or punishment increases.' In contrast, the less reason there is to do something inconsistent with one's beliefs, the *greater* will be the dissonance created by doing it. The principle of insufficient justification was used to predict and explain results in studies of what Festinger called forced compliance or what were later known as 'induced-compliance paradigms' (Harmon-Jones and Mills 1999). In the original well known experiment by Festinger and Carlsmith, subjects were asked, after taking part in dull and boring experimental tasks, to tell a person who was represented as a member of the next group of subjects that the tasks were 'interesting, enjoyable and lots of fun.' Some of them were paid $20 and others $1 to 'assist' the experimenter by briefing new subjects, in the process expressing an opinion that was contrary to what they believed. The excuse they were given for undertaking this paid deception was that the regular assistant was absent, and that the experimenter would be happy to pay them to be available to assist in the future. Those paid $1 later rated the experiment as more enjoyable than did those who were paid $20. The interpretation was that being paid a small amount offered little justification for the paid behaviour which remained dissonant with the subjects' beliefs, whereas the larger sum provided cognitive elements consonant with their behaviour and so generated less dissonance. The higher dissonance in those paid less led to dissonance being reduced by their making changes to their beliefs (Festinger and Carlsmith 1959).

Another finding demonstrating the same principle of insufficient justification leading to a change of attitude was obtained using a negative rather than a positive incentive. (Remember this was in the 1950s, when sex was not so readily talked about as it was in later generations.) Those in a severe initiation condition, that had required women to listen to embarrassing sexual references to prepare them to join a discussion group that turned out in fact to be rather dull and boring, evaluated the group more favourably than did those in the mild initiation condition whose qualifying activity was not very embarrassing (Aronson and Mills 1959).

In a mirror image extension of the Festinger and Carlsmith's experiment, Aronson and Carlsmith (1963) demonstrated the dissonance effect of bringing about compliance by threat of punishment instead of inducement by a reward. They used either mild or severe threats to prevent children from continuing to play with some very attractive toys. The children's ratings of the attractiveness of the toys decreased under mild threat, but increased with severe threat, as predicted from the theory. The authors reasoned that a threat of severe punishment would be perceived as sufficient justification for ceasing the action, but that if a person ceased the desired behaviour after a mild threat, they would need to convince themselves that the formerly desired act is no longer desirable. Festinger had said, 'If one wanted to obtain private changes in addition to public compliance, the best way to do this would be to offer just enough reward or punishment to elicit overt compliance' (Festinger 1957, p. 95).

The alternative view of opinion change had been that of reinforcement theory. Dissonance theory was gladly taken up by social psychologists in its early days because, as Aronson observed, the experimental findings 'represented a striking and convincing act of liberation from the dominance of general reward-reinforcement theory ... dissonance research sounded a clarion call to cognitively oriented social psychologists, proclaiming in the most striking manner that human beings think, they do not always behave in a mechanistic manner' (Aronson 1999, pp. 107–108).

It is an interesting fact, however, that, while its appeal to many at the time was that cognitive dissonance was not mechanistic, compared with reinforcement theory, physical concepts remained, such as equilibrium, force and tension, which, it appears, Festinger took from Lewin who claimed that the fundamental concepts of dynamics were 'in no way special to physics' (Lewin 1935, p. 40). In Lewin's field theory, however, all the relevant causal factors are represented in the present time, whereas Festinger described processes that extended over time: 'He viewed the psychological phenomena in dynamic terms – as processes occurring over time' (Zajonc 1990, p. 662).

Compared with *attribution theory* as expounded by Weiner (see Chapter 6), cognitive dissonance theory was relatively mechanistic. Weiner's first requirement of a theory of motivation was that it 'must be based on a concept other than homeostasis' (Weiner 1986, p. 15). So, purposive behaviour could not be expected to return a system to a previous state. The outcome might not be predicable. The difference of the attribution approach compared with dissonance theory will be examined further in Chapter 6.

Physiological Arousal in Dissonance

Zanna and Cooper argued that it was insufficient to design experiments like the Festinger and Carlsmith study by treating people 'as if' they experienced arousal: '[T]he internal mechanism which Festinger and Carlsmith relied upon to make their prediction was the uncomfortable arousal state of the participants. However, no direct measurement of the "arousal" was undertaken' (Zanna and Cooper 1976, p. 200). In a reflection upon his theory 30 years after its original publication, Festinger commented, in reference to some recent work by others, that 'the demonstration that there is some physiological evidence for arousal I think is an extremely important finding and needs more research' (Festinger 1987/1999, p. 384). It was to be expected that physiological components of affective arousal would be found if cognitive dissonance is concerned with uncomfortable feelings.

In one interesting experiment by Zanner and colleagues certain subjects were given a tranquilizer (30 mg of phenolbarbitol) and a comparable group amphetamine (5 mg) prior to being asked to write an essay strongly expressing an opinion on favour of President Ford pardoning President Nixon, which was contrary to their beliefs (Zanna, Higgins and Taves 1975; Zanna and Cooper 1976). Another group was given a placebo. Some were given less opportunity than others not to undertake the dissonance-inducing task. The drug-induced arousal interacted with decision freedom to affect dissonance-reducing behaviour. It is an important and well-demonstrated principle of dissonance theory that cognitive dissonance is much more likely to be aroused under conditions of high choice than low choice, so that people feel more discomfort knowing what they have done if they freely chose to do it. It was found by Zanner and colleagues that cognitive inconsistency between behaviour and beliefs was associated with aversive arousal and greater attitude change under the amphetamine treatment. There was no evidence of dissonance in the tranquilizer condition for both the high-choice and low-choice conditions. A change of attitude was observed under the high-choice but not the low-choice condition for the placebo group, as predicted.

The findings showing that arousal had occurred under conditions of cognitive dissonance are perhaps what one would expect, but the opposite effect in which dissonance was associated not with arousal of tense feelings, but found in their absence, was the result in a previous study by Zanner and Cooper. The expectation of such feelings was suggested by a placebo that subjects were told could have the effect of making them feel tense in one condition and relaxed in the other. Dissonance theory then predicted correctly that when the discomfort aroused by dissonant cognitions could be attributed to an external cause, a drug they were told they had taken, that explanation was allowed to account for the feelings of arousal and so did not require dissonance reducing behaviour (Zanna and Cooper 1974, 1976). In the 1974 study, Zanna and Cooper had found that attribution of arousal to having taken a pill which the subjects believed to have side effects leading them to feel tense virtually eliminated the dissonance effect, but when the subjects felt they should have been relaxed by the pill, the dissonance effect was significantly enhanced.

So dissonance produced physiological arousal, but when arousal could be attributed to some other cause, the behavioural consequences of dissonance did not occur. The dissonance-reducing effects subsequent to arousal were observed when there was no alternative way for a person to account for the feelings of discomfort. That is, the cognitive representations of emotion, the physical aspects of which had been demonstrated, were shown to be elements in cognitive motivation. These findings illustrate the signalling function of emotion that I discuss in Chapter 8. Cooper recalled at a later date Festinger's foresight in regard to the cognitive representation of emotion and its function in motivation:

> More impressive than the impact of the original experiments was Festinger's foresight to recognize the careful interplay between motivation and cognition. Festinger recognized, before it was fashionable, that ... emotions were represented cognitively and that it was the relationship among the cognitive representations that prompted motivation. (Cooper 1999, p. 149)

That cognitive function of emotions is what I have assumed in the general theory of cognitive motivation, in which the cognitive representation of emotion plays an important part along with personal responsibility. Such results also point to the importance of a sense of agency and other functions of the self that we will discuss shortly.

Another, more recent demonstration of arousal, one in which direct physiological measures were employed, was found when skin conductance changes were measured after subjects had written a counter-attitudinal statement (Harmon-Jones, Brehm, Greenberg, Simon and Nelson 1996; Harmon-Jones 1999). Skin conductance responses are believed to be associated with increased sympathetic nervous system activity during emotional arousal. It was found to be higher in subjects who were given a high degree of choice whether to write the counter-attitudinal statement than in those in a low-choice condition. In addition to showing evidence of emotional arousal, those in the high-choice condition also rated a boring passage as more interesting, thus indicating the behavioural effects of dissonance reduction in association with physiological arousal.

Dissonance as an Aversive Drive

Cognitive dissonance was *not* originally presented as a different kind of drive – different, that is, from supposedly biological drives like hunger, thirst, fear and sex – as it might be in cognitive theories of motivation. It was seen by Festinger as another drive that creates an aversive condition in the same way as typical biological drives do, and its reduction was understood to be reinforcing. 'Successful reduction of dissonance is rewarding in the same sense that eating is rewarding' (Festinger 1957, p. 90). The approach of many of Festinger's contemporary theorists in the 1950s had been to include newly named drives, such as exploration and manipulation, in the same class as other drives and then try to demonstrate their drive properties, often, but not always, with Hullian learning theory principles in mind. In fact, it was found that novel and conflict generating stimuli that increased arousal could sometimes be positively rewarding (Montgomery 1954; Montgomery and Segall 1955; Dember and Earl 1957; Barnett 1958).

With the properties he designated for cognitive dissonance, Festinger had a conflict theory similar in its arousal processes to Berlyne's conception of cognitive conflict as aversive, except that in Berlyne's exposition it was aversive only when arousal is too high, above an optimal level below which an increase in arousal would be sought (Berlyne 1955, 1960). Berlyne modified his original position on tension reduction, as we noted in Chapter 2, to recognize evidence that 'moderate rises in arousal can be rewarding in a way that has nothing to do with subsequent relief of arousal' (Berlyne 1971a, p. 191). Tension reduction models gave way to theories which recognized at least some positive reinforcing effects of increased arousal. Nevertheless, no matter how much the language used about it invoked biological drive concepts, cognitive dissonance theory is a cognitive theory, and it is a theory of motivation, one that shares much in common with other consistency theories.

In various theories it is suggested that cognitive conflict will motivate searching for new information. But the cognitive dissonance explanation differs in the reasons given for seeking new information: for example, in the cognitive process theory of curiosity (Chapter 2), the highly curious person seeks a 'good' resolution that might lead to a completely new understanding of the phenomenon or fill gaps in knowledge in the process of creating a new conception. That is, the highly curious person does not merely seek to reduce inconsistency. In a more broadly applicable cognitive theory, the purpose of seeking additional information would not only be to 'provide cognition consonant with existing cognitive elements,' thus reinforcing existing ideas, but sometimes to place one's cognitive map in jeopardy for the sake of better knowledge. Highly curious people, having a high regard for the uniqueness of new information and also for the integrity of their cognitive maps, prefer to avoid shortcuts to an easy resolution. In contrast, dissonance may be manipulated in accordance with the theory of cognitive dissonance to produce maladaptive behaviour, to reinforce prejudice or to give up belief in what is objectively true.

Despite its shortcomings, Festinger's theory has inspired a great deal of interesting research, often affirming the original formulation. The high degree of generality in the original formulation has been both a bane and a blessing, which Aronson discussed in terms of 'scope versus tightness in theory building' (Aronson 1999, p. 112). The focus tends to shift, but it has continued to suggest new ideas. Among these are several which move beyond the simple dissonance ratio of negative to positive cognitive elements to consider more complex functions of the self in new versions of dissonance theory such as self-consistency theory (Aronson 1968), responsibility theory or the New Look at dissonance theory (Cooper and Fazio 1984), self-affirmation theory (Steele and Liu 1983) and radical dissonance theory (Beauvois and Joule 1996). Except for radical dissonance theory, these new developments tend to be more consistent with the general theory of cognitive motivation than is the original cognitive dissonance theory.

Self-Referent Modifications to Dissonance Theory

Forty years after its publication, the study by Festinger and Carlsmith was described by Aronson in glowing terms: 'I regard this experiment, because of the enormous impact it had on the field, as the single most important study ever undertaken in social psychology' (Aronson 1999, p. 106). Zajonc was no less laudatory in his obituary following Festinger's death in 1989:

> Festinger's is the first name that comes to mind in association with social psychology. For Leon is to social psychology what Freud is to clinical psychology, and Piaget to developmental psychology. I say *is* not *was* because his intellectual influence is permanent. (Zajonc 1990, p. 661)

The investigations and theoretical discussions which followed his original work on cognitive dissonance, especially the Festinger and Carlsmith experiment, have led to thousands of experiments, a great many publications and a number of fruitful modifications to the theory. A revision of particular interest, having regard to my proposal for a general theory of cognitive motivation applied to the integration of the whole person in a social context, is Aronson's alternative explanation of the findings of Festinger and Carlsmith in terms of *self-consistency theory*.

Aronson's Self-Consistency Theory of Cognitive Dissonance

Aronson interpreted the Festinger and Carlsmith's results as due to dissonance being created by inconsistency between the self-concept and behaviour, that is, inconsistency in regard to a person's self-concept as a moral and capable person that was in conflict with the person's knowledge of his or her having been induced to tell a lie to another person who might be affected by it (Aronson 1968, 1992). Aronson was led to propose self-consistency theory as a result of having argued with Festinger that his favourite example of a situation in which dissonance theory did not apply did not make sense. Suppose a man is driving on a lonely country road and has a puncture. He prepares to change the tire, only to find that he has no jack in the car. Festinger said that he might experience frustration and a number of other emotions, but that there were no dissonant cognitive elements, and Aronson declaimed: 'Of course there was dissonance! What kind of idiot would go driving late at night on a country road without a jack in his car?' (Aronson 1999, p. 110). Eventually Aronson saw that he needed to recognize a new principle: that is, that dissonance would occur when a person's self-concept was threatened. The driver's 'cognition about his idiotic behaviour' was dissonant with 'his self-concept of being a reasonably smart guy' (p. 110). The second dissonant cognition here was not an element in the immediate situation, but a continuing attribute of the person. This revision led to further examination of variables related to the self.

Aronson concluded that there was a hidden assumption in the original theory and early experiments. We normally assume that people have a reasonably positive self-concept; but, he wondered what would happen if negative, rather than positive, self-expectancies were violated? Aronson and Carlsmith carried out an experiment in which it was discovered that when students did *better* than they had come to expect from repeated failures in a task, they subsequently *underperformed* on that task. That is, they brought their behaviour into conformity with their low expectations of themselves (Aronson and Carlsmith 1962). This required a self-consistency theory, not merely the maintenance of a positive self-concept.

Aronson claimed that

> at the very heart of dissonance theory, where it makes its clearest and neatest prediction, we are not dealing with just any two cognitions; rather, we are usually dealing with the self-concept and cognitions about some behaviour. If dissonance exists it is because the individual's behaviour is inconsistent with the self-concept. (Aronson 1968, p. 23)

A somewhat similar but competing explanation of dissonance effects is offered in the *self-affirmation theory* proposed by Steele and colleagues (Steele and Liu 1983; Steele 1988; Steele, Spencer and Lynch 1993). They argued that the results of Festinger and Carlsmith are not due to either cognitive inconsistency or self-inconsistency, but to subjects being forced to behave in a manner that threatened their sense of moral and adaptive integrity. They found that dissonance-reducing attitude change could be eliminated by having subjects complete a value scale questionnaire in which they affirmed a positively valued part of their self-concept immediately after writing an essay expressing an opinion contrary to their beliefs (Steele and Liu 1983). The results were interpreted to imply that salient, self-affirming cognitions may help to objectify reactions to self-threatening information. They developed a theory that self-affirmation overcame a threat to self-worth and restored personal integrity (Steele 1988).

Steele and colleagues predicted that people with more favourable self-concepts would be more resilient to specific self-image threats than people with less favourable self-concepts (Steele et al. 1993). High and low self-esteem groups were identified from scores on a personality inventory. Self-esteem was also manipulated experimentally. It was found that false feedback on their self-esteem score affected resilience by either enhancing or challenging self-esteem amongst those predisposed to low self-esteem, but there was little effect in people already well equipped to deal with a challenge to self-esteem. Providing increased or decreased resources to deal with a threat to self-esteem had a strong effect where resources were otherwise lacking. The results were thus interpreted to support self-affirmation theory rather than self-consistency theory.

Different interpretations were debated, and these debates illustrate the importance of self-concepts, agency and responsibility in cognitive motivation. Joshua Aronson and colleagues argued that, 'We want to see ourselves as good, capable, and able to predict and control outcomes in areas that matter. Awareness of information that threatens this image motivates us to restore it to a state of integrity … the objective is global self-worth and not cognitive consistency' (Aronson, Cohen and Nail 1999, p. 128). This is not far removed from Elliot Aronson's insight that behaving as something of an idiot threatened one's self-concept as a competent person able to control outcomes, but that insight gave rise to self-consistency theory. The role of the self has continued to be a focus of ongoing research with various proposed amendments to the theory of cognitive dissonance, and I will return to it at the end of this chapter. Harmon-Jones argues, and E. Aronson appears to agree, that while feeling responsible for producing aversive consequences might add strength to dissonance, it is not a necessary condition for it to occur (Harmon-Jones et al. 1996; Aronson 1999; Aronson et al. 1999; Harmon-Jones 1999).

A sense of personal agency was implied in the idea that feeling responsible for the adverse consequences imposed upon another person by what one did as a matter of choice would produce dissonance. This would follow from inconsistency with one's self-concept as a caring person, according to both self-consistency and self-affirmation theories, as well as a separately proposed *responsibility theory* to explain the results of Festinger and Carlsmith. An amendment was proposed to the original theory, named the *aversive-consequences* revision by Harmon-Jones et al. (1996, 1999), in which it was proposed that feeling personally responsible for the production of foreseeable aversive consequences was a necessary and sufficient condition for the observed effects of induced compliance (Cooper and Fazio 1984). At first sight such a revision seems to be consistent with both self-consistency theory and self-affirmation theory, but Elliot Aronson found in his studies of hypocrisy with various colleagues that dissonance effects could be produced without the subjects being aware of any possible adverse consequences.

Hypocrisy, Responsibility and Integrity

Aronson's principal study of hypocrisy (Aronson, Fried and Stone 1991; Stone, Aronson, Crain, Winslow and Fried 1994; Aronson 1999) was conducted as part of a practical effort to find an effective way to persuade sexually active people to use condoms to control the spread of HIV/AIDS. The students concerned were already well informed on the risks of unprotected sex but often did not take the recommended precautions. Common methods of persuasion by giving information about possible consequences seemed to be ineffective. The students already agreed that condoms should be used. They just weren't using them. The hypothesis was set up from self-consistency theory that if students could be induced to tell others about the risks and the need to practice safe sex by using condoms they could be brought to see themselves as hypocrites if they did not practice what they preached. Then dissonance would be likely reduced by changes of behaviour in their using condoms. The students concerned reported in follow-up studies (Stone et al. 1994) that they had in fact increased their use of condoms. In a behavioural test, a significantly higher proportion of students in the hypocrisy condition actually purchased condoms. Three months after the induction of hypocrisy, 92% of the students in that group were found in a telephone survey to be still using condoms.

Aronson and colleagues interpreted the hypocrisy experiment not only to demonstrate the powerful effects of dissonance manipulation in a public health program but also to argue for the lack of support for the responsibility theory that was proposed by Cooper and Fazio in their 'New Look' version of dissonance theory (Cooper and Fazio 1984). It was claimed by Aronson and colleagues on the basis of the condom hypocrisy study and another similar experiment on attitudes to water conservation (Dickerson, Thibodeau, Aronson and Miller 1992) that Aronson's early modification of dissonance theory emphasising the importance of the self-concept offers greater predictive and explanatory power than the New Look (Cooper and Fazio 1984). The early study of dissonance caused by positive achievements against an expectation of failure (Aronson and Carlsmith 1962) was also interpreted to support self-consistency theory rather than the New Look, although it was acknowledged that 'a New Look interpretation cannot be ruled out' (Thibodeau and Aronson 1992, p. 600).

In comparison with the original theory, the effect of cognitive dissonance in revisions such as the self-consistency theory, responsibility theory and self-affirmation theory can be seen as changes of focus from the micro to the macro level of cognitive motivation. In the original form, demonstrated in the Festinger and Carlsmith experiment, dissonance was brought about by inconsistency between cognitive elements representing aspects of the present situation, e.g., one's opinion that the task was boring, and one's knowledge of having said that it was interesting. In a self-consistency type of explanation, a more complex interaction is seen to occur, in which a cognitive representation of the self is found to be inconsistent with the knowledge of what one has done. The explanatory power of an incomplete gestalt is transferred from the effect of insufficient justification in a particular situation to striving for completeness in self-understanding as a person of integrity which would extend beyond the present situation. Integrity can have a special meaning in regard to individual identity that is expressed in both contemporaneous and longitudinal or narrative images of the self. Identity and integrity in cognitive motivation at the macro level are discussed in more detail in Chapter 11. In the general theory of cognitive motivation, they are components in processes of integration that are introduced in Chapter 7 in reference to the role of consciousness.

Radical Dissonance Theory and Metatheories of Consistency

Not surprisingly, there has been a reaction against the introduction of self-referent concepts into later versions of dissonance theory. A 'radical dissonance theory' was proposed by Beauvois and Joule, recommending a revival of emphasis upon the central tenet of the original theory in which it is proposed that all hypotheses in dissonance theory research must be derived from the dissonance ratio (Beauvois and Joule 1996; Beauvois and Joule 1999). Beauvios and Joule claimed that Festinger left open the possibility of distortion by combining the basic idea of dissonant cognitions with a metatheory derived from more general cognitive consistency theories, especially those based on Heider's balance theory (Heider 1946, 1958). The form of that metatheory was seen in the measurement of 'structural imbalance: a generalization of Heider's theory' (Cartwright and Harary 1956). The structural balance measure concerned the whole structure of the cognitive field with no particular status assigned to any of the cognitions involved, 'in perfect conformity with Heider's premises, which viewed the cognitive universe as a scene contemplated by the perceiver and that satisfied, to a greater or lesser degree, his or her preference for balance (Heider 1958)' (Beauvois and Joule 1999, p. 44).

Beauvois and Joule argued that Festinger' theory required a special element known as the *generative* cognition or the *focal* cognitive element (Mills 1999; see Beauvois and Joule 1999, p. 46). Cognitive representation of *behaviour* was then the key to the generative cognition. When it is dissonant from other relevant cognitive elements, it produces dissonance that results in the rationalization of behaviour. In addition, Beauvois and Joule did not see discomfort arising from the conflict between cognitive elements itself as for sufficient motivation, but suggested an additional proposition for the original theory: 'An act induces a state of dissonance only when there is commitment' (Beauvois and Joule 1999, p. 44). They derived this proposition from Brehm and Cohen (1962), and saw it as making dissonance theory part of the psychology of commitment (Kiesler 1971). Despite the strictures of radical dissonance theory, it opens that theory to modification by reference to whole person concepts. Without specifying one of the cognitions which is dissonant as the generative cognition, when he developed his self-consistency theory, Aronson specified the representation of behaviour as one of the dissonant elements and the self-concept as the other. As noted at the end of this chapter, Aronson envisaged later a more general application of dissonance theory with self-referent processes making sense of the world and one's own behaviour.

A Broader Integrative View of Self-Systems

Judson Mills is one who developed dissonance theory in the direction of general theories of integration. After working closely with Festinger in the early years, Mills came to regard the original definition of dissonance as deceptively simple. Rather than 'purify' the apparently simple concept of dissonance as Beauvois and Joule proposed in their radical theory by dropping out the metatheoretical elements of general consistency theories, he suggested changing the definition of dissonance to make self-functions more relevant (Mills 1999). That was to move towards what I have called a macro theory of cognitive motivation at the level of the whole person. Festinger's original weighting of dissonant elements of cognition according to their 'importance' was one way in which he allowed for the effects of dissonance motivation to be influenced by the self as a whole. Mills proposed that the theory be amended by incorporating a weighting of the consequences of behaviour according to a person's motivation for behaviour with those consequences.

Mills recommended a modification of the theory to allow for 'degrees of consequences' (by which he appears to mean the extent to which dissonant consequences follow from the behaviour) and degrees of desirability of consequences. He proposed amending the theory to provide that the degree of dissonance depends on how much the opposite behaviour follows from cognition about the consequences being desirable or undesirable (Mills 1999). This is not quite the same point as the 'New Look' responsibility modification (Cooper and Fazio 1984) which required that there be knowledge of consequences for dissonance to occur, that we now know not to be strictly necessary. It is rather a suggestion that when consequences are known, the effects will depend upon their desirability or undesirability in the light of one's motives apart from the motivational effect of dissonance.

After taking issue with the way that theories of self-consistency and self-affirmation view the involvement of the self in dissonance, and making a claim 'that there was no necessary role played by the self in dissonance reduction,' Cooper suggested that nevertheless 'the self is very much involved in dissonance if one takes a somewhat broader perspective' (Cooper 1999, p. 170). In the broader perspective Cooper argued that the self plays a role as a standard against which the consequences of behaviour can be assessed as wanted or unwanted, so that dissonance arises from unwanted consequences. More speculatively, he suggested that 'the self may be intimately connected to the ontogeny of dissonance' (Cooper 1999, p. 170).

As we have noted, Aronson took a contrary view to Cooper on the need for knowledge of consequences. When Aronson developed his *hypocrisy paradigm*, he argued that the production of aversive consequences is not necessary for the creation of dissonance, but he believed nevertheless that behaving inconsistently with beliefs about oneself remains an aversive condition. The difference of opinion between Aronson and Cooper remained, but not in that respect in which dissonance can arise from conflict between knowledge of one's behaviour and one's self-concept; rather, it was a matter of whether that knowledge must necessarily include knowledge of unwanted consequences of the behaviour. When both take the broader view, they have had similar things to say about the self.

In his later work Aronson made two quite different statements of the fundamental motivational properties of cognitive dissonance, in two successive sentences. The first is a narrow explanation in terms of its aversive quality in what cognitive psychologists might regard as an outdated type of drive theory, and the second is much more broadly conceived in cognitive terms as being concerned with making sense of one's experience:

> Because dissonance is an unpleasant drive state (like hunger, thirst, or pain), the person will attempt to reduce it – much like she or he would try to reduce hunger, thirst, or pain. Viewed more broadly, cognitive dissonance theory is essentially a theory about sense making: how people try to make sense out of their environment and their behavior and, thus, try to lead lives that are (at least in their own mind) sensible and meaningful. (Aronson 1999, p. 105)

Insofar as the first of Aronson's characterizations is apt in seeing cognitive dissonance as an aversive drive, it illustrates the fundamental weakness of Festinger's original version of cognitive dissonance. It provides explanations of why people will sometimes do strange things to escape from unpleasant conditions, but it has much less to say about where they will move to (in the Lewinian life space sense of movement). Festinger's cognitive dissonance theory deals mainly with arousal of motivation, not its goal-directing properties. A theory of motivation should do both. On the other hand, Aronson's second broader view points to a positive goal in making sense of dissonant cognitions.

There is a positively attracting character to the goals of cognitive motivation that is seen in examples such as epistemic curiosity, achievement motivation and self-efficacy. To the extent that positive attraction is typical of this class of motivation, it requires an account of goal setting and commitment that is difficult to incorporate into cognitive dissonance theory when it is based exclusively on aversive arousal. If, however, Aronson's second and broader view is taken, along with the modifications made by Mills, Cooper and others, the cognitive processes that make sense of diverse experience belong to a kind of purposive striving in which goal attainment gives *meaning*. Self-referent modifications of cognitive dissonance theory move the discussion in that direction. One recent development in the direction in which meaning-making is an enhanced self-referent modification in a process of cognitive integration is the meaning maintenance model of Heine et al. (2006; see also Proulx and Heine 2006, 2010).

We have noted how self-affirmation theory (Steele and Liu 1983; Steele 1988; Heine and Lehman 1997), concerned with sustaining the integrity of the self, may be compared with Aronson's self-consistency theory, from which it differs only in a small degree. It is one of the precursors to the meaning maintenance model of Heine and colleagues, which is offered as an overarching model of integrating processes that can account for a wide range of human motivations based on an impulse to relate all things to each other and to the self. The general theory of cognitive motivation is another formulation of the same kind, relating personal integrity and meaning to self-fulfilment. The theory of cognitive motivation presented in this book is intended to provide for both energizing and directing properties, and to do this in a theory that relates the motivational properties of basic cognitive processes in a specific situation to those that are found in long-term purposive behaviour of the person in a social context.

Summary

Festinger's theory of cognitive dissonance was a major influence on social psychology and personality research for several decades from the middle of the 20th century, and it has continued to receive attention in recent years. It shared a common background in Gestalt psychology with other consistency theories, but it was successful in part because it did not employ a simple generic model of cognitive consistency. While based on a few simple principles, it was presented with detailed exposition that led to some notable predictions that were counterintuitive. Festinger was concerned with more than logical inconsistency and included feelings together with thoughts in groups of cognitive elements, any two of which, if relevant, might be consonant or dissonant with each other. A dissonant combination was like a discord in music.

Dissonance gives rise to discomfort that people act to avoid or reduce, so for example if there is dissonance between the value that a person places on something and knowledge that they have chosen something else instead, they will tend to change their attitude towards it to make it less valuable to them. People gather information to enhance the value of what they have chosen or decrease the value of what they have rejected, thus reducing dissonance by making their attitudes more consistent with their behaviour. They might also change their behaviour to make it consistent with what they believe, but the conditions that reliably induce behaviour modification are quite complex, as was demonstrated, for example, in a study by Aronson and others making awareness of hypocrisy an effective means of inducing people to modify their sexual behaviour. Many empirical studies have shown effects of cognitive dissonance.

Evidence for alternative theories and modifications of Festinger's original theory is also discussed in this chapter. Among these modifications and alternatives are self-consistency theory, self-affirmation theory and responsibility theory, all of which emphasise self-functions at a higher level of cognitive organisation than dissonance elements in a simple behavioural paradigm in a specific situation. A recent radical re-affirmation of dissonance theory in comparison with metatheories of consistency is also discussed and contrasted with a renewed call for a broader view of self-systems. I conclude that the original cognitive dissonance theory deals largely with aversive arousal without effective means for giving positive direction to future behaviour, but that Aronson's self-referent broader view that dissonance is fundamentally about making sense of experience points to a theory of cognitive motivation that includes both energizing and directing properties.

5 Achievement Motivation

... success in competition with some standard of excellence.
– McClelland et al. 1953

Introduction

There was always a cognitive framework for affective processes in achievement motivation theory (McClelland 1965a; Heckhausen 1977). It is clear in the work of the two leading original authors, David C. McClelland and John W. Atkinson, who developed the field from the late 1940s through the 1950s and later, first at Wesleyan University and later at Harvard and Michigan. They defined an achievement goal as success in competition with some standard of excellence and the motive for it as a cluster of affectively toned cognitive associations – 'motives are "affectively toned associative networks"' (McClelland 1965a, p. 322). In this chapter I relate achievement motivation theory to the general model of cognitive motivation as one way in which a person may strive for completion of a self-image in a cognitive map of the person in relation to the field of his or her concerns.

The function of expectancies in motivation received a good deal of attention in the cognitive models that were proposed in the 1950s and 1960s. Atkinson was primarily responsible for development of expectancy-value theory that came out of his experience of research on psychogenic motives with McClelland. He acknowledged that it had some early roots in the gestalt type of theory proposed by Lewin and Tolman (see the introduction to Chapter 4.) His version of expectancy-value theory has continued to be a major point of reference for research on human motivation with a cognitive orientation. It has contributed also to the development of related theories, including Weiner's attribution theory that will be taken up in the next chapter.

Level of Aspiration and the Gestalt Heritage

The main bridge from the Gestalt theory pioneers, von Ehrenfels, Wertheimer, Köhler and Koffka, into the development of the later theories we are considering was the work of Kurt Lewin and his students, which was influential particularly after Lewin fled Germany in 1933 to live in the United States. Foundations had been laid in their work in Berlin. Early work there on level of aspiration directly influenced the original work of McClelland and Atkinson on achievement motivation (McClelland 1958b; Atkinson and Litwin 1960). Level of aspiration referred to a level of performance which would be acceptable to a particular individual's self-concept (Lewin et al. 1944; Heckhausen 1991). That definition in terms of consistency with the self-concept anticipated many later theoretical applications.

Tamara Dembo, one of Lewin's students who worked with him later in the United States, is credited with having developed the highly influential concept of 'level of aspiration' in her PhD thesis in Berlin in 1930 (Dembo 1931; Gardner 1940; Frank 1941; Lewin et al. 1944; see also Patnoe 1988). She discovered that after frustration with a difficult task, subjects would choose a task of an intermediate level of difficulty as a step towards a desired goal. She termed this preferred step the subject's *momentary level of aspiration*. Hoppe, another of Lewin's students, conducted the first experiment on level of aspiration phenomena (Hoppe 1930; Lewin et al. 1944). He reported that success or failure was shown to affect changes in the difficulty of preferred intermediate goals (Hoppe 1930; see also Gardner 1940). Subsequent work on level of aspiration in the United States was done by a team which included Festinger as well as Dembo, giving us a link with the theory of cognitive dissonance (Lewin 1935; Festinger 1942; Lewin et al. 1944; Festinger 1957).

Research on level of aspiration was a transition point to later extensive studies of achievement motivation. For example, Atkinson's summary specification of the resultant valences of success and failure was derived from Escalona's 'resultant valence theory' (Escalona 1940), which defined motivation for levels of aspiration as multiplicative functions of subjective probabilities and incentive values (Lewin et al. 1944). Escalona's 'resultant valence' formulation was elaborated by Festinger (1942). Their original formulae did not include the crucial variable of internal motive disposition or need. The necessity for it in a comprehensive theory was recognized, but as Hoppe had reported, they believed that more progress was needed on the measurement of such personality variables before they could be included in a quantitative description of motivation. That was the point at which McClelland and Atkinson made their original contribution a few years later.

Atkinson and Feather (1966a, p. 4), considered it 'something of [a] giant step to have recovered some basic ideas' from earlier analyses of level of aspiration (Escalona 1940; Festinger 1942; Lewin et al. 1944).

In *The Achievement Motive* the dynamics of achievement motivation are summarized in a diagram of an 'adjustive behavioural sequence,' (McClelland et al. 1953, p. 109), which is similar to diagrams of the life space employed by Lewin in his 'topological' theory of motivation (Lewin et al. 1936; Lewin 1938). Feather applied Lewinian field theory explicitly to represent 'topologically and dynamically' terms such as frustration when a person 'is separated at some psychological distance from a goal (or region of positive valence) by a barrier,' saying, 'This barrier is the source of restraining forces which oppose the driving forces acting upon the person in the direction of the goal' (Feather 1962, pp. 60–61). Feather elaborated a Lewinian type of theory into a general theoretical model of cognitive structures in which discrepancies produced an adjustive mechanism (Feather 1971). Feather's model of organization and discrepancy is more relevant to cognitive motivation in general than it is to achievement motivation in particular, and it will be discussed in general terms in Chapter 9.

In the general theory of cognitive motivation, striving for completeness may include striving for an achievement goal for which a need has been aroused. The motivational property of an incomplete gestalt of the person in a situation which includes a prospective achievement goal is implicit in the background of achievement motivation theory that will be discussed in the following sections. More recent developments, including individual differences in goal meaning by Dweck, and the hierarchical model of achievement motivation by Elliot, which have more definite cognitive terms for achievement goals, will be discussed at the end of the chapter.

The Approach to Need for Achievement through Measurement

McClelland and Atkinson, with colleagues Clark and Lowell, defined need for achievement operationally in reference to evidence in fantasy material for an achievement goal of *success in competition with some standard of excellence* (McClelland et al. 1953, p. 110). For achievement motivation to be aroused it was necessary that an achievement goal be one adopted by the person. It did not matter whether a standard of excellence was evident in competition with others in a race or in striving to reach a time standard measured by the clock, provided that the person competed with an *internalized* standard of excellence.

The Fantasy Method for Measurement of Achievement Motivation

Evidence of motivation was sought in the imagery found in stories told in response to pictures in a special purpose Thematic Apperception Test

(TAT), which was a modification of Murray's original TAT with more objective scoring (Murray 1938, 1953). McClelland's theoretical description of a motive as 'an affectively toned associative cluster' is exactly what is coded in a subject's fantasies to obtain an *n* Achievement score (McClelland 1965a, p. 322). The criteria for each category of imagery are defined in the scoring manual (Atkinson 1958a).

The functioning of an achievement goal was found to be different from that of the goal of a need like hunger. For example, when attempting experimental arousal of the need for achievement, it was found that it was a mistake to follow the model of hunger with attempts to find effects of deprivation and satiation, such as they had used in their previous investigations of 'The projective expression of needs' that studied hunger (Atkinson and McClelland 1948). The theory they were developing was a cognitive theory that does not apply a drive reduction model.

It is also significant for cognitive motivation theory in general that McClelland and colleagues drew the conclusion from their first experiment on the measurement of individual differences in achievement motivation using fantasy material that Tolman's basic theoretical concept of cognitive maps was not only useful for understanding purposive behaviour but had an affinity with their methods of measurement:

> One might even go so far as to suggest that by the use of this method Tolman could study much more directly the "cognitive maps" which the behaviour of his rats has led him to infer are the important intervening variables in determining behaviour (Tolman 1948). (McClelland, Clark, Roby and Atkinson 1949, p. 254)

Behavioural Correlates of n *Achievement in the Test Development Studies*

Scores on the test discriminated between subjects in their responsiveness to achievement arousal and in their performance on achievement-oriented tasks including scholastic achievement (Atkinson 1953). However, the correlations with academic achievement were not consistent and appeared to depend upon circumstances affecting arousal of the motive. There were also correlations with level of aspiration (McClelland et al. 1953). Linguistic correlates were found in situations which contained achievement cues. The linguistic results indicated that people who are highly motivated for achievement think more often in anticipatory and generalized terms. In his experiment on the Zeigarnik effect, Atkinson found more incomplete tasks were remembered by high *n* Achievement scorers under achievement-involved conditions, but in relaxed conditions more tasks were recalled by those subjects with low *n* Achievement scores. The dependence of effects on arousal conditions indicated the motivational character of the variable.

To test the developmental effects of expected cultural factors regarding independence, a cross-cultural approach was taken to compare evidence for achievement imagery in the folk tales of Native American cultures with ratings of independence training in ethnographic materials from those societies. Both the early age at which independence training was begun and the severity of the training were correlated with high *n* Achievement imagery. Questionnaire data were collected on how mothers of European-American children interacted with their children. The mothers of sons with high *n* Achievement stressed early independent achievement (McClelland et al. 1953). Observation of mothers interacting with their sons confirmed the effect on achievement motivation of affective rewards for ambition (Rosen and D'Andrade 1959).

Achievement Motivation as a Psychogenic Need

Atkinson and McClelland quickly differentiated their conception of psychogenic motives from the older type of drive theory with its need reduction mechanisms of reinforcement: 'to us this basic conception has not appeared entirely adequate' (McClelland et al. 1953, p. 8). In their break with a tension reduction model they noted other objections to it (Allport 1937a; Hebb 1949; Young 1949; Maslow 1954), and in particular Hebb's objection to the notion of motive as an *energizer* needed in order to explain the activity of the organism.

Maslow brought into focus more than Hebb's concept of self-activation and pointed beyond it to the principle of agency: 'Human beings seem to be far more autonomous and self-governed than modern psychological theory makes allowance for' (Maslow 1954, p. 326). It was an idea also present at that time in Allport's development of a theory of personal fulfilment in his book *Becoming* (Allport 1955). McClelland argued that for the achievement motive to be effective individuals must consider themselves responsible for the outcome, and make sense of it in terms of their understanding of themselves (McClelland 1961). He made reference back to Allport's earlier work: 'Evidence on the importance of the ego or the self-image [i]n controlling behaviour has been summarized by (Allport 1943)' (McClelland 1965a, p. 327). These ideas illustrate the macro version of cognitive integration in the completion of an incomplete gestalt of the person.

Personality-Situation Interactions for Arousal and Development of Motivation

Several developments led to the formulation of a systematic 'Expectancy × Value' theory of achievement motivation as a function of motive, subjective probabilities and incentives for success. Among these developments were Atkinson's theoretical work on achievement motivation and risk-taking (Atkinson 1957) and other related studies (McClelland 1958b; Atkinson, Bastian, Earl and Litwin 1960). Feather took persistence as evidence of motivation and mapped the relationship of it to expectation of success and the motive measures (Feather 1959, 1961, 1962, 1963). Feather drew on level of aspiration research in Lewin's group, Tolman's work on expectation of rewards, Rotter's social learning theory, Edward's subjective expected utility and Atkinson's paper on risk taking. Atkinson and Feather described two different types of personality, 'achievement oriented' and 'failure threatened', largely in terms of their difference in attitudes to risk taking (Atkinson and Feather 1966b, pp. 368–369).

Expectancy-Value Theory

The interaction of subjective expectancies, incentive values and two different achievement-oriented motives was nicely demonstrated in the experiment on risk taking and achievement motivation by Atkinson and Litwin (1960). In a ring toss game, similar to that devised by Hoppe, they had participants choose the distance from which they would attempt to throw a ring over a peg (Hoppe 1930). The prize money was greatest for the most distant attempts and least for throwing over a short distance. The rewards for success were calibrated so that the reward was balanced with the probability of success. Participants could expect to win in the long run about the same no matter which distance they chose. The level of difficulty chosen was then an expression of personal interest or motivation rather than being decided by objective rewards. The TAT measure of *n* Achievement was used for the achievement motive as a positive need for success (McClelland et al. 1953; Atkinson 1958a) and a Test Anxiety scale for fear of failure (Mandler and Sarason 1952; Mandler and Cowen 1958).

While it was found that participants on average preferred the middle distances, subjects with high need for achievement and low fear of failure tended more than others to choose intermediate distances, and those with high fear of failure and low need for achievement would choose more than others either near-certain success by standing up close or to throw from such a great distance that they could not have much hope of getting the ring over the peg. At neither extreme were those seeking to avoid failure risking much unexpected negative feedback. Theoretically, the most effective feedback on achievement should come from intermediate levels of risk because of the greater information value of events at that level. The information value of an event is a multiplicative function of the probability of success and the probability of failure. It is a curvilinear function with its maximum when there is an equal probability of success and failure and a minimum at the extremes (e.g. 0.5 x 0.5 = .25 in the middle, and 0.1 x 0.9 = .09 at the extremes). Subjects with a high need for achievement chose options with the greatest information value in feedback on success.

Atkinson's theory of the strength of achievement motivation as a function of motive, expectancy and incentive (Atkinson 1957) was later expressed in more detailed and quantitative terms (Atkinson 1964; Atkinson and Feather 1966b). It would be expressed as the multiplicative combination of strength of the motive, the probability of success and the incentive value of success, a function which was at maximum with equal probabilities of success and failure (McClelland 1961; Atkinson 1964). Similarly for fear of failure, avoidance or inhibitory tendencies will be greatest when there is a realistic challenge and expectancy of success is about equal to the expectancy of failure. The outcome will also be greatly affected by the relative strength of the two internal motive variables: the motive to achieve success and the motive to avoid failure. The combination will push the person towards the middle distance if the motive to succeed is greater and towards the extremes if the motive to avoid failure is greater. The outcome of this approach-avoidance conflict thus depends upon the cognitive integration of conflicting tendencies to resolve an incomplete gestalt.

Fear of Success and the Changing Sex Role Attitudes of Women

It had been well established that the effects of achievement motivation reflect both hope of success and fear of failure in *men*, but a new dynamic was brought into the discussion by Matina Horner with her concept of 'fear of *success*' that influenced the achievement of women (Horner 1971, 1972, 1974). She found that while there could be a conflict between motives of affiliation and achievement for both women and men, a consequent fear of success was particularly characteristic of women when they were in competition with men. Several different versions of the scoring manual for fear of success or (later) 'the motive to avoid success' were developed, and validation studies found relationships to arousal conditions quite different from those for the positive need for achievement. Fear-of-success scores were found to decrease rather than increase under conditions of arousal for some groups of women, indicating that a different motivational mechanism was in play. The third revision (Horner and Fleming 1992) shows 'the fear of success phenomenon as the conflicted expression of instrumental action in achievement situations' (Fleming and Horner 1992, p. 189).

Horner's original findings may have been to some extent a reflection of social conditions at that time, as was the previous paucity of research on achievement motivation in women. The test had been validated only on men. When both sexes were included, sex was sometimes found to be a moderator variable in the correlation of *n* Achievement with theoretically relevant variables: for example, the correlation with curiosity was found, at least in one situation, to be positive for boys but negative for girls (Beswick 1971). All the early work on the *n* Achievement measure by McClelland's team was done with men-only samples – it was said, to avoid such 'complications.' Need for achievement seemed to mean something different for women. After the 1950s some women began to investigate the nature and effects of achievement motivation in women. Horner, who worked with Atkinson at Michigan in the mid-sixties (Horner 1968), later joined McClelland at Harvard and contributed a 'fear of success' concept to the study of achievement and intrinsic motivation (Horner 1971). This was at the time when the women's movement for equality was beginning to gain strength.[1]

That there was a relationship of fear of success to changing social attitudes was evident in the results obtained by Peplau (1976). She found that the effect of fear of success as measured by Horner depended upon women holding traditional sex role attitudes. Women with traditional attitudes performed significantly better on a verbal task when working as a team with their boyfriend than when working in individual competition against the boyfriend; women with non-traditional attitudes showed the opposite pattern. Peplau commented that when Horner measured fear of success in her original study in 1965, 'the majority of women she tested held traditional sex-role attitudes. (She did not actually assess this, of course.) During the past decade, there has been considerable change in sex role attitudes. Today perhaps only women who maintain traditional beliefs about the feminine role are affected by fear of success' (Peplau 1976, p. 567). Nevertheless, that was in 1976, and later work by Horner and others still found evidence of fear of success affecting actual achievement behaviour with varying results depending upon the context (Fleming and Horner 1992). In the theory of cognitive motivation, contextual or cultural factors influence the resolution of the incomplete gestalt of an orientation to an achievement goal as they do other goal-oriented activities. It is a function of the whole self in a field of meaningful relationships.

[1] Horner herself contributed to accomplishments by many other women as president of Radcliffe College from 1972 to 1989.

Longitudinal Processes

The findings of McClelland, Atkinson and their associates in research on achievement motivation in the laboratory had parallels in the field, including achievement in contemporary business and historically in the rise and fall of entrepreneurial activity and economic development in different societies. After the initial phase of research on achievement motivation, McClelland gave attention especially to the business applications of his theory. Training programs were developed for improvement of performance through the acquisition and management of achievement motivation (McClelland 1961, 1965b; Litwin and Stringer 1968; McClelland and Winter 1969; McClelland 1976, 1978, 1984, 1985). There was good evidence for the effectiveness of these programs; one example is the training by McClelland of small businessmen in India, whose entrepreneurial success increased markedly through the acquisition of strong need for achievement, where other kinds of aid aimed at helping people to help themselves had failed.

After McClelland and Winter's *Motivating Economic Achievement* (1969) was published with positive findings, Winter extended his work on achievement and power motives into the study of personal responsibility. He invoked a sense of agency similar to the concept of personal causation proposed by deCharmes who also demonstrated effects of training (deCharms 1968; Winter 1973; deCharms 1987, 1992; Winter 1992b). The research of their team on the antecedent conditions affecting causal attribution supported the earlier conclusions of Rotter (1966) and Feather (1967) 'that individuals high in achievement motivation take responsibility for whatever outcome befalls them, while individuals low in achievement motivation regard achievement performance as relatively independent of their ability and effort' (Weiner and Kukla 1970, p. 15). (See Chapter 6 on attribution theory and the discussion of Winter's work on responsibility in Chapter 3.) These were long-term effects. Differences between short- and long-term effects of achievement motivation on career strivings are implied in Raynor's elaboration of achievement motivation theory concerned with conditional probabilities in a career path, which I will come back to shortly (Raynor 1969, 1970, 1974a).

Long-Term Effects of Cultural Change

In *The Achieving Society* (1961) McClelland presented an application of his theory and methods to explain different rates of economic development in various countries in the 20th century, as well as periods of rapid growth and decline in the history of certain ancient and modern societies over several centuries. Noting Max Weber's argument for an association between the Protestant Reformation and the rise of capitalism (Weber, Parsons and Tawney 1930), and his own observation that the characteristics of Protestant entrepreneurs described by Weber were similar to those of individuals with high *n* Achievement, he looked for evidence of the effects of this motive in contemporary and historical differences between societies which differed in economic activity. He postulated that an emphasis in child training on self-reliance, mastery and monitoring one's own behaviour would produce more active entrepreneurs. In a study of changes in 20th-century national economies, McClelland found that societies in which the literature chosen for children to read contained the most achievement imagery were those societies where there was the most economic growth in the next generation. He did not argue that the achievement imagery in the literature was an influence on the children who read those stories, but that strong achievement imagery in the stories represented cultures in which such motives were valued and encouraged.

McClelland also related the effects of *n* Achievement in British history to the cultural embodiment of the Reformation, Puritanism and the evangelical movement that was suggested in the sociological work of Max Weber on *The Protestant Ethic* (Weber et al. 1930) and the historical studies by R. H. Tawney in his *Religion and the Rise of Capitalism* (Tawney 1938). He noted similar cultural differences in comparisons between countries in recent times and related them to generative social factors such as child rearing, (see McClelland, Rhindlisbacher and deCharms 1955). McClelland had also written on 'The importance of early learning in the formation of motives' (McClelland 1958c). He cited research on how parents reinforce achievement striving in young children with signs of expectation and affective reward (McClelland et al. 1955; Winterbottom 1958; Rosen and D'Andrade 1959; McClelland 1961, 1985). Differences in the age of expected independence were found when Irish and Italian Catholic families were compared with Protestant and Jewish families (McClelland et al. 1955); similar differences were found between French Canadian and Italian Catholics versus Protestants and Jews (Rosen 1959; McClelland 1985). For a review of later research on the role of parents in children's achievement, see Pomerantz, Grolnick and Price (2005).

McClelland identified two periods of rapid economic growth in British history and found an association of them with a high level of need for achievement. These were the Elizabethan period in the 16th century and the Industrial Revolution of the 18th century. Similarly, in the history of ancient Greece, a period of increased prosperity and subsequent decline was related to changes in the cultural evidence of the achievement motive. Literature from early and later periods was compared in achievement imagery with that of the climax period 475–362 BC. An alternative to the literature method of scoring the motive in that study was a non-verbal graphic measure of need for achievement developed by Elliot Aronson in an ingenious study of doodles drawn by present-day students under varying conditions of achievement arousal (Aronson 1958). It was applied to designs on the ancient vases in which produce was carried, the distribution of which also marked the extent of trade. Both these, graphic and verbal, methods showed higher societal need for achievement immediately prior to the period of maximum entrepreneurial success in trade.

In general, a culture favouring the internalized setting of achievement goals and development of the psychological means for their attainment, such as commitment to standards of excellence and readiness to accept delay of gratification, was found to be characteristic of economically successful societies across different cultures and periods of history (McClelland 1961). Similarly, taking personal responsibility for one's achievement goals and preferring intermediate risks with high information value were shown to be features of an effective business culture in contemporary societies (McClelland 1961, 1965b, 1976, 1985).

Contingent Sequences of Achievement Striving

Raynor made a theoretical extension with a similar rationale in work which applied achievement motivation theory to career development. He made a distinction between *performance* and *intrinsic* components of achievement motivation. An activity might serve either as a means to an end in the long term or as an end in itself with 'intrinsic value' in the near term. Raynor referred to an earlier distinction which came out of the group dynamics tradition and was expressed in Lewinian terms contrasting the intrinsic valance of a goal region with its potential instrumental value (Thomas and Zander 1959, p. 126). Thomas and Zander demonstrated the strength of motivation for a sequence of behaviour that began with a proximate goal that was intrinsically rewarding but had a longer-term instrumental value. In Raynor's account, success on one task that was intrinsically motivated made possible a further opportunity to progress towards a long-term achievement goal that could be extrinsically motivated (Raynor 1974a, p. 152). This might occur in a career path. For example, a student might simply enjoy mathematics, but success in this subject could contribute to highly paid achievement in an engineering career.

At the heart of Raynor's concern was the contingent relationship of long-term outcomes to success on earlier tasks in a sequence such as a career (Raynor 1969, 1974a). Raynor argued that the original form of Atkinson's theory did not provide for this possibility. One consequence was that while *intermediate* levels of risk taking might be preferred in a single task situation, as found by Atkinson and Litwin, the contingency of future rewards on the outcome of earlier tasks would make a preference for tasks with a *high* subjective probability of success more likely in the short term, and this is what was found (Raynor 1974a, 1974b). The general rule about people with high achievement motivation preferring intermediate levels of risk was modified when contingencies in a sequence were taken into account. As part of his general theory of personality functioning and change in adult competence motivation (Raynor 1981), Raynor also proposed a theory of the self-system in relation to achievement motivation (Raynor 1982). He distinguished between arousal in the *behavioural system* and arousal in the *self-system*. This distinction applied to the difference between the intrinsic value of success in a task and striving by means of it to become a particular kind of person.

In Raynor's work, a long-term contingency could reduce the value of a short-term goal except as a means to an end, leading a person to take less risk for the sake of it. It is similar to Deci's finding that a contingent outcome can suppress interest in the immediate task (Ryan and Deci 2000a). It has been argued, nevertheless, in more recent work that it is possible in practice to manage an optimal combination of intrinsic and extrinsic incentives, particularly in education (Sansone and Harackiewicz 2000c). There are similar useful applications in business (Beswick 2009). One important condition found by Deci and Ryan was that *symbolic* as opposed to material rewards did not suppress intrinsic motivation. The macro model of cognitive motivation suggests that suppression or facilitation will depend upon the symbolic value or meaning of rewards for long-term personal achievement in a career path that is consistent with a person's self-concept.

The Continuous Activity Model

Atkinson made 'a radical revision' of his own theory of achievement motivation after reflecting over a number of years upon Feather's findings on persistence as evidence of motivation (Feather 1961, 1962; Atkinson and Birch 1970, 1974; Feather 1982a). Atkinson favoured a reconsideration of 'Expectancy X Value' theory within 'the framework of the new dynamics of action' (Atkinson 1982, p. 33). As we have noted, expectancy value theory had been elaborated into a more general theory with a longitudinal perspective by Raynor (1969, 1974a) in his contingent path model of the effects of distant goals. In Atkinson's understanding, a clue provided in Feather's conceptual analysis of persistence proved the foundation for a more extensive reconstruction of the theory of motivation.

Studying persistence in a continuous flow of action led Atkinson to abandon an episodic conception of motivation that had been applied in experiments on the expectancy-value theory, and to consider instead what might influence change in a continuous flow. He proposed to begin with a new premise: that the individual is already active in two senses, by (1) already doing something when observed and (2) being already motivated to do many other things, before being exposed to a new stimulus situation. 'The focus of interest shifts from … particular isolated activities to the continuity of behaviour and the juncture between different activities, a change from one to another' (Atkinson 1982, p. 34). A higher level of abstraction in the Atkinson and Birch elaboration of achievement motivation (Atkinson and Birch 1970, 1974) provided flexibility to account for empirical findings like those of Raynor that were not predicted from the episodic form of the expectancy-value theory.

> In the framework of the new dynamics of action, *the theory of achievement motivation is now to be considered a theory about the determinants of instigating forces to achieve success and inhibitory forces to avoid failure in various activities and not, as heretofor assumed, of the final strength of tendencies to achieve success and avoid failure in a particular situation.* (Atkinson 1982, pp. 35–36, original emphasis)

The distinction between 'instigating forces' and 'the final strength of tendencies' might be seen to foreshadow Elliot's distinction between the dispositional property of a motive and the overall motivational process in his hierarchical theory that depends upon the qualities of different achievement goals interacting with motives and expectancies, as discussed in the concluding sections of this chapter.

Achievement Goals

There was a significant change of emphasis in later work on achievement motivation, away from the motive as a dispositional property and towards achievement goals as cognitive structures directing goal-oriented behaviour. 'According to the now dominant achievement goal approach, behaviour is a rational attempt to reach consciously articulated (or accessible) ends or purposes, rather than a manifestation of underlying, affect-laden needs or desires' (Thrash and Elliot 2001, p. 3). In the words of one of the initiators of this new approach, 'An intentional view of behavior (Dennett 1978) is adopted. In this, action is construed as a rational attempt to attain goals or incentives' (Nicholls 1984, p. 328). Self-report measures then largely replaced projective or multi-method assessments of motivational propensities. McClelland continued to argue that questionnaire methods would risk sampling values more than motives (McClelland 1989), but the shift of emphasis from dispositional motive properties to goal properties led to a fruitful goal constructs theory (Dweck and Elliott 1983; Maehr 1983; Ames 1984; Nicholls 1984; see also Ames 1992).

Types of Achievement Goals

After many years of research focused on motives as dispositions, variations in achievement relevant behaviour came to be investigated as a function of different achievement goals. McClelland and his colleagues had described need for achievement in terms of concern with an achievement goal in which different examples of achievement motivation, such as unique accomplishment and long-term involvement with an achievement goal, were treated as functionally equivalent. The assumption had been that the aroused motive and its effects would be the same, as long as there was competition with a standard of excellence. In education (Sansone and Morgan 1992; Harackiewicz 2004) and more generally, researchers began to look for differences in specific achievement goals that might account for differences in achievement behaviour. This led to achievement goal theory articulated initially by Dweck and Nicholls (Nicholls 1984; Dweck 1985; Thrash and Elliot 2001).

It was said that global motives are ill-suited to account for specific ends towards which individuals strive (Dweck and Leggett 1988), while the motive approach neglected specific cognitive processes that are the proximal causes or mediators of achievement relevant outcomes (Dweck and Elliott 1983). The motive tradition was said to have neglected the subjective, meaning- and purpose-related experiences that accompany goal striving (Maehr 1974; Maehr and Nicholls 1980). This led to more concern with the symbolic nature of goal striving.

From studies of learned helplessness, Dweck and her colleagues documented two distinct patterns of affect, cognition, and behaviour in response to failure. Some children responded with a 'mastery' pattern attributing failure to insufficient effort while they attributed success to persistence, and they associated performance with positive expectancies and feelings in the pursuit of subsequent challenge. Other children of equal ability had a maladaptive 'helpless' pattern, attributing failure to insufficient ability, with negative affect and expectancies which were accompanied by decrements in persistence and performance and by avoidance of subsequent challenge. Dweck and Elliott[2] argued that children may pursue a *learning goal* or a *performance goal* as qualitatively different types of goals with different outcomes in achievement motivation (Dweck and Elliott 1983; Elliott and Dweck 1988).

Nicholls's (1989) goal theory approach was developed from investigations of developmental changes in how children conceive of ability. Initially it is undifferentiated. Nicholls found that by the age of 12 or 13, the child develops a 'differentiated' conception of ability, allowing for social performance norms and one's effort, while adults can work for either differentiated or undifferentiated goals.

While various definitions of goal categories have been advocated, the common distinction that was made particularly by Dweck and her associates has been widely adopted – that is, the distinction between a *performance goal* (sometimes referred to as an *ego* or *ability* goal) and a *learning goal* (which might be described as a *mastery, intrinsic* or *task* goal). In more recent work Dweck has referred to different 'mindsets' associated with two different types of achievement goals, in which a contrast is drawn between mindsets for fixed or for changeable personal qualities: belief that intelligence, for example, is fixed is then associated with performance goals, and belief that a person's intelligence is capable of growth is associated with mastery goals (Dweck 2006). In Dweck's argument, if the person believes that attributes such as intelligence are relatively fixed, a performance goal could be a threat as it has potential to indicate something about the person that is important but unchangeable. On the other hand, a person might believe that relative success on the task, when it is seen as a learning opportunity, could reveal progress in the development of changeable levels of skill.

Carol Sansone and Judith Harackiewicz and their colleagues, whose research on related topics is represented in the collected work *Intrinsic and Extrinsic Motivation: The Search for Optimal Motivation and Performance* (Sansone and Harackiewicz 2000a), made a different distinction, that is, between *purpose* goals and *target* goals, that I will come to shortly (Harackiewicz and Sansone 2000). They proposed a *process theory of intrinsic motivation* (Harackiewicz and Sansone 1991; Sansone and Harackiewicz 1996) that gave more room for a continuous process of motivation than concentration upon the dispositional motive alone. Arising from that background, in which he worked with Harackiewicz, Andrew Elliot's *hierarchical theory* combined the older tradition of

[2] Note: Elaine Elliott not Andrew Elliot with whom Dweck published later.

approach-avoidance conceptions from Atkinson and others with the performance-mastery goal formulation (Elliot and Harackiewicz 1996; Elliot 1997; Elliot and Church 1997; Elliot 1999; Elliot and Covington 2001; Elliot 2006, 2008). I will discuss the hierarchical model later in this chapter. At this point some consideration needs to be given to a developing understanding of the concept of 'goal' in achievement motivation.

A traditional description of a goal was that it is as a representation of an end or result that an individual aims to achieve (Tolman 1926; Pervin 1983, 1989; Austin and Vancouver 1996). In regard to achievement goals, Elliot and colleagues recommended a modification: 'However, achievement goal theorists have proposed a novel goal conceptualization (Maehr and Meyer 1997), defining a goal as the *purpose* for which one engages in a task (Maehr 1989, Dweck 1996) … or the alternative dictionary definition, "an intended or desired result; end; aim; goal"' (Thrash and Elliot 2001, p. 11). They note that this allows rich but diverse meanings of 'purpose.' As noted earlier, Nicholls adopts what he calls an 'intentional' view of behaviour – a rational attempt to obtain desired ends – while for Dweck goals represent what the individual is trying to do, and she distinguishes the states of ego and task involvement in terms of the ends that are sought. Going back some way in the history of these ideas, Woodworth made an early distinction between intrinsic and instrumental forms of achievement motivation, which might be seen to parallel the later mastery and performance distinction, when he said, in reference to Atkinson's work on achievement motivation and the Zeigarnik effect, that it makes a difference whether the subject is motivated by 'interest in the tasks or by concern for the ego' (Woodworth 1958, p. 93).

Sansone and Harackiewicz have included achievement goals in their work on intrinsic motivation with reference to the meaning an activity has for the person. They found support for the view that extrinsic rewards with *symbolic* value can *increase* intrinsic motivation by making competence salient as individuals are led to become more involved in the pursuit of competence (Sansone and Harackiewicz 2000b). They distinguished purpose goals from target goals (see Bandura 1986; Locke and Latham 1990). 'Target goals thus reflect a more specific idea of *what* individuals are trying to accomplish while performing an activity, whereas purpose goals reflect *why* they are engaging in the activity' (Harackiewicz and Sansone 2000, p. 99). In an apparent contradiction of Deci and Ryan's definition of intrinsic motivation (see Chapter 3), they began to include an understanding of the process of intrinsic motivation goals which may be separable from the activity. Individuals are seen to approach activities with some idea about what they want to accomplish in the longer term. Goals could then be pursued at a number of levels of abstraction, ranging from lower-order goals that are concrete and situationally specific to higher-order goals that are broad, cross-situational, and consistent over time (e.g., personal strivings, possible selves).

A consequent challenge addressed by Sansone and Harackiewicz, with Hidi and others, is to define the conditions under which activities that are directed towards 'higher-order goals,' which are rewarding in the longer term, can be undertaken in such a way as to maintain interest in the task and not suppress intrinsic motivation (Hidi 2000; Hidi and Harackiewicz 2000; Sansone and Harackiewicz 2000b, 2000c; Hidi, Ainley, Berndorff and Del Favero 2007). That is one of the issues examined in greater depth in the treatment of intrinsic motivation in Chapter 3. The key point is that maintaining interest depends upon the *symbolic* meaning of the higher-order goal for a person's long-term development.

The Hierarchical Theory of Achievement Motivation

Elliot's hierarchical model of achievement motivation (Elliot 1994, 1997) is a major contribution, relevant to cognitive motivation in general. In a conceptual analysis, Elliot and Harackiewicz proposed an integrated model combining the performance-mastery distinction between types of achievement goals with the classic approach-avoidance formulation of achievement motivation (Elliot and Harackiewicz 1994, 1996). Three kinds of achievement goals were defined: 'a mastery goal focused on the development of competence and task mastery, a performance-approach goal directed toward the attainment of favourable judgments of competence, and a performance-avoidance goal focused on avoiding unfavourable judgments of competence' (Elliot and Church 1997, p. 218). The utility of this distinction was investigated by experimental manipulation of achievement goals and observing its effect on intrinsic motivation (Elliot and Harackiewicz 1996). Performance avoidance goals undermined intrinsic motivation relative to both performance approach and mastery goals.

Elliot and Church presented the hierarchical model of achievement motivation in a step-wise process in which goals were seen as intermediate between motivational dispositions and motivated behaviour (Elliot and Church 1997). They also proposed that competence expectancies should be conceived as conceptually distinct from both motive dispositions and achievement goals. The hierarchical model then defined two sets of antecedent conditions: (1) motives as personal dispositions and (2) task-specific competence expectations. These conditions would together affect the adoption of achievement goals and subsequently achievement.

The dispositional properties of success-oriented achievement motivation and fear of failure were assessed using questionnaire methods which also assessed competence expectancy. For the intermediate goal variables, factor analysis confirmed three independent factors in the items selected for the three achievement goal definitions. For the *Performance-Approach* goal, the highest loading item was, 'It is important to me to do better than the other students'; the strongest of the *Mastery* goal items was 'I want to learn as much as possible from this class;' and for *Performance-avoidance* items it was 'I often think to myself, "What if I do badly in this class?"' The outcome variables were intrinsic motivation and final course grades. A new scale was developed for intrinsic motivation in which typical items were 'I think this class is interesting' and 'I enjoy this class very much.'

The principal findings in this study (Elliot and Church 1997) confirmed the path model of effects from antecedent conditions, through intermediate goal properties to outcomes. It showed significant differential effects of the antecedent motives and expectancy conditions on adoption of the three different types of achievement goals, which in turn completely accounted for the different effects of having those goals on the outcome measures of intrinsic motivation and performance.[3]

These results justify the conceptual distinctions Elliot and Harackiewicz had made between types of motives and kinds of achievement goals. Elliot and Church acknowledged, however, that there could be other relevant antecedent conditions, and more recent work has indicated support for at least one additional category of achievement goals. A 2 x 2 classification of approach-avoidance motives and mastery-performance goal types would indicate a fourth quadrant of mastery avoidance. This option was investigated subsequently (Elliot and McGregor 2001; Van Yperen 2006; Van Yperen, Elliot and Ansell 2009; Bartels, Magun-Jackson and Ryan 2010). It was found that mastery avoidance goals are more deleterious for performance improvement than each of the other three types of achievement goals (Van Yperen et al. 2009), but in their measure of mastery avoidance there was not a specific concern with a standard of excellence that is to be avoided, as there was in Horner's fear-of-success measure which was a function of interpersonal factors in tension with a person's self-concept. We do not know the implications of these different understandings of the negative type of mastery goals.

[3] In a regression analysis there was no remaining effect of the antecedent conditions on the outcome variables after the variance accounted for by the goals was taken out.

Towards a New General Theory of Goals

In Elliot's exposition, the renewal of a close association between motivation and cognition in the 1990s, after a period of unnecessary separation, brings approach-avoidance motivation into the foreground of motivational analysis (Elliot 2006). This understanding introduced a dynamic view in which a goal is not a fixed property but the result of and subject to continuing change and growth of organisation and may appear in a great variety of forms. Elliot uses the term 'stimuli' to refer to valanced objects/events/possibilities that may be concrete or abstract, and 'connote an essentially limitless, idiographic array of focal endpoints' (Elliot 2006, p. 113).

Elliot's suggestion of an essentially limitless range of focal endpoints matches my discussion in Chapter 12 of the basis in cognitive theory for expecting an infinite range of cognitive needs and emotions in an extension of Baumeister's 'needs for meaning.' In cognitive motivation these focal points involve emotions in anticipated feedback processes. Goals have receptors for emotion signals. In Chapter 8 I describe the function of emotions as a signalling system for orientation and movement towards a goal. The nature of goals in general and their development is discussed further in Chapter 9. Goals are not the whole story, but a component in the motivational process as Dweck, Harackiewicz, Elliot and others have demonstrated in regard to achievement. To understand the function of goals in cognitive motivation requires also an understanding of motives, expectancies, consciousness, agency, intention and commitment. Recent developments in the study of achievement motivation have emphasised the value of these traditional concepts that will be examined further in the following chapters.

Summary

Research on achievement motivation pioneered the study of specific motivational predispositions that were originally defined as psychogenic needs by Henry Murray. These are all examples of cognitive motivation. McClelland and Atkinson, who developed the field from the late 1940s through the 1950s and later, defined an achievement goal as success in competition with some standard of excellence and the motive for it as a cluster of affectively toned cognitive associations. The principal method used to develop an operational definition of 'need for achievement' (*n* Ach) combined experimental arousal of an internal disposition with standardized content analysis of fantasy material in a special form of Murray's Thematic Apperception Test (TAT). Scores on the test discriminated between subjects in their responsiveness to achievement arousal. This measure was correlated with academic achievement, as with other kinds of achievement, when there were appropriate arousal conditions. Child-rearing practices which emphasised independence training were related to the development of achievement motivation, both in the observation of individual instances and in cross-cultural differences. These differences were related by McClelland to entrepreneurial activity and rates of economic development.

Atkinson developed the expectancy value theory of motivation combining motive strength for seeking success, fear of failure, subjective probability of success and the incentive value of success or failure. Studying persistence in a continuous flow of action led Atkinson to abandon an episodic conception of motivation. A higher level of abstraction for representation of instigating and inhibiting forces in the Atkinson and Birch elaboration of achievement motivation provided flexibility to account for empirical findings like those of Raynor on sequential effects that were not predicted from the episodic form of the expectancy value theory.

There was a change of emphasis in later work on achievement motivation, away from motives as dispositional properties, towards achievement goals as cognitive structures developed from work by Dweck and others on the difference between interest and performance goals in self-theories. Particularly significant is the further development of a hierarchical theory of achievement motivation, proposed by Elliot, as a process involving dispositional properties of motives and competence expectations having effects on intrinsic motivation and performance that are mediated by achievement goal constructs.

6 Agency, Efficacy and Attribution

> We can object to any one who would frighten us away from the facts of human purpose for fear they would disturb some neat philosophical system.
>
> – Woodworth 1932

Introduction

The effects of attributions and self-efficacy beliefs are based on perceptions of agency. Weiner, in regard to attribution (Weiner 1986), and Bandura, in regard to self-efficacy (Bandura 1997), both emphasised the importance of a sense of agency, but from different perspectives. Weiner's attribution theory refers to a *retrospective* process in which a person infers a causal explanation of past behaviour, while Bandura's theory of self-efficacy relies upon a *prospective* process of goal anticipation and commitment. Both theories illustrate many of the essential features of cognitive motivation. The concept of competence, especially in White's theory of effectance motivation (White 1959), is important also in reference to both these theories and in the history of cognitive motivation. Weiner acknowledges White as one of the inspirations for his theory, but Bandura seeks to differentiate his theory of self-efficacy from White's conception of effectance motivation. Another approach to agency and free will is represented by the cognitive-affective processing systems theory advanced by Mischel and his colleagues (Mischel 1996; Mischel and Ayduk 2002, 2010). It is part of a more general discussion of self-regulation.

The Focus on Agency in Attribution and Self-Efficacy

A sense of agency has been increasingly recognized in personality and social psychology. In Chapter 3 I reviewed its importance for intrinsic motivation which was demonstrated by Deci and Ryan, among others, as a further development of deCharms's theory of personal causality and Heider's concept of a 'perceived locus of causality.' The sense of being the origin of our own actions and directing our purposive behaviour is an aspect of consciousness experienced by all people. It is central to Bandura's theory of self-efficacy (Bandura 1977a, 1982, 1997) as for White's earlier theory of competence or effectance motivation: '[T]he power of initiative and exertion that we experience as a sense of being an agent in the living of our lives may be called a feeling of efficacy' (White 1972, p. 209; see also White 1959, 1960).

Weiner's attribution theory was developed from Atkinson's expectancy-value theory of achievement motivation and is concerned with answers to a question such as, 'Who or what was responsible for that event?' Cognitive processes of seeking to understand *why* an action has occurred set up conditions for cognitive motivation. In Weiner's theory, understanding the past promises an understanding of what will be effective in the future (Weiner 1986, 2005).

In Bandura's 'social cognitive theory,' developed originally within 'social learning theory' (Bandura 1977a, 1977b, 1986), self-efficacy is concerned with 'the exercise of control,' so that in regard to self-regulation 'efficacy beliefs are the foundation of human agency'(Bandura 2001, p. 10). In his later work expounding 'an agentic perspective' Bandura discussed intentionality, forethought, self-reactiveness and self-reflectiveness as features of agency, and he extended individual human agency to collective agency in a social setting (Bandura 2001).

A Functional View of Agency

'To be an agent is to intentionally make things happen by one's own actions' (Bandura 2001, p. 2). In social cognitive theory, agency embodies a number of personal properties such as belief systems, self-regulatory capabilities and distributed structures through which personal influence is exercised. As Dennett would say, the agentic self is not a discrete entity that resides in a particular place and steers the ship as it were (Dennett 2003, 2004), but, in Bandura's theory, it is an effective functional characteristic of the system as a whole. The core features of human agency discussed by Bandura operate through phenomenal and functional consciousness. The function of consciousness in the process of cognitive integration is discussed in detail in Chapter 7. At this point we take up Bandura's advocacy of the functional value of conscious agency.

Moving on from recent views of human subjects as complex computational machines, Bandura recognized agency, with its subjectivity and conscious control, as an essential characteristic of humanness. Rejecting an epiphenomenal view of consciousness as a mere by-product of mental processes, he asked, 'Why would an epiphenomenal consciousness that can do nothing evolve and endure as a reigning psychic environment in people's lives?' (Bandura 2001, p. 2). He objected to the idea of people as essentially higher-level automatons without phenomenal and functional consciousness. 'Consciousness is the very substance of mental life that not only makes life personally manageable but worth living' (Bandura 2001, p. 3).

Bandura objected to the move from connectionist and computationalist models conceived as approximations to cognitive activities to the model of eliminative materialism in which people do not act on beliefs, goals, aspirations and expectations, but rather it is believed that their automatic networks at a sub-personal level make them do things. In his view, people employing belief systems as a working model of a complex world make good judgments about their capabilities, anticipate outcomes of their actions, and regulate their behaviour accordingly: 'Forethought, generative, and reflective capabilities are, therefore, vital for survival and human progress' (Bandura 2001, p. 3).

While rejecting eliminative materialism, Bandura was, nevertheless, a physicalist. He saw sensory, motor and other cerebral systems as tools people use to accomplish the tasks that give meaning and direction to their lives; and rather than people being mere receivers of structure built into their brains, they help to bring it about; and so he referred to research indicating that agentic action, such as exploring and manipulating, plays a role in shaping the neuronal and functional structure of the brain (Diamond 1988; Kolb and Whishaw 1998). Social cognitive theory subscribes to a model of *emergent* interactive agency (Bandura 1986, 1999), in which thoughts are 'emergent brain activities that exert determinative influence' (Bandura 2001, p. 4). In his agentic perspective Bandura understood the human mind as generative, creative, proactive and reflective, not merely reactive. These characteristics of the mind are emerging products of the physical brain that remain embodied functions of the brain. The philosophy of emergence is discussed in more detail in the next section, but first, here is Bandura's acknowledgement of agentic properties.

Intentionality: When people act intentionally, they are exercising agency as the originator of an action. The cognitive representation of a future course of action need not be simply an expectation or prediction, but can include a proactive commitment to bring it about. Bandura referred approvingly to Bratman's functionalist approach to intentional agency (Bratman 1999, Bandura 2001) that I discuss in Chapter 10, in which intentions are revised in the light of new information during the execution of an intention. However, in Bandura's theory, intentions are not sufficient for the fulfilment of future plans which will require other self-regulatory aspects of agency.

Forethought: Beyond forward planning, a future time perspective involves the creation and selection of courses of action designed to achieve the goals people set and anticipation of the likely consequences of their chosen courses of action (Feather 1982b, Bandura 1991). Bandura suggested that 'through the exercise of forethought people motivate themselves and guide their actions in anticipation of future events' (Bandura 1997, p. 7). The motivating effect of forethought is envisaged in a macro as well as a micro form, so that over a long period of time forethought 'provides direction, coherence, and meaning to one's life' (p. 7).

Self-reactiveness: In addition to adopting an intention and an action plan, agency requires the ability to shape appropriate courses of action and to motivate and regulate their execution. In self-efficacy theory, self-regulatory processes link thought to action through a set of self-referent sub-functions which include self-monitoring, self-guidance of performance via personal standards, and corrective self-reactions (Bandura 1986, 1991). These are all cognitive feedback functions in which self-reactive influences arise from comparisons of performance with personal goals and standards. Bandura believed that 'goals, rooted in a value system and a sense of personal identity, invest activities with meaning and purpose' (Bandura 2001, p. 8).

Self-reflectiveness: As agents, people are both actors and self-examiners. Metacognitive reflection on oneself, one's actions and thoughts, is another core, distinctively human feature of agency. Reflective self-consciousness enables people to evaluate their motivation, values and the meaning of their life pursuits. At this high level of self-reflectiveness people can address conflicts in motivational inducements and choose one over another. There is no more central or pervasive mechanism of personal agency than people's beliefs in their capacity to exercise a measure of control of their own functioning and environmental events (Bandura 1997). 'Efficacy beliefs are the foundation of human agency' (Bandura 2001, p. 10.)

These features of human agency are personal properties of the individual, but social cognitive theory distinguishes three different modes of agency: personal, proxy and collective. The conception of a proxy mode of agency, in which people's purposes may be achieved through others, goes back to Bandura's early work on vicarious learning (e.g. Bandura and Walters 1959; Bandura 1969). In addition to proxy agency, social cognitive theory extends human agency to collective agency, in which people cooperate in joint ventures. A key factor in collective agency is shared beliefs in their capacity to produce the desired results.

Agency, Free Will and the Emergent Properties of Systems

Bandura's views on agency are in stark contrast with the mechanistic and materialist views of Wegner and Dennett who argue that any sense of agency is 'ultimately' an illusion – that we can only imagine that we have free will.

Wegner attempted in his book *The Illusion of Conscious Will* to draw general philosophic conclusions favouring determinism from empirical observations that people can be mistaken in thinking that, by their freely chosen actions, they have caused things to happen. He favoured a deterministic philosophy, and even saw merit in fatalistic religious traditions (Wegner 2002, p. 333). While conceding that we might not always be mistaken about our thoughts causing actions, since better demonstrated by Baumeister et al. (2011), he reached a general conclusion that '[s]ometimes how things seem is more important than what they are. This is true in theatre, in art, used car sales', etc. … and 'in the scientific analysis of conscious will. The fact is, it seems to each of us that we have conscious will. It seems we have selves. It seems we have minds. It seems we are agents. It seems we cause what we do.' But, he says, '[I]t is sobering and ultimately accurate to call all this an illusion.' Then he concedes a human benefit: '[T]he illusions piled up atop apparent mental causation are the building blocks of human psychology and social life' (Wegner 2002, pp. 341–342). It seems that illusions are good for us, for our self-image, for our health, and they might even make us responsible citizens, but 'ultimately' there is no reconciliation between the machine model and human conscious agency. For Wegner, 'Our sense of being a conscious agent who does things comes at the cost of being technically wrong all the time' (p. 342).

A Neuroscientific Argument for Individual Responsibility

From a quite different point of view, Gray concluded from his extensive work 'creeping up on the hard problem' of consciousness that he had found 'the essentials of a reconciliation of the long-time irreconcilable: determinism and individual responsibility' (Gray 2004, p. 300). He argued that responsibility has to do with the correct functioning of feedback systems that operate largely unconsciously. This is a function of the reflexive self that includes both conscious and unconscious elements. In reference to the work of Libet and others that is discussed in Chapter 10, showing that conscious awareness of an intention to act may appear sometime after preparatory motor neuronal activity has commenced, he concluded, 'The conscious recognition of a decision to act and the ensuing action as *my* decision and *my* action comes after the event; but they nonetheless are mine' (Gray 2004, p. 300). Responsibility is a function of 'the entire system that is "me", its unconscious as much as its conscious part' (Gray 2004, p. 300). Gray's description of the unified nature of the reflexive self as a responsible agent distinguishes his position from that of Wegner in which a remnant of dualism remains. Baars and Dennett both, from different points of view, have discerned a kind of dualism in Wegner's conception of the person (Baars 2002b; Baars, Ramsøy and Laureys 2003; Dennett 2003, 2004).

In his concept of the person, Wegner has overlooked the non-reductive, autonomous nature of the reflexive self that Gray inferred from 'the correct functioning of feedback systems.' A contrasting dualist view is evident when Wegner said, 'The experience of will is the way our minds portray their operations to us, not their actual operation' (Wegner and Commentators 2004, p. 655), The dualism recognized by Baars and Dennett is revealed when we ask: Who is the 'us' to whom our minds portray their operations? The 'us' to whom our minds are portrayed in Wegner's theory appears to be something separate from the person who acts and whose actions are portrayed. Gray is saying that the self as object is the same entity as the self as observer, so that 'the actual operation of our minds' in the 'correct functioning of feedback systems' results in action that is '*my* decision and *my* action.' Agency is a function of the whole person, not of one part that acts upon another.

Cognitive-Affective Processing Systems Underlying Free Will

A different approach is represented by the work of Walter Mischel and his colleagues who proposed a theory of Cognitive-Affective Processing Systems (CAPS) underlying free will or willpower (Mischel 1996; Mischel and Ayduk 2002; Mischel 2004; Mischel and Ayduk 2004; Mischel 2009; Mischel and Ayduk 2010; Mischel 2012). Based on Mischel's work on delay of gratification, an early version of which is discussed in Chapter 2 in relation to curiosity, CAPS theory describes processes of self-regulation that are effective as control systems in freely voluntary behaviour. It is part of an extensive literature on self-regulation – see, for example, the two editions of the *Handbook of Self-regulation* (Baumeister and Vohs 2004; Vohs and Baumeister 2010).

The CAPS theory, as set out principally by Mischel and Shoda (1995), has its roots in Mischel's search for the role of ideation or cognitive images that may enable or reduce self-control for delay of gratification (Mischel 1973, 1974). Mischel and his colleagues found, contrary to expectations from psychoanalytic theory and behaviour reinforcement theories, that concentrating upon the physical presence of a reward object (e.g., either one or two cookies) reduced the time that children would wait for either a small or a large reward, but that abstract or iconic images could assist in delaying gratification to receive the greater reward (two cookies). This simple delay-of-gratification test was found to have long-term predictive value for the personalities of children who were followed into adult life (Mischel 1996). Apparently, the more abstract image enabled the subject to reconfigure and see the reward in a wider context, incorporating it into action plans which are cognitive representations that extend into the future.

Mischel referred back to William James who described 'preliminaries' that enable individuals to exercise 'will-power' (James 1890, Vol. 2, p. 488). Mischel reported support from his and his colleagues' research for the view that 'self-imposed delay of gratification, concern for the future and planfulness are essential prerequisites for mature human functioning' (Mischel 1996, p. 198). Self-regulatory ability influences 'self-concepts and self-esteem, interpersonal strategies (e.g. aggression), coping, and the ability to buffer or protect the self against the maladaptive consequences of chronic personal vulnerabilities such as rejection sensitivity' (Mischel and Ayduk 2010, p. 100). But it was not primarily a matter of stable habit types of traits that would direct behaviour with similarly adaptive strategies across a variety of situations (Mischel 2004).

In their cognitive-affective processing systems (CAPS) theory, Mischel and Shoda pointed beyond simple trait theory that Mischel had challenged so successfully in his book *Personality and Assessment* (Mischel 1968; Mischel and Shoda 1995, 2008; Mischel 2009). Situational determinism appeared for a period then to be reclaiming the dominant position that it had held in the behaviourist era. Mischel and Shoda, however, reintroduced cross-situational stability in the form of interactive signatures of an 'if-then' character. So, for example, a person might be more aggressive than others if certain attributes were found in a situation, but not otherwise. Such interactive invariabilities can characterize a person as readily as stable traits were once assumed intuitively to do. Personality was reconceptualised in terms of characteristic mediating processes that underlie and motivate behaviour.

Mischel and Ayduk employed 'a connectionist metaphor for a self-regulatory processing system' (Mischel and Ayduk 2004, p. 101; see also Mischel and Ayduk 2010). They considered the nature of *cognitive-affective units* (CAUs) consisting of cognitions and affects which combined in a stable network that constrains and guides activation. The CAUs are based on psychological variables originally proposed by

Mischel (Mischel 1973, 1974), and shown to be important in much subsequent research on self-regulation. These include personal appraisal of the situation, beliefs and expectancies (e.g. self-efficacy), personal values and goals, affects (e.g. anxiety, eagerness), as well as evaluative standards that are activated in specific situations; particularly important are the individual's self-regulatory competencies that include cognitive-attention strategies and scripts for diverse types of behaviour. CAUs are themselves composed of activation patterns at multiple levels (c.f. von Ehrenfels' idea of gestalts within gestalts discussed in Chapter 9). This is a system that has much in common with the cognitive motivation processing system. In a broader cognitive motivational perspective, the signature attributes of mediating personality systems and cognitive-affective units appear in the reflexive qualities of the unique self in which their self-regulation facilitates free will.

The Philosophy of Emergence

The reflexive self in the agency of a person can be seen as an expression of the *emergent* qualities of the person as an autonomous system. Bandura subscribes to such a model of emergent interactive agency, as do a number of contemporary scientists and philosophers. In her introduction to *Evolution and Emergence* (Murphy and Stoeger 2007), Nancey Murphy presented emergence as a departure from reductionism in which there is a search for 'understanding how complex (higher-level) entities become causal players in their own right, over and above the effects of their components' (Murphy 2007a, pp. 1–2).

The philosopher John Searle discussed emergent properties as 'system features.' He offers consciousness as an example of a 'causally emergent property of systems.' He believes that '[t]he existence of consciousness can be explained by the causal interactions between elements of the brain at the micro level' but not 'from the sheer physical structure of the neurons without some additional account of the causal relations between them' (Searle 1992, p. 111–112). This reference to consciousness resulting from causal interactions between elements of a system is consistent with the view recently developed in the neuroscience of consciousness as (an aspect of) information integration (see Chapter 7). Consciousness, in this view, is a feature of the brain as a system, not a component of the system. At that time Searle doubted that such an emergent system has causal powers that cannot be explained by the causal interactions between the elements of the system from which it emerged.

However, Searle made an interesting argument for a kind of emergence in the development of human capacity for free will in a later publication

(Searle 2010). He begins with the assumption that free will presupposes consciousness. Despite his earlier reservation about lack of causal powers in consciousness, he sees free will as a product of consciousness, and asks what basis there can be for a non-deterministic account of consciousness. In a speculative venture, while recognizing that much nonsense has appeared in applications elsewhere of the principle of indeterminacy in quantum mechanics, he suggests nevertheless that a basis for non-determinism in the effects of consciousness can be derived from that principle: i.e., because, he says, quantum mechanics is the only basis in physics for indeterminacy, 'if there is any factual reality to the conscious experience of non-determinism, that is to say freedom, there must be some connection between consciousness and quantum indeterminacy' (Searle 2010, pp. 129–130). Some scientists active in brain research, for example Christoph Koch (2012), have also considered this possibility favourably. Koch rejects determinism absolutely although he calls himself a reductionist, albeit 'a romantic reductionist', while saying that personally he finds determinism abhorrent.

Searle, like Dennett (2003), acknowledged the obvious point that randomness is not the same as freedom: 'Quantum randomness does not give us anything even remotely approaching free will' (p. 130). He says that lack of predictability does not in itself give us any kind of freedom worth having, but he observed that regularity at a gross system level could exist in systems in which there was randomness at a basic level in the behaviour of its constituent elements. The question was whether the indeterminacy of the quantum level could be carried through to the system level without its randomness. He argues that it is logically possible, although empirically unlikely, that 'the higher level consciousness of voluntary, free decision making would manifest the lack of causally sufficient conditions characteristic of the quantum level without inheriting the randomness of that level' (p. 131). Several other philosophers and neuroscientists have considered such a possibility favourably.

The Freedom-Enhancing Properties of Emergent Systems

The idea that some properties and not others evident at a lower level can carry through to a higher level of organisation without violating the laws of physics is advanced by other philosophers as well as Searle. Murphy has drawn on the work of Van Gulick, Peacocke and others for the emergence of freedom-enhancing properties at the system level when there is *selection* among the properties of constituent elements (Murphy 2007a, 2007b; Peacocke 2007; Van Gulick 2007). She considered the possibility of 'downward causation' in which a system exerts an influence on the selection of its constituent elements. An individual component behaves differently in the context of a system than it would outside it. Peacocke preferred 'Whole-part' constraint to the idea of downward causation. Similarly, Murphy supported Van Gulick in suggesting 'that the larger context of which a physical constituent is a part may affect which of its causal powers gets activated' (Murphy 2007b, pp. 31–32). We could draw an analogy with epigenetic effects on the expression of genes.

There is another argument for emergence in the neuroscience of Jaak Panksepp (see Chapter 8). In this understanding, the point of emergence for free will is at the boundary between secondary (conditioned) affective responses and tertiary emotions (social and cognitive attitudes). Dismissing 'bizarre and faulty views from psychology's past,' Panksepp and Biven declare that '"free will" is not a figment of our imagination as too many scientists are ready to claim these days. Free will is a higher tertiary-level neurocognitive function that we use on a regular basis (and quite effectively when we are not too emotionally aroused) for planning future actions.' The instinctive primary affective systems based largely in sub-cortical regions of the brain, and automatic conditioned emotions at the secondary level which result from classical and instrumental conditioning do not exhibit free will. 'That can only *emerge* from well-sculpted, deeply self-reflective, cognitive attitudes' (Panksepp and Biven 2012, p. 448, my emphasis). Reflexive self-functions, implying conscious and complex cognition, are necessary for the emergence of a capacity for free will.

The emergence of an autonomous system is only likely to occur when there is integration of information to form a new whole or gestalt that is distinguished from its context and possesses its own identity in a highly complex system. The most powerful effects of systemic relationships in cognitive motivation are those of consciousness that appear in processes of integration (see Chapter 7). The emergence of voluntary action coincides with the emergence of consciousness which is a necessary foundation for it (see the discussion of free will in Chapter 10).

Bandura's Theory of Self-Efficacy

Albert Bandura's 'agentic perspective' is employed in the introduction to this chapter to exemplify key concepts for the discussion of agency. It illustrates the general principles of his self-efficacy theory about the relationship of a particular kind of beliefs to actions, or 'perceived personal efficacy' that comes from 'beliefs in one's capabilities to organise and execute the courses of action required to produce given attainments' (Bandura 1997, p. 3). Self-efficacy theory, as a component of social cognitive theory, offers a way of accounting for cognitive control of behaviour.

Development of a Cognitive View from Social Learning Theory

To illustrate his dissatisfaction with trial-and-error learning, Bandura drew a contrast between the relatively benign allowance for errors that can be made in laboratory experiments and the lethal hazards of real life.

> For this reason, it would be exceedingly injudicious to rely primarily on trial-and-error and successive approximation methods in teaching children to swim, adolescents to drive automobiles, or adults to master complex occupational and social tasks. (Bandura 1969, p. 143)

In his view, typical human learning required complex cognitive processing, self-reflection and belief in one's ability to do as others are seen to do. Human agency was implied in self-efficacy which came to be expounded in terms of 'The exercise of control' – the subtitle of his mature exposition of the theory of 'self-efficacy' (Bandura 1997). Bandura thus linked a general belief in human agency as characteristic of humanity, at least in modern culture, with a cognitive theory of the way that beliefs function to produce behavioural outcomes: 'Beliefs of personal efficacy constitute the key factor of human agency' (1997, p. 3). Bandura made a distinction between 'people's hopes for favourable outcomes' and 'their sense of personal mastery' (Bandura 1977a, p. 194). His theory was 'based on the principle assumption that psychological procedures, whatever their form, serve as means of creating and strengthening expectations of personal efficacy' (p. 193). Later he placed greater emphasis on the person as the agent of his or her intentional actions: 'An intention is a representation of a future course of action to be performed. It is not simply an expectation or prediction of future actions but a proactive commitment to bringing them about' (Bandura 2001, p. 6. See Chapter 7 on consciousness and working memory and Chapters 9 and 10 on goals and intentions.).

In Bandura's social-cognitive theory, developed from social learning theory, reinforcement was seen to affect behaviour largely by creating expectations linking behaviour with anticipated outcomes, as Bolles had suggested in a cognitive approach to motivation a little earlier (Bolles 1972). Bandura nominated a second source of cognitively based motivation that operates through the intervening variables of goal setting and self-evaluation (Bandura 1977b), so that self-motivation employs standards against which to evaluate performance. Evidence for the motivational character of efficacy expectations was seen especially in how much effort people would expend in attempting to achieve those standards and how long they would persist in the face of obstacles and aversive experiences. 'The stronger the efficacy or mastery expectations, the more active the efforts' (Bandura 1977b, p. 80).

The conceptual shift from a response evoking stimulus to the input of information employed in meaningful processing points to intervening cognitive activity. Such an emphasis encourages development of a cognitive motivation theory (or a 'social cognitive theory') in which qualities of the self are integrated with planning and commitment to purposive behaviour.

Sources of Efficacy Expectations

Bandura made a clear distinction between *efficacy* expectations and *outcome* expectations. Many expectancy theories, such as Atkinson's expectancy-value theory of achievement motivation, at least in its original form (Chapter 5), embodied the motivational significance of the latter, outcome, type of expectation. As noted earlier, Bandura's particular emphasis was on the expectation a person has that he or she can be *effective in producing the behaviour which may have those desired effects*. He described four sources of efficacy expectations: (1) performance accomplishments, (2) vicarious experience, (3) verbal persuasion, and (4) emotional or physiological arousal (Bandura 1977a, pp. 195–200. See also Bandura 1977b, 1986, 1991, 1997).

In his discussion of the fourth source of efficacy information, Bandura suggested that *emotional (or physiological) arousal* elicited by stressful circumstances could have information value concerning personal competency. People tend to rely upon how they feel as a source of information, particularly about their self-efficacy. His social learning theory emphasized the informative function of physiological arousal. 'When motivation is conceptualized in terms of cognitive processes (Weiner 1972, Bandura 1977b), the informational and motivational effects of arousal are treated as interdependent rather than as separate events' (Bandura 1977a, p. 199). Cognitive representation both precedes and follows emotional arousal. The same principles concerning the information value of emotions are discussed in Chapter 8.

Cognitive Processing of Efficacy Information

People use many sources of information – enactive, vicarious, exhortative, and emotive – to judge their level of self-efficacy. In Bandura's theory, the impact of information on efficacy expectations will depend upon how it is cognitively appraised, so that even success experiences do not necessarily create strong expectations of personal efficacy. This might happen if past negative expectations have served self-protective functions, or when by virtue of the circumstances they could credit their achievements to external factors rather than to their own capabilities.

The relative balance of ability and effort as factors responsible for success is quite an ancient point of difference in human expectations elaborated extensively in recent decades by Dweck, Elliot, Weiner and others regarding differences between performance, ego or ability goals on the one hand and learning, mastery or task goals on the other. Bandura, similarly, noted that 'even under conditions of self-determination the impact of performance attainment on self-efficacy will vary depending on whether one's accomplishments are ascribed to ability or effort' (Bandura 1977a, p. 201). How the task is perceived affects the processing of information about success. When the information comes from emotional arousal, effects depend upon the meaning that is given to the arousal, especially in complex and ambiguous situations, as to whether failure is due to personal inadequacy or situational factors.

Self-Efficacy and Cognitive Motivation Theory

Bandura is one of the few theorists who have employed the term 'cognitive motivation' in a general sense with specific reference to some of the same examples, such as attribution theory and expectancy-value theory that are covered in this book. As we noted in Chapter 1, he distinguished 'three forms of cognitive motivators around which different theories have been built' (Bandura 1991, p. 71. For his extended discussion of cognitive motivation, see Bandura 1997, pp. 122–137). He postulated: 'that certain basic mechanisms of personal agency, such as perceived self-efficacy, operate in all of these variant forms of motivation' (p. 71).

Bandura sketched 'conceptions of cognitive motivation' which differed in the way that forethought, on the hand, and retrospective reasoning, on the other, related performance to 'anticipatory cognitive motivators' (Bandura 1989a, 1997, pp. 72, 123). The conversion of a prospective future state of affairs into current motivation is a process that requires more than goal definition: '[A] goal is not the agent of its own realization' (Bandura 1997, p. 122). In Bandura's formulation, forethought is translated into incentives and courses of action with the aid of self-regulatory mechanisms. In self-efficacy theory, people form beliefs about what they can do; they anticipate likely positive and negative outcomes; and they set goals and plan courses of action to realize valued futures and avoid aversive ones. These are cognitive processes in which efficacy beliefs play a central role in 'the cognitive regulation of motivation' (p. 122).

In the general cognitive motivation theory, motivation depends upon attempts to *make sense* of incomplete perceptual and conceptual images. Making sense requires more than cognitive consistency. To see a set of perceptual or conceptual elements together as a whole unit, distinct from its background and having its own identity, requires it to have gestalt qualities of good form.[1] While an incomplete form provides an incentive for change when its possible completion becomes the focus of attention, it is not the whole story. The image of a goal is compared with an incomplete gestalt of the present seen in relation to that prospect, and commitment to bring it about involves the allocation of resources of information and energy, leading to the initiation and maintenance of courses of action with guidance from affective feedback on the changing relationship of the person in the present situation to the goal. That is the general form, but the processes of integration which resolve incomplete gestalts operate on a wide range of particular contents. They include both conscious and non-conscious elements, both abstract and concrete knowledge, and both information about events and the cognitive representation of emotions which are responses to those events.[2] In these basic processes there are common operations on different contents with different goals and different motivational outcomes.

Belief in a person's capacity for behaviour that will produce desired outcomes is a necessary but not sufficient condition for linking an action plan with a goal. Two links are necessary for the process of cognitive motivation to be completed: (1) from the person to the action plan and (2) from the action plan to goal attainment. The person needs to believe not only in his or her capacity to put a plan into effect but also in the effectiveness of the plan. Bandura recognized this difference, and his assumptions about cognitive processes in motivation appear to envisage both links, but self-efficacy characterizes the first of them.

The examples of cognitive motivation given by Bandura point to certain parts of the overall process (see Chapter 1). His discussion of intentionality, forethought, self-reactiveness and self-reflectiveness as features of agency also illustrates parts of the process. His treatment is consistent with the role of agency in the general theory of cognitive motivation, but it does not address the process as a whole. Another apparent difference not yet discussed that is relevant to the general theory appears in regard to White's conception of effectance motivation. In what follows I argue that

[1] The nature of gestalt qualities is considered against its historical background in Chapter 9.

[2] The role of emotions as signs in the process of goal attainment is discussed in Chapter 8.

the differences Bandura saw are due mainly to some misunderstanding of White. Nevertheless, Bandura's overall conception of cognitive motivation is, like White's understanding, consistent with the general theory of cognitive motivation and describes many of its key features.

White's Effectance Motivation Theory

In his ground-breaking discussion of 'The concept of competence,' the subtitle of his article 'Motivation reconsidered,' Robert White put forward a theory of *effectance motivation* as a radical alternative to drive reduction theories which were the dominant model of motivation at that time (White 1959, 1960). The question naturally arises of whether the theory of effectance motivation differs significantly from Bandura's theory of *self-efficacy* that appeared a little later. White's pioneering work was an early source of concepts for theories of intrinsic motivation (see Chapter 3).

While it has been cited continuously since its publication, White's paper has received renewed attention recently. It has been a central reference in new developments of intrinsic motivation and self-determination theory (Deci and Moller 2005). Elliot and Dweck (2005b) have discussed it together with McClelland's theory of achievement motivation in reference to the operation of achievement goals – a new direction in the study of achievement motivation. It has also been described by Seligman (2011) as one of the historical foundations for the motivational assumptions underlying the development of positive psychology.[3]

White used the term 'efficacy' at several points, but in reference to a *feeling*, whereas Bandura used 'efficacy' to characterize a *belief*. White proposed to designate the motivation he was describing 'by the term effectance, and to characterize the experience produced as a *feeling of efficacy*' (White 1959, p. 329, emphasis in the original). It referred to a kind of satisfaction that could be experienced when there is no consummatory climax, 'as lying in a considerable series of transactions, in a trend of behavior rather than a goal that is achieved.' In the place of need satisfaction or drive reduction with goal attainment, White put that feeling: 'Effectance motivation similarly aims for the feeling of efficacy' (p. 323). The efficacy to which he referred was evident in the information feedback value of the stimulus field that might satisfy one's interest in it. So, White concluded that 'it may be that the satisfaction of effectance contributes significantly to those feelings of interest which often sustain us so well in day-to-day actions, particularly when the things we are doing have continuing elements of novelty' (p. 323).

[3] See the conclusion of Chapter 12.

In a later publication White specifically included a sense of *agency* in his description of effectance motivation. He referred to 'the power of initiative and exertion that we experience as a sense of being an agent in the living of our lives' that 'may be called a *feeling of efficacy*' (White 1972, p. 209). A sense of agency was always part of Bandura's conception of self-efficacy, and it became the major theme in his later writing (Bandura 2001). In this respect, as in others, White was closer to his own position than Bandura recognized.

Differences between White and Bandura

There is a difference of emphasis on focussed attention. According to White, effectance motivation is aroused by stimulus conditions which offer difference-in-sameness (Hebb 1949) and lead to behaviour which 'affects the stimulus so as to produce further difference-in-sameness' (White 1959, p. 322). The focussing of interest in White's concept of competence contrasts with Bandura's conception of competence varying across many fields of interest: 'In social cognitive theory, efficacy beliefs enter into the regulation of all types of performances' (Bandura 1997, p. 14); and 'What competent functioning is differs across time, milieus, social standards, and domains of activity' (p. 15). White would not have disagreed with this statement, but in his focussed account, 'The urge toward competence is inferred specifically from behavior that shows a lasting focalization and that has the characteristics of exploration and experimentation, a kind of variation within the focus' (p. 323). These two different perspectives are, nevertheless, mutually compatible. A different focus can produce competent functioning in different milieus.

In his original statement of the differences between his and White's theories, Bandura (1977a) claimed that the means by which an 'effectance motive' (a term White did not use) emerges from effective transactions with the environment are not spelled out in White's theory. In contrast, Bandura gives a good deal of detail on how expectancies are built up. He offered as another point of difference the view that 'in the social learning analysis, choice behaviour and effort are governed in part by percepts of self-efficacy rather than by a drive condition' (p. 203). The implication that effectance motivation is a kind of drive, and that it is not developed out of experience, was a misunderstanding of White at a crucial point.

White did not use the term 'effectance motive' (or 'need') in his paper, and he rejected the term 'drive,' but Bandura used the terms motive, need and drive repeatedly in his criticism of White. For example in the 1977 article he said, 'White (1959) postulated an "effectance motive," which is conceptualized as an intrinsic drive for transactions with the environment' (Bandura 1977a, p. 203). This statement is repeated at the beginning of his 1997 critical analysis (Bandura 1997, p. 13). There is a fundamental difference between ascription of a motive, need or drive as a dispositional property and describing a *process* of 'effectance motivation.' White called for 'a different kind of motivational idea' from that of a drive. He did not propose to add another motive or drive, to be called an 'effectance motive' to the common lists of motives like hunger, sex, affiliation, achievement, etc., but to examine a different understanding of motivation as a process.

What difference does it make to refer to *a process of motivation* rather than to a motive? It implies, in addition to (1) an internal disposition, at least the following: (2) giving attention to an environmental event; (3) evaluating the environment and one's present position in it in relation to ones goals and values; (4) processing the incoming information in relation to projected future events which might constitute goal attainment, frustration or facilitation; (5) the experience of particular feelings associated with those possibilities; (6) the allocation of resources and the making of commitments to specific purposive behaviour; (7) the processing of information about progress in a desired direction; and (8) about the attainment of objectives, in which emotions are effective signs of relationships to goals. White was concerned with motivation as a process, not a personal disposition.

White indicated a clear preference for conceiving of effectance motivation as a process in which satisfaction is not found at any particular point in a cycle of interaction between person and environment. There is no critical point in the cycle.

> It does not lie solely in sensory stimulation, in a bettering of the cognitive map, in coordinated action, in motor exercise, in a feeling of effort and of effects produced, or in the appreciation of change brought about in the sensory field. These are all simply aspects of a *process* which at this stage has to be conceived as a whole. (White 1959, p. 321, my emphasis)

Bandura was critical of a theoretical construct he called 'an automatic self-motivator' (Bandura 1977b, p. 164), in reference to White's theory of effectance motivation, and also Piaget's model of cognitive equilibrium and Deci and Ryan's theory of self-determination (Bandura 1997, pp. 13–15). He believed such a simple idea too readily explained too much. Bandura also claimed that, 'It is difficult to verify the existence of an efficacy or mastery motive because the motive is inferred from the very exploratory behavior it supposedly causes. This creates problems of circularity' (Bandura 1997, p. 13). White did not, in fact, postulate 'an efficacy or mastery motive,' not a particular motive as a trait or state, but rather an interactive process of motivation. He specifically rejected Hendrick's (1942) proposal of an 'instinct to master,' characterized as 'an inborn drive to do and to learn how to do.' It is a concept easily confused with effectance motivation.

In White's understanding effectance motivation has various forms, such as curiosity and achievement, derived from different types of interaction with the environment although it might begin in early childhood in a simpler basic form.

> In infants and young children, it seems to me sensible to conceive of effectance motivation as undifferentiated. Later in life it becomes profitable to distinguish various motives such as cognizance, construction, mastery, and achievement. It is my view that all such motives have a root in effectance motivation. They are differentiated from it through life experiences which emphasize one or another aspect of the cycle of transaction with environment. (White 1959, p. 323)

This is the same basic principle that I have employed in the discussion of various types of cognitive motivation that are expressed in different psychogenic motives.

Is Effectance an Innate Drive?

In his later work Bandura developed his theory of self-efficacy within a general theory of the exercise of control and raised the question of whether the motivation for control was innate: 'A major issue of contention is whether the exercise of control is impelled by an inborn drive for control or is motivated by anticipated benefits. There is a fundamental difference between the two. Drives push action, anticipated incentives draw it (Bolles 1975)' (Bandura 1997, p. 16). The terminology is different here from that of his 1977 reference to an automatic self-motivator, but the same criticism is implied in his direct reference to White and to Deci and Ryan: 'some theorists regard the striving for control as an expression of an inborn drive (White 1959, Deci and Ryan 1985)' (Bandura 1997, p. 16). In fact, as we have noted, White rejected Hendrick's 'instinct to master' and argued against explanation of behaviour exemplifying effectance motivation by reference to an inborn drive. In his view, effectance motivation was a developed capacity that depended upon learning. His concept of competence referred neither to an innate quality nor to a drive. He introduced his 1959 paper by making reference to 'deepening discontent with theories of motivation based upon drives' adding,

> I consider it necessary to treat competence as having a motivational aspect, and my central argument will be that the motivation needed to attain competence cannot be wholly derived from sources of energy currently conceptualized as

drives or instincts. We need a different kind of motivational idea to account fully for the fact that man and the higher mammals develop a competence in dealing with the environment which they certainly do not have at birth and certainly do not arrive at simply through maturation. Such an idea, I believe, is essential for any biologically sound view of human nature. (White 1959, p. 297)

In order to emphasize the 'intrinsic peculiarities' of tendencies like exploration, and 'to get them considered in their own right without a cloud of surplus meanings,' White said, 'I prefer in this essay to speak of the urge that makes for competence simply as motivation rather than as drive' (White 1959, p. 305). He understood motivation for the experience of competence not as a push type of drive, but as a process that we can say in Bandura's terms would draw people forward through the operation of 'anticipatory cognitive motivators' (Bandura 1997, pp. 122–123).

Bandura said there were two basic premises of the effectance motivation theory: 'that people are inherently driven to exercise control over their environment and that the achievement of control is inherently self-satisfying (Rodin, Rennert and Solomon 1980, Bandura 1986)' (Bandura 1997, p. 15). But White argued against effectance motivation being understood as a kind of drive and denied that any such motivation in human beings was innate: in 'the mammals and especially man, with their highly plastic nervous systems, fitness to interact with the environment is slowly attained through prolonged feats of learning' (White 1959, p. 297).

Rodin et al. (1980), whose research on the supposed premises of White's theory is cited by Bandura in support of his criticism, referred to White's conceptualization as probably the most influential attempt to account for behaviours that were inadequately explained by theories of motivation based on primary drives, but they quoted White incorrectly as referring to 'an innate need to manipulate the environment' (Rodin et al. 1980, p. 132). White's exact phrase was 'an intrinsic need to deal with the environment' (White 1959, p. 318). 'Intrinsic' does not normally mean 'innate', although it might mean the same as Bandura's term 'inherent' that could be understood to mean an essential quality – but the misunderstanding is clear: they thought White believed that effectance motivation was innate when White had said it was not. In addition to its not being innate, White argued for a different idea of motivation as a process.

Weiner's Attribution Theory

Attribution theory also illustrates many of the essential features of cognitive motivation. There are many kinds and sources of attribution theory in which beliefs about causes of behaviour affect motivation. I will mention several of them briefly, but this section deals mainly with the theory proposed by Bernard Weiner that has been a key point of reference in recent decades. These theories are all concerned with the motivational effects of forming hypotheses to explain observed behaviour.

Weiner was a student of John W. Atkinson, and he built his attribution theory (Weiner 1985a, 1986) partly on modifications to Atkinson's expectancy-value theory of achievement motivation and other basically Gestalt types of theory. The personal causation theory of deCharms (1968) discussed in Chapter 3 was another influential source of ideas about the internal control of behaviour that was acknowledged by Weiner, as was White's theory of effectance motivation.

Past Causes and Future Expectations

Weiner interpreted *shifts* in level of aspiration described by Kelly (1973) as processes giving rise to causal thinking. Kelly proposed that to satisfy a need to control the environment, people gather information to test ideas about what causes particular changes to occur. What a person expects to happen in future, and who would be responsible for it, would then develop from causal attribution of events in the past. Causal attribution implies personal responsibility that is a necessary condition for cognitive motivation.

In an early paper with colleagues at UCLA, Weiner classified theories of motivation as falling into two contrasting groups, often labelled mechanistic and cognitive approaches (Weiner, Frieze, Kukla, Reed, Stanley and Rosenbaum 1971). The major difference was in the extent to which explanations of behaviour could be formulated without reference to higher mental processes, as in the writings of Hull and Spence (Hull 1943a, 1943b; Spence 1956), in contrast with the extent to which the goal is represented mentally or anticipated cognitively. Such a cognitive representation of anticipated future events was suggested in the theories of Lewin, Tolman and Atkinson (see Chapter 5). As Weiner and colleagues saw it, the preferred model, which is similar to what emerged in cognitive theories in later decades, was one in which 'an incoming stimulus, viewed as a source of information, is encoded into a belief system that gives it "meaning"' (Weiner et al. 1971, pp. 95–96). The attribution model of achievement motivation was 'based on the assumption that beliefs about the causes of success and failure mediate between antecedent stimulus-organism transactions and ensuing achievement behaviour' (p. 96).

Looking back over the history of his ideas at the time when he received the E. L. Thorndike Research Award for Career Achievement, Weiner restated his cognitive motivational assumptions about mediation between representations of past experience, the present and the future:

> Thorndike pointed out a motivational sequence takes place over time and a critical issue is how to represent the past so it may influence the present and the future. As an attribution theorist, I also focus on how the past makes its way into the present and future. But rather than having reinforcement or past hedonism as the bridging mechanism, I contend that the interpretation of the past, that is, the perceived causes of prior events, determines what will be done in the future. (Weiner 2010, p. 29)

It followed from the general nature of his explanation of the future effect of past causes that the 'attributional theory of achievement motivation' (Weiner 1985a) was generalized to become 'An attributional theory of motivation and emotion' (Weiner 1986).

Sources of Causal Structure in Attribution Theory

Weiner credited Fritz Heider with the first analysis of causal structure in this field, acknowledging him as the originator of attributional conceptions (Heider 1944, 1958; Weiner 1985a, 1986). There is another paper by Heider that makes an explicit link with Gestalt theories of motivation (Heider 1960), which I discussed in Chapter 4. In not taking account of that publication of Heider, Weiner left out the idea of perceived incompleteness being a source of motivation. That omission is significant in the difference between attribution theory and the more general cognitive motivation theory that I propose. The possibility remains for us to integrate attribution theory into a more general framework as a form of cognitive motivation theory, as Bandura seems to suggest (Bandura 1989b, 1991).

Weiner illustrated elements of his theory that he took from Heider in the example of a man rowing a boat across a lake on a windy day, the outcome being attributed to either the external factor of the wind or the internal factor of the man's strength and skill, or to both in varying degrees on a bipolar continuum. Degrees of internality and externality, or alternatively a dichotomous attribution, had been proposed by George Kelly in his personal constructs theory (Kelly 1955). Weiner also acknowledged the inner-directed and other-directed typology suggested by David Riesman in his widely read book *The Lonely Crowd* (Riesman 1950) which characterized the community oriented, rather conformist, post–World War II American society with consensus-seeking values, in contrast with the longer American tradition of self-reliance. That post-war consensus was deeply challenged in the cultural revolution of the 1960s and 1970s, when conflict theories were given more attention. These differences were prefigured to some extent in those cognitive consistency theories which made provision for conflicts as we have noted in the discussion of cognitive dissonance in Chapter 4.

Initially Weiner had accepted Rotter's *locus of control*, internal-external dimension (Weiner 1974a; Weiner, Russell and Lerman 1978), but he and his colleagues separated locus from control when effort and ability were shown to have independent effects as attributed causes, both being internal, but with ability being stable and effort varying on a second dimension, *stability*. A third dimension was originally described as 'intentionality,' but intentionality was later subsumed under *controllability*, and Rotter's concept of locus of control in the first dimension was recast as *locus of causality*. Multi-dimensionality of attribution is central to Weiner's theory. He described the 'so-called causal dimensions,' i.e. locus, stability and controllability, as 'the very heart and soul of my approach to motivation' (Weiner 2005, p. 76). Different dimensions of attribution were associated with different emotions.

The influence of expectancies on behaviour was recognized by Weiner as 'the empirical center for those using the theories of Atkinson, Bandura, and Rotter' (Weiner 1986, p. 252), but he preferred to give more attention to the role of emotion in which he linked different emotions with the effect of different attributions. So, for example, feelings of pride and self-esteem were linked with the locus of causality dimension, hope of success with the stability dimension, and shame and guilt with controllability (Weiner et al. 1978; Weiner 1986, 2005). In attribution theory, emotions generated by different attributions have different effects in 'a temporal sequence going from attributions to affects to evaluations' (Weiner 1986, p. 253). If a student is perceived as having tried hard, but with little ability, praise is likely; failure might evoke pity in such a case, but anger perhaps when help is sought in a situation where the student was seen to be at fault. Weiner and his associates conducted many experiments demonstrating such effects (Weiner 1986, 1995, 2005).

Weiner's Principles for the Development of a General Theory

Weiner enunciated twelve principles that form the foundation for his general theory of motivation and emotion known as attribution theory, saying that a theory of motivation must:

1. Be based on a concept other than homeostasis
2. Embrace more than hedonism
3. Include the full range of cognitive processes
4. Be concerned with conscious experience
5. Include the self

6. Include the full range of emotions
7. Be neither too general nor too precise
8. Be built upon reliable (replicable) empirical relations
9. Be based on general laws rather than individual differences
10. Include sequential (historical) causal relations
11. Explain rational and irrational actions, using the same concepts for both
12. Account for achievement strivings and affiliative goals. (Weiner 1986, p. 15)

These principles are very close to those that I adopted for a general cognitive motivation theory without making them explicit. To be clear about where we are heading then, it might be helpful to note some differences. There are differences at three points: (a) I did not aim to cover the full range of emotions (his point 6) but only those emotions associated with *cognitive* motivation as set out in Chapters 8 and 12; (b) I drew upon insights from the measurement of individual differences while also seeking general laws, and in the process made the uniqueness of the individual personality a primary principle rather than merely an unexplained exception to general laws (cf. his point 9); and (c) curiosity was my initial focal point rather than achievement and affiliative goals named by Weiner at 12. However, my starting point was within the same research culture as that shared by Weiner with McClelland and Atkinson in their studies of achievement and affiliation.[4] Further, while I agree with point 7, I would make a different emphasis in seeking a theory with both a high degree of generality and specific forms. Weiner added a confession: 'The principles listed above were not *a priori* axioms upon which a theory of motivation was constructed. Rather, a theory slowly emerged, and with it came a set of sometimes justifying, sometimes clarifying, often bootstrapped principles' (Weiner 1986, p. 150). That, surely, must be a common experience.

Beyond the general principles for construction of a theory of motivation that Weiner enunciated retrospectively, attribution theory has several basic assumptions or defining propositions. The first and most comprehensive is the proposition that, 'Causal perceptions are instrumental to goal attainment and aid in the pursuit of cognitive mastery' (Weiner 1986, p. 21). The term 'mastery' adopted by Weiner is quite commonly used in recent work on distinctions between different kinds of achievement goals discussed in Chapter 5, and by Bandura in his theory of

[4] See remarks in the Preface on my indebtedness to David McClelland, which I imagine has much in common with what Weiner received from John W. Atkinson.

self-efficacy (Bandura 1977a, 1982, 1997, 2001). Mastery in this context does not imply a concern with social dominance. Fundamentally, it is White's 'concept of competence' (White 1959) that I have discussed in relation to curiosity and cognitive motivation in general. Weiner clearly recognized its association with curiosity, even while it also had an aspect of utility, when he asked of the idea that people constantly seek causal explanations:

> Why this constant pursuit of 'why'? A number of explanations come to mind (see Forsyth 1980, Weiner 1985b). We might just want to know, that is, to understand the environment, to penetrate ourselves and our surroundings. This familiar motivational interpretation is known as the principle of mastery (White 1959). In addition, it clearly is functional to know why an event has occurred. As Kelly (1971) stated, 'The attributor is not simply an attributor, a seeker after knowledge; his latent goal in attaining knowledge is that of effective management of himself and his environment' (p. 22). (Weiner 1985a, p. 548)

Weiner's formulation of the principle of self-regulation embodies two contrasting assumptions about motivation: one is hedonistic – in which a goal is sought to maximize pleasure and avoid pain – and the other is concerned with understanding. 'A central assumption of attribution theory, which sets it apart from pleasure-pain theories of motivation, is that the search for understanding is the (or a) basic "spring of action"' (Weiner 1979, p. 3). In the attribution of a cause, a person seeks to understand *why* an action has taken place. There is an obvious affinity of this component of attribution theory with aspects of the cognitive process theory of curiosity (Chapter 2) and with striving to make sense of things in general that is fundamental in cognitive motivation.

Without its always being specified what causes what, in Weiner's work we have reference to 'links' between attributions and emotions, and to different emotions being associated with different dimensions of attributions, i.e. locus, stability and controllability. Weiner allowed for a degree of 'bidirectionality' in causal links: '[O]utcomes determine general affective states, and general affective states influence outcome perceptions; attributions influence expectancy, and expectancies guide attributions; attributions influence communicated emotions, and communicated emotions provide attributional information; causes are placed in dimensions, and dimensional focus might direct attributional decisions' (Weiner 1986, p. 241). These pairs of causes are not in the form of one cause exactly reversing or contradicting the other: the second action that feeds back on the first has been modified by the first and it modifies the second in turn. It is a recursive type of function, typically found in functions of the self with its basic quality of reflexive action. As G. H. Mead, the early theorist of the self, said, 'But there is nothing odd about the product of a given process contributing to, or even becoming an essential factor in, the further development of that process' (Mead 1934, p. 226). We perceive ourselves and are changed in the process. These are common processes in cognitive motivation.

Common Concepts for a General Theory

Reflexive processes involving the self in purposive strivings are evident in achievement motivation and cognitive dissonance as well as attribution theory. These three, together with curiosity, competence and self-efficacy, are prime examples of cognitive motivation. Ideas common to these theories involving the self are seen in their history. Weiner's development of attribution theory had deep roots in the study of achievement motivation, and this relationship continued in recent work by others on achievement goals (Elliot and Dweck 2005a). In Chapter 1, in my discussion of the scope of cognitive motivation, I made of a point of Appley's emphasis on self-discrepancy as a general theme of cognitive motivation theories (Appley 1991). In a development in line with Aronson's self-consistency version of dissonance theory (see Chapter 4), Dweck and Molden also developed their theory of the function of self-theories in competence in this direction (Dweck and Molden 2005). Reflexive processes with recursive effects are incorporated into a theory of cognitive motivation when self-functions are introduced.

Besides achievement motivation theory as the cradle in which it was nurtured, there was a relationship of attribution theory also with cognitive dissonance (Zanna and Cooper 1976). At first harmonious, it became hostile when self-concepts were introduced. Zanna and Cooper concluded that one of the effects of attributing failure to an external cause in order to resolve dissonance was to preserve one's view of oneself. Attribution theory is just like cognitive dissonance in being 'about putting our own cognitive houses in order' (Zanna and Cooper 1976, p. 199).

Bridging the Gap

Weiner related his attribution theory to White's concept of competence (Weiner 2005). He construed competence as a subjective inference or social construction that can pertain to the self and to others, illustrating especially the feeling of being effective in one's interaction with the environment (White 1959, p. 329). Bringing attribution theory into a relationship with effectance motivation and with achievement motivation is part of a potentially much larger project in theory construction. Another step is to relate achievement motivation to the concept of competence.

Elliot and Dweck (2005b) have sought to incorporate research on achievement motivation within the range of a 'general concept of competence,' or effectance motivation. They say about the origins of the two lines of research that flowed from the work of McClelland on achievement and White on competence,

> At about the same time that the need for achievement was being established, White (1959, 1960) offered his analysis of effectance motivation. White posited a fundamental need for individuals to be effective in negotiating their environment, the prototypical manifestation of which is the infant's curiosity and exploratory play. Although need for achievement and effectance motivation would seem to be conceptually related, the pioneers of the two constructs made almost no reference to the work of the other, and subsequent proponents of the two traditions have followed suit. To this day, although the need for achievement construct is considered a central part of the achievement motivation literature, effectance motivation is rarely mentioned (for exceptions, see Veroff 1969, Nicholls 1984, Elliot and Reis 2003). (Elliot and Dweck 2005b, p. 5)

There has, indeed, been too little cross-reference between these fields, even though they were not developed in isolation from each other. The founders, McClelland and White, were, for many years, in the same department at Harvard. Their work continued in parallel as separate theoretical domains, but they did appreciate each other's work. At the beginning of my research on curiosity in 1959 in McClelland's research centre, he suggested that I should have a talk with White about his article on 'the concept of competence' just then being published in the *Psychological Review.* I tried from the beginning to relate their somewhat different conceptions of basic motivational processes. At that time I suggested my cognitive process theory could form the basis of a more general theory of motivation (Beswick 1964). But it was not until I came back to the field in 2000 to work on intrinsic motivation again that I began to see the potential for a general theory of *cognitive* motivation that would apply to both White's and McClelland's ideas. It required another level of abstraction to relate the different theories.

Elliot and Dweck have since pointed in this direction. I have been trying to go further and develop a theory of cognitive motivation that covers not only achievement motivation and competence but also curiosity, cognitive dissonance, attribution theory and other self-referent cognitive motivation theories such as self-efficacy, self-determination, implicit self-theories and various conceptions of intrinsic motivation. That is what this book is about. In the next chapter I begin Part II in which the basic processes of cognitive motivation, evident in these different examples, are explored systematically.

Summary

The effects of attributions and self-efficacy beliefs are based on perceptions of agency. Weiner, in regard to attribution, and Bandura, in regard to self-efficacy, both emphasised the importance of a sense of agency, but from different perspectives. Weiner's attribution theory refers to a *retrospective* process in which a person infers a causal explanation of past behaviour, while Bandura's theory of self-efficacy relies upon a *prospective* process of goal anticipation and commitment. Both theories illustrate many of the essential features of cognitive motivation theory.

Attribution theory is concerned with answers to a question such as, 'Who or what was responsible for that event?' Weiner's theory was developed from Atkinson's expectancy-value theory. He also employed concepts inherited more directly from Gestalt psychology through Heider's work and from Lewin and Festinger, and concepts from Kelly's theory of causal attribution. Cognitive processes of seeking to understand *why* an action has occurred set up conditions for cognitive motivation in which attribution shares basic processes with curiosity. Dweck and her associates added further understanding of this in reference to the ways in which people attribute causes to malleable or fixed qualities of a person.

The sense of being the origin of our own actions and directing our purposive behaviour is central to Bandura's theory of self-efficacy. Belief in the efficacy of one's actions for attaining certain ends helps to motivate activity aimed at achieving those ends. This theory was developed originally within 'social learning theory' which Bandura revised into 'social cognitive theory.' Self-efficacy is concerned with 'the exercise of control,' so that in regard to self-regulation 'efficacy beliefs are the foundation of human agency.' In his later work expounding 'an agentic perspective', Bandura discussed intentionality, forethought, self-reactiveness and self-reflectiveness as features of agency, and he extended individual human agency to collective agency in a social setting. In its agentic perspective Bandura's theory has much in common with the general theory of cognitive motivation.

The concept of competence in White's theory of effectance motivation is important in reference to both these theories. I discuss misconceptions which have developed in the comparison of White's effectance motivation theory and Bandura's self-efficacy, arguing that they are mutually compatible and that both illustrate important features of cognitive motivation in general. Elliot and Dweck have sought to bring McClelland's achievement motivation within the scope of White's concept of competence, and I suggest that a wider general theory of cognitive motivation can embrace also others including cognitive dissonance, attribution theory, and self-efficacy.

Part II

Basic Processes and Applications

7 Working Memory, Consciousness and Attention

> Working memory requires conscious processes, not *vice versa*.
>
> – Baars 2003

Introduction

In cognitive motivation, processes of integration employ the executive functions of working memory that manage attention. New whole images are formed in a person's cognitive map of the world and of themselves. These processes integrate disparate information arising from novel input, conceptual conflict and gaps in knowledge, so as to resolve an incomplete gestalt that is the goal of purposive behaviour. I will review research on the neural correlates of consciousness that show a close relationship between consciousness and processes of integration. Consciousness becomes effective particularly in the transition from automatic parallel processing to explicit serial processes that achieve cognitive integration. I will discuss a suggestion that voluntary attention facilitates the integrative function of consciousness in working memory and provides a basis for the exercise of personal agency.

Working Memory

The basic processes of cognitive motivation that take place in working memory facilitate certain kinds of purposive behaviour which develop through cognitive processes that manage incoming information in relation to what is already in the system. Similarly, the relationship to the system as a whole of discrepant elements already present in a person's thoughts and feelings is managed by the same basic processes of integration, resolving conflicts and gaps in knowledge. The aim of these processes is completion of incomplete images or gestalts.

The Developing Concept of Working Memory

There is a rich background of research on cognitive processes that relate the contents of perception on the one hand and long-term memory on the other to thinking, feeling and action through an intermediate set of processes that are the functions of working memory. Many steps in the development of the theory of working memory began at the time when short-term and long-term memory were defined separately in what became known as the modal or multi-store model (Atkinson and Shiffrin 1968). Baddeley's work has been central to extensive research on it over many years. With Hitch, he introduced the current concept of working memory to replace the earlier model of short-term memory (Baddeley and Hitch 1974; Baddeley 1986, 2007). Foreshadowing the need for such a concept, the term 'working memory' had appeared previously without elaboration in the early days of cognitive theory (Miller et al. 1960) and without the specific meaning given to it by Baddeley and his colleagues. For a personal view of the history of this field by its leading proponent, see Baddeley (2012). I employ Baddeley's model for the most part in the discussion of working memory, and other sources for the treatment of consciousness and attention.

In Baddeley's mature model of working memory (Baddeley 1986, 1996; Baddeley and Della Sala 1998; Baddeley 2007), the functional units which interact in the storage and retrieval of information comprise a central executive that controls attentional processes, an episodic buffer, and at least two different subsystems of temporary storage and manipulation: the visuospatial and phonological subsystems. The functional units depend upon anatomical and physiological features of the brain which are becoming known to an increasing degree, but the mental structures are conceived theoretically in terms of their functional properties.

The cognitive theoretical system of working memory does not deal directly with motivation, although emotion, goals and consciousness enter into its higher-level complex expression. Baddeley has, however, recognised the need for a better understanding of motivation in relation to it, saying, 'Once again I suggest that we clearly need to reintroduce concepts of energy and motivation into cognitive psychology' (Baddeley 2007, p. 344). In a later review, in his comments on the central executive Baddeley asked, 'Do we need a concept of cognitive energy?' (Baddeley 2012, p. 23). It should become clear in what follows that to address motivation, and cognitive motivation in particular, the theory of working memory needs to be developed further to deal with concepts of energy, the construction of goals as objects of attention, the function of goals in directing behaviour and the identification and manipulation of available means for the attainment of goals. These additional concepts are introduced here and discussed in the following chapters. Nevertheless, important processes in cognitive motivation take place in working memory as it is currently understood.

According to the cognitive motivation theory, cognitive processes have motivational effects when attention is directed towards an incomplete gestalt. Attention is directed to an incomplete gestalt in such a way that imagining the completion of the incomplete image creates awareness of possible means for its completion, without the final form being fully defined. Awareness of possible means for the completion of an incomplete gestalt generates activity to bring those potential means for completion into an effective relationship with what already exist in the cognitive map. The sources of information that could be useful in resolving problems of integration may be sought internally or externally. So we have exploratory behaviour, asking questions, thinking about a problem, hypothesis formation, testing expectancies, tentative moves into creativity, imagining future possibilities, wondering, doubting, subjective epiphanies and reflections upon oneself and the world.

The means of resolution for an incomplete gestalt will also include skills and cognitive operations by which the information is manipulated. At the same time, sources of physical energy required for those operations are accessed (see Chapter 10 on willpower). These processes take place in working memory and are at least in part conscious, and consciousness is known to be related to processes of integration. It is, then, important to explicate the function of consciousness in working memory.

Working memory is a temporary storage system under attentional control, which enables complex human thought and commitment to action. This description of working memory is a slight modification of the definition given by Baddeley. I have modified his most recent formulation by adding 'commitment to action'. Adding commitment to action to the definition of working memory extends and re-applies the modification that Baddeley and Hitch made to include some processing of information together with a store in short term memory. As Baddeley put it much later, 'We chose the term working memory in order to emphasise the functional role of the proposed system, rather than simply its storage capacity' (Baddeley 2007, p. 6).

Two characteristics of working memory in the Baddeley and Hitch model are particularly relevant to cognitive processes with motivational properties: (1) the limited capacity of working memory, and (2) its multi-component structure. Empirical demonstrations of these properties were given by Baddeley and others in experiments using dual task methods. For example, when people were asked to undertake a problem-solving, comprehension or learning task, while maintaining various amounts of extraneous information short term, such as rehearsing a string of digits, they took longer on the task as the extraneous information load increased, although accuracy was not affected (Baddeley 1986). Besides limited capacity, results such as these, particularly in the effect on time taken to complete complex tasks, indicated the multicomponent nature of working memory. It was not simply the capacity of short-term memory as a storage system but the effects of processing demands that affected performance. Processing functions were then added to the model of short-term memory to make it working memory.

Baddeley and Hitch thus proposed a multicomponent model of working memory comprising 'an attentional control system – the *central executive* – together with two subsidiary storage systems, the *phonological loop* and the *visuospatial sketchpad*' (Baddeley 2007, p. 7). The two subsystems are means of processing the two main types of distal stimuli, i.e. perception by means of sound and sight. They are means for rehearsing or maintaining representations of verbal and visual input in their different modalities while coding operations are performed under control of the executive. While the executive was understood in the original version of the theory to have some storage capacity itself, this was changed at a later stage to place the temporary storage function of the central executive in a separate 'episodic buffer'.

Functions of the Central Executive

The central executive came to be understood, after experiments using dual-task methods (Baddeley 2007), and particularly after studies of patients with frontal lobe damage, as a functional unit without storage capacity but with several identifiable functions which could operate independently:

> The first, a capacity to focus a limited capacity system, is quite broadly accepted as a feature of most current attentional theories (Pashler 1998). The second, a capacity to switch attention, on closer examination seemed unlikely to be based on a single executive subprocess. The third, the capacity to divide attention, appears more promising, though by no means firmly established. The fourth function proposed for the executive (Baddeley 1996) [... is] the capacity to link long-term and working memory. (Baddeley 2007, p. 138)

A somewhat different description of differentiated executive functions was given by Miyake and colleagues from a study of individual differences. Using confirmatory factor analysis and structural equation modelling, they found evidence for three separate but correlated functions in complex executive tasks: (a) shifting between tasks or mental sets,

(b) updating and monitoring of working memory representations, and (c) inhibition of dominant or prepotent responses (Miyake, Friedman, Emerson, Witzki, Howerter and Wager 2000). We should not expect to identify exactly the same properties from correlational studies of individual differences as from experimental manipulation, but they imply similar qualities and effects, especially in the role of attention, the supervision of working memory and its relationship to long-term memory. Despite their different formulation, Miyake and colleagues still adhered to Baddeley's model claiming that their results 'support recent theoretical attempts to fractionate the central executive (e.g., Baddeley 1996, Baddeley and Logie 1999)' (Miyake et al. 2000, p. 89).

A similar study with older adults by Hull and colleagues replicated the findings of Miyake and colleagues in regard to their first two factors but not the third, 'inhibition' (Hull, Martin, Beier, Lane and Hamilton 2008). The difference could have been due to methodological differences, the effects of aging (West, Schwarb and Johnson 2010) or to some continuing uncertainty in identifying the underlying dimensions. Chan and others in a major review from a physiological perspective concluded that more research is needed to fractionate the executive system by assessing a wide range of functions and to verify their neuroanatomical correlates (Chan, Shum, Toulopoulou and Chen 2008). Even if there are varying accounts of the range of functions performed by the central executive, and much remains to be discovered, there is sufficient agreement for us to conclude that the driver for the operation of the central executive in working memory is the focussing of attention, and that there are several related functions of the executive.

When the role of consciousness in working memory is taken into account, as it must be in the operation of the central executive, we need to be able to envisage a working-memory system in which the effects of attention can be discerned and there is integration across a range of perceptual channels and storage locations. One aspect that becomes relevant is the modularity of some of its component processes. Modularity is seen in the functional independence of components such as the verbal and visual subsystems of perception and their related temporary storage. The effects of attention should be evident in the separate modalities and also in their combinations – see the discussion of the 'binding problem' (Gray 2004) in the later section on the integrative function of consciousness.

Two (or More) Temporary Storage Systems

The phonological loop was initially conceived simply as a mechanism for rehearsing perceived sounds. 'The phonological loop was assumed to be capable of holding speech-based and possibly purely acoustic information in a temporary store' (Baddeley 2007, p. 7). Subsequently, rehearsal and storage functions were found to be distinct: each was capable of being affected independently by different experimental procedures, and by lesions in different regions of the brain. Each was related to different patterns of activity found in neuroimaging, so that the storage component was located especially in the temporo-parietal region of the left hemisphere, while rehearsal was more frontally located in Brocas area (Paulesu, Frith and Franckowiak 1993; see also Jonides 1998).

These findings tend to reinforce Baddeley's functional separation of store and process, and to have relevance for Baars's account of the role of consciousness. So Baars, for example, referred to Paulesu et al. (1993) in support of his global workspace theory of consciousness (Baars 2005a). His theory sees inner speech as 'a particularly important source of conscious auditory-phonemic events, and visual imagery is useful for spatial memory and problem-solving.' It is consistent with the Paulesu et al.'s (1993) study showing that 'areas of the left hemisphere involved in outer speech are now known to be involved in inner speech as well' (Baars 2005a, p. 49).

An alternative theory challenging Baddeley's model has been offered by Jones and colleagues (Jones 1993; Jones, Macken and Nicholls 2004; Jones, Hughes and Macken 2006). They have proposed a 'perceptual-gestural view' of short-term memory which suggests that a concept of 'perceptual organization' can replace the hypothesized phonological store. In their view the 'old' model of Baddeley and others (Broadbent 1958; Atkinson and Shiffrin 1968; Baddeley and Hitch 1974; Baddeley 1986; Cowan 1995) applies to cognitive processes which occur *after* a critical dividing point where categorizing occurs, but they question this traditional distinction and refer to more peripheral processes of perception which in their view meet the demands of short-term memory.[1] However, in Baddeley's system with its emphasis on the processing of incoming information as much as storage, the working memory can include perceptual processes. It combines some features of both memory and perception, bridging the 'fundamental division' described by Pashler (1998, p. 33), that Jones and colleagues questioned.

A suggestion by Jones and colleagues that 'the perceptual process feeds directly into the output planning process, or rather the output planning process can "pick up" residual information from the perceptual

[1] Jones and colleagues refer to a 'fundamental division in cognitive architecture' between pre-categorical perceptual processes and post-categorical mnemonic processes named by Pashler, which they question.

process' (Jones et al. 2006, p. 278) points to the same set of operations as I suggested by adding 'commitment to action' to the definition of working memory. The more dynamic concept of perceptual organisation recommended by Jones and colleagues as a *process*, which can replace the idea of a supposedly static store, is a significant departure from the early short-term memory model, but not so very different from rehearsal in the phonological loop as it was elaborated with the recognition of some cognitive processing in Baddeley's later more dynamic concept of temporary storage.

There are other points at which the alternative model reinforces rather than contradicts the working memory model when it is combined with Baars's global workspace theory of consciousness that we will be taking up shortly. According to Baars's theory, the 'broadcasting' of information that is facilitated by consciousness makes it available to widely separated systems. That some 'picking up' may occur or begin at a precategorical stage of dealing with new information is not the fundamental point. Perception always includes some central processing whether or not a process of coding for meaning is completed. Perceptual organisation joins sensory input with central processing that gives access to wider aspects of cognition including memory. That has been well enough known at least since Bruner's discussion of perceptual readiness and Broadbent's treatment of attention (Bruner 1957; Broadbent 1958).

Baddeley responded to Jones and colleagues with criticism of their assumption of a single multi-modal system which he described as 'inconsistent with the data from other groups, and with data from neuropsychology and neuroimaging'. Such data favoured short-term multi-modal storage being understood to include a specific temporary store for phonological information (Baddeley 2007, pp. 56–57). Baddeley believes, nevertheless, that there is much in common between his theory of the phonological loop and Jones and colleagues' alternative theory featuring perceptual organisation, although that alternative is expressed in terms that favour perception over memory. There might not in the long run be a great difference between them. In the cognitive motivation theory, 'perceptual organization' can do the same job as a temporary store if the store is linked with cognitive processes such as coding operations. The working memory model is likely to remain a useful set of ideas for understanding the motivational properties of cognitive processes.

Similarly, in regard to the *visuospatial sketchpad*, its original conception as a subsystem of working memory has been further differentiated into components, visual and spatial at least, each interacting with the central executive and the episodic buffer, and hence with long-term memory. Baddeley concluded from a number of studies that 'the evidence suggests a clear difference between the short-term storage of features representing visual objects, and of their spatial location' (Baddeley 2007, p. 83). He noted in particular the conclusions of Klauer and Zhao (2004) who found that short-term visual memory of objects was more disrupted by visual than by spatial interference, and a spatial memory task concerned with the location of objects was simultaneously more disrupted by spatial than visual interference. This indicated a degree of functional independence of visual and spatial units within the visuospatial subsystem of working memory.

Baddeley suggested also that there was evidence for a third subsystem concerned with the storage of information about actions, which may rely upon motor or kinaesthetic code. Indeed, we could postulate a multiple component system in which the central executive operates on information in a wider range of temporary storage and processing subsystems corresponding to all modes of perception.

Historically, the question was whether the kind of automatic processing in modules originally envisaged by Fodor in his *Modularity of Mind* (Fodor 1983) could be applied to the central processing of novel stimuli and higher mental processes. That is the point at which consciousness would have its integrating effects across modular systems. Fodor later proposed that central processes were not themselves modular – 'the mind doesn't work that way' (Fodor 2000, 2005, 2006; see also Pinker 2005a, 2005b).

Klauer and Zhao's (2004) interpretation of the results of their six experiments as demonstrating fractionation of the visuospatial component of short-term memory is relevant to the question of modularity. The theory is that the differentiated set of temporary stores, referral and manipulative processes is made available, together with other sources of information from long-term memory, for the integrative function of working memory. The effects of conscious integration are seen in this, according to Baddeley, primarily in the operations of the episodic buffer.

The Episodic Buffer and Consciousness

Although he originally included a storage function in the central executive of working memory, Baddeley concluded from the findings of a wide range of empirical research that the central executive need not include a storage capacity but could operate on information in long-term memory and the temporary storage subsystems (Baddeley 1986, 1996; Baddeley and Della Sala 1998; Baddeley and Logie 1999). The function of temporary storage was conceived by Baddeley initially to be represented in the phonological loop and the visuospatial sketchpad, but that idea was not sufficient for all the kinds of information from internal and external sources that needed to be available somewhere for processing to achieve meaningful results. Having taken storage out of the central executive, Baddeley suggested the episodic buffer to meet this need.

In Baddeley's later work, the episodic buffer is postulated to be a temporary storage system that is able to combine information from several input sources. Although in his initial version (Baddeley 2000), the flow of information from the phonological loop and the visuospatial sketchpad was conceived as occurring indirectly through the executive, empirical investigations led to a direct link being postulated between the episodic buffer and the perceptual subsystems. The episodic buffer had a degree of independent function intermediate between perceptual input, long-term memory and the central executive (Baddeley 2007, p. 148).

The episodic buffer processes both thoughts and feelings. The argument for greater attention to feelings in cognition has not been developed by Baddeley, although he called for re-introduction of concepts of energy and motivation into cognitive psychology. In his 2012 review he relates emotion, a key element of motivation, to the episodic buffer: 'What about emotion? Elsewhere (Baddeley 2007) I have suggested that it impacts WM via a hedonic detector system; where within the M-WM [multicomponent working memory] system is this located? I assume that the buffer provides access to conscious awareness' (Baddeley 2012, p. 23). This might appear to suggest that working memory is necessary for consciousness, whereas Baars claimed that 'working memory requires conscious processes, not *vice versa*' (Baars 2003, p. 11), but they both agreed that Baars's conception is nevertheless compatible with Baddeley's theory. We might wonder whether their models, respectively of conscious access and the episodic buffer, could be two models of the same basic processes.

Baars had argued some years earlier in his cognitive theory of consciousness that short-term memory cannot be used to explain consciousness, but rather that it might be the other way around (Baars 1988, pp. 37–38). He also concluded that short-term memory is not the same (does not have the same functions) as consciousness. The same kind of dual task interference experiments as those used in studies of working memory have indicated, in studies of consciousness, a limited capacity to process different conscious events simultaneously, while it is well established that unconscious or automatic processes can proceed in parallel without interference (Baars 1988, p. 36). There is certainly a close similarity between the supposed integrative functions of consciousness and those of working memory. A number of theorists have suggested that a principal function of consciousness is to bind together information gleaned from separate perceptual channels and memory locations into coherent objects (Baars 1997, Dehaene and Naccache 2001). This corresponds to the function of the episodic buffer in Baddeley's account.

Baddeley relates the reflexive character of conscious awareness to the multicomponent structure of working memory: 'the reflexive character of conscious awareness, the fact that we can be aware of our experience and reflect upon it, implies a system that has both temporary storage and manipulative processes' (Baddeley 2007, p. 149). He presents the idea of the episodic buffer as a conceptual tool with heuristic value for the purpose of explaining how the subsystems of working memory integrate the contents of temporary storages and interface with long-term memory. The process of integration, carried out through the episodic buffer, is taken up again in the following section on consciousness, but first we need to acknowledge that there are alternatives to Baddeley's model of working memory.

Alternative Views of Working Memory

Despite the distinctions made some decades ago, there have been challenges to the idea of more than one kind of memory, such as short-term and long-term memory. In one alternative, short-term memory has been conceived as a subset of long-term memory (Cowan 1993, 1995). Then even if we do need to treat *short-term* memory differently from long term memory, some have questioned whether the *working* memory concept is necessary (Nairne 2002). And there are many variants of the working memory model (Miyake and Shah 1999a). Different accounts of the executive functions associated with the frontal cortex do not necessarily have the same components as those Baddeley proposed in his working-memory model (Miyake et al. 2000), although they might still be compatible. There are many diverse contributions in the very extensive literature in this field. Our interest in its relevance for motivation theory is selective and is concerned with those aspects of working memory most relevant to the integrative function of consciousness and commitment to purposive behaviour.

Nairne has argued that Baddeley's model was mistaken in retaining the notion of memory trace in short-term memory with simple processes of rehearsal and decay (Nairne 2002). He challenged what he saw as an assumption made by Baddeley that, purely as a function of time, information would disappear from short-term memory (in the absence of reactivation by some means). Nairne appealed to an argument put forward at an earlier time when McGeogh criticized Thorndike's 'law of disuse,' arguing that mere time is not a causal factor, that is, that something has to happen in time for conditions to change (McGeogh 1932; McGeogh and Irion 1952).

Baddeley, in defence, said that the brain is always active. Functional magnetic resonance imagery (fMRI) studies have recently given evidence from spontaneous fluctuations in the blood oxygen level dependent (BOLD) signal in support of the common claim, repeated by Baddeley, that the brain is very active even in the absence of explicit input or output (Fox and Raichle 2007). Baddeley argued that decay of memory could be caused by interference from spontaneous activity as well as from a more structured source: 'A more appropriate distinction would therefore be that between decay, seen as forgetting due to general neural activity (occurring during a delay), and forgetting due to specific interference. My own view is that both are likely' (Baddeley 2007, p. 37). He argued that it was not merely a matter of keeping a trace in existence as a kind of store: '[T]he issues Nairne raises are problematic only for a model that limits itself entirely to a very simple rehearsal loop that does not even involve a potentially separable phonological store. This was not true of the phonological loop hypothesis, even in its earliest form' (Baddeley 2007, p. 37).

Nairne was also critical of the concept of activation, arguing that the 'strength' of an item in memory was better understood as the result of a combination of storage and retrieval cues: 'As Endel Tulving put it, "Every phenomenon of episodic memory depends on both storage and retrieval conditions" (Tulving 1983)' (Nairne 2002, p. 69). Baddeley was more concerned with the differentiated structure of working memory, evident in the relative independence of its various functions, than he was with mechanisms of recall. Even so, he recognised that the game was far from over in regard to agreement on structures. If we are to continue to base our theory construction on Baddeley's model, it would be wise for it be taken *pro tem* as a guide to the form of theory that should be useful. He said himself that the model could be changed in a particular component like the idea of a trace 'without seriously threatening its usefulness as a tool for analyzing performance on complex cognitive tasks, its principal aim' (Baddeley 2007, p. 38).

A different approach is that of Cowan, whose emphasis on the role of attention makes it relevant to our interests (Cowan 1988, 1993, 1995, 1999, 2005). Cowan proposed a 'conception of short term memory ... with the focus of attention depicted as a subset of the activated portion of long term memory' (Cowan 1995, p. 162). His 'embedded-processes model' is a hierarchical or nested sets model of memory with a small set of current ideas, objects or events, which are the current focus of attention and awareness, at the centre, and a wider activated set not in the focus of attention but accessible to immediate recall in short-term memory surrounding it, these all being within the domain of long-term memory. He saw these features as *necessary* in 'the most basic memory faculties that must exist according to all available evidence'. Cowan described a view in which 'working memory refers to cognitive processes that retain information in an unusually accessible state suitable for carrying out any task with a mental component' (Cowan 1999, p. 62). In his view 'working memory is central to cognitive psychology because it is assumed to be the vehicle for the retrieval of all information that is needed to carry out a particular task' (Cowan 1999, p. 97).

In cognitive motivation, this creative aspect of working memory, in building resources for future use, is relevant to the formation of goals and purposive cognitive processes in which the possible means for reaching goals are recognised and resources are committed to their attainment. Cowan's emphasis on the role of attention is consistent with the means proposed in cognitive motivation theory by which those processes of goal definition and commitment come about through selective attention.

Consciousness

Without relying exclusively upon it, I am accepting Baddeley's multicomponent model as background for the role of consciousness in working memory:

> The multicomponent working memory model assumes a four-component system, comprising (1) an attentional controller, the central executive, and three temporary storage systems, namely (2) the visuospatial sketchpad, (3) the phonological loop, and (4) a more general integrated storage system the episodic buffer. (Baddeley 2007, p. 14)

The Workspace Model of Conscious Access

The working together of all these components is seen in Baddeley's application of Baars's cognitive theory of consciousness, in which the workspace model was concerned with the integrating effects of consciousness by means of increased accessibility (Baars 1988, 1997, 2002a, 2003, 2005a; Baars and Gage 2007).

Baars used the metaphor of an audience seated in a darkened theatre with a spotlight illuminating items on the stage, 'a bright spot on the stage of immediate memory, directed there by a spotlight of attention under executive guidance' (Baars 2005a, p. 46), so making information that is conscious available to many potential recipients.

This is the primary functional role of consciousness: to allow a theater architecture to operate in the brain, in order to integrate, provide access, and coordinate the functioning of very large numbers of specialized networks that otherwise operate autonomously. (Baars 2005a, p. 47)

As Mandler put it, 'Momentary states of consciousness are the final step in the reduction of information that floods the organism' (Mandler 2002, p. 107). Many others have put forward or discussed similar ideas on the integrative functions of consciousness, although some have emphasised consciousness as a process extending over a period of time rather than as a momentary state. Baars's formulation is a convenient link with Baddeley's model of working memory. Baddeley himself explicitly adopted it (Baddeley 2007, pp. 302, 306–308).

Together with Baars's theory, Baddeley relied in his latest work significantly on the functions of consciousness in working memory described in a review by Dehaene and Naccache (2001), who used the global workspace cognitive architecture originally developed by Newell and Simon and their associates (Newell and Simon 1972; Newell 1990; Newell, Laird and Rosenbloom 1993). Dehaene and Naccache aligned Baars's conception with similar concepts from others, including the central executive (Baddeley 1986), the supervisory attentional system (Shallice 1988), the anterior attention system (Posner 1994; Posner and Dehaene 1994) and the dynamic core (Tononi and Edelman 1998). They synthesised those ideas by postulating that in addition to modular components that can function unconsciously, independently, and in parallel,

the architecture of the human brain also comprises *a distributed neural system or "workspace" with long-distance connectivity that can potentially interconnect multiple specialized brain areas in a coordinated, though variable manner* (Dehaene, Kerszberg and Changeux 1998). Through the workspace, modular systems that do not directly exchange information in an automatic mode can nevertheless gain access to each other's content (Baars 1988). (Dehaene and Naccache 2001, p. 13)

The great potential for interconnectivity that is provided by the global workspace with its wide scope and flexibility is purchased at a cost in the functions of consciousness being subject to the limitations of serial processing. The analogy of a bottleneck has been employed since the early discussion of the effects of consciousness, suggesting a process of squeezing together disparate elements in working memory as we move from parallel to serial processing. Serial processing comes about when different sets of information cannot be processed simultaneously. This typically happens when conscious attention is required. The serial processing limitation may be seen to arise from any or all of several constraints that are inherent in the working memory model: (1) the limited capacity of short term memory, (2) the focussing of attention in the executive of working memory, and (3) the necessity for commitment from time to time to a single course of action for the organism as a whole.

One of the peculiarities of research on consciousness and attention is that the same processes seem to be implicated in both the narrowing of attention and the broadcasting of information to a wide range of receivers. It is that object, percept, concept or schema that is the present focus of attention which is made widely available in the global workspace. Baars's conscious access hypothesis is that consciousness enables dominant information to be widely distributed in the brain and made available to many structures performing different functions. While he used the analogy of a theatre where there is a spotlight focussed on the stage (Baars 1997), Crick had used the image of a searchlight (Crick 1984, Crick and Koch 1990). Global workspace (GW) theory emerged from the cognitive architecture tradition. 'Newell and co-workers were the first to show the utility of a GW or "blackboard" architecture in a distributed set of knowledge sources, which could cooperatively solve problems that no single constituent could solve alone' (Baars 2005a, p. 45). For Newell and colleagues, see Newell and Simon (1972), Newell (1990) and Newell et al. (1993). On the 'blackboard' architecture for a common place of interaction, see Hayes-Roth (1985).

The Integrative Function of Consciousness

The point of these various analogies – a theatre stage, a searchlight, a blackboard – as shared points of reference is that consciousness enables whatever is the focus of attention to be made widely available. If we were to insist instead that consciousness must be no more than an epiphenomenon, it might be said that when wide availability comes about, by whatever means it does, consciousness is what we experience or what may be inferred by observers when whatever is the focus of attention becomes widely available. Such an account pointing to nothing in particular as an explanation of how wide availability occurs is unconvincing. It makes more sense to accept consciousness as a state of the system which has consequences. Consciousness itself has effects in the distribution and integration of information.

The idea that consciousness has an integrating function in working memory has a converse demonstration in the conditions under which people (and animals) become unconscious. It is known that anaesthesia induces unresponsiveness and amnesia, and also unconsciousness, but the extent to which it causes unconsciousness is harder to establish. Certain anaesthetics do not necessarily cause unconsciousness. There is evidence that unconsciousness is a likely result when a complex of brain regions in the posterior parietal area is inactivated, interrupting cortical communication and causing a loss of integration. Alkire and colleagues in a review of the literature on consciousness and anaesthesia concluded that 'anesthetics seem to cause unconsciousness when they block the brain's ability to integrate information' (Alkire, Hudetz and Tononi 2008, p. 876). The general conclusion is that there is agreement across fields of study that the capacity to integrate is necessary for consciousness.

Tononi, a co-author with Alkire of the aforementioned article, has put forward separately an information integration theory of consciousness (IITC) (Tononi 2004, 2005; Tononi and Koch 2008). Tononi's theory relies upon a detailed review of findings which relate the phenomena of consciousness to evidence for greater interconnectedness of areas in the cortico-thalamic system which are critical for consciousness compared with the more modular character of other areas. He interprets those findings in terms of the information storage and processing capacity of integrated combinations compared with parallel processing in separate modules such as is found in the cerebellum. He saw the global workspace theory of Baars as compatible with the IITC, but there are some differences in emphasis. Tononi noted that 'global workspace neurons, characterized by their ability to send and receive projections from many distant areas through long-range excitatory fibers, are especially concentrated in prefrontal, anterior cingulate, and parietal areas' (Tononi 2005, p. 123). He concluded in regard to Baars's theory and the findings of Crick and Koch (Baars 1988; Crick and Koch 1990, 1995; Baars 2002a; Crick and Koch 2003; Koch 2004; Baars 2005a) that 'there is broad convergence on certain key facts: that consciousness is generated by distributed thalamo-cortical networks; reentrant interactions among multiple cortical regions are important; that the mechanisms of consciousness and attention overlap but are not the same, and that there are many "unconscious" neural systems' (Tononi 2005, p. 123). That assessment was reconfirmed in his later joint review and update of the neural correlates of consciousness with Koch (Tononi and Koch 2008). (On awareness and consciousness as distinct processes, see also Koch and Tsuchiya 2007.)

Baars suggested, in a manner similar to Tononi, that '[c]onsciousness might be a gateway to brain integration, enabling access between otherwise separate neuronal functions' (Baars 2002a, p. 51). Where Tononi identifies consciousness with integration, Baars refers to an enabling role of consciousness in processes of integration. He treats 'consciousness as a variable' that has observable effects. He made predictions on the effects of consciousness and summarised evidence in favour of each of seven predictions. The last three of these predictions are directly relevant to the following discussion of selective attention and voluntary control, i.e.:

- Voluntary control is enabled by conscious goals and perception of results.
- Selective attention enables access to conscious contents, and vice versa.
- Consciousness enables access to "self" (Baars 2002a).

It is significant for a theory of cognitive motivation that Baars gave special emphasis to the role of the self in consciousness in his comments on the final prediction (number 7): 'The last point might turn out to be so fundamental that the order should be reversed' (Baars 2002a, p. 51). First there is more evidence of the integrative functions of consciousness.

There is evidence of much more widespread activity in various regions of the brain during conscious compared with unconscious states. Dehaene and colleagues found that fMRI images showed higher intensity in the visual cortex and widespread activity in parietal and frontal cortex for conscious perception of visually presented words, and lesser regional activation concentrated in the early visual cortex for unconscious processing (Dehaene, Naccache, Cohen, Le Bilan, Mangin, Poline and Rivire 2001). Similar results indicating widespread coordinated activation in conscious states were reported by Alkire and colleagues using transcranial magnetic stimulation (TMS) (Alkire et al. 2008). Kjaer and colleagues' (Kjaer, Nowak, Kjaer, Lou and Lou 2001) PET scans showed that greater blood flow in parietal and prefrontal cortex differentiated between subliminal and supraliminal perception. Baars listed a number of similar findings on the widespread activation that is correlated with conscious perception (Baars 2002a, p. 49). The type or pattern of widespread activity is significant, the frontal, parietal and anterior cingulate areas often being important for consciousness (Tononi 2005; Tononi and Koch 2008).

Differences between patterns of neural activity that are related to conscious compared with unconscious or automatic processing are matched in important respects when highly skilled performance on practiced tasks is compared with patterns observed during new and challenging tasks which are in the process of being learned. A well-learned skill can be performed to a large extent automatically, but conscious attention will be required when conditions change. Baddeley points out that a subject who is finding it difficult to hit a target under water can improve by consciously allowing for refraction (Judd 1908), and a sports coach will assist a player to improve a particular skill by first consciously controlling movements which, with practice, can become automatic (Baddeley

2007, p. 307). The neurological difference that is correlated with a change from conscious to unconscious activity in the process of learning a complex skill has been nicely demonstrated experimentally by Haier and colleagues (Haier, Siegel, MacLachlan, Soderling, Lottenberg and Buchsbaum 1992). They observed the brain imagery of people playing a computer game (Tetris) with which they were initially unfamiliar, at which time, while learning the game, wide areas of the brain showed a high level of activity; but later, after extensive practice over two weeks, the level of activity was much lower in general and concentrated in limited areas.

A different approach to the integrative functions of consciousness was made by Gazzaniga from studies of split-brain patients whose corpus callosum had been surgically severed in a treatment for epilepsy. He postulates a 'left-hemisphere interpreter' which has the function of discerning patterns (Gazzaniga 1970, 1995, 2000; Wolford, Miller and Gazzaniga 2004). Gazzaniga and his colleagues found from numerous experiments and clinical observations that people are so ready to discern patterns that they will make up meaningful but completely false stories to account for novel inputs when brain dysfunction prevents access to relevant information. In normal functioning, the interpreter, by seeking patterns, is extremely useful, whether at the level of a minor perceptual task or in applying more general belief systems in one's perspective on life and ethical behaviour (Gazzaniga 2005).

Gray brings another perspective to the association of integration with consciousness in his treatment of the 'binding problem' (Gray 2004). The binding problem is the challenge of understanding the integration in conscious perception of information from different sources. It has two aspects. One is the fact that *inter*modal integration takes place, combining information that is processed in clearly identified different parts of the brain for visual, auditory, olfactory and other stimuli, so that in conscious perception a single object is 'seen', although there is no specific location for processing an integrated percept. The other is *intra*modal, in which not only are conscious perception and unconscious visual action systems brought together, but such different aspects as the shape, colour and name of an object are integrated in the perception of a single object. Although different aspects are processed separately, nonetheless, all the senses do come together in consciousness – at any particular moment there is just one unified scene. Gray saw integration as a system property not predicable from the properties of the individual components that make up a system.

The emerging consensus on neural processes associated with integrative functions tends to support a theory that consciousness enables cognitive integration to take place in working memory.

Fundamental Self-Referent Processes

It is a basic proposition of cognitive motivation theory that the same fundamental processes that are found in perception of whole figures at the micro level contribute to integration of images at the level of the organisation of the self in a social context. This integration at the macro level depends upon the reflexive nature of the self. Damasio saw consciousness to be a function of this reflexive nature of the self: that is, when the self as knower reflects upon the self as object. 'I believe conscious minds arise when a self process is added onto a basic mind process. When selves do not occur within minds, those minds are not conscious in the proper sense' (Damasio 2010, p. 8).

Appley has a similar conception for motivation theory in 'the notion of self as a superordinate, integrating fulcrum' (Appley 1991, p. 30), which I discussed in Chapter 3 in reference to McReynolds's cognitive motivation theory. Here Appley refers to a later mature aspect of McReynolds's work on the widely recognised reflexive nature of the self, in the interaction between the 'executive self' and the 'perceived self' (McReynolds 1987 p. 199; see also Appley 1991, p. 34). Appley related McReynolds's discussion of planning and control to the executive self and its efforts to maintain internal consistency and positive self-esteem: 'to reduce dissonance, incongruity, incompatibilities, and internal inconsistencies in personality functioning, "including cognitive, affective and conative elements" (McReynolds, p. 202)' (Appley 1991, p. 35).

As we noted earlier, it is significant for a theory of cognitive motivation that Baars gave special emphasis to the role of the self in consciousness in his concluding comments on the prediction that consciousness would enable access to functions of the reflexive self as well as executive control of the body:

> Conscious perceptual input to frontal regions might lead to executive interpretation and control, which enables working memory, voluntary control, voluntary selective attention, and accurate report. Even the role of consciousness in learning could be a consequence of voluntary attention. Thus conscious access to self-systems of the prefrontal cortex might enable the other functions. (Baars 2002a, p. 51)

It is a reasonable hypothesis that in the central executive functions of the prefrontal cortex voluntary attention becomes an explicit aspect of a person's sense of agency, but there is no simple correlation between prefrontal activity, self-functions, attention and consciousness. Quite separate areas of the brain are engaged for perception and reflexive self-processes (see Goldberg, Harel and Malach 2006).

The executive functions of the prefrontal cortex are involved in the management of both thought and feelings, as we noted in the discussion of the function of the episodic buffer in working memory. Cognition and emotion are combined in the control of purposive behaviour in processes such as making plans and commitments to action. Damage to the prefrontal cortex, for example, can result in a person losing appropriate feelings in social situations, typically leading to such changes as marriage breakdown, a general inability to recognise and articulate feelings, and loss of the kind of judgement in interpersonal situations that can be necessary to hold a job (Damasio, Tranel and Damasio 1991; Saver and Damasio 1991; Damasio 1994, 1996; Damasio and Anderson 2003). We need to include in our understanding of consciousness and working memory the role of feelings and emotion as well as action, thinking, learning and perception as Damasio has argued in *The Feeling of What Happens* (Damasio 1999), and again in his later work, *Self Comes to Mind* (Damasio 2010). A similar position is taken by Panksepp and Biven (2012). In the next chapter I will consider the cognitive representation of emotion in relation to reflexive self-processes. First we need to take the topic of attention more comprehensively into our understanding of working memory and consciousness.

Attention

Attention plays a major role in the functions of working memory and hence in cognitive motivation. In Baddeley's model, the central executive of working memory directs purposive behaviour by managing attention, but there is a very basic question about what it means to give attention to something. In his influential review of research on attention Pashler warned against too great a readiness to imagine that we know what we talking about when we speak of attention (Pashler 1998). For example, attention is not identical with consciousness, although we often speak of it as if it were. Research in recent years has found an incomplete empirical overlap of attention and consciousness: for example, it is possible to demonstrate that people have given attention to some things without being conscious of them, that one can recall consciousness of something that was not the focus of one's attention, and that consciousness and attention are associated with two distinct brain processes (Koch and Tsuchiya 2007; Tononi and Koch 2008). Similarly, attention can be separated from voluntariness. It has long been known also that there are some forms of attention, such as the orienting reflex (Sokolov and Vinogradova 1975; Sokolov 2002), which are involuntary, or automatic.

Attention is not a simple concept. On the one hand it is easy to agree with William James that everyone knows what attention is, while on the other Pashler can take a 'more skeptical tack, assuming instead that no one knows what attention is, and that there may even not be an "it" there to be known about (although of course there might be)' (Pashler 1998, p. 1). It is implicit in Pashler's approach that attention can be given meaning in the context of empirical research, but in his view it is likely to retain some of its common language meaning. Partly for this reason he wished to avoid the reification inherent in folk psychology that would allow the intrusion of assumptions about mental life that are misleading.

The subject matter of the scientific study of attention deals with much the same subject as the common-sense approach, but Pashler sought to avoid the metaphysics of folk psychology and stay close to the data, using the term 'attention' as little as possible. He has proceeded 'within the framework of the contemporary information-processing approach'. As he sees it, 'The ultimate goal is to work out some account of how the mind processes information, an account that is mechanistic but posed at the functional level' (Pashler 1998, p. 6–7). For my purposes, a functional account is sufficient to recognise the role of attention in working memory, especially in regard to the integrating effects of consciousness.

Baars relates consciousness to only some of the components of working memory, but it is to those components in which the role of attention is crucial. Similarly, the components of working memory in Baddeley's model that invoke the effects of attention, for the most part, are those of the central executive where attention is managed and to a lesser extent the episodic buffer where the integrating effects of consciousness are evident. That is a significant step, especially when it is combined with conscious control being a function of voluntary attention.

Early and Late Selection Theories

Research on the topic of attention, like others in cognition, underwent renewed interest in the 1950s, especially in Britain. It was one of the first roots of 'the cognitive revolution' (see Chapter 2). An experimental study by Cherry at this time nicely demonstrated the importance of attention and its most intriguing nature (Cherry 1953). Cherry used the dichotic listening technique in which people listened to two different messages, each played to one ear through headphones. When they were asked to repeat back one particular message rather than the other – that is, to 'shadow' a message delivered to one ear only – they were able to do so, but they could not report anything about the message received in the other ear. They did not even notice changes of the language or when a message was played backwards on the non-attended side, although they might notice acoustic changes such as a change of pitch from a male to a female voice or when the message disappeared. Subjects were able to follow a message when it was switched from one ear to the other, thus indicating a semantic feature in their performance. Cherry's interpretation employed an information-processing approach as a conceptual framework that was then relatively new in psychology.[2]

At that stage two competing theories of attention appeared, employing 'early' and 'late' selection models. Broadbent, following up Cherry's work with additional experimentation, put forward the information processing theory of attention known as 'Early Selection Theory' or 'Filter Theory' (Broadbent 1958). In Broadbent's model, incoming information is first analysed in both channels at the physical level whether or not it is in the attended channel. This initial processing of the messages in both ears did not employ symbolic properties of the input, but in further analysis the attended message in one channel only is processed to the point of identification of words, or semantic interpretation. In this model selective attention occurs before identification of incoming signals, and semantic processing is then sequential or serial from that point on. This led to important work on the distinction between parallel and serial processing. There was evidence that at the level of semantic interpretation people showed some physiological responses to non-attended messages that were emotionally arousing or personally significant. Such responses as the galvanic skin response indicated that some semantic processing of the non-attended message must have occurred. For example, Morey showed that using a person's own name in the non-attended channel could 'grab' a person's attention, at least in a minority of cases. This effect was replicated by Wood and Cowan in more recent research with improved methods (Moray 1959; Treisman 1960; Corteen and Wood 1972; Wood and Cowan 1995).

These findings led to formulation of 'late selection theories' in which early recognition of *familiar* objects was seen to proceed unselectively and without capacity limitations (Deutsch and Deutsch 1963; Norman 1968), but *novelty* requires more focussed attention that is likely to occur at a late stage which involves central processing. This is the point at which consciousness is effective and serial processes supplant parallel processing.

[2] It was from Cherry that I took the basic concepts of information theory that were employed in the original version of the cognitive process theory of curiosity in 1960, in which coding difficulties created by novel stimuli aroused conceptual conflict, leading to exploratory and problem solving behaviour. See Chapter 2.

Parallel and Serial Processing

According to the late selection theories, irrespective of what a person might choose to attend to or to ignore, the neural network operates to bring about apparently automatic recognition of stimuli as belonging to categories that are *familiar*, to the degree that there is adequate information in the incoming stimuli. 'One cannot voluntarily choose to identify or recognize something, according to these theorists' (Pashler 1998, p. 16). Denial of the need for voluntary attention amounts in this instance to saying that processing of search information about several objects is occurring simultaneously, in parallel, and automatically, without the need for conscious comparisons. The distinction between parallel and serial processing, and the need for conscious voluntary attention, are significant questions for a theory of cognitive motivation.

Many experiments on the difference between parallel and serial processing followed Treisman and Gelade's (1980) publication of 'A feature-integration theory of attention.' They proposed a new hypothesis that when more than one separable feature, such as shape or colour, or separate parts of a figure were needed to identify an object, candidate figures in a field of observation must be attended to serially. In contrast, parallel processing was assumed to be effective when a target figure could be identified by a particular feature. Integration of two or more features to identify a figure would require serial processing, although it was found later that some simple combinations of attributes could be processed in parallel, or very nearly so (Pashler 1998). In general, complex cognitive processing requires a queue to be formed for serial attention. Consciousness would then facilitate integration of the separate elements that are required for meaningful identification. This is a key point in cognitive motivation.

There was, however, a question of whether the parallel vs. serial distinction proposed by Treisman and Gelade is as sharp in reality as might have been supposed in the original discussion of early and late selection theories. Wolfe, for example, argued that, rather than a dichotomy, there is a continuum between parallel and serial processes in studies of selective attention (Wolfe 1998). He and his colleagues have advocated a 'Guided Search' model (Wolfe, Cave and Franzel 1989; Cave and Wolfe 1990; Wolfe 1994b). Pashler proposed that the existence of both perceptual selectivity and parallel processing naturally suggests the simple and obvious account that he termed *controlled parallel processing* (CPP). 'On this view, we may *voluntarily choose* to analyze a single stimulus (suppressing the perceptual analysis of other stimuli) or we may choose to analyze several stimuli in parallel, or even analyze a number of stimuli in parallel while suppressing the analysis of others' (Pashler 1998, pp. 400–401, emphasis added). As Wolfe and others observed, a person is not limited necessarily to serial or parallel processing as discrete alternatives.

In human perception, parallel processing has generally been thought to be pre-categorical, terminating when semantic outcomes are generated; but we may conclude from Pashler's review and other sources such as Wolfe, and Tononi and Koch (2008), that there is a stage of transition from parallel to serial processing that is broad enough to allow some overlap. The conditions in which parallel processing is likely to be supplanted by serial processing in the bottleneck effect are those offering the greatest challenge in complexity, especially when relating novel input to existing knowledge. It appears to be the cognitive load imposed by such features as novelty and complexity that triggers transition to conscious serial processing.

If working memory and consciousness operate as proposed in the theories of Baddeley and Baars, we can see attention as facilitating the availability of focussed information for widespread use in the meaningful outcomes of serial processing. Such meaningful integration is a function of consciousness. In Baars's conscious access hypothesis, conscious perception gives access to widespread brain sources of information and processing. Similarly, attention enables the comprehension of a novel input when it is broadcast widely. 'Selective attention enables access to conscious contents, and *vice versa*' (Baars 2002a, p. 50).

Voluntary Attention

There is a well-recognised distinction in the experimental literature between voluntary and involuntary attention. While there is always in the background the implicit philosophical question of whether a sense of voluntary action can ever be anything but an illusion, interesting theoretical conceptions concerning the nature and effects of voluntary actions have arisen from empirical studies. Pashler concluded from a range of research findings, in reference to his hypothesis of controlled parallel processing, that we may 'voluntarily choose' to analyse a particular stimulus or decide to attend to several stimulus items provided that the processing demands are not too great. How sharply a person focuses attention is to some extent a matter of choice.

Voluntary attention depends upon the central allocation of resources to achieve specific goals (Prinzmetal, Ha and Khani 2010, p. 255 fn). Among the historical precedents, Prinzmetal and colleagues referred to Posner's discussion of the distinction between exogenous and endogenous control of attention (Posner 1978). In more recent work Posner has reported PET scan studies of brain mechanisms involved in voluntary attention and noted how, when meaning is sought, left frontal areas join with the posterior parietal areas, thus pointing to association of perceptual with executive functions in the voluntary condition, which would be necessary for the allocation of resources (Posner 1994; Posner and Raichle 1994).

While consciousness differs from attention in what is known of the brain areas involved in each, Posner nevertheless said, 'I do believe that an understanding of consciousness must rest on an appreciation of the brain networks that subserve attention' (Posner 1994, p. 7398). Posner envisaged many mechanisms which jointly underlie awareness and phenomenal experience, and an anterior attention network playing a role in the executive functions of awareness and control.

Norman and Shallice proposed a structure similar in function to both Posner's anterior attention network and Baddeley's central executive. They called it the *supervisory attention system* (SAS) (Norman and Shallice 1986; Shallice 1988; see also Shallice and Burgess 1998; Jack and Shallice 2001). They suggested that while attention to commonly observed stimuli would normally trigger a routine response automatically, non-routine control of behaviour requires intervention by the supervisory attention system in which attention is centrally managed. Voluntary attention might in this way be experienced as *causing* cognitive, affective and behavioural outcomes; in other words, one would have a sense of agency by virtue of the voluntary focussing of attention. If we add response selection to the semantic outcomes of attention, *an act of will could then be seen as voluntary attention linked with a commitment to action through response selection and allocation of resources.*

Jack and Shallice have argued for a reciprocal feedback model for the role of consciousness in voluntary action (Jack and Shallice 2001, p. 184). In their view, a model which includes the encoding of information in episodic memory as a result of conscious modulation by the supervisory system provides a basis for conscious choice between alternative courses of action. Jack and Shallice suggest that this process is 'of central theoretical importance' because 'the ability to remember a stimulus or thought is the principal criterion for the self-ascription that we were conscious of that stimulus or thought (Allport 1988)' (Jack and Shallice 2001, p. 184). Episodic memory encoding arises whenever supervisory system modulation of lower-level processes occurs. That is the crucial step from non-conscious to conscious processing, from parallel to serial processes, in the preparation of voluntary action. So they say, 'There is a fundamental principle that pervades work on perceptual awareness. This is the principle that *awareness is necessary for intentional action*' (Jack and Shallice 2001, p. 166, emphasis in the original).

It is implied that there is a connection between voluntary attention and an intention to act. (Etymologically, 'attend' and 'intend' share a common Latin root implying a sense of direction, as in 'tend.') The connection between voluntary attention and intention raises additional issues concerning the nature and function of intention that I will examine further in Chapters 9 and 10. At this stage it is reasonable to conclude that the integrative role of consciousness in working memory is facilitated by voluntary attention, and that this process is one of the means by which an incomplete gestalt functions to produce cognitive motivation with a sense of agency. Before returning to the function of the incomplete gestalt in Chapter 9 in regard to goals and intentions, we first need to bring emotion more directly into the picture as a phenomenal and effective guide to purposive behaviour. This is our task in the next chapter.

Summary

The theory of cognitive motivation that was introduced in Chapter 1 describes processes of integration in which new whole images are formed in a person's cognitive map to make sense of disparate experiences. These processes employ the executive functions of working memory that manage attention. In this chapter I discuss the theory of working memory, its structure and functions, and relate it to the integrative processes of cognitive motivation. These integrative processes are described in this chapter as a function of consciousness and attention, which are each examined in the light of recent research.

Working memory is a temporary storage system under attentional control, which enables complex human thought and commitment to action. I discuss Baddeley's multicomponent model as background for the role of consciousness in working memory 'comprising (1) an attentional controller, the central executive, and three temporary storage systems, namely (2) the visuospatial sketchpad, (3) the phonological loop, and (4) a more general integrated storage system the episodic buffer' (Baddeley 2007, p. 14). This model has been elaborated by other recent theorists, and some alternatives are discussed, but most remain in basic agreement with Baddeley's model.

There is close similarity between the supposed integrative functions of consciousness and those of working memory. In working memory, incoming information is integrated with what is already in the system. A principal function of consciousness is to bind together information gleaned from separate perceptual channels and memory locations into coherent objects. The binding role of consciousness is suggested by Baars in his workspace model of conscious access and by others who have proposed models of integration. Tononi's 'information integration theory of consciousness' is discussed with reference to his and Koch's review of the neural correlates of consciousness. In several theories the integrative processes are related to reflexive self-processes which are distinct from but integrated with perceptual processes. I envisage a model in which these integrative processes in working memory underlie the completion of incomplete gestalts in cognitive motivation.

Research in recent years has found an incomplete empirical overlap of attention and consciousness. Similarly, attention can be separated from voluntariness. Two early competing theories of attention, employing 'early' and 'late' selection models, are reviewed together with studies of parallel and serial processing. Consciousness comes into play as processing moves from parallel automatic modular processes to serial consciously regulated processes, especially when a novel stimulus appears and semantic outcomes are facilitated. When voluntary attention is added, I suggest that *an act of will could then be seen as voluntary attention linked with a commitment to action through response selection and allocation of resources*. The integrative role of consciousness in working memory is facilitated by voluntary attention, and this process is one of the means by which an incomplete gestalt functions to produce cognitive motivation with a sense of agency.

8 The Function of Emotion in Cognitive Motivation

My heart leaps up when I behold a rainbow in the sky.
–William Wordsworth 1802

Introduction

The cognitive representation of emotions is an essential component of the means by which goals are formed, commitments made and purposive behaviour is directed. Emotions are essential for both the energizing aspect and the directing aspect of motivation. The information value of emotions becomes particularly important in providing the core dynamics of cognitive motivation. In this theory emotions are signs along the pathway to fulfilment and signals for the initiation of action in pursuit of a goal. Feelings, the conscious aspects of emotions, are thereby elements in cognitive motivation together with nonconscious[1] affective components which can also be represented in cognitive processes. LeDoux, in his review of research on the neuroscience of emotion (LeDoux 2000), saw promise in an information-processing approach to emotion, much along the lines of what had been developed over a longer period in studies of cognition. He suggested that such an approach would be mutually beneficial:

> Minds are not either cognitive or emotional, they are both, and more. Inclusion of work on emotion within the cognitive framework can help rescue this field from its sterile approach to the mind as an information-processing device that lacks goals, strivings, desires, fears, and hopes.
>
> Once a processing approach to emotion is taken, emotion and cognition can be studied similarly: as unconscious processes that can, but do not necessarily, lead to conscious experiences. This would open the door for the integration

[1] The term 'nonconscious' is often preferred to unconscious by authors in this field, but not by LeDoux, as quoted in this paragraph. There are some components of an emotional response, such as a range of physiological changes, preparatory motor actions and some cognitive processing, of which a person might be unaware; these are nonconscious components. The term 'unconscious' might or might not imply hypothetical mental processes preventing certain thoughts and feelings from being consciously recognised.

of emotion and cognition, and such integration should be a major goal for the immediate future. (LeDoux 2000, p. 157)

The Information Value of Emotions

The suggestion by LeDoux that emotion can be taken into the same hypothetical set of information-processing operations as cognition, although relatively new in its context, is in line with recent developments in the neuroscience and psychological literature. In his preface to *Cognitive Neuroscience of Emotion*, Davidson agreed that 'emotion should properly be included in cognitive neuroscience since emotion requires cognitive operations that are indistinguishable from those essential to other processes such as attention and memory' (Lane and Nadel 2000, p. v). In the same vein Clore, with various colleagues, has advanced a theory of 'affect as information' in which it is proposed that people monitor their feelings as feedback to help evaluate a situation (Swartz and Clore 1983; Clore 1992, 1994; Clore, Wyer, Dienes, Gasper, Gohm and Isbell 2001). 'Emotional sensitivity represents a very fundamental and general process of evaluation, and emotions can be understood to represent a process of relevance signalling' (Frijda 1994, p. 113). Frijda envisaged centralised signalling in which harmony or disharmony between 'end' and 'current state' are centrally signalled to the action system: 'Affects are just those signals' (p. 113). Gray and his colleagues have offered a meta-theory of emotion-cognition organised around the concept of control dilemmas in which emotions provide feedback information (Gray et al. 2005).

The information value of emotions and their feedback functions have been studied in recent work on the *Psychology of Self-Regulation* (Baumeister and Vohs 2004; Forgas et al. 2009; Vohs and Baumeister 2010; see also Schwarz 1990; Mischel and Ayduk 2002; Mischel 2012). The model of an affective feedback system of self-regulation proposed by Carver and Scheier (1990, 1998, 2000, 2009) is an influential theory built upon the function of affects derived from a comparison of information about present conditions and an envisaged goal state (Tice 2009). Those cognitive comparison processes have been elaborated in what is called mental contrasting in combination with a second process of implementing intentions (Oettingen and Gollwitzer 2009). Higgins had previously contended that emotion serves to signal discrepancies between actual and desired states (Higgins 1987; see also Higgins 1997). Baumeister and his colleagues argued for an understanding of how emotion shapes behaviour through feedback, anticipation and reflection rather than as a direct cause of behaviour (Baumeister et al. 2007).

Motivation and Emotion

It was commonly expected by theorists of the 1970s and 1980s that emotion and motivation would be related in *some* way. There was an 'increasingly wide acceptance of emotions as motivational processes that influence cognition and action' (Izard 1993, p. 68; see also Izard 1977). Izard said, 'Fundamentally, emotion is about motivation – positive and negative feelings, readiness or tendency to cope, and cues for cognition and action' (Izard 1993, p. 73). McClelland had defined motivation in terms of affectively toned cognitive processes (McClelland 1965). As I have noted in Chapter 2 in reference to curiosity, as Higgins et al. (1997) have argued, a simple hedonic mechanism of pleasure signalling approach and pain signalling avoidance is inadequate, and I will discuss this matter further at several points in this chapter and later.

In the strong traditions of the experimental psychology of learning and motivation, which has relied increasingly on neuroscience, Rolls defined an emotion as a state elicited by a reinforcer (Rolls 1999, 2005). Because stimuli which act as reinforcers function as goals, he is also concerned with motivation. 'Thus motivation may be seen as a state in which one is working for a goal, and emotion as a state that occurs when the goal, a reinforcer, is obtained, and that may persist afterwards' (Rolls 2005, p. 37). This simple definition does not explicitly make provision for those emotions that are associated with the anticipation of a goal, but in his 'refinements of the theory' Rolls says that 'the stimulus that produces the emotional state does not have to be a reinforcer when producing the emotional state – it simply has to be *capable of being shown to have instrumental reinforcing properties*' (Rolls 2005, p. 22, emphasis in the original.)

Buck presented 'An integrated view of motivation and emotion' (Buck 1985), in which he postulated a set of adaptive primary motivation/emotional systems, or 'primes', from which emotion provided an expression or 'readout' of motivational potential. At the highest level of his hierarchical system Buck envisaged a syncretic cognitive output above more basic indications of motivational potential derived from acquired drives, primary affects and effectance motivation.

Another information-processing account of motivation with a neuroscience base has appeared recently (Anselme 2010), but it makes no explicit reference to emotion except in citing Buck's uncertainty processing theory (UPT): '[M]otivation is an information processing (cognitive) system including anticipation and attention, and devoted to collecting information about particular events in order to optimise the reaching of goals' (Anselme 2010, p. 292). Anselme's 'uncertainty processing theory' does not specify the affective qualities that form part of the information which signifies relationship with a goal in cognitive motivation theory. 'This signal function is precisely the core of what affective states are about' (Bless 2002, p. 30).

Higgins was one of several theorists[2] who have described an association of particular emotions with particular motivational conditions. In regard to his regulatory focus theory, Higgins said, 'Evidence is presented that people's emotional experiences of the objects and events in their lives involve different kinds of pleasure and different kinds of pain depending on their regulatory focus, a variability not covered by the hedonic principle' (Higgins 1997, p. 1283). As noted in Chapter 2 in the discussion of approach and avoidance, Higgins described two different strategies associated with differences in *regulatory focus*. One strategy is preventive, concerned with defence of the status quo, while the second seeks to exceed the status quo through the attainment of growth and accomplishments. The first is characterised by vigilance and the second by eagerness. In a social context, 'regulatory focus theory distinguishes between the following two kinds of desired end-states: (a) aspirations and accomplishments (promotion focus) and (b) responsibilities and safety (prevention focus)' (Higgins 1997, p. 1282). These differences give rise to differences in the quality and intensity of emotions associated with different kinds of positive and negative goals.

Based partly on his earlier work on self and affect, in his self-discrepancy theory (Higgins et al. 1985; Higgins 1987), Higgins gave an account of emotions associated with different kinds of discrepancy between actual and desired end-states (Higgins 1997, 1998, 2000, 2001). Different emotions are associated with differences between (1) approaching matches and (2) avoiding mismatches. Higgins and colleagues found that an inclination to approach matches is more likely when there is a promotion focus, and that a strategic inclination to avoid mismatches is more likely for a prevention focus (Higgins, Roney, Crowe and Hymes 1994), thus questioning a simple approach-avoidance paradigm. When there was a mismatch between actual and desired states, individuals with a promotion focus tended to have discrepancies between actual and 'ideal' outcomes, and those with a prevention focus were more concerned with what 'ought' to occur compared with what actually occurred. Feelings of disappointment, dissatisfaction or sadness were associated with failure to attain hopes and ideals, and feelings of agitation such as feeling uneasy, threatened or afraid were associated with failure to match obligations or the 'ought' type of aspiration: '[A]s the magnitude of participants' actual-ideal discrepancies increased, their suffering from

[2] See also the discussion of Weiner's theory of attribution in Chapter 6.

depression symptoms increased, and as the magnitude of their actual-ought discrepancies increased, their suffering from social anxiety symptoms increased' (Higgins 1997, p. 1288). According to their regulatory focus, people experience *different kinds of pain* from not attaining their goals.

Other studies have shown that regulatory focus underlies *different kinds of pleasure* people experience from attaining their goals. Higgins and colleagues found that the stronger the promotion focus, the stronger the cheerfulness-related emotions experienced when *promotion* was working with actual-ideal congruency, and the stronger were the dejection-related emotions when promotion was not working. The stronger the *prevention* focus, the stronger were the quiescence-related emotions when prevention was working in the actual-ought contingency, and the stronger were the agitation-related emotions when prevention was not working (Higgins, Shah and Friedman 1997).

These findings from Higgins and colleagues represent emotion as a consequence of motivation, but at the end of this chapter I summarise the role of emotion in cognitive motivation as an element in motivational processes, as a means to an end; i.e. I suggest that we see emotion primarily as a servant of motivation, as Baumeister has recently recommended for a general theory of motivation (Baumeister 2016). Before we reach that point, many different facets of the motivation-emotion relationship need to be examined, beginning with the question of what we mean by emotion.

The Definition of Emotion

LeDoux's preference for understanding both emotion and cognition in information-processing terms contributes to an information-processing approach to motivation in which emotion signals information about the fulfilment of purposes. This basic idea is found also in Rolls's theory of emotion and motivation and in Damasio's theory of images and somatic events in emotional arousal (Damasio 1994, 1999; Rolls 1999; Damasio 2003; Rolls 2005; Damasio 2010). Both cognitive and somatic qualities might be recognised, but they have had different emphases in competing theories such as those of Lazarus and Zajonc. Panksepp's account combines an emphasis on basic affective systems at the subcortical level with higher brain processes of a cognitive nature (Panksepp 1998, 2000, 2011a). A different emphasis is made by Barrett with her claim that emotions are made real in the social world by top-down conceptual knowledge that shapes perception (Barrett 2012). Discussion of the differences between somatic and cognitive emphases leads to a multicomponent definition of emotions.

Cognitive and Somatic Emphases

Emotion was seen in cognitive approaches, such as those of Lazarus, or Clore, Ortony and colleagues, to be an outcome of a computation evaluating the relationship of goals to behaviour in the present situation (Ortony, Clore and Collins 1988; Lazarus 1991; Clore and Ortony 2000). Oatley and Johnson-Laird's communicative theory was similar in regard to evaluation, except that they sought to integrate the biological approach of Darwin with the information-processing or cognitive science approach of Simon (Darwin 1872/1998; Simon 1967; Oatley and Johnson-Laird 1987, 1996). Others with a somatic approach described emotion in terms of a range of physiological responses that may be represented cognitively (Zajonc 1998; Damasio 2010, Panksepp and Biven 2012). Zajonc agreed with Damasio that 'the primary and fundamental reaction to external stimuli is not a perceptual or cognitive reaction, but an emotional reaction modulated by what Damasio called *somatic markers*, essentially "gut feelings"' (Zajonc 1998, pp. 591–592), which Damasio saw as determining subsequent reactions, including cognitive processes.

Although they make contrasting emphases, there is a bond between cognitive and somatic theories of emotion. Ekman (1977) was one of the first, in addition to Lazarus (1974), to put forward the idea of appraisal as a fundamental process in the generation of emotions. He presented an evolutionary view in which emotions are patterns of physical responses that have an adaptive value. Lazarus, whose cognitive emphasis built much on the effects of appraisal, put forward a 'cognitive-motivational-relational theory' based on appraisal of the present situation in terms of its *relational meaning*: 'Thus anger could be said to involve the relational meaning of an unwarranted offense against me and mine, anxiety an existential threat, guilt having acted against a moral standard, and sadness having experienced an irrevocable loss' (Lazarus 1994a, p. 82). The relational meaning depends upon deep cognitive processing.

Differences of opinion about the necessity for prior cognitive processes to produce emotional arousal takes us back to the high-profile dispute in which Lazarus argued for the priority of cognition over emotion and Zajonc for the primacy of affect (Lazarus 1984; Zajonc 1984). Lazarus said later that 'primacy' did not necessarily mean priority in time: '[T]he question of which is temporally first is an epistemological error' (Lazarus 1999, p. 8). He invoked the principle of reciprocal causation that we commonly find in functions of the self: 'In other words, although emotion is a response to meaning, it can also occur prior to the next thought, which is, in its turn, a response to the experienced emotion and its perceived impact on oneself and others' (Lazarus 1999, pp. 8–9).

Part of the problem lay in the definition of emotion, and specifically whether it should be defined to include a cognitive component, as distinct from being engendered by cognitive processes, if indeed it was. The definition of emotion turned out to be no easy matter. After some decades of struggle with it, Mandler declared that 'it should be obvious that a non-contested definition of emotion is not within our reach' (Mandler 2002, p. 103). Izard saw the definition of emotion as 'a very thorny issue' that 'will not be resolved to everybody's satisfaction', although 'it is possible to identify basic characteristics of emotion on which there is considerable agreement' (Izard 1993, p. 71). Nevertheless, multicomponent definitions combining cognitive and somatic approaches, as well as contributions from affective neuroscience, have largely solved the problem.

Lazarus foreshadowed later multicomponent definitions when he described emotion as a complex disturbance with three main components: subjective affect (which includes cognitive appraisal); physiological changes related to species specific forms of mobilization for action; and behavioural components (Lazarus 1974, pp. 21–22). Zajonc was critical of Lazarus for *defining* emotion as necessarily including a cognitive component and then arguing that cognitive appraisal is, *as a matter of fact*, a necessary precondition for emotional arousal. He believed that there was evidence of emotional reactions occurring without prior cognitive appraisal of environmental input (Zajonc 1980, 1984).

There was evidence that object identification, and thus complex cognitive processing, was not required for stimuli to produce an emotion response (Zajonc 1998). Rolls, however, argued that this 'low road' to emotion (LeDoux 1996; Izard 2000) was an *exception* to the general rule that processing stimulus input to the level of object identification is necessary for emotion arousal (Rolls 1999, 2005). In a significant resolution of these competing points of view, Panksepp has proposed that basic or primary emotions result directly from neural activity in sub-cortical affective systems, but that cortically mediated cognitive and social influences typically contribute to the greatly varied qualities of human emotions at what he calls a tertiary level that I will discuss further (Panksepp 1998; Panksepp and Biven 2012).

Multicomponent Views of Emotion

Izard, in his article on 'cognitive and non-cognitive approaches', posits four hierarchically arranged arousal systems for emotion, 'with neural systems, the simplest and most rapid, at the base and cognitive systems, the most complex and versatile, at the top' (Izard 1993, p. 68). 'The four types of systems that activate emotions are neural, sensorimotor, motivational, and cognitive' (p. 73). Izard's view with his multicomponent understanding of emotion has much in common with that of Lazarus, and with Clore and Ortony, who gave a multicomponent formulation following Ortony and colleagues' emphasis on the cognitive determination of emotions (Ortony et al. 1988). They made basically the same point that 'Emotions always involve cognitive appraisal processes' (Clore and Ortony 2000, p. 24). Clore and Ortony noted especially the work of Frijda and colleagues who described an interaction or sequence of several components in processes of appraisal: an eliciting condition, a cognitive evaluation, physiological activation, a change of action readiness and finally an action (Frijda 1986; Frijda, Ortony, Sonnemans and Clore 1992, Frijda, Manstead and Bem 2000). Similarly, Clore and Ortony gave a definition, or comprehensive description, of human emotions, with four major components: cognitive, motivational-behavioural, somatic and subjective-experiential.

Although one of the components might be labelled 'cognitive' in cognitive motivation theory, the various components of emotion can each be conceived as having cognitive representations capable of being related to one another and to other sources of information about goals, behaviour, body states and the self. The central claim of the cognitive accounts of emotion according to Clore and Ortony was that emotions depend upon the perceived meaning or significance of situations. This view was found previously in Mandler's studies of cognition and emotion, which were conducted together with his work on consciousness (Mandler and Mandler 1964; Mandler 1975, 1984, 1985, 1997, 2002). 'Appraisal,' in a cognitive approach to emotion, referred to the assignment of value or emotional meaning as a result of evaluation. Emotions thus required cognitive processes sufficient to generate or retrieve preferences (Zajonc 1998), to generate evaluative meaning (Mandler 1984; Clore and Ortony 2000 p. 26) or to make sense of emotionally arousing stimuli. 'Meaning' implied complex cognition in which long-term memory is utilised together with the processes of working memory that are in part conscious (on working memory, see Chapter 7). Evaluative meaning is applied to a symbol in relation to a purpose and thus to motivation. This understanding applies specifically to the function of emotion in cognitive motivation and not to all the effects of emotions which also include homeostatic regulation of bodily functions.

Basic Emotions and Complex Feelings

Whether there is indeed a common set of basic emotions that may be developed into greatly varied complex feelings through learning has been a matter of serious debate. The idea of 'basic emotions' was advanced particularly by Ekman, who followed Darwin's classic contribution (Darwin 1872/1998). The first list of basic emotions in recent scholarship appears to have been produced by Tomkins, who carried out cross-cultural comparisons, claiming universality for a list of emotional expressions. His work inspired similar cross-cultural work by Ekman and Izard (Tomkins 1962–1963; Izard 1971; Ekman 1973; Russell 1994; Ekman 1998). They produced lists of basic emotions from studies of agreement about facial expressions such as fear, anger, sadness, happiness, disgust and surprise.

From a different research base, Panksepp has been a major contributor to the theory of basic emotions from a 'neuroevolutionary' approach. He distinguishes between (1) seven or more *primary* process neural systems that are evolutionarily given discrete brain systems of affective response; (2) *secondary* process emotions developed from the basic emotions by classical conditioning and instrumental learning; and (3) *tertiary* affects and neocortical 'awareness' functions with cognitive executive, regulatory and working memory decision-making effects (Panksepp 1998, 2005; Panksepp and Biven 2012). The evidence leaves 'little question about the existence of basic emotional feelings in the basement of the mind (Panksepp 1998)' (Panksepp and Biven 2012, p. 9). They cite a meta-analysis of recent neuroimaging studies that found support for the basic emotions model: 'Each of the emotions examined (fear, anger, disgust, sadness, and happiness) was characterised by consistent neural correlates across studies, as defined by reliable correlations with regional brain activations' (Vytal and Hamann 2010, p. 2864).

An alternative to the basic emotions theory is a 'dimensional' view combining a bivalent dimension of positive and negative feelings with another dimension of high and low arousal arising from what Russell has called Core Affect (Russell 2003, 2009). Russell says, 'The concepts of emotion, fear, anger, and so forth are parts of a folk theory inherited from human shepherding and farming ancestors' (Russell 2003, p. 145). He argues that each folk concept must be scrutinised for its scientific value, and he throws doubt on the idea of a simple set of basic emotions. Russell describes several processes of 'psychological construction': one to account for components such as facial movement or tone of voice in a particular emotional episode; another for relations between components; and a third for 'the categorisation of the pattern of components as a specific emotion' (Russell 2009, p. 1259).

There has been extensive discussion of the fundamental difference between Russell's dimensional view and Panksepp's categorical view of basic emotions (Zachar and Ellis 2012). Ekman has argued against 'Russell's mistaken critique', saying that strong evidence for the universality of specific emotions remains (Ekman 1994b). Panksepp has suggested in response to Russell that the conflict between theories of basic emotions and the dimensional view arises from the different levels of analysis in which basic emotion theory is dealing with primary process systems and dimensional theories with tertiary processes (Panksepp 2011a). Given this distinction between analyses at different levels, both views have significant empirical support – and they can be held together: 'A hybrid view combining dimensional descriptions of emotion states in terms of arousal and valence with additional characterization provided by basic emotion categories would be consistent with the current findings' (Vytal and Hamann 2010, p. 2881). The difference between primary and tertiary emotions provides for multiple dimensions at the tertiary or more cognitive level, with specific neural systems operating at the same time at the primary level. Complexity at the tertiary level provides great scope for the function of emotions in cognitive motivation.

The difference between primary and tertiary emotions in Panksepp's theory corresponds in part with a distinction made by Lisa Feldman Barrett between the biological basis for emotions evident in physical changes and 'socially shared conceptual knowledge that perceivers use to create meaning from these physical changes' (Barrett 2012, p. 413). I will discuss her contribution, which challenges Panksepp's account, and also Izzard's noted earlier in the chapter, after a general review of the question of whether there are a limited number of basic emotions. (See also Barrett 2006a; Barrett, Lindquist, Bliss-Moreau, Duncan, Gendron, Mize and Brennan 2007; Izard 2007; Panksepp 2007).

Darwin, Ekman and the Evolution of Basic Emotions

The idea that there are a limited number of basic emotions has been widely held. Oatley and Johnson-Laird suggested a set of basic emotions in their cognitive and communicative theory of emotion (Oatley and Johnson-Laird 1987; Oatley 1987; Johnson-Laird and Oatley 1989; Oatley and Johnson-Laird 1996; Oatley, Keltner and Jenkins 2006). While there have been doubts over a long period about the composition of a universal set of basic emotions (Russell 1994), some agreement has emerged. Oatley and Johnson-Laird specified much the same set from cognitive studies as Ekman and Izard did from cross-cultural studies of facial expressions (Ekman, Sorenson and Friesen 1969; Ekman and Friesen 1971; Izard 1971; Ekman 1998). Yet, the fact that the various lists of basic emotions are not identical has been taken as evidence against the general idea (Russell 1994; Zajonc 1998). Taking a completely different approach, Panksepp has produced a strong case, from the arousing effects of direct brain stimulation, for his proposed set of seven primitive affective systems in the brain that he has named seeking, fear, rage, lust, care, panic/grief and play. These are postulated evolutionary developments still evident in *The Archaeology of Mind* (Panksepp 1998, 2005, 2011a; Panksepp and Biven 2012). Damasio, too, has described brain structures and functions for a range of specific emotions and their evolutionary development (Damasio 2004, 2010).

Although the idea that emotions can be reliably inferred from facial expressions has a long history in Western literature, going back as far as Aristotle, the classic attempt to enumerate basic and universal emotions from facial expressions in modern times is that of Darwin in his book, *Expression of the Emotions in Man and Animals* (Darwin 1872/1998). Ekman, a recent interpreter of Darwin, has found support in his own research for Darwin's claim of cross-cultural agreement on certain common emotions (Ekman 1973, 1992b, 1998, 1999b). Darwin had requested travellers and people working and living with indigenous populations in remote places around the world to report to him on how emotions were expressed in different cultures. He found common patterns of facial expressions and gestures for many emotions, such as fear, anger, disgust, sadness, surprise and enjoyment, which he believed to be innate.

Darwin also described parallels with human emotions among the expressions of emotions in primates and other mammals. He placed the evolutionary emergence of some emotional expressions very much earlier than others. So, 'laughter, as a sign of pleasure, or enjoyment, was practiced by our progenitors long before they deserved to be called human' (Darwin 1872/1998, p. 356). Of the typically human emotions that appeared later, Darwin suggested that weeping came at a rather late date. He said of late developments, 'Of all expressions, blushing seems to be the most strictly human' (Darwin 1872/1998, p. 359). The implication is that the most typically human expressions appeared at a late date when the cognitive capacity for refection upon experience, and similar discernment of emotions in others, had begun to mature as humans developed a theory of mind capacity (I know that you know that I know, and so forth). Others have suggested in the context of recent work on human evolution that the development of a capacity for theory of mind took place within the last 250,000 years, and perhaps as recently as 70,000 years ago (Tomasello and Call 1997; Tomasello et al. 2005). Darwin and Ekman claimed that human emotions are universal and many are shared with other mammals, while the most typically human appear to have evolved recently together with the greater cognitive capacity that enables reflexive self-processes.

There have been reservations about Ekman's claims for matching human expression of basic emotions with homologous facial expressions in other primates. Research reported from the Yerkes National Primate Research Center, Atlanta, GA, using an objective Facial Action Coding System (FACS), indicates that while several patterns of facial expressions can be matched to a considerable degree between humans and chimpanzees, 'many of the matching human expressions are not identical to those described by Paul Ekman as basic emotions (anger, fear, happiness, sadness, surprise, and disgust) but represent some variation of these' (Parr 2010, p. 624). According to Parr, sadness shown in a pouting face in young children may be the most similar. While happiness in humans may be aligned with the 'play face' in chimpanzees, there is a difference in the way the upper teeth are revealed in the human smile that is not found in chimpanzees. Anger is similar in humans, but chimps lack the human knitting of eyebrows. Parr concluded however that, despite minor differences, their analysis provided 'a clear visual representation of how similar many of the facial expressions are between chimpanzees and humans, enabling informed assumptions about the underlying emotional content' (Parr 2010, p. 624).

In support of Darwin's theory of the universality of emotional expressions, Ekman reported that both he (Ekman et al. 1969) and Izard (1971), working independently, 'obtained consistent evidence of agreement across more than a dozen Western and non-Western literate cultures in the labelling of enjoyment, anger, fear, sadness, disgust, and surprise facial expressions' (Ekman 1992b, p. 34). To rule out the effects of mass media, he and Friesen replicated these findings with isolated preliterate societies in New Guinea (Ekman et al. 1969; Ekman and Friesen 1971; Ekman 1972). He claimed that further support was found in West New Guinea (West Papua) by Heider and Rosche. They confirmed Ekman's results, but work in other parts of Indonesia later by Heider, when he was working largely with variations in the use of words naming emotions, led to more complex findings (Heider 1991, Ekman 1992b, 1998). Ekman has argued in reply to Russell that there is still strong evidence for universality of specific emotional expressions (Ekman 1994b).

There are, in fact, three different questions being addressed in these cross-cultural studies: (1) Is there a useful degree of similarity in the physical expression of different emotions in culturally separate populations? (2) Is there social agreement on the recognition and naming of different expressions within and across cultures? (3) Are there several different underlying affective systems for universal basic emotions in the brain? There was a tendency to infer answers to the first and the third questions from answers to the second.

Panksepp presents a new approach in which it is suggested that there are a limited number of universal sub-cortical primitive affective systems in the brain that can be demonstrated by electrical stimulation. These are said to be supplemented by learning at higher cortical and cognitive levels from which a great variety of human emotions have developed (Panksepp 1998, 2007, 2011a). Lisa Feldman Barrett, to whose work we will come shortly, argues on the contrary that the finding of specific neural structures for specific emotions has been influenced by the use of suggestive verbal labels for emotions, while humans create ontologically subjective categories to serve social functions (Barrett 2006a; Barrett et al. 2007; Barrett 2012).

Panksepp's Primary Emotional Affective Systems

Because he postulates that feelings can enter consciousness directly from sub-cortical systems, Panksepp distinguished his understanding of emotion from what he called the 'read-out' theories of Damasio, LeDoux and Rolls. In contrast with them, and with William James's somatic theory, and those quite different theories such as the cognitive approach of Lazarus, 'The affective neuroscience approach does not envision emotional feelings being "read out" by higher cognitive brain functions, although there are pervasive interactions with those regions of the BrainMind' (Panksepp and Biven 2012, p. 75). It is proposed that there is a kind of core consciousness of emotions that humans share with other mammals based on sub-cortical systems. Homologous 'old' brain regions found in other mammals are postulated to have the same affective functions as in humans where their effects are modified (but not 'read out') by the much more highly developed cerebral cortex (Panksepp 1998, 2005, 2011a, 2011b; Panksepp and Biven 2012). He described seven basic affective systems:

> We have at least seven primary-process (evolutionarily engraved, but experientially refined) unconditional emotional affective systems in the brain: SEEKING, RAGE, FEAR, LUST, CARE, PANIC, and probably PLAY, with many overlapping controls and functions (Panksepp 1998). They all exist in brain areas shared homologously in all mammals. The capitalizations highlight a new way of speaking – they are assertions of the existence of brain networks that govern class-similar emotional behaviors as well as distinct types of class-similar affective experiences in all mammals. (Panksepp 2011b, p. 550)

Panksepp and Biven recognise, in regard to the 'read out' conception of Damasio, LeDoux and Rolls, that 'these esteemed colleagues may have been referencing secondary-process emotions based on learning (LeDoux and Rolls) and tertiary feelings that arise when cognitions and basic emotions are combined into complex amalgams (Damasio)' (Panksepp and Biven 2012, p. 69). At the phenomenal level what we commonly observe in people is unavoidably composed of complex amalgams of primary with secondary and tertiary systems.

One of Panksepp's primary affective systems is, however, of particular relevance to cognitive motivation – the SEEKING system, with its emotion of excited, euphoric anticipation, most evident in curiosity. It is an affective system that moves the animal 'to search for, find and acquire all the resources that are needed for survival ... the system produces all kinds of approach behaviours, but it also feels good in a special way' (Panksepp and Biven 2012, p. 95). 'This positive feeling of anticipatory eagerness ... is entirely different from the pleasurable release of consummation' (p. 96). The distinction from a consummatory response is exactly what I have specified from psychological and literary sources for curiosity. While it can be positively attractive, Panksepp's SEEKING system also has some of the same undifferentiated excitement and ambivalent character which is typical of curiosity. However, the human curiosity I have described in Chapter 2 is experientially refined and culturally modified, not the raw basic emotion that Panksepp and Biven refer to when they say: 'When the SEEKING system is aroused, animals exhibit an intense, enthused, curiosity about the world' (Panksepp and Biven 2012, p. 98). This is the primitive basis on which the higher-level cognitive processes of human epistemic curiosity and the intrinsically rewarding aspects of other forms of cognitive motivation are formed.

There is also a contribution to certain forms of cognitive motivation in three other basic affective systems described by Panksepp: *CARE, PANIC/GRIEF, and PLAY*. PLAY is a system that is fundamental for many forms of intrinsic motivation such as effectance motivation (see Chapter 6). Two of them – CARE and GRIEF – have a mutually complementary relationship, bonding parents and infants while they develop into more broadly applicable foundations for empathic relationships that have many consequent beneficial effects. Each has its own basis in subcortical systems, but they are related to each other and interact with the SEEKING system in ways that promote various processes of unification. Composites of these three at the tertiary level facilitate social relationships that are beneficial in promoting individual development. They provide protection and recovery from threats or trauma to which the cognitive motivation of belief systems and spiritual strivings at the highest level of personality organisation have been shown to contribute (Emmons 1999a).

Panksepp identified another system that is also relevant to cognitive motivation. In his theory, *the core SELF* is the basic affective foundation for a sense of self. It is not another basic affective system, but a common base of overlapping systems. It embodies what is known as 'core consciousness' (Panksepp 1998, 2005; Baars 2005b; Damasio 2010; Panksepp and Biven 2012). Higher manifestations elaborating basic emotional processes at the secondary and tertiary levels have been proposed by Panksepp to develop from what he calls the core SELF, a system represented in the midbrain where the various primary process affective systems converge (Panksepp 1998; Panksepp and Biven 2012). He describes also common centres that are richly connected to widespread cerebral structures, especially the premotor cortex and frontal lobes where planning and control systems are concentrated and intentions are generated. Panksepp postulates the gradual emergence of 'idiographic selves' that are not isolated cognitive processes, but linked with affective evaluation of the world. In Chapter 12, I have further extended the idea of the idiographic development of emotions to suggest a theory of an infinite range of emotions and a corresponding infinitely varied pattern of cognitive motivation that is typical of human beings.

Barrett's Conceptual Act Theory of Emotions

According to Lisa Feldman Barrett's theory, an array of sensations from the world and the body counts as an emotion when categorised as such by adding information from past experience that is not intrinsic to those sensations (Barrett 2006a, 2006b, 2012). 'People experience an emotion when they conceptualize an instance of affective feeling. In this view, the experience of emotion is an act of categorisation, guided by embodied knowledge about emotion' (Barrett 2006b, p. 20). In her discussion of whether emotions are 'natural kinds,' the categories of which 'cut nature at its joints' (Barrett 2012, p. 416; see also Barrett 2006a, 2006b; Barrett et al. 2007; Izard 2007; Panksepp 2007; Barrett 2012), she claims that the method of studying specific brain activation systems by electrical stimulation that was employed by Panksepp does not produce subjective experiences of specific emotions, but rather of 'general pleasure, displeasure, or arousal' (Barrett 2012, p. 414). Her claim for cultural influence is similar to Russell's (2009) suggestion for the definition of particular emotions by cultural categorisation of physical signs. Barrett suggests that observations are biased by the way words are used to suggest culturally defined feelings. She notes many sources of discrepancy in the relationship of physical signs to particular emotional experiences. She refers to findings that brain lesions in areas supposedly responsible for processing particular emotions do not correlate well with behavioural observation or subjective reports of specific emotions. She concludes from studies of biological profiles that 'it is not possible to literally verify whether or not a person (or non-human animal) is angry, sad, or afraid (or is in any other emotional state) using methods that do not rely on a human perceiver' (Barrett 2012, p. 415.)

Barrett argues, among other things, that categories for definition of particular emotions suggested by physical signs can be both too narrow and too general; for example, on the one hand, the study of 'behavioural adaptations' in other mammals has revealed distinct neural circuits that control flight, fighting and freezing. These categories are too specific for the common emotional category of fear, one of Panksepp's seven also named by others such as Izard from cross-cultural studies. On the other hand, signs generated by electrical stimulation have been claimed to lack specificity, although Panksepp reports otherwise. For Barrett, whether it is in regard to differences in specificity or generality, the evidence for physical changes correlating with subjective and behavioural categories of emotion is not very good. She then argues for a social constructionist view of emotions with specific emotions defined by conceptual acts.

In commenting on Barrett's paper on emotions as natural kinds (Barrett 2006a), Panksepp reiterated his claim that there is abundant neurobehavioral data to support the existence of a variety of core emotional operating systems in ancient subneocortical regions of the brain (Panksepp 2007), as he has argued in detail since (Panksepp 2011a; Panksepp and Biven 2012). In an approach that agrees well with the holistic emphasis in cognitive theories, he said, 'Mechanistic science is only adept at explicating "parts" rather than describing the "wholes"' (Panksepp 2007, p. 293). In reference to other reviews, he concluded that it is now widely accepted that emotions are both biologically grounded and culturally shaped, as he has since elaborated on the differences between his categories of primary, secondary and tertiary emotions. Differences between Barrett and others such as Panksepp and Izard are substantial enough to remain for some time, but at what point cultural knowledge combines with physiological information to define the composite experiences of human affect may not be a matter of fundamental importance for a cognitive theory; the fact is that we experience combined effects. It is important to acknowledge such a combination as typical of human feelings. At the phenomenal level, emotions will function in much the same way as signs for purposive behaviour, whether Barrett or Panksepp is followed.

Affective and Non-Affective Feelings

Emotions have often been defined as affective states with positive or negative valence. On the other hand, besides curiosity, there are feelings like hope or the feeling of understanding, or what Averill has named intellectual emotions (Averill 1991), or what Clore has called cognitive feelings (Clore, Ortony and Foss 1987, p. 751). Clore and colleagues questioned the status of such terms as sleepy, tired, relaxed, puzzled, curious, receptive, boredom, impatience, inspiration, luckiness, conflict and rectitude. Do these words refer to emotions? In their empirical investigation of 'the affective lexicon' they found that people discriminated emotional terms from others when asked to respond in a context that referred to *feeling* something rather than *being* something: so, for example, in the context of *feeling* abandoned, the word 'abandoned' was rated as referring to an emotion, but in the context of *being* abandoned, it was not. From discriminant analyses of the meaning of emotion words they discovered multivariate functions that discriminated between four major categories of words in a taxonomy specifying categories of Affective, Cognitive, Bodily and External conditions. Another discriminant analysis yielded an eight-class set of categories. Affective vs. non-affective feelings is not a simple distinction.

Whether it makes sense theoretically to speak of 'non-affective feelings' is an issue that raises basic questions about emotions, particularly in regard to whether we must characterise emotions as valenced. The affect associated with forms of cognitive motivation like curiosity can be an ambivalent state of excitement, or wonder, or a feeling of puzzlement or partial insight, not necessarily positive or negative (see Chapter 2). Clore and colleagues classified curiosity among 'cognitive conditions' for the meaning of emotion words where it is grouped with cognitive feelings such as a feeling of understanding or not understanding something, or 'the feeling of knowing'. Damasio also refers to a feeling of knowing as a conscious experience that marks a sensory event – it is 'the feeling of what happens' – but he says it is not an affect (Damasio 1999). Clore and colleagues said that '[a]ll emotions are affective, but not all affective conditions are emotions' (Clore et al. 1987, p. 751). Clore and colleagues cannot be right if, as seems to be the case, there are non-valenced affects, but it is a semantic problem to some extent. Some states that are not valenced can be called feelings, and feelings are the conscious aspects of emotions.

Culturally Modified, Subtle, Complex and Refined Emotions

'We have many emotional terms that are cognitive elaborations built upon and out of the neural energies of our basic emotions' (Panksepp and Biven 2012, p. 147). What we commonly observe in everyday life are these learned and encultured expressions. Human emotional expression is a cognitive and social process that takes place within a culture. Ekman argued that all emotions are basic in the sense that all include innate factors and play a functional role in evolutionarily significant adaptive behaviour (Ekman 1994a; see also Ekman 1992a, 1992c). On the other hand, Prinz has argued that no emotions are basic in the evolutionary sense of being selected combinations of fixed responses to specific environmental cues, but '[e]very emotion that we have a name for is the product of both nature and nurture' (Prinz 2004, p. 69). In Panksepp's terms, this would apply to learned secondary and tertiary emotions.

Margaret Mead maintained strongly her commitment to cultural relativism in opposition to what she apparently perceived as programmatic in Ekman's conception of the innate basis of universal expressions, in which she saw the menace of Nazism (Mead 1975). In distinction from the programmatic view of which Mead accused him, Ekman proposed that emotional expressions are not instinctive and being 'embedded in a context, may be elicited by different stimuli, be operated upon by different display rules, be blended with other affects, and followed by different behavioral consequences' (Ekman 1998, p. 386). In his argument with Mead he adopted a distinction made by the noted zoologist Earst Mayr between an 'open program' and a 'closed program'. An open genetic program allows for additional input from experience during the life of an individual. There is always a nature-nurture mix, but the mechanisms proposed by Ekman tend to strengthen the argument for an adaptive function based on evolutionarily effective basic processes with modification in the individual by the influence of culture and individual experience.

Differentiation of feelings by reference to their personal and social significance is implied in a suggestion by Ellsworth that a sense of agency can be responsible for differences where people feel better able to deal with an event if they know the cause of it (Ellsworth 1994, p. 153). She found that negatively evaluated events perceived as having been caused by other people evoke anger, but shame when they are one's own responsibility, and sorrow when seen to be due to fate or uncontrollable circumstances. This view is consistent with the widely held more general hypothesis that the varied qualities of emotions are derived at least in part from perceptions of the situations in which they occur, and these may extend to the understanding of agency.

Perception of agency implies a useful degree of certainty about the causes of psychologically significant events, and this is a point at which individual differences can arise. The concept of *causal uncertainty* and a scale of measurement for it were developed by Weary and Edwards (1994, 1996) to account for individual differences in the ability of people to attribute causes in a social context. Attributed causes might range from external circumstances to the dispositional properties of other persons. The effects of causal uncertainty can depend upon personal resources for information processing as well as external factors (Weary, Vaughn, Stewart and Edwards 2006) and the accessibility of thoughts about the self (Edwards, Wichmanm and Weary 2009). Their model postulates that causal uncertainty has two components: (1) a cognitive construct consisting of beliefs about the self, which may suggest that a person does not understand or may be unable to detect causal relations in the social world; and (2) 'metacognitive feelings of uncertainty' (Edwards et al. 2009, p. 695). Beliefs about the self are important for a sense of agency.

The conception of more differentiated emotions being a product of differences in our sense of agency, particularly in complex social situations, could be a further step on the way towards a better understanding of the richly varied qualities of human emotion. The more we approach distinctively human qualities, the more room there is for diversity, complexity and subtlety in the experience and communication of feelings. The multidimensional semantic space in which emotions can be described signifies the many dimensions on which people can be psychologically separated from and approach their goals. We can expect the multiplicity of dimensions to depend upon the degree of cognitive complexity in the individual and in the culture. Variation in cognitive complexity is a factor in the subtle differentiation of feelings on many dimensions.

Averill has discussed 'intellectual emotions', taking *hope* as an example, saying that some emotions tend to be primarily cognitive or intellectual in nature (Averill 1991). It is the common experience of academia, and of people working in the arts and sciences, that intellectual passions have motivating properties directly, and not because they serve or mask other ends. So, for example, it is fitting to find such comments as: 'Readers will recognize in these essays and exchanges the motivating power of intellectual passion' (Bennett, Dennett, Hacker and Searle 2007, p. viii). Most people within and many outside the academy have experienced, at least on occasions, the excitement of mere ideas. Averill says that intellectual emotions have more power over us than the passions from which they differ, and that hope is similar to anger and love in the power it has to influence the way people behave, and also in that it is difficult to control. He suggests that because contemporary theories have a strong physiological emphasis, the effect is to 'dumb down' the character of human emotions that he described elsewhere as 'many splendored things' (Averill 1994).

It remains possible to reconcile an approach to emotions in terms of different degrees of complexity in subjective experience with the idea that there is a limited set of basic affective systems in the brain which underlie a great variety of emotions developed with personal experience in a shared culture. But it takes a poet or a novelist to even approach the complexity and subtlety of human experience. George Eliot, in *Middlemarch*, for instance, achieved something of it, but she admitted in her characters to struggling with its demands:

> Yet Dorothea had no distinctly shapen grievance that she could state even to herself; and in the midst of her confused thought and passion, the mental act that was struggling forth into clearness was a self-accusing cry that her feeling of desolation was the fault of her own spiritual poverty. (Eliot 1965, p. 224)
>
> Will again feared that he had gone too far; but the meaning we attach to words depends on our feeling, and his tone of angry regret had so much kindness in it for Dorothea's heart, which had always been giving out ardour and had never been fed with much from living beings around her, that she felt a new sense of gratitude and answered with a gentle smile. (Eliot 1965, p. 253)

Invocation of Consciousness

There is a fundamental question about consciousness of feelings and their role in motivation that requires more attention in a basic theory than it has received to date. It has been suggested that in the evolution of mammals affective arousal was the original source of consciousness. Panksepp has described 'consciousness-creating affective circuits', and Mandler referred to emotional arousal from novel stimuli giving rise to 'consciousness-constructing mechanisms'. Consciousness is associated with processes of integration (see Chapter 7). Could it be a basic biological function of emotion to bring consciousness into effect in a process of cognitive integration? It is suggested by Mandler, Damasio, Panksepp and others that a level of neural development is reached in which emotions triggers consciousness. When aroused by a novel stimulus or conceptual conflict, feelings reinforce attention to arousing conditions, thus initiating an amplifying reverberation that 'keeps the ball bouncing' until discrepancies are resolved. (See curiosity and the resolution of conceptual conflict in Chapter 2.)

Mandler's Hypothesis of Emotion Causing Consciousness

Mandler proposed a 'discrepancy detection mechanism' which is 'important in bringing to bear consciousness-constructing mechanisms' in troubleshooting and in the awareness of unusual and unexpected events. 'Thus, any situation which will arouse the visceral system will also set the stage for a conscious construction' (Mandler 2002, pp. 102–103).

This setting of the stage for conscious construction, in which Mandler postulates an association between consciousness and emotion, points to the crucial role of novelty in constructive cognitive processes. This effect of discrepancies calls for an adaptive response to unexpected situations: i.e. more adaptive than automatic responding. These are the situations in which consciousness enables integration of information from diverse sources for the development of new ways of seeing the world and acting effectively with originality.

In an organism with sufficient cognitive capacity a response to discrepant stimuli would, in the absence of debilitating anxiety, potentially include conscious construction of goals and hypotheses about choices and commitments that can be made. Potential commitments have a cognitive representation in a manner analogous to thinking 'I am thinking of doing X', as in prospective memory. Commitments consist of the allocation of resources with attention to a response alternative. Voluntary attention, when combined with response selection and resource allocation, is an expression of willpower in purposive behaviour. (See the conclusion of Chapter 7 on volition and the discussion of conscious will in Chapter 10.)

It is in the processing of novel input, in which the prefrontal and parietal cortices are critically involved, and when automaticity is not adaptive (Shallice and Burgess 1998), that consciousness is required, or 'consciousness-constructing mechanisms', in Mandler's terms, are brought to bear. By bringing initially unconscious somatic elements of emotion together with consciousness-constructing cognitive reactions to novelty, Mandler incorporated into his theoretical framework what Damasio claimed was commonly missing in evaluative accounts of emotion (Damasio 1994, 2000a).

Damasio's Regulatory Function of Emotions

Damasio conceived the feedback function of emotions as being derived from the regulation of bodily functions: 'Processes of emotion and feeling are part and parcel of the neural machinery for biological regulation, whose core is constituted by controls, drives, and instincts' (Damasio 1994, p. 83; see also Damasio 2010). In his view, initially, homeostasis was the basic process for bodily regulation. Later he preferred Stephen Rose's term homeodynamic as 'more appropriate than homeostasis because it suggests the process of seeking an adjustment rather than a fixed point of balance' (Damasio 2003, p. 302, n. 5). He made a positive emphasis in his review of William James's theory of emotion, saying that 'Emotions are also conducive, directly or indirectly, to well-being,' and so the point of stability being sought was 'located in the positive range of the affective spectrum rather than being neutral' (Damasio 2004, p. 4). It is then closer to the cognitive motivation theory in which we rely upon the dynamic effects of an incomplete gestalt that moves the action towards a new set of conditions, never returning to a previous state of affairs as would be assumed in a homeostatic model.

In any case, Damasio understands the purposeful regulatory functions of emotion as definitive, with a consequent effective role for the subjective elements of emotion. Referring first to emotion as a set of unconscious reactions, he says that emotions are part of the basic mechanisms of life regulation. 'Emotions and related phenomena are the foundation for feelings, the mental events that form the bedrock of our minds' (Damasio 2003, p. 28). Damasio saw the emotional state as being induced by an appraisal or evaluation of an *emotionally competent stimulus* in a process that encompasses a number of physiological steps and cognitive outcomes. This regulatory combination includes the information value of both feelings and the bodily aspects of emotion. Damasio referred to Spinoza's preference for the word 'affect' used with different qualifications to signify *internal* or *external* phenomena[3] as corresponding to his terms 'feeling' and 'emotion'. 'If an emotion is a collection of changes in body state connected to particular mental images that have activated a specific brain system, *the essence of feeling an emotion is the experience of such changes in juxtaposition to the mental images that initiated the cycle*' (Damasio 1994, p. 145, emphasis in the original). This is implied in the somatic marker hypothesis that we will come to shortly. In the light of contemporary multicomponent definitions of emotion, a simple construction is to prefer the term 'feelings' for the conscious elements of emotion, and 'emotion' for the inclusive concept of unconscious somatic and information processing elements together with feelings.

Rolls's Reflexive Theory of the Consciousness of Emotions

Rolls presented a theory of consciousness based upon cognitive processes of reflection:

> [C]onsciousness may be the state that arises in a system that can think about (or reflect on) its own (or other peoples') thoughts, that is in a system capable of second- or higher-order thoughts (Rosenthal 1990, Dennett 1991, Rosenthal 1993, 1997).... [A]ccording to the analysis, having a higher-order thought about

[3] In Damasio's understanding of the translation he prefers, 'Spinoza uses neither the word emotion nor the word feeling but rather affect – in Latin, *affectus* – a word that is appropriate for both concepts. He says that, "By *affectus* I mean the modifications of the body, whereby the active power of the said body is increased or diminished, aided or constrained, and also the ideas of such modifications" (Spinoza, The Ethics, Part III).'

a lower-order thought is necessary for the lower-order thought to be conscious. (Rolls 2005, p. 404)

Although the last point in this quote suggesting that a lower-order thought cannot be conscious unless it is reflected upon by a higher-order thought has been rejected by other theorists (Izard 2000; Katz 2000; Panksepp and Biven 2012), the reflective nature of consciousness described by Rolls is widely shared with others including Mandler and Damasio. This reflexive function is a fundamental attribute of the self (Baumeister 1998; Baumeister and Vohs 2004). Baars and colleagues, whose work was important in our consideration of the role of consciousness in working memory (Chapter 7), said, controversially, in a later work, 'Humans seem to have a common intuition of an observing self that has access to conscious sensations, inner speech, images and thoughts' (Baars et al. 2003, p. 671). They specifically rejected Gilbert Ryle's famous philosophical denunciation of this idea of an observing self (Ryle 1949), saying that current evidence seems to be broadly supportive.

Rolls depends upon the representational function of language in his reflective or meta-cognitive theory of consciousness, but it need not imply an interpreter or perceiver as an independent agent separate from what is perceived. A phrase like 'the observing self,' used by Baars, may be unfortunate terminology in some contexts, although it is not intended in the sense that Jackendoff wishes to avoid in suggesting that 'representation' and 'symbol' imply an interpreter or perceiver such that a symbol represents or symbolizes something 'to so-and-so' (Jackendoff 2008, pp. 5–6). The use of terms such as 'the observing self' and 'representation' need not imply a dualist conception of the person, but rather the reflexive nature of the self, in which what is observed is included in our understanding of the observer. We look at ourselves. We who look at ourselves are ourselves.

Some writers like Baars have encouraged an expectation that the self is engaged fundamentally in all conscious perception, but it does not always include reflexive functions of the self (Baars 2002a; Baars et al. 2003; Baars 2005a; see also Chapter 7). Recent studies that employed brain imaging have found well-described patterns associated with consciousness of sensory events (involving the sensory cortex) to be different from those for self-referent events (involving prefrontal areas). You can be aware of a sensory event without reflecting upon it. 'Do you really have to think about the thought of stubbing your toe in the dark (or any unanticipated trauma) before feeling pain or anger?' (Izard 2000, p. 203). Rolls's speculative theory of consciousness being constituted by higher-level thoughts reflecting upon lower-level thoughts appears unlikely to survive in its entirety, but as one possible mechanism among others it is compatible with the reflexive nature of the self which remains typical of human consciousness. Even with that limitation, the relationship of 'self' to consciousness can still apply to aspects of self-consciousness, introspection, self-image, personality characteristics, planning and decision-making in which feelings are important.

The Somatic Marker Hypothesis

Damasio's somatic marker hypothesis (SMH) states that signals from the body originating in homeostatic (or preferably homeodynamic) adjustments are represented and regulated in the emotion circuitry of the brain, particularly incorporating functions of the ventromedial prefrontal cortex (VMPFC, other authors refer to the orbitofrontal cortex, that is to the area located just above the eye). It is important to note that in his later work Damasio (2010) agreed with Panksepp that the emotion circuitry of the brain need not always include such higher cortical processes as those of the prefrontal cortex, but we should also note that in the quote below Damasio defined somatic markers as feelings generated by *secondary* emotions that *have been connected, by learning, to predicted future outcomes of certain scenarios*. They cannot be aligned with Panksepp's basic emotions which are mainly subcortical. Panksepp himself gave a similar definition of secondary emotions.

According to Damasio, when a bad outcome comes to mind, you experience an unpleasant gut feeling, so a somatic state 'marks' an image of a response alternative, and that marker is utilized directly in decision-making. It depends on more than pure reason: 'In short, *somatic markers are a special instance of feelings generated from secondary emotions*. Those emotions and feelings *have been connected, by learning, to predicted future outcomes of certain scenarios*' (Damasio 1994, p. 174, original emphasis).

A somatic marker focuses attention, allowing the individual to choose from fewer alternatives. In some people, frontal-lobe patients in particular, lack of emotional arousal before decision-making results in failure to direct attention to a limited set of potentially beneficial alternative responses. Sociopaths and psychopaths may be cool in the same way that patients with damaged prefrontal lobes are (Saver and Damasio 1991). A 'sick culture' can affect normal adults similarly (Damasio 1994, p. 173ff). Failure to limit the range of options from which to choose has been called Hamlet's problem (Fodor 1987). It is a version of the frame or search problem. The search for and testing of consequences can expand indefinitely when attention is not sufficiently focussed. Damasio's theory of somatic markers has been recommended as a solution to the frame problem (Evans 2004).

Damasio's Images of Somatic Events

Damasio's use of 'image' as a basic term in his theory makes it a cognitive theory – albeit one that employs images of somatic events. He refers to two kinds of image, i.e. to images of response options and to representations of somatic changes. The somatic marker hypothesis (SMH) refers to an association between these two kinds of image. Response options are said to be 'marked' by association with bodily changes either directly or by representation in the brain of bodily actions that are expected to occur. Damasio defined an image as 'a mental pattern in any of the sensory modalities,' in which the brain turns neural patterns in its nerve cell circuits into 'the explicit mental patterns which constitute the highest level of biological phenomena' (Damasio 1999, p. 9).

It was in the use of images of somatic events that Damasio defended the theory of William James against claims that Cannon's experiments (Cannon 1927, 1929) had shown that James was wrong in basing his explanation of emotion on awareness of changes in the body (Damasio 2004). Beside direct representation of somatic events, Damasio includes in his theory images of *simulated* somatic events. He agreed with James that some feelings can have purely cognitive origins. It is commonly believed that William James represented feelings as due only to somatic events, but in fact, in his original article 'What is an emotion?,' James made allowance in exceptional cases for 'the liveliest subjective feelings, either of eye or ear, or of the more visceral and emotional sort, as a result of pure nerve-central activity, with complete peripheral repose' (James 1884, footnote p. 200).

The Contribution of Emotions to Decision-Making

In his formulation of the somatic marker hypothesis, Damasio drew on his and his colleagues' experience with patients who had suffered damage to the orbital cortex, especially the ventromedial prefrontal cortex (VMPFC). They reviewed the famous case of Phineas Gage, a railroad construction worker who suffered damage to his prefrontal cortex in a blasting accident when an iron rod passed right through his skull, entering his eye and coming out the top of his head (Damasio, Grabowski, Frank, Galaburda and Damasio 1994). Although Gage made a remarkable recovery and appeared in many respects to be able to think and act normally, he showed great changes of personality. He changed from being a conservative and responsible foreman and family man to one prone to outbursts of swearing and anti-social behaviour, and who had a general inability to make good judgements in social situations so that he could no longer hold a job or maintain a marriage and friendships. Damasio reviewed many cases with similar prefrontal damage and 'all had decision-making defect and flat emotion and feeling. The powers of reason and experience of emotion decline together even when the normal knowledge and intelligence functions remain' (Damasio 1994, pp. 53–54).

Patients with damage to VMPFC had difficulty in expressing emotion, experiencing feelings, making plans and envisaging the consequences of their actions. Damasio hypothesized that such emotional changes were the cause of their decision making deficit and that these changes were a result of a loss of normal capacity in the VMPFC to monitor and process information on body states represented by signals from the viscera, internal milieu, and the skeletal and smooth muscles (Damasio, Tranel and Damasio 1990; Damasio et al. 1991, Damasio 1994). He concluded that emotions combining somatic and cognitive functions distinguish between alternative courses of action and are necessary for decision-making in complex social situations.

Conscious Strategies as an Alternative to the SMH

Although at first developed from clinical observations, much of the research on the somatic marker hypothesis (SMH) subsequent to Damasio's original publications (Damasio et al. 1991; Damasio 1994, 1996) has employed an experimental procedure developed by his colleague Bechara and used initially to explore 'insensitivity to future consequences following damage to human prefrontal cortex' (Bechara, Damasio, Damasio and Anderson 1994; Bechara, Damasio, Tranel and Damasio 1997). Bechara's procedure became known as the Iowa Gambling Task. This experimental paradigm appeared to represent very well the processes postulated by Damasio and his colleagues, but it has come under challenge on several grounds, and particularly in regard to whether the resulting advantageous decision-making could be a consequence of conscious cognition rather than the hypothesized emotional arousal affecting decisions by nonconscious 'marking' of response alternatives.

The principal critics of the Iowa Gambling Task experiments, Maia and McClelland, concluded that 'our data provide no reasons to posit that nonconscious biases guide advantageous behavior in this task before knowledge that is consciously accessible does' (Maia and McClelland 2004, p. 16075). Bechara and Damasio and colleagues replied that the SMH was not about the difference between conscious and nonconscious processes: 'The central feature of the SMH is not that non-conscious biases accomplish decisions in the absence of conscious knowledge, but rather that emotion-related signals assist cognitive processes even when they are non-conscious' (Bechara, Damasio, Tranel and Damasio 2005, p. 159). This represented at least a change of emphasis, and it directly supports our use of the signalling function of emotions in motivation theory.

A Cognitive Theory of the Function of Emotion in Motivation

The key point of research findings reviewed in this chapter is that cognitive representations of emotions can contribute to cognitive processes having motivational properties. Among similar conceptions, Damasio's SMH offers a framework for discussing how the somatic aspects of emotion may be represented in cognitive processes that are motivating and contribute to decision-making. The cognitive processes of decision-making include both conscious feelings and those components of emotion that do not enter consciousness, but in cognitive motivation it is in the integrative functions of consciousness described by Baars, Tononi, Koch and others that emotion has its principal effects.

The Joint Operation of Cognitive and Emotional Processes

The processing of information on both the cognitive and the somatic components of emotion is itself a cognitive operation. We noted in Chapter 1 how Bolles envisaged the future construction of a theoretical 'system which contains just one matrix containing both motivational and structural mechanisms; I predict that both kinds of mechanisms will be cognitive' (Bolles 1974, p. 19). As we have seen in this chapter, there have been many recent developments in the kind of theory that brings together affective and cognitive functions in a single frame of reference. Some are the result of debates on the relative importance of cognitive and somatic factors a generation ago, and some are substantial independent new formulations. Such developments help to overcome the dichotomy that motivation psychologists such as Deci and Ryan believed was necessary in their distinction between cognitive and motivational perspectives (Deci and Ryan 1985).

Many of us have reinforced that unfortunate division between motivational and cognitive approaches. This chapter is testimony to the fact that I was only half right when I said many years ago, 'The pleasurable integration of a signal with a category system is assumed to be a general principle of learning, but it is from the process of integration and not the attendant quality of pleasure that explanatory principles are derived' (Beswick 1971, p. 159). I was right about the process of integration, but too keen to exclude anything that might support drive reduction theories derived from Hull and Freud, and so missed the feedback function of emotions as signals in the cognitive processes of motivation. That was a fundamental mistake.

Overview of Emotion as a Factor in Cognitive Motivation

In the general theory of cognitive motivation, as in other formulations of self-regulation and goal-oriented behaviour (Forgas et al. 2009), the function of emotion is to act as a signalling system for purposive behaviour. (See also Baumeister et al. 2007 in regard to emotion having a signalling function rather than being a direct cause of behaviour, and Tice 2009 on how emotions affect self-regulation.) Early in this chapter similar contributions on the information value of emotions by Clore, Frijda, Gray and others were noted. The theories and supporting empirical research reviewed in this chapter suggest a theoretical system along the following lines:

1. Emotions are signals that provide feedback on goal-oriented activities, both initiating and guiding motivated behaviour.
2. All components of emotion, peripheral and central, somatic and cognitive, conscious and nonconscious, are represented centrally in cognition.
3. Images of goals are represented together with memories of past experience of adaptive behaviour in purposive sequences.
4. This information is processed in working memory and will often involve conscious processes of integration across brain systems.
5. Feelings, the conscious aspects of emotions, are employed in conscious planning, adjustment of ongoing action, and in the appreciation of salient features of the environment and the person.
6. Nonconscious components of emotion, which might include bodily processes that are not consciously monitored or which are simulated cognitively without conscious recognition, and other unconscious cognitive elements of emotion such as memories processed without becoming conscious, can act as further information on the relationship of the person's present position to a goal.
7. Feelings and the nonconscious elements of emotion can be processed either separately or together in the cognitive evaluation of a situation in relation to the fulfilment of purposes.
8. Emotions also have the potential to change goals. The process of monitoring the disparity between a goal and the present situation, signalled by emotions, may result in modifications not only to an action

plan but also to the goal itself in a creative process of progressive feedback.

9. While there appear to be a limited number of basic affective systems in the brain for such emotions as fear, anger, care, grief, lust, play and seeking, mature human emotions are subtle and complex compositions. We receive and employ signals that are not merely positive or negative indications of whether we are on course or off course, near or far from a limited number of goals, but human emotions have meanings that vary greatly in a multidimensional semantic space.

One key quality in the conceptualization of emotion as a signalling system in motivation is that it represents emotion as a means to an end, not an end in itself. There are reasons why sentient organisms have been selected in evolution to have emotions. It may be helpful to contrast such a utilitarian understanding of emotion in motivation, the practical reason why we have emotions, with the effect of drugs taken to achieve a subjective experience. Motivated behaviour that is adaptive is not aimed at achieving the feedback of emotional experience for its own sake, but at goals which are behavioural and cognitive objectives defined by individual and collective survival needs and by personally meaningful outcomes. The effect of drugs taken to induce an affective state makes emotion an end in itself. While drugs with direct effects on consciousness have many admirable uses, not least in the relief of pain or perhaps in social facilitation, it is not uncommon for people to intuit the prospect of cheating oneself by cutting across the evolutionarily significant and personally fulfilling function of emotion as a means to an end.[4] The effect of addiction is to reduce purposive behaviour except in pursuit of the drug, and thus to traduce the adaptive function of emotions. Human autonomy embodies the means to facilitate choice amongst, and the capacity to create, a great range of options, with varieties of affective value, not all of which will demonstrate adaptive functional relationships between emotion and motivation. The function of emotion in purposive behaviour is thus subject to human agency and freedom, which may facilitate, vary or limit its adaptive potential.

There is another important qualification to the purposive function of emotions that has not been given attention in this work. That is that our

[4] I remember discussing this point, or something very like it, with Ralph Metzner, a fellow graduate student at Harvard around 1960 and well known later for his research on psychedelic drugs which he had already begun with Timothy Leary and Richard Alpert (later known as Ram Dass). He commented then that Arthur Koestler had a point when he suggested that the view from the summit was better when you had actually climbed the mountain.

feelings are not an altogether reliable guide for goal-oriented behaviour. We sometimes need therapeutic interventions, but that is a subject for a different book.

In the next chapter I develop a view of goal formation in which the cognitive representation of emotions in an incomplete gestalt plays a part in setting up expectations of the kind of feedback that will guide purposive behaviour. That feedback takes place in a process of cognitive completion. In previous chapters I have advanced the idea of an incomplete gestalt as the heart of an explanation of the motivating power of goals in a cognitive theory. The nature of commitments to goal seeking was introduced briefly as an aspect of volition at the conclusion of the previous chapter and will receive further attention in the next chapter. Willpower is an important topic in this field. It is one on which significant research has been conducted in recent years (Baumeister and Tierney 2011). We need to examine these points in regard to the nature of goals and intentions. This will be our aim in the next two chapters.

Summary

In the general theory of cognitive motivation, emotions are signs along the pathway to fulfilment and signals for the initiation of action in pursuit of a goal. In this way emotion can be taken into the same hypothetical set of information-processing operations as cognition. It is an essential component of the means by which goals are formed, commitments made and purposive behaviour is directed. Feelings are elements in cognitive motivation together with nonconscious affective components of emotions. The function of emotion demonstrates fundamental processes in cognitive motivation together with those of consciousness and working memory that were discussed in the previous chapter.

There was an early contrast between cognitive and somatic emphases in theories of emotion, which led to multicomponent definitions of emotion that included cognitive and behavioural components together with subjective states and physiological changes. Emotions were also defined in terms of the reinforcing value of stimuli as rewards and punishers which in their interaction with different situations may produce greatly varied affective states. The question arose of whether there is a limited number of evolutionarily shaped basic emotions, such as fear and anger, which Darwin suggested humans share with other mammals. Panksepp has described seven primary affective systems (SEEKING, RAGE, FEAR, LUST/LOVE, CARE, PANIC/GRIEF and PLAY). He suggests that secondary conditioned emotions, and tertiary cognitive and social emotions, are developed from the seven basic affective responses.

I review arguments for recognising complex and subtle emotions among an infinite range of human feelings in a multidimensional semantic frame of reference.

Emotion is seen by some theorists to be an instigator of consciousness, and thereby a contributor to the construction of meaning, given the integrating function of consciousness. These theorists envisage reflexive conditions for the experience of an emotion in which there is a correlation of the ongoing representations of the body with the neural representations constituting the self. Damasio's somatic marker hypothesis (SMH) is that emotions 'mark' response alternatives as favourable or unfavourable, and thereby facilitate decision-making without relying upon rational thinking; but critical reviews have established that conscious strategies can be adopted from knowledge of response alternatives to account for the same choices. Cognitive theories take us beyond the limitations of somatically based theories of emotion, such as the somatic marker hypothesis, at least in its original form.

In conclusion, I propose a theoretical framework for understanding the function of emotion in cognitive motivation by treating both cognition and emotion in information-processing terms. Processes of evaluation that result in the elicitation of somatic responses are cognitive, and the consequent affective elements are primary sources for cognitive operations that have the potential to bring emotions into consciousness and working memory as signs of relationships to a goal. Goals may then not only be sought but redefined in a creative process of progressive feedback in the resolution of incomplete gestalts.

9 Goals

> The pursuance of future ends and the choice of means for their attainment are the mark and criterion of the presence of mentality in a phenomenon.
>
> – James 1890

Introduction

'Human beings are by nature goal oriented. This is no longer a controversial truth in psychology, but neither is it a trivial one' (Emmons 2005, p. 15). In the Introduction I developed the idea that purposive behaviour implies motivation, so that we can look for internal processes that give direction to behaviour and initiate action. In this chapter and the next I seek an understanding of the nature of internal representations of possible future states of affairs and the commitment to attain them.

The Definition of Goals and Intentions

'A goal is a cognitive representation of a future object that one is committed to approach or avoid' (Elliot 2006, p. 113); or we could 'define goals as internal representations of desired states, where states are broadly construed as outcomes, events, or processes' (Austin and Vancouver 1996, p. 338). Goals may also be represented as personal strivings which uniquely characterize a person (Emmons 1989, 1999a, 2005). When such goals are conscious, voluntariness in commitment to action may be implied besides cognitive representation and desire in striving for a goal defined as 'an imagined or envisaged state condition toward which a person aspires and which drives voluntary activity' (Karoly 1993, p. 274). Summing up the work of many contributors to a collected work on the study of goal concepts, Pervin defined a goal as 'a mental image or other end point representation associated with affect towards which action may be directed' (Pervin 1989, p. 474). These definitions all point to commonly recognised properties of a goal that are included in the general theory of cognitive motivation, although none of them is a complete description in cognitive theoretical terms.

In the general theory of cognitive motivation *there is a changing relationship of unrealized potential between cognitive elements representing present and future states of affairs as goal-directed behaviour proceeds.* Feelings signify that relationship between the present and the future that is represented in an image of a goal in relation to the present situation. This is the incomplete gestalt of a *goal orientation.* The goal itself is a more limited incomplete gestalt. Goals are representations in the present cognitive map of possible future outcomes, events or processes, which are identifiable unitary components of the map with potential to guide purposive behaviour. Awareness of incompleteness in an incomplete gestalt implies some idea of what the complete image might be like and suggests how it might be completed. In that way it gives direction to future behaviour. In the general theory I have been developing, an incomplete gestalt is a crucial component of the cognitive map which gives rise to cognitive processes with motivating properties.

An intention is implied in a commitment to reach a goal (Bandura 2001, p. 6). It is a kind of goal orientation in which agency is assumed on the part of a person so committed. In the next chapter I will be examining various approaches to intentional agency in the pursuit of cognitively represented goals, and the means of their attainment. This chapter is focussed on the concept of a goal which is included in the idea of an intention.

Pervin (1989) enunciated a principle that is typical of cognitive motivation theories, namely that the cognitively defined concept of goal characteristically departed from physiological deficit views of motivation (see also McClelland 1965; Pervin 1983). On the other hand, Pervin also suggested that the concept of a goal represents a more motivational view of personality than theories referring mainly to traits. Goals can be tied to the information-processing and purposive concepts of action plans, strategies, beliefs and self-regulation. These are cognitive concepts of purposive behaviour so that many aspects of personality may be represented cognitively in reference to goal concepts. As Pervin noted, goals and self-concepts are intimately linked. Goals have both cognitive and affective features and contribute to the definition of the self, while self-knowledge and self-efficacy beliefs influence goal-directed action. Having both affective and cognitive features, and being closely related to broad aspects of the self, in this understanding goals play a major role in the activation and organisation of behaviour.

Consciousness and the Organisation of Goals

The development of cognitive psychology was concerned with a shift away from external stimulus-based control towards understanding actions as being guided by an internal representation of a desired state of affairs; however, it came to be questioned whether that kind of cognitive control necessarily required consciousness of a goal. 'Cognitive control of thought, feeling, and behaviour differs from stimulus-based control because it involves actively maintained internal representations. There is no requirement that a goal be conscious, or even accessible to awareness, just that it be actively maintained' (Gray et al. 2005, p. 70).

Consciousness enters into the function of goals in cognitive motivation theory in a quite a different way. In Chapter 7 I have discussed the integrating function consciousness. It is not so much that conscious attention is focussed on a goal, though it may be, and that could be important, but that the relationship between a goal and the present situation requires a resolution that involves integration of disparate or conflicting elements in a cognitive map. Some of the elements to be integrated might not be conscious, and these might include non-conscious components of emotion, but consciousness facilitates integration of the whole.

A common theme in the literature is that goals are organised into a system, and that such a system is capable of change over time, remaining flexible to meet challenging demands (Allport 1961b; Pervin 1989). In the dynamics of goal systems, strategies are developed to achieve multiple goals by adaptive sequencing of aspirations if the simultaneous seeking of certain goals is not possible. Such planning is characteristic of conscious intentionality. It is one of the marks of foresight and planning (Feather 1982b) that it is under intentional and voluntary control which I discuss in the next chapter. This is not to say that setting priority among goals is always a rational cognitive process. Emotion plays a critical role. Indeed, it is one of the functions of emotion in cognition to mark the priority of goals. Many theorists have suggested that emotions assign value or prioritise processing and serve as interrupting signals redirecting ongoing behaviour (Simon 1967; Oatley and Johnson-Laird 1987; Dolan 2002; Gray et al. 2005).

Goal constructs can be organised in a variety of ways. From a wide-ranging review of goal constructs in psychology Austin and Vancouver (1996) discussed the complex taxonomy of personal goals that had been developed by Ford and Nichols (1987). Ford later proposed 24 goal categories including such diverse and sophisticated goals as exploration, understanding, superiority, resource acquisition, mastery, creativity, happiness, safety and belongingness (Ford 1992). It was one of many such classifications (Murphy and Alexander 2000). In his comments on Murphy and Alexander, Pintrich contrasted Ford's list of 24 general goals with more specific task goals:

> There are a large number of other general goal content constructs such as personal strivings, personal projects, current concerns, possible selves, and life tasks that reflect a more general perspective on goals and reflect different goal contents that individuals may be striving for in many contexts (see Austin and Vancouver 1996, Emmons 1997); for reviews). (Pintrich 2000b, p. 93; see also Pintrich, Conley and Kempler 2003)

'Goals influence the selection, organization, and retrieval of information' (Pervin 1989, p. 478). Goals are thus fundamentally important cognitive components of motivation. Pervin had noted at an earlier time, when commenting on 'the cognitive revolution and what it leaves out', that the rise of cognition as an area of interest had tended to supplant motivation, but that in later years theories derived from the cognitive revolution were 'leading the way in exploring relations between motivation and cognition' (Pervin 1989, p. 2). These are the theories that contributed to the recent conceptions of consciousness and working memory (see Chapter 7), and the role of emotion (Chapter 8), which are required for understanding the basic processes of cognitive motivation.

The Gestalt Heritage

Gestalt ideas provided roots for later theories of cognitive motivation. In addition to Allport, Lewin was a key link, as shown in Chapter 4. In Tolman's work it gave rise to the view that behaviour is purposive and cognitive (see Chapter 3). Tolman said of behaviour in general, "These purposes and cognitions are its very warp and woof' (Tolman 1932/1949, p. 6). Pervin claimed that '[g]oal concepts have almost always been part of cognitive models' (Pervin 1989, pp. 6, 8). They are present in micro processes of situational adjustment, while in the macro model of cognitive motivation goals are critical elements in the dynamic organisation of cognitive maps at the level of the whole person. In this forward-looking perspective, Pervin saw Gordon Allport's ideas on conscious purposive integration (Allport 1955) as reflecting Gestalt theory. It undoubtedly influenced his emphasis on the purposive processes of 'becoming' in personality theory. Long-term goals of personal fulfilment are part of the high-level processes of personality integration that contribute to a sense of purpose and meaning that I discuss in Chapter 12.

Gestalt psychology offered what was essentially a cognitive theory of goal states, perceived situations and the dynamic interactions between them (Lewin 1926; Lewin et al. 1936; Heider 1960). Tolman's theory of learning employed the concept of goals in a cognitive explanation of purposive behaviour (Tolman 1948), but it was nevertheless seen by Tolman himself, and later by sympathetic critics such as Bruner (see Chapter 2), to be a revision of behaviourism rather than a departure from it (Tolman 1927, 1932/1949, 1948; Bruner 1990). Nevertheless, his concept of cognitive maps describing a context for goal-directed behaviour was taken up by many others who favoured cognitive theories of motivation. There was a second route to cognitive theories of goals that developed in part from feedback ideas in cybernetic models, which were at the same time inspired in part by Tolman and influenced by Gestalt psychology (Kimble, Wertheimer and White 1991; Murray 1995).

Early Gestalt Theories

The systematic empirical investigation of Gestalt concepts began with what became known as the Berlin group, principally Wertheimer, Köhler and Koffka, around 1910. The concept of gestalt qualities had been defined a generation earlier by von Ehrenfels (1890, 1890/1988). He used the term 'form quality' or 'Gestalt quality' to refer to the direct perception of a melody as distinct from the sensations of the individual notes, and to a square as the squareness aspect of the appropriate combination of four lines. In reference to the 'sensing' of a melody, he extended the notion of 'form' from simultaneously present visual patterns to sequential patterns in auditory phenomena. The form of a melody referred to the preservation of relationships between notes in spite of changes in the particular physical stimuli when a tune is played in a different key or on a different instrument. With both visual and auditory data a gestalt appears directly without rational inference as a clear image that reduces ambiguity (Smith and Ehrenfels 1988; Ash 1995; Murray 1995). In Gestalt theory it is not inferred; it enters consciousness directly; but it came to be understood that it did so only after much unconscious processing as distinct from conscious inference. The same gestalt principles were applied to thinking as to perception. Ehrenfels also conceived of higher levels of abstraction forming gestalts of gestalts.

Ehrenfels took from 'the analysis of the sensations' by the physicist and philosopher of science Ernst Mach (1886, 1897) the key idea that 'we are able directly to "sense" spatial shapes or tone-Gestalten or melodies' (von Ehrenfels 1890/1988, p. 82). Such perceptions or 'impressions' of whole figures or forms were distinct from the summation of the elements of sensation which gave rise to them. Ehrenfels defined a gestalt quality as 'a positive content of presentation bound up in consciousness' in the presence of separable elements (p. 93). The philosopher of phenomenology, Husserl, an associate of Ehrenfels, in his 1891 *Philosophy of Arithmetic* had a similar idea in regard to the direct perception of the quality of a whole figure perceived in a collection: 'a certain characteristic quality [Beschaffenheit] of the unitary total intuition of the given collection, capable of being grasped in a single glance' (Smith 1988, pp. 18–19). Ehrenfels relied upon examples such as melody or shape, rather than a formal definition of 'gestalt'. Significantly, it is in consciousness that the gestalt quality is 'bound up' with the 'complex' of elements that he called the 'foundation' of that quality. However, being 'bound up in consciousness' does not mean that conscious rational processes produce gestalts. We might now say that consciousness facilitates the integration of cognitive elements (see Chapter 7). There is a process of cognitive integration that may be unconscious in part, which leads to conscious awareness of a new form.

Many years after his 1890 foundational paper, von Ehrenfels recalled that 'The theory of Gestalt-qualities began with the attempt to answer a question: What is melody?'[1]

> The decisive step in the founding of a theory of Gestalt-quality was my own assertion: when the memory-images of successive notes are present as a simultaneous complex in consciousness, then an idea *(Forstellung)*, belonging to a new category, can arise in consciousness, a unitary idea, which is connected in a manner peculiar to itself with the ideas *(Vorstellungen)* of the complex of notes involved. The idea of this whole belongs to a new category, for which the name "founded contents" *(jundierte Inhalte)* came into use.[2] (von Ehrenfels 1937, p. 521)

Ehrenfels applied the same notion of gestalt as in the example of a melody to visual figures and to moods, feelings and emotions. He included in the concept of a gestalt the integration of data from different modalities, complex memories and inner perception. These qualities were described later by Wertheimer who had attended lectures by von Ehrenfels when a student at Prague. He developed the basic concepts of Gestalt theory in discussions with Köhler and Koffka in Berlin around 1910.

The Concept of Prägnanz

Wertheimer's concept of Prägnanz, meaning the goodness of form or precision, succinctness, clearcutness or pithiness of an image, defines the

[1] 'Like so many of the leading figures in the Gestalt movement, Ehrenfels was a passionate musician. He took lessons in composition from Anton Bruckner, and made a name for himself as the librettist of a number of Wagner-inspired music-dramas performed in Elberfeld and Prague between 1904 and 1925' (Smith 1988, pp. 10–11).

[2] This short paper was dictated by Ehrenfels to his wife in 1931 shortly before his death and published some years later.

essential qualities of a gestalt. In his historical review of Wertheimer's concept, Barry Smith followed distinctions between the various 'dimensions' of Prägnanz made by Edwin Rausch (Rausch 1966) that he described as distinctions 'between the several varieties of order given in experience' (Smith and Ehrenfels 1988, p. 62). These dimensions or aspects of *order* were lawfulness, originality and integrity, as general principles of organisation, and two further formal dimensions of Prägnanz, simplicity and diversity, 'both of which are of particular relevance in the sphere of aesthetics' (p. 65). In Smith's summary (pp. 62–64),

> The first dimension, *lawfulness*, is a matter of regularity. A whole lacking this quality appears arbitrary or accidental, as if its parts have been thrown together at random; whereas lawfulness presupposes some intelligible context or reference system such that the structure or structures instance some species or kind.
>
> The second dimension of Prägnanz, *originality*, is a matter of the primacy, the autonomy of a phenomenon, its capacity to serve as a prototype or master. When this quality is lacking the figure signifies that something is derived, secondary, obtained from some initial structure by a systematic process of transformation. Originality, in this understanding, presupposes lawfulness.
>
> Prägnanz as *integrity* constitutes its third dimension. It is a matter of that which is whole, complete, intact, integral, as opposed to that which is disturbed, or incomplete.

The Possibility of an Incomplete Gestalt

Given the importance in Wertheimer's description of these qualities of Prägnanz for the definition of a gestalt, there might appear to be something self-contradictory in the very idea of an *incomplete* gestalt. Are not gestalts by nature complete? Is completeness not what the idea of a gestalt is all about? Do not whole figures click into place when a gestalt switch occurs? Wertheimer's principle of *Prägnanz* as the fundamental principle defining a gestalt includes completeness, even fullness, as in the cognate word 'pregnant'. In Gestalt theory we automatically join the dots to see a complete figure. In the classical tradition of Gestalt theory, from Wertheimer, Köhler and Koffka, the perception of a gestalt is immediate, *sui generis*, not derived or inferred, or the result of a judgement being made.

Although he allowed for the possibility of the foundation complex of stimulus elements entering consciousness without the experience of a gestalt, saying that not every claimant need be crowned, Ehrenfels nevertheless insisted that when a gestalt was perceived, it was an immediate direct perception and not a rational inference: 'Gestalt qualities are given in consciousness simultaneously with their foundations, without any activity of mind specifically directed toward them' (von Ehrenfels 1890/1988, p. 112). So could a gestalt be anything other than complete?

Von Ehrenfels approached the idea of an incomplete gestalt when he postulated degrees of 'formedness', saying: 'The fact that there is such a thing as a *degree of formedness* [*Gestaltung*], that every Gestalt has a certain *Gestalt level*, is of fundamental significance' (von Ehrenfels 1916/1988, p. 118). He said that for a given degree of multiplicity 'those Gestalten are higher which bind this multiplicity into a stronger unity' (p. 118). In the same paper he speculated upon gestalt level and purity being '*values* for our human feeling and desiring' (p. 119). 'Perhaps all valuing of psychic and psychoid beings can be reduced to a drive towards level and purity of Gestalten – all desire to satisfaction of this drive, all pain to its inhibition' (p. 120). This is close to the possibility I have entertained elsewhere, of the incomplete gestalt being a general model of all motivation, including need satisfaction, although I apply it only to cognitive motivation.

Wertheimer held a similar view on degrees of formation in the production of gestalts. Michael Ash quotes a translation of an obscure report of Wertheimer's lectures at Frankfurt in 1913 by Gabriele, Countess von Wartensleben, who had recently completed a doctorate with an experimental project in which Wertheimer and Köhler were subjects. She said that Wertheimer described a new epistemology based on the claim that not sensations, but structured wholes, or Gestalten, are the primary units of mental life. She noted his reference to incomplete new forms in the process of being realized:

> Almost all impressions are grasped either as chaotic masses – a relatively seldom, extreme case – or as chaotic masses on the way to sharper formation, or as Gestalten....
>
> The process of knowing ... is very often a process of 'centering,' of 'structuring,' or of grasping that particular aspect which provides the key to an orderly whole, a unification of the particular individual parts that happen to be present; what results is that a structured unit emerges as a whole due to, and through, this centering. The result of just this knowledge process is a springing forth [*Herausspringen*] of the Gestalt from the 'not yet formed' [*noch nicht gestaltet*]. (Ash 1995, p. 123)

The concept of an incomplete gestalt was present at the beginning of the Gestalt movement. It appears, however, that the English language term 'incomplete Gestalt' was found in Gestalt literature only at a later stage in what became the gestalt therapy movement: 'Any incomplete Gestalt represents an "unfinished situation" that clamors for attention' (Perls, Hefferline and Goodman 1951, p. ix). In the same passage Perls and colleagues also represented gestalt formation as being accompanied by awareness, anticipating the later association of cognitive integration with the neural correlates of consciousness (Baars 2002a, 2003; Tononi

2005; Baars and Gage 2007; Tononi and Koch 2008). The motivational effect implied by Perls is the same as what Heider proposed when he cited Koffka on the tendency to form as good a whole unit as conditions allow (Heider 1960).

Other cognitive theories have entertained similar ideas in regard to pattern completion. At a time when there were many consistency theories (see the introduction to Chapter 4), Feather offered a general theory of 'organization and discrepancy in cognitive structures' (Feather 1971, p. 355) in which an unbalanced structure is a condition for cognitive adjustment that could have motivational consequences. His analysis prefigured some of the later conceptions of integration. Feather drew particularly on the cognitive motivational concepts of Heider (1946. 1958, 1960, see also Newcomb, 1968a). He described three structural models which applied respectively to communication, recall, and attribution of responsibility. In each case there could be perceived structures that mirror the current situation and are discrepant with underlying abstract structures. These abstract structures were assumed to be relatively stable and to be organized in a balanced or consistent way, representing an organized residue or summary of past experience. When a perceived structure is unbalanced there would be pressure to resolve the structural discrepancy with the underlying corresponding abstract structure by cognitive adjustment in the direction of the abstract structure. There may also be behavioural adjustments such as seeking more information. In some cases the abstract structure might change as new and discrepant information is continually experienced. In Feather's account, new information might also be sought and new elements of structure developed in the process of adjustment as I have proposed in the cognitive process theory of curiosity in Chapter 2. He also draws a parallel with curiosity, which in cognitive motivation theory is a basic model for completion for an incomplete gestalt.

Feather recognised that Heider's use of the principle of balance was similar to the Gestalt principle of *pragnänz* making an emphasis on 'good form' (Heider 1958), but he agreed with Zajonc (1968) that the perception of forms considered by Heider had an additional component of particularity which may resist adjustment of a discrepancy in any way that would deny unique or conflicting qualities. He concluded that '[t]he use of the balance principle in the three models described previously should not be taken as endorsement of Gestalt principles of *pragnänz*, closure, etc.' (Feather 1971, p. 273). This might appear to challenge the position I have taken in support of those principles. However, Feather has commented recently, in reference to his 1971 paper, 'Maybe it was overstated at the time. I would not want to exclude the possibility that there may be intrinsic forces that push towards a "good" structure. I have a lot of sympathy for structural approaches. In my paper I wanted to bring in the normative component which relates to the distinction between "is" and "ought", which underlies the distinction I make between perceived and abstract structures' (Feather 2017, personal communication).

In the general theory of cognitive motivation, Wertheimer's principle of integrity with its necessary particularity, noted earlier, can be incorporated with Heider's principle of balance and seen to be consistent with Wertheimer's exposition of pragnänz. Closure is a deceptively simple concept that can be understood in different ways. I have discussed conflicting accounts at several points. See the concluding section of Chapter 2 in relation to curiosity, and Chapter 11 in regard to Arnheim's distinction between the effects of integration processes in open and closed systems and the corresponding interplay between distinctive structure and the simplifying tendency.

In the general theory of cognitive motivation, if we can 'see' a possible completion, and yet know that we have not yet achieved a satisfying complete image, then fundamental processes of integration will ensure that we have motivation for its attainment. 'Many of the most basic forms of thought can be understood as pattern completion (Barsalou, Niedenthal, Barbey and Ruppert 2003)' (Baumeister and Masicampo 2010, p. 959). It is emphasised in the recognition of intentions discussed in the next chapter. The work of Rudolph Arnheim, a student of Wertheimer and Köhler, on the psychology of art, which further illustrates these processes, is discussed in Chapter 11.

Goals and Emotions in the Function of an Incomplete Gestalt

In addition to the representation of a desired state of affairs as a goal, in the cybernetic type of model characterized by feedback processes, there was also representation of the current state with which it is compared (Miller et al. 1960, Powers, Clark and McFarland 1960, Powers 1973). In the TOTE (test-operate-test-exit) theory of G. A. Miller and colleagues, which was one of the historical foundations for later cognitive theories of motivation, the difference between desired and current representations impels the organism towards reducing the difference. In the TOTE model of Miller and colleagues the match is retested after adjustment and the loop is exited when a match is found. In the theory of Powers and colleagues there is no exit, but provision for continual monitoring and hence for both parallel and serial processing (Austin and Vancouver 1996). In cognitive motivation theory, an incomplete gestalt functions as a way of modelling feedback processes for purposes of integration.

The Signalling Function of Emotions in Feedback, Anticipation and Reflection

In the previous chapter I considered a theory of the function of emotion in motivation in which emotions serve as signals of the relationship between the present situation and relevant goals. In cognitive motivation, these signals may be subtle and complex, with meanings that vary in a multidimensional semantic space (see Chapter 8). The varied qualities of emotions have sometimes been understood to be the result of interpreting simple positive and negative signals in the light of the situation in which they arise. I have argued against such a simple bivalent conception of emotions. Rolls had such a theory, but with a sophisticated view of interaction with the situation, in which a wide range of emotions can result from different reinforcement contingencies and related factors (Rolls 2005).

There is a detailed discussion of the function of emotions in Chapter 8, in which I envisage their having a utilitarian value in motivation as feedback on changing relationships to a goal. Many others have promoted similar ideas. For example, a cognitive theoretical view of the function of emotions in feedback, anticipation, and reflection, rather than direct causation, in which situational interpretation plays a part but not as the sole source of varied meanings, has been advanced by Baumeister et al. (2007). Varied and complex emotions are not mere epiphenomena, interesting phenomena though they may be in their own right, but they have a function in arousing and directing purposive behaviour in ways that are subtle and complex as well as being sometime overwhelming.

The Integration of Goals with Dispositional Properties and Situational Cues

Goals are commonly conceived in terms of any purpose or reason for action giving both energy and direction to behaviour. Elliot argues for 'a more restricted definition of and role for the goal construct, that it not only affords clarity with regard to the nature of goals, but also affords clarity with regard to how goals fit in the overall motivational process' (Elliot 2006, p. 113). He says that 'it is also necessary to consider the motivation underlying goals.' We can agree that goals are but one part of motivation as a process. In addition to the definition of a goal, and to underlying dispositional properties such as motives, another part of the process in cognitive motivation theory is the signalling value of emotions giving information on the relationship of a goal to directed behaviour in the present situation.

The idea of an incomplete gestalt is similarly a way of relating the present to a possible future state of affairs, but it is different from the cybernetic feedback model in two respects: (1) like Lewin's field theory diagrams (Lewin 1935; Lewin et al. 1936; Lewin 1951), it envisages a single image which is a composite of the representation of a goal and the representation of its relationship to the present situation; and (2) in the incomplete gestalt, the envisaged future state is not fully defined, but suggested by representative elements in an image with the unrealized potential to make sense of the present somewhat incoherent state. The mere existence of a goal representation which differs from the representation of the present state of affairs is not sufficient to create motivation for change. *The two representations must be brought together to interact in such a way that conflicts and gaps between them become the focus of attention.* In the processes which form and resolve an incomplete gestalt there is a vision of a future whole figure, in which both the energizing and directing properties of motivation are activated.

Recent work on goal constructs in achievement motivation by Elliot and his colleagues has led to a similar conception of energizing and directing properties by combining the dispositional properties of a motive with cognitive representations of the relationship of a goal to the present situation within a single complex. They have suggested a functionally coherent integrative concept of a goal *complex*, following early proposals by Murray and Allport:

> Rather than conceptualize the energizational aspect as an abstraction residing at the personal level (i.e., a motive) which is then made available to specific goals or aims in a particular situation or context, it may be preferable to view goal adoption as the creation of a new, context-specific cognitive-dynamic entity. Again we may look to Murray (1938, see also Murray 1936), for guidance: 'One might say that traces (images) of cathected objects in familiar settings become integrated in the mind with the needs and emotions which they customarily excite, as well as with images of preferred modes. A hypothetical compound of this sort may be called a *need integrate*, or *complex*' (Murray 1938 p. 110). Allport (1937a) argued, 'Now this conception of a need integrate is a great improvement over the skeleton need. It fulfils well our demand for a unit of analysis that is concrete, life-like, and personal, provided only that the need integrate is understood to be not only a momentary organization but a mental structure that endures ...' (pp. 241–242). (Thrash and Elliot 2001, pp. 17–18)

Where Thrash and Elliot have referred to a goal *complex* and a *need integrate*, I have employed the idea of a goal *orientation*. More than goal definition is required. Their reference to a 'cognitive-dynamic entity' catches up the affective qualities that were explicitly included by Murray in his need integrate or complex and which figure in my conception of emotions as feedback signals. In a *process* view of motivation the integrating properties of an incomplete gestalt always operate with the feedback functions of emotions, but it would be helpful to know more about how processes of integration form such a cognitive-emotional complex. Although gestalt properties, such as simplicity, consistency, symmetry and identity, which contribute to the formation of a whole image, have been recognised for a long time, the forces that make a whole image cohere and stand out from a background are not fully understood. It seems to be a basic property of neural systems that brains function to create such images.

Self-Organising Systems

When we suppose that the brain functions, by means that are not fully understood, produce images which represent order at the edge of chaos, we might conceive an incomplete gestalt to be an instance of what has become known in mathematical, physical and biological sciences in recent times as a self-organising system (Kauffman 1993; Camazine, Deneubourg, Franks, Sneyd, Theraulag and Banabeau 2001; Camazine 2003; Skår 2003; Kauffman 2008).[3] According to Skår, the original ideas on self-organising systems in Schrödinger's thoughts about life (Schrödinger 1944, 2000) are now considered to be very strong suggestions for system qualities in the relevant disciplines. Similarly, Turing's mathematical conception of a self-organising system (Turing 1952) could have more than analogical relevance to cognitive psychology. Examples are easily recognised: 'Self-organisation refers to a broad range of pattern-formation processes in both physical and biological systems, such as sand grains assembling into rippled dunes, chemical reactants forming swirling spirals, cells making up highly structured tissues, and fish joining together in schools' (Camazine et al. 2001, p. 7). Camazine and colleagues give the following definition:

> Self-organization is a process in which pattern at the global level of a system emerges solely from numerous interactions among the lower-level components of the system. Moreover, the rules specifying interactions among the system's components are executed using only local information, without reference to the global pattern. (Camazine et al. 2001, p. 8)

[3] On the current understanding of self-organising systems, see, for example, the special issue of the Royal Society journal *Philosophical Transactions: Mathematical, Physical and Engineering Sciences*: No. 1807, 2003.

Kauffman has suggested a process of autocatalysis in which a feedback cycle is set up that grows stronger and stronger in complex systems, forming a self-reinforcing web of reactions, which can move spontaneously into a new form of organised complexity. Following Kaufman's ideas, Paul Davies noted that computer models show that any network with enough components will tend to flip spontaneously into a state of organised complexity. He then suggested that this could be the basis for the organisation of life, but he saw a conceptual problem in that idea. Davies drew a distinction between order and self-organisation. Order could occur in the repetition of events in a system with simple components and form patterns, but he argued that for organic life something like a software program was needed in addition to local information. 'Life is not an example of *self*-organization. Life is in fact *specified*, i.e. genetically directed, organization. Living things are instructed by genetic software encoded in their DNA (or RNA)' (Davies 1999a, p. 108). So he says order refers to simple patterns, and that cited examples of self-organising systems are often nothing of the sort, but spontaneous ordering instead, well short of the organised complexity of biological organisms that require some kind of software to guide their organisation. The emergence of new forms with system qualities is a phenomenon that has attracted a great deal of attention. I have discussed it in relation to curiosity in Chapter 2. In Chapter 6 I have discussed the psychological implications, especially for agency and free choice, of the concept of emergence as it applies to the development of whole systems with properties not evident in their components at a lower level of organisation, as we see in the concept of a gestalt.

As noted previously, in the early days of the Gestalt movement, Köhler wrote a book on the occurrence of simple patterns in physical phenomena, *Die physischen Gestalten*, specifically for biological scientists and philosophers. He argued for the existence of such patterns as natural events in the brain (Köhler 1920/1924; see the English translation of the Introduction, Arnheim 1998). Köhler took examples such as the shape that a drop of oil takes in water and how it spreads on the surface of water, and compared it to what he postulated as gestalt tendencies towards patterns on the surface of the cerebral cortex.

> When Wertheimer formulated his principle [of Prägnanz] in psychology I happened to be studying the general characteristics of macroscopic physical states, and thus I could not fail to see that it is the psychological equivalent of Mach's principle in physics. (Köhler 1938, p. 254f)

Köhler believed that the propensity of physical systems to form patterns provided the basis for psychological patterns (Köhler 1920/1924;

Arnheim 1998). His principle of isomorphism, assumed for simple patterns on the surface of the cerebral cortex, was dismissed after research by Lashley and others on brain functions in animals had discredited the electric field theory of cerebral integration (Lashley, Chow and Semmes 1951; Sperry, Miner and Myers 1955; Pribram 1971, 1984; Gardner 1985). We can now acknowledge that he was wrong only in the grossness of the physical processes in the brain that he assumed, when a more complex neural network could have been implied. We can see now instead functional similarity to physical patterns in neural networks.

There is something very much like the understanding of patterns in Gestalt psychology in the way that physical scientists have been speaking of self-organising systems: 'With self-organization, complexity and emergence, the realization increasingly shared by many scientists is that behaviour at one "level" is then more than the "sum" of the behaviour of individual entities' (Skår 2003, p. 1054).[4] Köhler had introduced his first book in 1920 referring in the opening sentence to this basic concept, pointing back to the original use of the term 'gestalt' with the meaning given by von Ehrenfels (1890/1988): 'psychological states and events, whose characteristic properties and effects cannot be reduced to the sum of their so-called parts.' He said, 'One came across gestalten in visual space, and the name was then adopted for all other gestalten, not only in vision but also for melodies or intellectual conceptions. Gestalten are fundamental patterns, whose particular properties are by far superior to those of the materials of which they consist' (Köhler 1920/1924, English translation of the introduction, Arnheim 1998, p. 22.)

The parallel of Köhler's ideas with those of physical and biological scientists in recent years is nicely summed up in a biographical memoir of Wolfgang Köhler by Ulrich Neisser:

> There are indeed many organized wholistic systems in the world: Why should there not be? On this point the triumph of Gestalt psychology has been so complete that it is hard to understand how this was ever disputed or why Köhler had to demonstrate it. Interestingly, his demonstration anticipated many of the dynamic concepts that are now the 'bread and butter' of cognitive science. Self-organizing systems, parallel distributed networks, and attractor states (for example) are all physical Gestalten. It is unfortunate that the scientists who developed those concepts in the 1980s and 1990s were largely unfamiliar with this aspect of Köhler's work. (Neisser 2002, p. 190)

The propensity to form organised patterns is common to physical and psychological phenomena. This propensity is a very general thing,

[4] The gestalt psychologists could have told them that long ago, although Wertheimer, Köhler and Koffka seemed to prefer *different from* rather than *greater than* the sum of the parts.

appearing in the arts and philosophy as well as science. A compelling image of the potential of perceived incompleteness, even in well-formed objects as diverse as justice and beauty, is seen in Scarry's literary reference, quoting Simone Weil to 'beautiful things acting "like small tears in the surface of the world that pull us through to some vaster space"' (Scarry 1999a, p. 112). Beauty, of course, suggests something already well formed and yet still open to unrealized possibilities. Points of opportunity for a larger vision can invite directed action more readily than the immediate prospect of closure with its finality requiring a kind of surrender. The whole configuration of cognitive elements from which a partially ordered whole figure, in a state of tension and liability to change, stands out from a background constitutes an incomplete gestalt. It can then specify the range of potential new elements which may be engaged for its completion. The lock defines a key.

Einstein's Incomplete Gestalt of Relativity

In the report of his conversations with Einstein about the thought processes Einstein was engaged in when he developed the theory of relativity, Wertheimer described how a radical change of cognition took place in terms we can now see to be remarkably consonant with Scarry's and Weil's literary usage. In his last book, published posthumously, Wertheimer recalled:

> Those were wonderful days, beginning in 1916, when for hours and hours I was fortunate enough to sit with Einstein, alone in his study, and hear from him the story of the dramatic developments which culminated in the theory of relativity. During those long discussions I questioned Einstein in great detail about the concrete events in his thought. He described them to me, not in generalities, but in a discussion of the genesis of each question. (Wertheimer 1945, p. 168)

Wertheimer gave a brief formulation of the crucial steps in Einstein's creative thought processes:

> In a passionate desire for clearness, Einstein squarely faced the relation between the velocity of light and the movement of a system; confronting the theoretical structure of classical physics and the Michelson result [which raised a question about the adequacy of the classical system to account for the speed of light in a system in motion].
>
> A part-region in this field became crucial and was subjected to a radical examination.
>
> Under this scrutiny a great gap was discovered [in the classical treatment of time.]
>
> The necessary steps for dealing with this difficulty were realized.

> As a result, the meaning of all the items involved underwent a change.
> When a last arbitrariness in the situation had been eliminated, a new structure of physics crystallized. (Wertheimer 1945, p. 186)

'A great gap' in the old system which emerged from giving attention to a particular discrepancy, as in any example of curiosity at the micro or macro level, was not filled, but the system was re-ordered with changed meanings and in a new structure. Nor was it, in the way it happened, an exclusively rational process as in a mathematical derivation from a set of axioms. According to Wertheimer, Einstein said, 'No really productive man thinks in such a paper fashion.' 'The way the two triple sets of axioms contrasted in the Einstein-Infeld book is not at all the way things happened in the process of actual thinking. This was merely a later formulation of the subject matter, just a question of how the thing could afterwards best be written' (Wertheimer 1945, pp. 183–184, fn. 7). It began with a passionate desire and was completed with a visual image. 'These thoughts did not come in any verbal formulation.'

Einstein agreed with Wertheimer that a sense of direction is an important factor in creative thought processes: 'Such things were very strongly present. During all those years there was a *feeling* of direction, of going straight for something concrete. It is very hard to express that *feeling* in words .... Of course, behind such a direction there is always something logical; but I have it in a kind of survey, in a way *visually*' (Wertheimer 1945, p. 184, fn). Here we find an iconic (visual) type of newly forming whole or gestalt being approached with emotions guiding the direction of movement towards a cognitive goal, as should be the case according to cognitive motivation theory, whether it be in specific limited problem-solving tasks approached with curiosity, the formulation of a scientific theory or the development of a personal identity.

In Wertheimer's report of his conversations with Einstein, we are told that when considering the results of the Michelson experiment which disconfirmed expectations about the speed of light in a system in motion, Einstein '*felt* a gap somewhere' without being able to formulate it. 'He *felt* that the trouble went deeper than the contradiction between Michelson's actual and the expected result. He *felt* that a certain region in the whole structure was not as clear to him as it should be' (Wertheimer 1945, p. 174, emphasis added). Rather than follow logical steps of reasoning as he might when demonstrating a proof, Einstein was guided by his feelings to a new holistic conception. The gestalt flip came from focusing on an irritant and realizing in this case that the presence of an observer seemed to introduce a fundamentally arbitrary and subjective factor. In getting rid of the arbitrary element Einstein realized (Wertheimer 1945,

p. 196) that a basic invariant was needed. This led to the introduction of the velocity of light as a constant.

Guided Processes of Cognitive Completion

The key components of goal-directed behaviour in the function of an incomplete gestalt are all illustrated in Wertheimer's account of Einstein's creative thinking, but there are many ways in which new elements of information and structure can be found and incorporated in the resolution of an incomplete gestalt. In that sense it has the property of equifinality as well as creativity. Those two properties might not readily coexist, for equifinality presupposes a useful degree of constancy in the goal (Emmons 1989; Pervin 1989). Originality implies that there need not be a well-defined pattern with an empty space into which a missing piece might easily fit, as seems at first sight to be implied in Loewenstein's theory of curiosity (Loewenstein, Adler, Behrens and Gillis 1992; Loewenstein 1994), but because the fit is not likely to be perfect, an incomplete pattern must be expected to change shape when new elements are added. Commitment to action should follow perception of the possibility of completion when it is combined with the allocation of resources for the instrumental acts in which the required new information is found and incorporated.

As discussed in Chapters 2 and 5, the concept of change in the cognitive map is metacognitive. It has to do with thinking about thinking. It provides reasons for change in the relationship between cognitive elements which are implied, for example, in expectancy theories. Expectancy theories have features of an incomplete gestalt, but those features that are present in expectancies theories are not sufficient for cognitive motivation. A comprehensive theory of cognitive motivation requires the idea of a gestalt itself to be employed in a description of the motivational system with reference to the function of emotions (Thagard 2002).

To reiterate: Realization of the potential of a goal through a process of change which moves towards the completion of an incomplete gestalt is guided by feelings that signal differences between the goal and the present situation. It requires meaningful integration of new information reconciling discrepancies and enabling the creation of a new gestalt. Missing pieces and missing structure are found, or created, and incorporated into the resolution. One big difference from the old need satisfaction theories is that goal attainment does not constitute the restoration of equilibrium in a previous state of affairs. Although Damasio reasserted homeostasis as a general model of motivation he asked and answered the question, 'Is homeostasis enough ... Not really,' because anticipation is more effective than restoration (Damasio 2010, p. 44). Nor, for cognitively defined goals, can there be a universal and lasting definition of a particular goal. When a goal is attained, there is a new creation. The tension between present and future states is open-ended, and not comparable with looking back to a lost state of equilibrium that might be restored.

Personal achievement goals will have unique qualities, although they might be classified as the goals of commonly observed achievement or other social-cognitive motivation. More so with curiosity, the particular object of attention will be seen in different ways by different people, and different aspects of a situation will arouse interest in different individuals, so that curiosity could be understood as a collection of a great variety of uncommon needs, as discussed in Chapter 2. There are many points in the process of cognitive motivation at which there are individual differences in the creation, maintenance and resolution of conceptual conflicts and gaps in knowledge. At the same time, flexibility of response is greatly increased as the agency of the person becomes more apparent with increased cognitive capacity.

The processes of imagination (literally the formation of images) and the completion of incomplete images are the fundamental processes of cognitive motivation. These are cognitive processes which can be modelled in information-processing terms, but some of the variables represent affective qualities. Emotions as signals provide feedback on the changing relationships represented in the image of a goal in relation to the present state of affairs. Those relationships are multidimensional. The present state can differ from the envisaged state in many ways.

Thus goals indirectly specify, but only in part, in their nature and their relationship to the present situation, the kind of emotions that will guide their attainment (or avoidance). Affective qualities are included in the definitions of specific goals by specification of the emotional signals relevant to them. Feelings are associated with expectations. The incomplete gestalt, as it were, includes 'receptors' for relevant emotional signals. The feelings associated with a personal goal tend to be complex and sometimes ambiguous because of the uncertain shape of the outcome, the varied attractive and unattractive features of the goal, the kinds and degrees of separation from it that are possible, the great range of possible means likely to be available for attainment of the goal, and because of the additional complexity of conscious agency involving the reflexive nature of the self. The agency of the person in this process will be discussed further in regard to intentions in the next chapter. The role of cognitive motivation in the development and functioning of the self is treated more fully in Chapters 11 and 12.

Summary

Goals are representations in the present of future states that a person is seeking. Goals become active when attention is focused upon the incomplete gestalt of a future state and a person's relationship to it. Differences between goals and present states are marked by emotions. Having both affective and cognitive features, and being closely related to broad aspects of the self, goals play a major role in the activation and organisation of behaviour.

Gestalt ideas provided roots for later theories of motivation in which conscious goals and intentions have a role. I review the contribution of Gestalt principles, for example Wertheimer's presentation of the basic concept of Prägnanz (completeness, singularity, clear-cut-ness or pithiness) with lawfulness, originality, and integrity as general principles of organisation, and two further formal dimensions of simplicity and diversity. The work of early Gestalt theorists is reviewed in reference to the question of whether a gestalt can be incomplete, e.g. Ehresnfels approached the idea of an incomplete gestalt when he postulated degrees of 'formedness.' I discuss Wertheimer's report of his conversations with Einstein on the thought processes that led to the theory of relativity, as an example of the formation and creative resolution of an incomplete gestalt.

Theories of self-organising systems have been presented recently in biological and physical sciences which are very similar to those put forward much earlier by Köhler and others in Gestalt psychology. Köhler's original conception has been shown to be mistaken in so far as it refers to electrical processes on the surface of cerebral cortex, but a functional view of integrating processes in which dispersed networks provide the basis for the same conceptual organisation remains acceptable.

Principles of purposive behaviour were discussed in terms of goals, cognitive maps and an incomplete gestalt in the cognitive process theory of curiosity in Chapter 2. These principles are generalized to the full range of cognitive motivation which depends upon the guidance of feelings signifying relationship to a goal. Affective qualities are included in the definitions of specific goals by specification of the emotional signals relevant to them. The incomplete gestalt, as it were, includes 'receptors' for relevant emotional signals. Realization of the potential of a goal through a process of change which moves towards the completion of an incomplete gestalt requires meaningful integration of new information reconciling discrepancies and enabling the creation of a new gestalt.

10 Intentions

> I have often felt much difficulty about the proper application of the terms, will, consciousness, and intention.
>
> – Darwin 1872

Introduction

The concept of an incomplete gestalt introduced in Chapter 1 was applied to goals in Chapter 9. That application is part of the cognitive motivation theory of intentions, but intentions require more than goals. An incomplete gestalt relating the person to a goal, a future state of affairs that is being sought, constitutes a *goal orientation*, as discussed in the previous chapter. In cognitive motivation theory, an intention is a particular kind of goal orientation. It is a particular kind of goal orientation because it includes commitment to a course of action. Commitment is an attribute that might not be included in an orientation to the future that is concerned with expectations and evaluations. 'An intention is a representation of a future course of action to be performed. It is not simply an expectation or prediction of future actions but a proactive commitment to bringing them about' (Bandura 2001, p. 6). Agency is implied in this commitment. Take the example of a climate scientist who builds predictive models for future changes of global temperature. From such models the scientist might have strong expectations, but his or her orientation to the future will become intentional only if he or she does something to intervene in the process of climate change, such as meeting a government official to advocate a policy to control carbon emissions. The scientist would then be an agent behind future-oriented action with an intention to do something about what might otherwise only be expected.

In his founding conception of gestalt qualities, Christian von Ehrenfels conceived the possibility of gestalts within gestalts (von Ehrenfels 1890/1988). In the cognitive motivation theory, the same applies to *incomplete* gestalts in the relationship of goals to intentions. A goal is itself an incomplete gestalt of a future state, but a broader incomplete image including the person in a particular situation together with a goal is the dynamic composite image of an intention, the prospective completion of which in a course of action is a source of cognitive motivation. Action plans, expectations and evaluations may be included in the composite image of the person in relation to a goal, but an intention requires, in addition, a commitment to reach a goal. Commitment to an action plan is the key point.

Gollwitzer's distinction between goal intentions and implementation intentions captures much of the same difference as I describe in reference to a goal and the broader image of a relationship between the person and a goal that includes action plans (Gollwitzer 1999; Gollwitzer, Fujita and Oettingen 2004; Oettingen and Gollwitzer 2009). Gollwitzer and his colleagues agree that while choosing or accepting a goal is the central act of willing in the pursuit of goals, further acts of willing facilitate goal implementation. In their view these further acts introduce an element of automaticity into the relationship of particular situations to specific courses of action. Implementation intentions link action plans to situational triggers which to some degree free the person from having to make new decisions on the means of goal attainment at every turn of events. Gollwitzer referred to a sharp divide like crossing the Rubicon in reference to the transition from a deliberative to an implemental mindset. There is a question, however, of whether additional deliberative decisions about goals might have to be made after the Rubicon has been crossed. The implementation stage that follows the deliberative decision might not be limited to the means for attaining the chosen goal but, as I suggest in Chapter 8 in regard to the role of emotions, experiences of success and failure can lead to revision of the goals themselves. The automaticity of implementation intentions will be limited by the need for agency when unexpected events occur.

The relationship of intentions to agency has been analysed conceptually by Bratman (1999). He put forward a *planning theory of intention*, in which intentions are seen as elements of stable, partial plans of action concerning present and future conduct. The function of incomplete or imperfect images of future possibilities that is relevant to cognitive motivation theory is evident in his idea that by settling on plans we commit ourselves to future conduct in ways that help support imperfect forms of coordination and organisation over time. That is, settling on plans carries forward the link between present conditions and future action. Bratman conceived plans of action as having a hierarchical structure, with embedded means and preliminary steps, and specific as well as general intentions. These plans are typically partial, and details are filled in as needed when purposive action develops. His theory helps to explain how intentions and plans impose structure on practical reasoning and justify the rationality of the case for non-reconsideration of plans.

The Relationship of Intentions to Agency

Bratman's theory helps to explain how intentions and plans impose structure on practical reasoning. While recognising that many animals are purposive agents who pursue goals in the light of their representation of the world, Bratman understands human agency as possibly distinctive in the function of plans as cognitive structures: 'Our agency is typically embedded in planning structures' (Bratman 1999, p. 5). The appeal to planning structures allows us to articulate basic features of intention and decision-making, and to distinguish those features from belief and ordinary desire. Bratman recommends that we seek a view of intentional commitment that respects the fact that a planning agent is not only a planner but also a temporally and causally located agent.

In this chapter I examine various approaches to the intentional agency that is evident in deliberate pursuit of cognitively represented goals. It is in conceiving of future possibilities that human cognitive capacity gives purposive behaviour its great strength as an innovation. These approaches address in different ways issues raised by Bratman. And his question of whether it might be possible to hold together the two classic attitudes to causation found in Hume and Kant can usefully remain in the background of our discussion. He followed Korsgaard (1983) in highlighting 'two main views in the theory of action: first, a Humean view that sees desires as causes of action, and the will as at most a by-product of the underlying causal processes; and second, a Kantian view that emphasises the role of the agent, will and universal principles of action in the reflective endorsement of desires as potential grounds of action' (Bratman 1999, pp. 11–12). This comparison points to two questions on which we will need to take a position, i.e. (1) whether a sense of will is a mere epiphenomenon, and (2) what the role of reflective cognition might be. I consider both of these as critical questions in the understanding of intentions.

The general case for intentions as expressions of conscious agency with observable effects contrasts with the contrary arguments seen in Wegner's book, *The Illusion of Conscious Will* (Wegner 2002; Wegner and Commentators 2004). I will consider Wegner's argument after Libet's quite different construction of the role of consciousness in the formation and enactment of intentions (Libet, Gleason, Wright and Pearl 1983; Libet 1985, 1999, 2004). In that context I will return to Dennett's arguments on intentions, consciousness and free will (Dennett 1971,

1987, 1991, 2003), and will make further reference to Baumeister and colleagues on free will and self-control (Baumeister, Mele and Vohs 2010; Baumeister and Tierney 2011; Baumeister and Monroe 2014). On the powers of conscious thought, see also Baumeister and Masicampo (2010).

Conscious Intentions

When a person has an intention he or she has determined to take a course of action in pursuit of a goal. A goal and a course of action are cognitive representations of possible future events, although action might not yet have been initiated when commitment is made to seek a goal (Bandura 2001; Baumeister et al. 2010). As an expression of personal agency, an intention is a *conscious* commitment, but there is also now good evidence that not all components of an intention are conscious. I have discussed in Chapter 6 Bandura's argument for regarding intentions as legitimate explanations of purposive behaviour, although not all purposive behaviour need have conscious intentions. In his understanding, an intention is a representation of a future course of action in which commitment is added to expectations. In the general theory of cognitive motivation, that commitment will induce a process of integration that is facilitated by consciousness.

Baumeister and his colleagues have provided strong evidence for conscious 'causation' of behaviour in a summary of recent research (Baumeister et al. 2011). They carried out a meta-analysis of evidence from experimental studies on whether there is a causal relationship between conscious thought and behaviour (Baumeister et al. 2011; see also Baumeister and Masicampo 2010; Baumeister et al. 2010). As discussed in Chapter 7, Baars similarly has summarised supporting evidence for the effects of 'consciousness as a variable' (Baars 2002a). From an opposing point of view, Wegner (2002) has argued from a range of different types of research that conscious will is an illusion, and I will discuss his argument shortly. Baumeister and his colleagues concluded that

> [t]he evidence for conscious causation of behavior is profound, extensive, adaptive, multifaceted, and empirically strong. However, conscious causation is often indirect and delayed, and it depends on interplay with unconscious processes. (Baumeister et al. 2011, p. 331)

Their results were set against the claim of others that '[b]ehavior does not originate with a conscious decision' (Dijksterhuis, Chartrand and Aarts 2007, p. 52). Baumeister and colleagues claimed that such an argument from observation of the immediate precursors of an action is irrelevant because the effects of consciousness are often offline and indirect, depending in part upon earlier unconscious processes. Baumeister and colleagues, here and elsewhere, emphasised the integrating and reflective functions of conscious processing which brings together conscious and unconscious elements (DeWall, Baumeister and Masicampo 2008; Baumeister and Masicampo 2010; Baumeister et al. 2010; Baumeister et al. 2011). Empirical research, such as that of Libet, indicates that the roots of consciously intended behaviour often have precursors in unconscious processes. These conclusions will be discussed in the following sections. They provide a useful framework for looking closely into the effect of conscious intentions.

Libet's Research on Delayed Recognition of Intentions

At the centre of the debate on the conscious causation of behaviour over several decades have been the findings of Libet and his colleagues on the timing of neural events in relation to consciousness of an intention or decision to take a specific action (Libet et al. 1983; Libet 1985, 2004). In carefully managed experimental investigations subjects reported becoming conscious of an intention or an urge to act some 300 ms or more *after* the beginning of measured brain activity preparatory to that action. The question was whether such a delay ruled out any causal role for a conscious decision to act. Previous work had documented the occurrence of a 'readiness-potential' (RP) (Kornhuber and Deecke 1965), probably indicating cerebral activity in the pre-supplementary motor area, measured from the scalp with an electroencephalogram (EEG), that precedes self-initiated 'freely' voluntary *acts*. Where there was scope for conscious planning, the RP might appear up to a second or more before the act, and at a shorter time before more spontaneous activity (Libet, Wright, Feinstein and Pearl 1979; Libet, Wright and Gleason 1982). For the critical experiment Libet and colleagues considered the possibility that '[t]he appearance of preparatory cerebral processes at such surprisingly long times before a freely voluntary act raises the question of whether conscious awareness of the voluntary urge or *intention* to act also appears with such similar advance timings' (Libet et al. 1983, p. 624, my emphasis, to contrast intention with acts). It was the timing of such a voluntary urge or intention in relation to the neural RP that was investigated in the critical experiment.

More recent work has confirmed the general principle that some relevant brain activity can occur well before people report that they became aware of an 'urge', or decision, or intention to act (Haggard and Eimer 1999; Haggard and Magno 1999; Haggard 2008; Soon, Brass, Heinze and Haynes 2008). As Soon and colleagues said,

> There has been a long controversy as to whether subjectively "free" decisions are determined by brain activity ahead of time. We found that the outcome of a decision can be encoded in brain activity of prefrontal and parietal cortex up to 10 s before it enters awareness. This delay presumably reflects the operation of a network of high-level control areas that begin to prepare an upcoming decision long before it enters awareness. (Soon et al. 2008, p. 543)

In the original study by Libet and colleagues, subjects were instructed to watch a clock-face type of display to report the time of a conscious event and to perform a quick abrupt movement of the fingers and/or wrist. They were 'to let the urge to act appear on its own at any time without any preplanning or concentration on when to act.' '[T]he subject was asked to note and later report the time of appearance of his conscious awareness of "wanting" to perform a given self-initiated movement. The experience was also described as an "urge" or "intention" or "decision" to move, though subjects usually settled for the words "wanting" or "urge"' (Libet et al. 1983, p. 627). The actual time of the beginning of muscle movement in the arm in the voluntary act relative to the 'clock position' timing of the monitored awareness events was recorded from an electromyogram (EMG) of an appropriate muscle. Similarly, EEG recordings of the 'readiness-potential' (RP) were related to the same time measure.

The result of great interest was in the timing of the onset of the 'readiness potential' (RP), evident from the EEG, in comparison with the subjectively reported time of 'wanting' to act. For three types of RP and two different methods of measurement, the RP appeared a significant length of time, ranging from 800 ms to about 100 ms, before the reported feeling of 'wanting' or intending to act. In the most typical case of spontaneous movement with a sharply defined type of response the RP appeared about 350 ms before awareness of the 'urge' or 'wanting' to act. Delays were longer when the instructions allowed for awareness of planning a movement compared with shorter times for spontaneous movement. Initially two types of RP had been distinguished according to whether the instructions called for preplanning or spontaneous voluntary movement (Libet et al. 1982).

The reported time of awareness of 'wanting' to act was interpreted as 'the time of the appearance of the *conscious* intention to act' (emphasis in the original). The word 'intention' is an interpretation of the subjects reporting a time of awareness of an 'urge' or 'wanting' to act, as they were not normally asked when they became aware of an intention. The time of the inferred conscious intention was compared with what was called 'the onset of cerebral processes before the act (as evidenced in the RP)' (Libet et al. 1983, p. 634). With few exceptions, onset of the RP occurred before reported awareness by substantial amounts of time, irrespective of which measure of RP onset was employed. The differences were highly significant, statistically, for all methods of measurement. 'It is clear that neuronal processes that precede a self-initiated voluntary action, as reflected in the readiness-potential, generally begin substantially before the reported appearance of conscious intention to perform that specific act' (Libet et al. 1983, p. 635).

Libet had long argued that validity of the operational criteria for time of intention to act necessarily depends upon acceptance of introspective reports (e.g. Libet 1965). Only the subjects themselves had access to the subjective event in their own awareness of where the spot of light was on the dial when they became aware of the 'intention' to act. Libet discussed this principle at some length in his later work (Libet 2004), especially in regard to the possibility and meaning of free will.

Because there was evidence of preparatory cerebral activity in the early appearance of the 'readiness potential', it was inferred by Libet and colleagues 'that some neuronal activity associated with the eventual performance of the act has started well before any (recallable) conscious initiation or intervention could be possible.' They suggested that, 'Put another way, the brain evidently "decides" to initiate, or at least, to prepare to initiate the act at a time before there is any reportable subjective awareness that such a decision has taken place' (Libet et al. 1983, p. 640). As we saw in the discussion of consciousness in Chapter 7, there is a philosophical objection to this 'other way' of putting it that was put forward by Bennett and Hacker (2003), for example, who argued that it is not brains or parts of bodies but people who experience and decide things. Empirically, in any case, the data do not refer to reports of having made decisions. We are concerned with the *process*, not an instantaneous event of decision-making in forming intentions. It is a process that extends over a period of time, and, as Libet said, it usually begins *unconsciously*. Libet had much earlier (Libet 1965) proposed that some substantial period of time for appropriate cerebral activity was required for eliciting all specific conscious experiences.

While accepting the conclusion that spontaneous voluntary acts could be initiated unconsciously, Libet and colleagues proposed that there were conditions in which conscious control could operate: (1) there could be a conscious 'veto' that aborts performance; and (2) in those voluntary acts that are not spontaneous, in which conscious deliberation precedes the act, conscious initiation and control could not be excluded. On the first of these conditions for conscious control, Libet argued, especially in his later work (Libet 2004, e.g. p. 197), that the fact that conscious intention appears about 200–150 ms before the motor act, allows sufficient time for a conscious function to 'intervene' in the process. In this way it may provide a trigger to enable the volitional process to go to completion, or to be 'vetoed'; and this, he argued, gives rise to our feeling that free will could control the outcome. Sensing volition then becomes to some extent a function of giving attention to only part of the process of forming an intention. Viewed in the wider context of the literature on consciousness and attention (see Chapter 7), it should not be at all surprising that the experimental evidence Libet and his colleagues provided should indicate that the process of decision making extends from non-conscious modular parallel processing of information to serial conscious commitment to action. Typically consciousness resolves conflicting prescriptions for action that have arisen from parallel processes in transition to serial processes (Morsella 2005). (See the section of Chapter 7 on parallel and serial processes in relation to consciousness.)

Objections to Libet's Theory of Voluntary Acts

There have been various objections to Libet's conclusions, particularly in regard to the possibility of the free exercise of an act of suppression after becoming conscious of an intention to act. Some commentators have questioned whether 150 ms is long enough for any conscious activity of choice to be effective. This was Wegner's claim questioned by others, such as Bogan and Mandler (Mandler 2004; Wegner and Commentators 2004). Libet commented later that while Wegner accurately described his experiment, he made no reference to the suggested opportunity for a 'veto' of intended behaviour (Libet 2004, p. 144), which was of prime importance in providing appropriate circumstances for the exercise of free will.

Many commentators have interpreted Libet's findings as confirming the view that the experience of will is an illusion (Norretranders 1999; Velmans 2000; Sommerhoff 2002; Wegner 2002; Velmans 2003; Soon et al. 2008). Gazzaniga too gives an interpretation in line with his claims for the propensity of the brain to create illusions of this kind (Gazzaniga 1998), but he has also argued in support of a sense of agency as a basis for responsible action in society (Gazzaniga 2005). Others have been supportive of Libet's general conclusion on the possibility of conscious intentions affecting voluntary behaviour (Haggard and Eimer 1999; Sirigu, Daprati, Ciancia, Giraux, Nighoghossian, Posada and Haggard 2003; Haggard 2005, 2008; Batthyany 2009; Baumeister and Masicampo 2010; Baumeister et al. 2010, 2011). Bandura noted Libet's 'concern over the automaton view of human nature and the characterization of humans as blissful illusionists'. He acknowledged Libet's case for a dual control system in which people control not only initiation but whether to enact an action plan, saying, 'Hence people are held responsible for their conduct' (Bandura 2008, p. 119). Bandura joined Libet in dismissing the regress argument that the conscious veto is itself the product of preceding neural processes, saying that it 'strips unreservedly any capacity for self-regulative influence over behaviour that is morally consequential' (Bandura 2008, p. 119).

Libet claimed as evidence supporting a belief in free will the reports by some of his subjects that they voluntarily suppressed or allowed the action to proceed after becoming aware of the urge or intention to act. While he said that belief in free will or determinism was simply that, a belief not verifiable by empirical methods (Libet 2004), he nevertheless placed much store by the observation of an apparent opportunity for voluntary action in the period immediately following awareness of the urge or intention to act:

> It should be added that some subjects volunteered reports that, in some of the individual trials, they felt an urge or intention to move which did not consummate in an actual movement, accompanied in some cases by an experience of voluntarily suppressing the act; in such cases, the subject waited until another urge to act arose suddenly, without deliberate planning (see Discussion of "Volitional processes"). (Libet et al. 1982, pp. 329–330)

Libet argued that such subjects' reports should be accepted like any other data, and that the onus is on the sceptic to demonstrate that the subjects were mistaken (Libet 2004).

Further empirical work has directly investigated the neural correlates of a conscious intention being subsequently cancelled. In a functional MRI experiment voluntary inhibition of voluntary action was localized to an area of the anterior frontomedian cortex rostal to the pre-supplementary motor area which had previously been designated for preparatory action in the Libet type of experiments (Brass and Haggard 2007). An identifiable event for analysing brain activity on 'veto' trials was found when action was cancelled consciously at the last possible moment. Haggard commented that '[s]uch decisions might have a key role in self control, and also raise the important possibility that voluntary actions can be prepared in order to simulate them but not execute them, as in imagined action or in prediction by forward models (Wolpert and Miall 1996)' (Haggard 2008, pp. 939–940). In cognitive motivation theory such forward models are incomplete gestalts of goal-oriented activity.

The procedure employed by Libet did not require an inference that 'a decision' had been made at the time of awareness, as the instruction to subjects was 'to let the urge to act appear on its own at any time without any preplanning or concentration on when to act'. This letting-the-urge-appear did not constitute an instance of active decision-making (Batthyany 2009). The word 'decision' was not normally used by either the subjects or the experimenter. It could still apply to any subsequent voluntary provision to allow the act to proceed or to the commitment process as a whole. A case for or against conscious agency cannot be built upon a *decision* having been made at the time of becoming conscious of an 'urge' to act, but the later results of Brass and Haggard point to a more secure basis for inferring a neural process for voluntary acts in the subsequent period in which Libet proposed that a 'veto' was possible.

Although Libet himself allowed for the possibility of voluntary acts, his findings were taken up with enthusiasm by some adherents to materialistic determinism, such as Dennett and Wegner. Damasio described those interpretations of Libet's work as 'superficial and unjustified reactions to findings whose interpretation is still being discussed' (Damasio 2010, p. 269). Wegner's claim for an illusion and Dennett's argument for compatibilism, and some alternatives to them, are discussed in the following sections.

Wegner's Claim That Conscious Will Is an Illusion

Wegner's argument from a deterministic philosophy that conscious will is an illusion (Wegner 2002) is introduced in the general treatment of agency in Chapter 6. Wegner makes a strong claim that not only can we be mistaken about being the origin of our actions, but that we are 'technically wrong all the time' (Wegner 2002, p. 342) in our sense of agency.

It is a complex question, and Wegner's position is nuanced in many ways. The case for mental events having effects on behaviour continued to be acknowledged by Wegner, and hence the possibility remained for conscious intentions to be seen to have effects. In his response to Mandler's comments on *The Illusion of Conscious Will* (Mandler 2004) Wegner said, 'Mandler reports that "Wegner threatens to throw the baby out with the bathwater when he implies that mental events can never be causal agents for thought and action." I never said never' (Wegner and Commentators 2004, p. 683). Acknowledging the arguments advanced by Tweney and Wachholtz (2004; see also Tweney 1997) that they could prove that there is free will by pointing to biofeedback studies in which people can learn (within limits) to control their own autonomic functions, such as heartbeat, Wegner responded that, 'In saying this, they reveal their assumption that the actual relationship between thought and action is at issue here. It is not' (Wegner and Commentators 2004, p. 683).

Wegner's scepticism was directed towards the *experience* of will, not 'the actual relationship' to action. Mandler saw Wegner's distinction between phenomenal will and empirical will as largely acceptable to current psychological thinking, particularly in regard to the function of 'empirical will – the actual relationship between mind and action … relationships between people's thoughts, beliefs, intentions, plans, or other conscious psychological states and their subsequent actions' (Wegner 2002, p. 15), which he contrasted with the experience of will. Mandler questioned whether the psychological causal factors in this account should have been described as *conscious* states, and made the point that empirical will could include the effect also of unconscious factors. Libet's work also points to the presence of unconscious precursors to conscious intentions in the development of voluntary acts, but the main point here is the conceptual separation of conscious will from the full set of 'causal' conditions which include factors additional to conscious experience.

Wegner suggested that it was helpful to know what we cannot attribute to ourselves. He used the famous example of subjective certainty in Penfield's patient who raised an arm in response to direct brain stimulation by an electrode and said, 'I didn't do that. You did' (Penfield 1958, 1975). The sense of being a responsible agent accords with our general conclusion from a wide range of literature that the unifying functions of consciousness are found in the formation and implementation of intentions, so Wegner could say that 'the experience of conscious will acts as a unifying clue in our causal analysis, leading us to do a better job of appreciating our own potential causality than the causality of anyone else. Conscious will puts the agent self together in the in the puzzle of life' (Wegner 2002, p. 329). That is a beautiful phase that 'puts the agent self together in the puzzle of life' (p. 329). It fits well the macro model of cognitive motivation at the level of the whole person, except that, as in Bandura's theory of self-efficacy, it would not work if it were not true enough of the time for us to have confidence in our own effectiveness. As Wegner says, 'Perceived control is usually understood as a global feeling of competence or confidence' (p. 330), and he claims value for the person in that perception even when it is not strictly true.

Wegner sought support for the idea that positive illusions provide an opportunity for 'creative self-deception' (Taylor 1989). How much does it matter if perceived control is not in fact true? Placebos, for example, do work. There is a mechanism for the effect. 'People do not get better simply because they think they are going to get better. Rather, believing that one will get better releases a number of chemicals in the body that may actually promote healing' (Taylor 1989, p. 118). The same beneficial effect can be claimed for positive self-enhancement through psychological procedures. Wegner suggests that whether we embrace the illusion of control or reject it, the experience of agency in our intended behaviour remains a useful clue to what is real.

The truth cannot be demonstrated empirically with finality. For Libet, free will remained a matter of belief: 'The assumption that a deterministic nature of the physically observable world can account for subjective conscious functions and events is a speculative *belief*, not a scientifically proven proposition' (Libet 2004, p. 153). Libet wished to allow for non-determinism as an option in which 'conscious will may, at times, exert effects not in accord with known physical laws', although that is 'also a non-proven speculative belief' (Libet 1999, p. 56). There are alternatives to Libet's indeterminism as a basis for freedom that we will discuss shortly, chiefly in reference to the theory of emergence in complex structures, and in regard to free will and self-control.

A pervasive problem with Wegner's argument is that it appears to assume some kind of dualism. This unexpected dualism was discerned by Baars and by Dennett (Baars 2002b; Baars et al. 2003; Dennett 2003, 2004) in 'the way our minds portray their operations to us' (Wegner and Commentators 2004, p. 655) and the idea that 'we inhabit an extraordinarily complicated machine' (Wegner 2002, p. 27). Baars made the point that, 'Conceptually, the argument suffers from dualism – implicitly assuming that consciousness is only a by-product of brain activity, as if it were a non-physical substance' (Baars 2002b, p. 268). He said if we adopt the viewpoint of modern neuroscience, these arguments lose their force because consciousness and volition are aspects of brain functioning. Dennett discerned the same fault, recognising Wegner's apparent indebtedness to dualist ways of thinking he would have him repay the 'Cartesian loans' (Dennett 2004). Dennett identified a Cartesian ghost in the machine, the 'we' who inhabit it.

Dennett objected to Wegner's (2002) idea that '[c]onscious will is particularly useful, then, as a guide to ourselves' (p. 328), because for him it implied that one part of the brain could have a controlling influence on another. He did not want any 'boss' in the system.

> It seems as if there has to be some central Agent or Boss or Audience, to take in (to transduce) all the information and appreciate it, and then 'steer the ship.' The idea that the network itself – by virtue of its intricate structure, and hence powers of transformation, and hence capacity for controlling the body – could assume the role of the inner Boss and thus harbor consciousness, seems preposterous. Initially. But some version of this claim is the materialist's best hope. (Dennett 1996, p. 73)[1]

The 'we' who inhabit and guide ourselves was an idea for which Gray also criticized Wegner. In Chapter 6 I contrasted Wegner's apparent dualism with Gray's description of a unified reflexive self. It helps to explain

[1] Dennett's position on this matter is also a *non*-materialist's but physicalist's best hope. A physicalist view does not rely upon eliminative materialism. See Chapter 6.

the difference between his basic approach and the emphasis in cognitive motivation theory on processes of integration as a basis for conscious intentional acts.

Dennett had, however, previously accepted Wegner's comment on the *experience of will* serving as a marker that could be useful in the future: 'A *person* has to be able to keep in contact with past and anticipated intentions, and one of the main roles of the brain's user-illusion of itself, which I call the self as a center of narrative gravity, is to provide *me* with a means of interfacing with myself at other times. As Wegner puts it, "Conscious will is particularly useful, then, as a guide to ourselves" (p. 329)' (Dennett 2003, p. 253). Narrative conceptions of the identity of a person are discussed in Chapter 11 as relatively realistic and functional. In this instance, however, Dennett appears to be reinforcing Wegner's view of experience as an illusion, albeit a useful illusion: 'one of the main roles of the brain's user-illusion of itself' (Dennett 2003, p. 253).

'Conscious thought is sometimes mistaken about inner processes and reasons for acting, may be too slow to initiate behavior, succumbs to false explanations of external events, is not needed to produce many important behaviors, and can be mistaken about whether it exerts control' (Baumeister and Masicampo 2010, p. 965). But this might not be the principal function of conscious thought, which these authors suggest is not in the enhancement of sensory input or direct control of behaviour, but in simulating past experiences, future possibilities and other people's perspectives. Its great value lies in bringing together information from diverse sources. Such constructed images of past and possible future activity, in addition to providing the images for committed action, enable reports of one's own mental processes to have social as well as personal functions. These images make it possible to share thoughts about intentions with others, thus enabling cultural as well as personal integration. Socially, conscious thought is required for people to be able to talk and thereby share cultural benefits, and it allows mistakes made by individuals to be corrected in society.

Baumeister and Masicampo claim that Libet's results pose no problem for the position they advocate because direct control of motor movement is not the purpose of conscious thought, and the brain has work to do in advance to create conscious thought. Similarly, in reference to Wegner, they claimed that their account can be reconciled with the fact that the conscious mind can be mistaken about whether a response was caused by oneself or others (Wegner 2002). 'It affirms that any input from consciousness is upstream and that the conscious feeling of agency is itself a construction rather than a direct pipeline to reality. Still, it is probably right most of the time, even if it is a simulation' (Baumeister and

Masicampo 2010, p. 966). A somewhat stronger position in favour or conscious effects was taken by Haggard.

Haggard's Account of Conscious Intentions

Patrick Haggard and his colleagues provided wider support for the main thrust of Libet's findings in several investigations (Haggard and Eimer 1999; Haggard and Magno 1999; Sirigu et al. 2003; Haggard 2005; Brass and Haggard 2007). He concluded from these and a later neuroscience review that networks of brain areas, including the pre-supplementary motor area, the anterior prefrontal cortex and the parietal cortex, underlie voluntary action. 'These areas generate information for forthcoming actions, and also cause the distinctive conscious experience of intending to act and then controlling one's own actions' (Haggard 2008, p. 934). In one of these investigations that Haggard conducted with Eimer, the voluntary aspect of the movement was enhanced by introducing an additional element of choice. Subjects chose not only when to move but whether to press a key by moving a finger on the left *or* the right hand. They found that conscious awareness of intentions was associated with the prior onset of the readiness potential in the pre-supplementary motor area (preSMA) on the opposite side of the brain to the hand that was chosen for movement (where representation of that hand is located). This confirmed their view that awareness of an intention to move was related to neural preparation for a specific motor action and not to a general readiness to act (Haggard and Eimer 1999; Haggard 2008, p. 942). Conscious intention to act is then a function of integrating the cognitive simulation of specific projected motor acts with subjective awareness of an emotionally tinged 'urge,' or 'wanting' to act, that constituted the final stage in a commitment to action.

Soon and colleagues identified similar patterns of brain activation before movement that predicted whether participants would perform a forthcoming action with the left or the right hand. They found patterns of activation in the frontopolar cortex that predicted participants' choices up to 8 s before the action itself was performed, which Haggard suggested may represent an earlier stage in the causal chain that generates actions (Haggard 2008; Soon et al. 2008). Among the other supporting reports was the finding, in a study that replicated Libet's findings, that patients with parietal lesions could report when they started moving but not when they became aware of their intention to move. It was thus proposed that when a movement is planned, activity in the parietal cortex generates a predictive internal model of the upcoming movement, which forms the neural correlate of motor awareness (Sirigu et al. 2003). In cognitive motivation it represents construction of an image of a goal and the means for its attainment. Again, consciousness of a specific action plan links behaviour with intention as it forms part of the process of forming and making conscious commitments.

Haggard saw volition as consisting of a *series* of decisions regarding whether to act, what action to perform and when to perform it. The decision on whether to perform an act had both an early motivational component and a late predictive final check, with action selection occurring between these decision points. Others also have suggested a decision-making process that extends over time (Dennett 2003). Haggard argued that everyday versions of voluntary action as a moment of mental choice can be contrasted with a set of processes in specific brain circuits which 'jointly specify several kinds of information that determine our actions, so … voluntary action is therefore a form of decision making' (Haggard 2008, p. 937).[2]

Haggard approved an important model of cognitive control in the theory of supervisory processes formulated by Shallice and his associates (Norman and Shallice 1986; Shallice 1988; Shallice and Burgess 1998). They suggested that while commonly observed stimuli would normally trigger a routine response, non-routine control of behaviour requires intervention by the supervisory attention system in which attention is centrally managed. It is a process that invokes consciousness. Voluntary action in regard to goals was understood in terms of choosing between several simultaneous goals to schedule them in a series. This switch to serial processing is again what we have seen as a common function of consciousness. Such a choice between goals and courses of action is also a function of free will as described later in the chapter in the section on free will and self-control, particularly in reference the work of Baumeister and his associates (see Baumeister and Monroe 2014).

According to Haggard, late decisions on whether to act synthesize information from several independent action specifications, while they predict possible outcomes, and evaluate the costs, before the motor system is committed in voluntary action. In this model a check on whether to proceed is achieved by comparing the output of a predictive forward model with a goal description, the motor commands then being adjusted accordingly. Some predictive checking could result not only in correction of specified actions but in cancelling the action, as Libet proposed. Haggard suggested that a decision on when to act could be a form of the decision on whether to act, as a result of further evaluation of the

[2] Haggard described a range of different types of decision with reference to a large number of neuroscience and behavioural studies of the particular brain circuits (pp. 937–940).

cost of acting in the light of changing external conditions and internal motivations. When an intention is being maintained for later action that might be dropped 'prospective-memory situations particularly highlight the need for "late whether decisions" or "veto decisions"' (p. 940). This is the point at which Libet saw the possibility of conscious control.

Conscious experience figured at several points in Haggard's account of the 'cognitive processes that underlie the experience of voluntary action' (p. 941), specifically in reference to intention, action and outcome. These conscious elements, each 'caused by' separate neural signals, are synthesized (integrated, we might say) to form an overall impression of an action as a single event. In this synthesis, intentions predict the actions, together with the goal effects to which they refer, and the sensory experiences of the action. These processes bind together the various components of the experience of an intended action to produce awareness of the action as a whole, and hence representation of the self as an agent that is capable of voluntary control.

Dennett's Compatibilism and Conscious Intentions

Philosophers have been active in attempting conceptual clarification of psychological theories of intention and consciousness, and they have sometimes promoted particular theories and approaches. Daniel Dennett is one whose work in this area has been extensive and prominent. Many people have found it both fascinating and contentious. A reviewer of one of his books (Dennett 1998) remarked in *Philosophical Psychology*, 'There may be method in his madness, but it is madness still. But it is gripping, intriguing, gifted madness that rightly commands our attention' (Polger 2001, p. 250). Both intentionality and consciousness have been central themes in his wide-ranging and controversial contributions as a philosopher to cognitive psychology over the past 40 years or so. His books, especially *The Intentional Stance* and *Consciousness Explained* (Dennett 1987, 1991), and some of his later related work have attracted a great deal of attention.

Dennett presents himself as a 'compatibilist', one who holds that free will is not incompatible with determinism, although he hedges his position somewhat by saying that he is talking about practical, not theoretical, free will.[3] He distinguishes determinism in human behaviour from inevitability. Dennett argues that all human acts are subject to physical

[3] Theoretical free will is a hypothetical construct entertained and dismissed in the determinist philosophy in which Dennett asserts that there can be only one physically possible future.

determinism, but that 'holding people responsible is still the best game in town' (Dennett 1984, p. 162. See also Dennett 2003). People are sufficiently responsible to be punished or praised because their behaviour is a function of who they are. He claimed that freedom is compatible with the immediate causal conditions being within an agent who is not unduly subject to external constraints. Dennett argues that the only sort of free will 'worth wanting' is compatibilist. A compatibilist can consider that the self is part of the world of causes and effects, so that when we say the agent could have done otherwise we mean that 'had the causal factors internal to the self (a subsystem of the brain) been different, this self would have exerted a different causal action on the rest of the world' (Gomes 1999, p. 74).

Pointing out the etymological connection of 'inevitable' with 'unavoidable,' he argued that it is possible to imagine, and to construct, logical or mathematical models of entities whose every move is determined by strict rules but which can reliably avoid many threats by acting in accord with regularities in their imagined world, just as people are quite good at avoidance in the interests of self-preservation. Avoiders are programmed to avoid. In a completely determined imaginary world, an avoidable event is not inevitable because threats can be avoided but they are nevertheless determined. 'Determinism is the friend, not the foe, of those who dislike inevitability' (Dennett 2003, p. 60). It is easier to dodge events determined in a regular pattern than it would be in chaotic conditions. Compatibilism is thus demonstrated as a conceptual possibility. We can still argue about whether it fits the world we live in, but hypothetically it allows considerable room to talk of freedom while still holding with determinism if we are convinced of its necessity.

In Dennett's view, 'freedom evolves' (Dennett 2003) together with the increasing complexity and information-processing capacity of higher organisms. We 'leap up' from 'the basic level of atoms and space to higher ontological categories' concerning vagueness, subjectivity, and intentionality (p. 65). With such development, 'the whole can become more *free* than its parts' (p. 48). In this view of freedom being enhanced by increased complexity Dennett comes close to the philosophy of emergence that I discussed in Chapter 6. In that philosophy, a dynamic view of the reflexive self in the agency of a person can be seen as an expression of *emergent* qualities of the person as an autonomous system. In her introduction to *Evolution and Emergence* (Murphy and Stoeger 2007), Nancey Murphy presented emergence as a departure from reductionism in a search for 'understanding how complex (higher-level) entities become causal players in their own right, over and above the effects of their components' (Murphy 2007a, pp. 1–2).

In Dennett's view, freedom being based on a person's capacity to make intelligent use of his or her knowledge of the regularities observed in the world presents a different, and 'deterministic', model of free will compared with either Gray's reconciliation (see Chapter 6) or that which Libet entertained when he referred to indeterminism as allowing for free will (Libet 1999, 2004). Dennett rejected Libet's 'vision of "conscious will" as being out of the loop' (Dennett 2003, p. 245). He wants to say, 'You are not out of the loop. You are the loop.' Being the loop implies a non-instantaneous causal process for which an agent is responsible. This 'being the loop' is what Gray was describing in his reference to responsibility as a function of the entire system that is me.

Dennett quotes Wegner approvingly when Wegner says, 'A micro analysis of the time interval before and after action indicates that consciousness pops in and out of the picture and *doesn't really do anything*' (Wegner 2002, p. 59, Dennett's italics, p. 245), but he suggests in addition that one needs to think in terms of a longer-term process, not instantaneous conscious causation. Dennett argued that rather than consciousness not really doing anything, it is implicit in Wegner's work that

> [c]onsciousness has lots of work to do, but its accomplishments seem to disappear when we ask ourselves what work it is doing *right now* (at time *t*). Since at each moment it 'doesn't really do anything,' it can seem that it is an entirely epiphenomenal accompaniment, along for a free ride. An evolutionary perspective shows us why this is mistaken. (Dennett 2003, p. 246)

In this understanding, consciousness is an expression of the need and capacity for self-monitoring that makes the difference between most animals' adaptation and human cognitive control. Selection of appropriate behaviour does not, for most animals, require *experience* of the capacity to cause it, but self-monitoring became advantageous as creatures acquired more and more behavioural options. Dennett suggested that it was communication, and especially of actions and plans, that brought about evolution of the *less unwitting* forms of behavioural control. This is quite close to the understanding of freedom that I have argued for as a consequence of the completion of an incomplete gestalt at the macro level of the whole person.

Dennett suggested, in regard to intentionality, that people come to anticipate the behaviour of animate entities by taking an intentional stance towards them, treating them as *agents* with *beliefs* about the world and specific *desires*, who have enough common sense to do the *rational* thing given those beliefs and desires. If we assume they have intentions, it is easier to predict what they will do. 'When we adopt the intentional stance we have to know *at least roughly* how the agent picks out the objects of concern ... We typically don't need to know exactly what way the agent conceives of his task' (Dennett 1996, p. 41). In this he is similar to Bratman in his planning theory of intentions in regard to the exercise of partial plans.

This knowing approximately how an agent conceives of a task or situation means that in adopting an intentional stance we attribute a capacity for 'theory of mind' (Premack and Woodruff 1978) to an agent. In having a theory of mind an agent knows that another person is also an agent who knows something and may intend some action in regard to it, and probably that the other knows that we know that he knows, and so on. At one point Dennett gave as an epigraph (Dennett 2006, p. 108), an illustration from Coventry Patmore's poem, 'The Kiss':

> 'I saw you take his kiss!' 'Tis true.'
> 'Oh Modesty!' 'Twas strictly kept:
> He thought me asleep; at least I knew
> He thought I thought he thought I slept.' (Patmore 1856)

In thinking about thinking we make sense of things, including ourselves as intentional beings, and we know others can do this too.

Dennett relates his conception of the relevant basic cognitive processes to curiosity, saying 'that the only work that the brain must do is whatever it takes to *assuage epistemic hunger* – to satisfy "curiosity" in all its forms' (Dennett 1991, p. 16) – hence the central role of curiosity in the theory of cognitive motivation. The 'one necessary thing' for the brain to do is to bring together in a meaningful way whatever is required to make sense of things – and that, in challenging circumstances, is where consciousness confers great advantages.

He then goes on to build up a picture of the more complex adaptive cognitive processes in consciousness and their neural correlates. These correlates of consciousness include: (1) auto-stimulation to 'broadcast' information from one specialist module to many, or the global access hypothesis (Baars 1988; 1997, 2005a); (2) the use of language to replicate ideas seen in the concept of cultural 'memes' (Dawkins 1989, p. 192); and (3) transition from multiple competing modular channels to narrative-like sequences in serial processing exemplified by Schank in his work on scripts (Schank and Abelson 1977; Schank 1990; Schank and Schank 1999). That transition from parallel to serial processes is marked by consciousness, at least in human beings (see Chapter 7.) Dennett later described the invention of language as 'a slingshot that has launched it (the human species) far beyond all other earthly species in the power to look ahead and reflect' (Dennett 1996, p. 147). These reflexive and other capabilities evolved to establish adult human consciousness as a uniquely capable system of *anticipation* – a necessary component of an intention. Dennett claimed in the end that description of these processes is all that is needed to 'explain' consciousness (Dennett 1991). Ten years later he observed:

> Theorists are converging from quite different quarters on a version of the global neuronal workspace model of consciousness, but there are residual confusions to be dissolved. In particular, theorists must resist the temptation to see global accessibility as the *cause* of consciousness (as if consciousness were some other, further condition); rather, it *is* consciousness. (Dennett 2001, p. 221)

The claim that consciousness *is* accessibility makes the same emphasis as Tononi does in his saying that consciousness *is* integration (Tononi 2004, 2005). I argue in Chapter 7 that such a description of information-processing mechanisms is an incomplete account of consciousness because, except by arbitrary assertion, it does not include sentience, the subjective qualities known directly to a conscious person. As for Dennett's rejection of the idea of accessibility *causing* consciousness, Baars, the author of the global access hypothesis, would agree, but he turns the necessary conditions around the other way, saying that 'working memory requires conscious processes, not vice versa' (see his global workspace account: Baars 2002a, 2003, 2005a). This claim for consciousness having a causal role would be a problem for Dennett, but in agreement with Baars, in the general theory of cognitive motivation, the processes of integration for purposive behaviour, that take place in working memory, are facilitated by consciousness.

The lingering historical puzzle about conscious intentions goes a long way back, even in the modern era, well before Dennett's sensitivities, and Woodworth's early claim. It was present in the influence of Brentano on the original Gestalt theorists whose contribution to the psychology of goals was reviewed in the previous chapter. Early in the development of 'dynamic psychology', Woodworth included a role for consciousness: 'unless there is some *conscious anticipation* of the result we should hardly speak of purpose' (Woodworth 1932, p. 243). In more recent times Searle has argued for what he called a 'strong claim' that '[o]nly a being that could have conscious intentional states could have intentional states at all' (Searle 1992, p. 132; see also Searle 1983, 2010). These theoretical and philosophical positions have been strengthened in recent years by such empirical research as I have cited here from Baars, Haggard, Gray, Baumeister, Panksepp and others, which bypasses Dennett's compatibilism. The critical point is that cognitive integration of information that defines purposes and commitment to action is a function of consciousness that operates at the level of the whole person, while it includes both conscious and unconscious processes. Agency is a property of the system as a whole.

Free Will and Self-Control

It is an essential human characteristic to act with conscious intentions. As we have discussed in reference to the work of Libet, Haggard, Gray and others, invoking conscious intentions assumes a capacity for free will. In this work I have regarded free will as being, like consciousness, an emergent property which has appeared at the system level in the evolution of complex mind/brain systems. This is a position not uncommon among contemporary philosophers and psychologists. Baumeister and his colleagues have in recent work described free will as an emergent capacity that is 'simply another kind of cause' (Baumeister and Monroe 2014, p. 6). Dennett accepts it for practical purposes but denies it in a deterministic theory that he shares with Wegner. Many studies of laypersons' opinions strongly affirm belief in free will – the belief that I am responsible for what I choose to do, that I am the cause of what I do consciously and deliberately. Nevertheless, it is not entirely a conscious process. When we act with deliberate conscious commitment, we typically recruit action plans and resources that are in part unconscious. Sometimes a resource of energy that we depend upon might, colloquially, be called 'willpower' (Baumeister 2008; Baumeister and Tierney 2011). On willpower and self-control, see also the work of Mischel and his colleagues that is discussed in Chapter 6 (Mischel 1996; Mischel and Ayduk 2002, 2004, 2010; Mischel 2012). It is a concept with quite profound implications even if it is a folk psychological idea:

> Much work in recent years has suggested that this capacity [for free will] involves the expenditure of a limited resource, akin to strength or energy. Most likely the traditional folk term 'willpower' is an intuitive expression of the idea that persons must put energy into regulating themselves. (Baumeister and Monroe 2014, p. 30)

Motivation implies both a sense of direction and a source of energy. Colloquially, 'willpower' might be spoken of as a kind of energy without it being clear whether this energy is metaphorical, cognitive or physiological. The concept of willpower is an idea imported into psychological theory from folk psychology without strict definition, but regardless of its origin it has been a significant research question in recent years whether 'willpower' refers to something 'real' or physical, not merely metaphorical, and especially whether it refers to some physical property of a person.

An evidence-based argument has been made for seeing willpower as a real property of a person that is both cognitive and physiological, a source of energy necessary for people to exercise their capacity for free will. This, of course, makes the assumption that people do have that capacity. Sometimes authors like Baumeister and Monroe might avoid an irrevocable commitment and argue that *if people have free will*, they must be able to do certain things, like exercise self-control and make rational choices, and then proceed by empirical methods to demonstrate a capacity to do those things, and in the case of Baumeister and his colleagues to relate that capacity to a source of physical energy in glucose stored in the body: 'Research on volition indicates that self-regulation, intelligent reasoning, decision making, and initiative all deplete a (common) limited energy source, akin to the folk notion of willpower and linked to the body's glucose supplies' (Baumeister and Monroe 2014, p. 2).

The role of glucose, making willpower more than metaphorical, was demonstrated in evidence elucidating the strength model of free will (Gailliot et al. 2007). This model came from studies showing that after one act of self-control, performance on a second act of self-control is impaired (Baumeister, Bratslavsky, Muraven and Tice 1998; Hagger, Wood, Stiff and Chatzisarantis 2010). Baumeister suggested that some form of energy or strength is involved in self-regulation, and that a source of such energy for self-control may be depleted by acts of free will. People will even show a tendency to conserve energy by underperforming on a second task when they know that performance on a third task is going to be required (Muraven, Shmueli and Burkley 2006).

A simple explanation that the level of blood glucose was reduced by the effort put into self-regulation has not been replicated consistently (Baumeister and Monroe 2014). What has been shown more clearly is that low levels of glucose predict poor self-regulatory performance (Gailliot et al. 2007) and, significantly, there is evidence that rather than the level of glucose itself, it is its availability for metabolic use that produces the effect. So diabetics, who have restricted availability but high levels of glucose in the blood, have been shown to have problems with self-control. That this availability could be a function of cognitive-motivational as much as physiological factors is suggested by a related finding that comes from a different line of research: Type 1 diabetics were characterized by an implicit motivational syndrome of high need for affiliation and low need for power that represented a risk factor in blood sugar control (McClelland 1989). McClelland's 'Easygoing Affiliative Syndrome' reflects the same correlation as found by Gailliot and colleagues but suggests causal processes in both directions. Baumeister and Monroe proposed a similar bi-directional process when they discussed the mutual depreciation of decision-making and self-regulation, suggesting that the exercise of free will depends upon a common limited resource. Another finding is that receiving a dose of glucose can counteract the depletion effect. 'Linking self-control to blood glucose levels provides a new perspective on free will, especially if one regards it as a variable capacity' (Baumeister and Monroe 2014, p. 34).

The proposition that decision-making itself is depleting was challenged on the grounds that the autonomy of people is restricted when cognitive dissonance procedures are employed to induce people to make choices guided by external influences. When people made two successive *pleasant* self-consistent choices, they did not show ego depletion (Moller, Deci and Ryan 2006). However, Vohs and colleagues confirmed that choosing among a wide range of choices does cause ego depletion. While the results of Moller and colleagues' study were replicated for a small number of pleasant choices, as the number of successive choices was increased, the effect of pleasantness decreased and disappeared (Vohs, Baumeister, Schmeichel, Twenge, Nelson and Tice 2008). In the long run, choosing is depleting, regardless of the level of enjoyment. Baumeister and Monroe conclude that there are common processes based on the same underlying resource in self-control and decision making by rational choice. 'That is, there is arguably a single psychological phenomenon that underlies the popular understanding of free will' (Baumeister and Monroe 2014, p. 40).

In addition to self-regulation and rational choice, as classic defining cases, Baumeister and Monroe propose initiative and planning as forms of free will that also have the effect of ego depletion. Their general conclusion was that human beings have a form of volition that enables people to guide their behaviour based on much wider cognitive and social considerations than apply to other species, including incorporation of 'meaningful ideas into the causation of action' (Baumeister and Monroe 2014, p. 45). In cognitive motivation theory, the integrating effects of consciousness, meaningfulness and the ability to discern theory of mind in other agents are distinctively human aspects of intentional behaviour that I will discuss in reference to comparative studies in the next section.

Discerning Intentions as a Distinctly Human Characteristic

Awareness of our own ability to act with conscious intentions is a step towards recognition of the same quality of intentionality in another person. Understanding how to discern the intentions of another agent also facilitates self-reflection on one's own intentional thinking. A considerable amount of research has been undertaken on the discernment of intentions in other people as a characteristic human attribute. The evidence available from comparative studies of human beings with other primates, and of human infants with older children, leads to a conclusion on the uniqueness of adult human social perception. In this research implicit processes (non-conscious or automatic) have been distinguished from explicit processes that require consciousness in the recognition of intentions (Frith and Frith 2012). Much of this research, which has been concerned with such questions as whether chimpanzees have a theory of mind and whether very young infants can detect false beliefs, is only of marginal relevance for our task of understanding intentions, but the implicit-explicit distinction reinforces the importance of consciousness for intentionality. As an aspect of human consciousness, intentionality is seen in such theories as Bandura's account of human agency (Bandura 2001) to be an essential part of what it means to be human. Comparative studies are therefore of considerable interest for discussion of human intentionality.

Tomasello's Evolutionary Anthropology of Intentionality

A case was made by Michael Tomasello (Tomasello 1999) and his colleagues at the Max Plank Institute of Evolutionary Anthropology, Leipzig, Germany, for consciously shared intentionality being a uniquely human characteristic. Later research has indicated that the human ability to discern the intentions of another might not be entirely unique (Call and Tomasello 2008); others have argued since that it depends upon how that ability is defined (Frith and Frith 2012). Tomasello and colleagues proposed a simple model of intentionality 'based on control systems principles – in which goal, action, and perceptual monitoring are all seen as components in the larger adaptive system that serves to regulate the organism's behavioural interactions with the environment' (Tomasello et al. 2005, p. 676). Tomasello suggested that this capacity for understanding self-regulation depended upon individuals understanding other members of their species as beings *like themselves* who have intentional and mental lives like their own.

Tomasello argued that there was not enough time in recent human evolution for the normal processes of evolution by natural selection to have created each of the necessary cognitive skills for a species-specific culture one by one. He proposed that there need have been only one genetic innovation enabling a cascade of social-cognitive changes that could have occurred quite recently, perhaps as late as the last 250,000 years (Stringer and McKie 1996). In any case, his argument was that there is only one known biological mechanism that could bring about these changes in so short a time. It was the mechanism of social and cultural transmission, a moderately common evolutionary process, but different in different species. Modifications would have accumulated over time with inventions being improved by recursive feedback progressively incorporating new adaptations into the same but modified objects and practices in successive generations with a 'ratchet effect' (Tomasello, Kruger and Ratner 1993). In this process people have to 'imagine themselves "in the mental shoes" of some other person, so that they can learn not just *from* the other but *through* the other' (Tomasello 1999, p. 6). This implies 'theory of mind' in an observer imputing subjective qualities to another. To learn socially the conventional use of a tool, children have to understand the *intentional* use of the tool or symbolic practice – what it is 'for', what 'we' do with it. Groups develop a culture by individuals identifying with one another, understanding conspecifics as intentional agents.

Until recently, comparative studies had tended to highlight the common features that human beings share with other primates. A different picture emphasising the uniqueness of human capacity for social perception and cumulative cultural learning has recently come out of comparative studies in primate laboratories. An example is Hauser's description of unique human neural capacities for advanced cognitive operations (Hauser 2009) that we noted in Chapter 3. Hauser referred to many researchers having pointed to 'fundamental changes starting some 800,000 years ago, with a crescendo of change at around 45,000 to 40,000 years ago' (p. 193). A genetic revolution had taken place that provided humans with an unprecedented capacity for generating novel cultural expressions and created a gap between humans and other primates. He proposed that the human brain was transformed from a system with a high degree of modularity to a system of modules with numerous promiscuous and combinatorially creative interfaces. 'This system provided a universal framework on which cultural options could be realized (Dehaene, Duhamel, Hauser and Rizzolatti 2005, Jackendoff 2008)' (Hauser 2009, p. 193). This transition suggests that extended consciousness (see Chapter 7) became characteristic of humans at the same time.

Human beings 'identify' with conspecifics more deeply than do other primates. According to Tomasello, human children understand other persons as beings like themselves, and sometimes try to see things from their point of view. Tomasello referred to this process generally as 'understanding others as intentional (or mental) agents (like the self)' (Tomasello 1999a, p. 14). This understanding of others as intentional agents has many cascading effects making possible collaborative creation of cultural artefacts and processes of cultural learning.

Research on non-human primates, chimpanzees and orangutans in particular, originally led Tomasello and Call to the general conclusion that chimpanzees and other non-human primates do not understand the psychological states of others (Tomasello and Call 1997; Call and Tomasello 1998; Tomasello et al. 2005). While other primates could use insightful strategies to influence what happened next, human beings could do something different: inferring a goal so that they can attempt to influence this and other intentional and mental states, not just behaviour. Later research has modified these findings, especially in regard to the evolution of a capacity for theory of mind. Other primates were then seen to have a greater capacity for understanding others than was at first thought, although a significant difference remains in regard to explicit (conscious) reasoning about the beliefs of others.

The Evolution of Emotionally Modern Minds

Non-human primates possess many of the cognitive abilities that humans do (Baumeister and Masicampo 2010). The major differences lie in the human improvements in identifying with each other and understanding each other. These qualities, added to the primate mental abilities that were similar to human abilities, 'transformed them into new, culturally based cognitive skills with a social-collective dimension' (Tomasello 1999, p. 7). A battery of mental tests given to human children, chimps and orangutans confirmed that the three groups were largely similar on most tests but differed consistently on social-cognitive skills (Herrmann, Call, Hernandez-Lloreda, Hare and Tomasello 2007). More generally, primates (especially chimps) can pass some tests of theory of mind but not others (Corballis 2004; Call and Tomasello 2008; Corballis 2009; see also Hauser, Chomsky and Fitch 2002). Hence, group action in other primates is limited and does not show the kind of intentional collaboration that is common to almost all human groups. The crucial advances that enabled human minds to create culture consisted of acquiring the ability to understand the inner, mental states of others and the motivation to communicate one's own inner thoughts to others (Tomasello et al. 2005). As noted earlier, Baumeister and his colleagues have proposed that the capacity for exercising free will emerged as another factor in the development of human culture through social interaction. The creative outcome of mutual understanding probably depends upon a complex of such factors.

In her book *Mothers and Others: The Evolutionary Origins of Mutual Understanding*, Sarah Blaffer Hrdy argues for early development by infants of their capacity to discern acceptance and commitment on the part of their carers and their mother in particular (Hrdy 2009). She has proposed an account of the evolution of emotionally modern minds in which the need for emotional bonding between infants and mothers

(Bowlby 1969, 1979) is associated with the infant's capacity to attribute mental states to another person. She presents the recent common view, which has come from studies of false beliefs, that young children develop an understanding that others may hold beliefs different from one's own – an understanding that is derived from the experience of interaction with adults and older children that was described in the influential paper, 'Theory of mind is contagious: You catch it from your sibs,' by Perner, Ruffman and Leekam (1994). This kind of reasoning on the part of young children presupposes that they have a sense of self and a capacity to conceptualize others as separate selves with their own mental states and feelings. 'Beginning around age three, children are able to interpret the feelings and intentions of others and even to imagine what it is like to be someone else altogether' (Harris 2000, pp. 54–55ff). By age four, children display sensitivity to other people's self-image, beginning to flatter and attempting to ingratiate themselves with them (Fu and Lee 2007; Burkart 2009).

The key point of Hrdy's theory of human development is the advantage in understanding others that she attributed to the effect of other caretakers sharing with the mother in the care of the child. It multiplies the advantage that comes from the opportunity to interact with older, more experienced caretakers. Hrdy suggests that the capacity of human children to discern the intentions of others developed when the infant had to learn to perceive and trust the mother's emotional attachment even when she is not present, with the result that 'babies cared for by multiple caretakers would be more aware of distinctions between self and others, better able to read the mental states of conspecifics, and capable of integrating information about their own intentions and those of others – indeed, perhaps several others' (Hrdy 2009, pp. 138–139). She suggested

> that some of these emotional qualities that distinguish modern humans from other apes, especially mind reading combined with empathy and developing a sense of self, emerged earlier in our evolutionary history than anatomically modern humans did (Fonagy, Gergely, Jurist and Target 2002). The critical factor in this emergence of intersubjective capacities was the novel developmental context in which generation after generation of early humans grew up, different from that of any other ape before. (Hrdy 2009, pp. 137–138)

The question posed by Hrdy of when humans became emotionally modern in the course of evolution is relevant to our understanding of the nature of intentions. The suggestion is that a Bowlbian type of attachment could have developed from shared infant care before language and symbolic culture in the last 200,000 years. It could have laid the foundation for the explosive rate of cultural evolution that followed. Tomasello also suggested that the discernment of intentions appeared before language, although the two continued to develop together.

Implicit and Explicit Intentions

One point at which human children behaved in a significantly different way compared with other primates was in the recognition of false beliefs. Call and Tomasello concluded from early false belief paradigms that chimpanzees showed no understanding of others holding false beliefs, (Call and Tomasello 1998, 1999). Later experiments have confirmed this difference from humans in regard to *explicit* beliefs, but some signs have been found of incomplete *implicit* understanding of false beliefs (Frith and Frith 2012).

A simple homely example of the false belief test is given by Hrdy:

> Ask a two-year-old sitting in his mother's lap to watch while you carefully set a cookie on the table. Next, ask his mother to shut her eyes, and hide the cookie on your lap, under the table. Then ask the two-year-old where his mother (eyes still shut) thinks the cookie is. A child younger than three or four years lacks sufficient 'theory of mind' to be able to understand that his mother has a different understanding of the situation than he does. He will almost always tell you that his mother thinks the cookie is under the table (where the cookie actually happens to be), even though she could not see the cookie being put there and thus could not know that. Almost all four-year-olds and a few children as young as three will announce that their mother thinks the cookie is still on the table, where it is not. (Hrdy 2009, p. 136)

Reviewing the evidence for non-human primates having theories of mind, and perceiving intentions, 30 years after the original publication of the seminal article 'Does the chimpanzee have a theory of mind?' by Premack and Woodruff (1978), Call and Tomasello (2008, p. 187) concluded that, contrary to Tomasello's previous argument, 'there is solid evidence from several different experimental paradigms that chimpanzees understand the goals and intentions of others, as well as the perception and knowledge of others'. Nevertheless, despite several seemingly valid attempts, there is currently no evidence that chimpanzees understand false beliefs. Failure on false belief tasks points to a fundamental difference of theoretical importance, which Frith and Frith (2012) suggest can be explained by reference to the distinction between implicit and explicit processes of belief reasoning made by Apperly and Butterfill (2009).

Some authors claim that very early false belief understanding can be demonstrated (Leslie 2005; Onishi and Baillargeon 2005), and that it provides the 'conceptual foundation' for later development of the ability to reason about false beliefs (Surian, Caldi and Sperber 2007). Others say that the results can be explained by infants adopting simple behavioural rules, like 'people look for objects where they last set eyes on them' (Perner and Ruffman 2005, p. 214). Apperly and Butterfill (2009) suggest that both sides in this conflict are mistaken, but that progress can be made by postulating two types of belief reasoning and belief-like states which differ across human infants, non-human animals and human adults.

The general conclusion of Apperly and Butterfill is that the difference between infants and non-human primates on the one hand and older children and adults on the other on tests of understanding false beliefs can be explained by postulating two quite different processes of making inferences about the beliefs of others: one that develops early in human infants, and is found in non-human subjects, is implicit, efficient and inflexible; and the other, requiring the greater cognitive capacity and maturity found only in older human subjects, is explicit, flexible and cognitively demanding. They make this distinction by reference to the nature of explicit adult human theory of mind reasoning as an attitude to content that is propositional (sentence like) and has a psychological role of interacting with other beliefs and desires causing and justifying actions; and they postulate that infants' theory of mind may be limited in respect to either or both content and psychological role.

'One of the proudest achievements of human beings is the ability to reflect on themselves and their past, present, and future,' yet 'most of our cognition occurs automatically and without awareness' (Frith and Frith 2012, p. 289). There is a tradition of cognitive psychologists to make a fundamental distinction between implicit (automatic, unconscious) processes and processes that generate explicit, conscious products (Kahneman and Frederick 2002; Adolphs 2009). In a different context, Gollwitzer and colleagues have made a distinction between implicit and explicit intentions (Gollwitzer et al. 2004). Apperly and colleagues draw the contrast that human adults seem quick and efficient in their social interaction and communication, yet most direct investigation suggests that adults' belief reasoning is relatively effortful and dependent upon limited cognitive resources for memory and executive control (Apperly and Butterfill 2009; Apperly, Samson and Humphreys 2009). Belief reasoning is, then, not automatic, but there is an important role for strategic control in theory of mind tasks which can be disrupted by simultaneous tasks interfering with working memory or language processing or if working memory or other aspects of executive control are impaired as a result of brain injury (Apperly and Butterfill 2009, p. 959). The explicit reasoning required for making strategic judgements in social cognition is marked by the same requirement for reference to executive functions that we saw in Chapter 7 in regard to the transition from parallel implicit processes to serial explicit processes that are associated with the role of consciousness in working memory. It appears that we are dealing here in social cognition with the same cognitive capacity for explicit processing as is required for conscious intentional planning and commitment.

Frith and Frith (2012) suggest that it is through reflective awareness that humans manage to outstrip the performance of other social species. Reflective awareness is found in human behaviour together with reflective discussion. We frequently talk to each other about our mental states, and Frith and Frith suggest that such interactions would be impossible without a special high-level ability for meta-cognition, which may be uniquely human (Metcalfe 2008). They suggest that the human meta-cognitive ability to reflect upon our own mental states 'may well lie at the heart of conscious awareness' (Frith and Frith 2012, p. 305), while it enables people to teach and learn in a deliberately interactive way and to share intentions and experiences, thus making possible joint endeavours such as cultural institutions of the arts and sciences or political and religious activities.

This chapter began with the definition of an intention in terms of an envisaged future state to which a person is committed. Cognitive motivation arises from the conscious comparison of imagined future states with the present states of a person and a situation. This comparison depends upon a meta-cognitive ability to reflect upon our own mental states. The focus of the next chapter is how this type of reflection leads to the construction of meaning and the iconic and narrative images which constitute the identity of a person.

Summary

In cognitive motivation theory, an intention is a particular kind of orientation to the future requiring more than expectations and evaluations. Commitment to reach a goal is the key. Intentions require not simply an expectation or prediction of future actions but a conscious commitment to bring them about. This conscious commitment depends upon some initial preparation that is in part unconscious. Goals and intentions are elements in a cognitive map with potential to guide purposive behaviour towards a desired future state which is partially defined by an incomplete gestalt.

Research by Libet and his colleagues on delayed consciousness of intentions, until after there is some neural preparation for action, has been used by some writers to claim that a sense of agency is always an illusion. However, an integrated conception of agency can be advanced in which the whole *process* of intention formation and enactment is emphasised as distinct from a momentary state of consciousness that may be associated with a commitment to act. In this context I discuss Libet's research on unconscious factors in intentions and his theory of voluntary acts, in comparison with Wegner's argument for the experience of agency being an illusion. Haggard's alternative account of the relationship of intention to action is preferred. I note Libet's own defence of voluntary action. Dennett's compatibilism of free will and determinism is discussed with some reservation, and recent arguments for reaffirmation of willpower by Baumeister are presented in preference to it.

The ability of people to discern the intentions of others has been presented as distinctively human in recent work by evolutionary anthropologists such as Tomasello. This leads to further consideration of the nature of intentionality and the evolution of emotionally modern minds with an understanding of intentions as both implicit and explicit processes. Recent research on the capacity of non-human primates to satisfy theory-of-mind criteria is considered in relation to the claims of human uniqueness. Human capacity for forward thinking and responsibility for intended actions depends upon reflexive self-processes in which a person reflects upon his or her own thoughts and feelings.

Cognitive motivation, which arises from the comparison of imagined future states with the present states of a person and a situation, depends upon this meta-cognitive ability to reflect upon our own mental states.

11 Identity

> I credit poetry ... for making possible a fluid and restorative relationship between the mind's center and its circumference.
>
> – Seamus Heaney 1995

Introduction

The search for and celebration of identity, purpose and meaning are sources of cognitive motivation. These high-level cognitive processes, which are the subject of this chapter and the next, operate on images of ourselves and of our place in the world. Those images are often experienced as incomplete, and the fundamental process of motivation is to move towards their completion. In curiosity we become aware of conceptual conflicts and gaps in knowledge as we are puzzled by strange or novel things, and we try to move from an incomplete understanding of the object towards completion of what is otherwise an incomplete gestalt (see Chapter 2). In the same way at the macro level of the whole person striving for self-understanding in a long-term view of life, we attempt to move towards a complete and meaningful image of ourselves. Cognitive motivation theory articulates a particular approach to identity based on the principle that people seek meaningful integration at all levels of personality organisation. In this chapter I consider first the nature of images of our own identity and the cognitive processes which facilitate their development. This leads to the discussion of meaning and purpose in the next chapter.

People have images of themselves in much the same way as they have images of physical objects, relationships, abstract ideas and other people, about which they often have visual and other images and can tell stories. The images we have of our own identities are similar, but they have special qualities: (1) they include a deep bodily sense of ourselves as living creatures; (2) they are part of our reflexive self-consciousness, including both the self-as-object and the self-as-knower; and (3) they are purposive. Images of identity are meaningful patterns of thought and feeling about ourselves which are formed in the process of seeking the fulfilment of our purposes.

Iconic and Narrative Images of Identity

Meaningful personal integration is experienced largely in two forms that I refer to as *narrative* and *iconic* patterns of meaning. These patterns, forms or images can be illustrated in examples provided by the Irish poet Seamus Heaney, in his lecture, 'Crediting poetry', given when he received the Nobel Prize for Literature in 1995. He began by describing how, as a boy, his exploration of radio broadcasts from different cities in Europe, including Stockholm, where he was then speaking, contributed to the development of his understanding of the wider world from his home in Ireland:

> I had already begun a journey into the wideness of the world. This in turn became a journey into the wideness of language, a journey where each point of arrival – whether in one's poetry or one's life – turned out to be a stepping stone rather than a destination, and that is the journey which has brought me now to this honoured spot. (Heaney 2006, pp. 150–151)

That is a narrative pattern of meaning, particularly significant in its 'stepping stone' imagery, and hence in its sense of purposeful progress in which he said he had dared to 'walk on air.' He credited poetry 'for making this space walk possible'. It gave one kind of meaning to his life. He went on to refer to another kind, a conceptual type of integration that gave meaning in a different way: an iconic form, a visual image with a centre and a circumference, for which he credited the same creative aesthetic sense: 'I credit poetry … for making possible a fluid and restorative relationship between the mind's center and its circumference' (Heaney 2006, p. 151).

These narrative and iconic forms of self-integration, which I suppose to be derived from generic cognitive structures formed in the process of making sense respectively of verbal and visual information, are, while the most common, not the only forms. The distal modes of perception by means of sound and light commonly provide the images used in abstract thought, and together with bodily feelings they tend to dominate everyday conscious thought. These images figure in our dreams and imagination, but other kinds of image can also be employed in higher-level cognition: Francis Galton, for example, reported an experimental investigation of doing 'Arithmetic by smells' in the first issue of the *Psychological Review* (Galton 1894).

In our sense of self there are also proprioceptive and other proximal sources, and some evolutionary neurobiological theorists (Panksepp 1998;

Damasio 2010; Panksepp and Biven 2012) would attribute a primary sense of self to a deeply based feeling or bodily experience of being a living creature. Anticipating the reflexive view of the self, it is 'an intrinsically reverberating neural network linked to basic body tone' – the basis of primary affective consciousness, '*that ineffable feeling of experiencing oneself as an active agent in the perceived events of the world*' (Panksepp 1998, p. 310, emphasis in the original). Damasio refers to feelings that are based on direct signalling from the body as 'primordial and indispensible components of the self' and adds that they 'constitute the very first and inchoate revelation, to the mind, that *its* organism is alive' (Damasio 2010, p. 76). Awareness of the body plays a role in Gestalt therapy with its attention to images of wholeness (Perls et al. 1951), and in traditional and contemporary forms of mindfulness and in mindfulness-based cognitive therapy (Crane 2009; Kashdan and Ciarrochi 2013).

Proximate and distal modalities may be combined in images that last for many years and can be evoked in distressing or fond memories, like the call of birds once heard combined with the scent of a dimly remembered garden. The combination of diverse modes and sources is particularly striking in Sarah Scott's account of curiosity in a group of travellers passing through a varied scene discussed in Chapter 2. Combinations of modalities may be found, for example, in the creative imagination of culinary expertise, where varied tastes, smells and textures combine with visual impressions, and perhaps the story of an enjoyable evening, to form agreeable whole images of particular dishes. By whatever empirical means images of the self are formed, they similarly result from processing inputs in the various modalities in which meaning is given to disparate elements by processes of integration into patterns.

We come now to the elucidation of basic concepts of image formation with some help initially from the Gestalt tradition and the study of aesthetics, but concepts of image, pattern, map and the like are not restricted to those approaches. A similar set of ideas is found, for example, in Damasio's neurobiological approach to the study of self-images similar to Panksepp's ideas cited earlier. Damasio believes that 'conscious minds arise when a self process is added onto a basic mind process' (Damasio 2010, p. 8). 'Conscious minds begin when self comes to mind' (p. 22). In a manner reminiscent of the role of consciousness in organising patterns across widely separated brain regions described by Baars, Tonini, Koch and others (Baars 1997; Tononi 2005; Baars 2005a; Tononi and Koch 2008), Damasio refers to patterns across large networks: 'Those maps are experienced as *images* in our minds, and the term *image* refers not just to the visual kind but to images of any sense origin such as auditory, visceral, tactile, and so forth' (Damasio 2010, p. 18).

The patterns of objects and events in the external world that we perceive and imagine are most commonly but not exclusively iconic or narrative, and so it is with images of the self.

Gestalt Theoretical Foundations

In cognitive motivation, the generation and resolution of an incomplete gestalt plays a central role. Gestalt ideas are indispensable in my exploration of cognitive motivation, but Gestalt theory on its own does not have very much that is useful to say about underlying processes in the way that integration takes place. For that task I have suggested the processes of conscious integration in working memory discussed in Chapter 7, and the function of emotions as a signalling system described in Chapter 8. In this chapter and the next, these ideas are combined with a theory of identity which invokes a personal orientation to the future that was introduced in the discussion of goals and intentions in Chapters 9 and 10 and is tied up with concepts of purpose and meaning.

Aesthetic Principles of Image Formation

Seamus Heaney, in the passages quoted earlier in this chapter, credits poetry with making possible a *fluid and restorative* relationship between the mind's centre and its circumference. His image points to gestalt principles in the integration of elements to form a whole unit. In the general theory of cognitive motivation, when a person is engaged in purposeful activity resolving the difference between a goal and the present state of affairs, purposeful change requires resolution of tensions in an incomplete gestalt that functions as a goal orientation. Applied to the person as a whole, the resultant image is the kind of representation that can express personal identity in a coherent form.

We should not be surprised to find a poet providing insights into the psychology of identity. Goals and gaps and incomplete images are completed in a process that is *creative*. The emotional qualities of speech commonly found in the rhythm and tone of poetry contribute to such creative processes. The creation of images can then be linked with the function of emotions as signals in purposive behaviour, and hence with processes of integration in which poets can bring about unexpected conjunctions to evoke feelings and insights. Metaphors, the use of which tends to characterize poetry, typically combine concepts in that way: in his 'Education by Poetry,' another poet, Robert Frost, referred to '[t]he metaphor whose manage we are best taught in poetry' (Frost 1931, in Richardson, 2007, p. 108), and in a recent essay on Frost and his understanding of metaphor we find that '[p]oetry, speech, metaphor, are the ways human beings transform the brute materiality of the world into meaning' (Kirsch 2014, p. 48).

The resolution of challenges to meaningful images of the self requires the kind of creative processes often best expressed in poetic metaphors in which we attempt to say one thing in terms of another (Frost 1931). In Frost it was in striving for unity: 'Greatest of all attempts to say one thing in terms of another is the philosophical attempt to say matter in terms of spirit, or spirit in terms of matter, to make the final unity' (see Oster 1991, p. 299). In similar literary usage discussed in Chapter 9, it is seen in images of reaching for the incomplete wholeness of beauty, as in Elaine Scarry's powerful image, suggested by Simone Weil, of beautiful things acting 'like small tears in the surface of the world that pull us through to some vaster space' (Scarry 1999, p.112).[1] We come shortly to the notable contribution of Scarry's predecessor, Arnheim, on aesthetics.

There is necessarily some creative genius in the resolution of an incomplete gestalt. New forms of cognitive organisation are required because there is no neat fit of new information to fill a gap in knowledge, as one might assume there could be from Loewenstein's analysis of curiosity with its emphasis on the filling of gaps (Loewenstein 1994). The gap-filling idea was taken up by others who have researched curiosity, such as Kashdan and Litman (Kashdan 2004; Litman and Jimerson 2004; Litman 2005, 2008; Kashdan 2009; see also Chapter 2). But the same authors not only have allowed for the dynamics of deprivation in awareness of gaps in knowledge but also refer to the combination of deprivation with a positive interest in novelty. There is a similar conception of holistic integration in making sense of one's life as a whole in Emmons's *Psychology of Ultimate Concerns* (Emmons 1999a). What we find is not simply the filling of gaps. We see a reordering of cognition in the process of integrating new information to form a new order. The general principles of the theory of cognitive motivation introduced in Chapter 1 acknowledge that the adaptive aim is not merely to fill a gap, or resolve a conflict, but to create a new order.

Creative writers have seen this prospect of creating new forms as a process of 'recentering' (a concept found in gestalt theory) that implies initial 'decentering.' So Scarry envisaged 'radical decentering' in a process of transformation, again quoting Weil (1951/1979, p. 159/99), in which beauty 'requires us "to give up our imaginary position as the center … A transformation then takes place at the very roots of our sensibility."' She spoke of being lifted up,

[1] Eysenck, Berlyne, Koffka, Arnheim and other significant authors of psychological works in this field have contributed in a similar way to the psychology of art.

letting the ground rotate beneath us several inches, so that when we land, we find we are standing in a different relation to the world than we were a moment before. It is not that we cease to stand at the center of the world, for we never stood there. It is that we cease to stand even at the center of our own world. (Scarry 1999, pp 111–112)

Scarry apparently has a liking for images of levitation as a way of depicting processes of cognitive restructuring by momentary detachment. In a different work, concerned with the difficult task of understanding representation, she used such an image to allow an iconic form to give a narrative account:

Forms of art that have no temporal element (painting) or a very repetitive relation to time (music) convey the 'activity' of work with more ease than does literary narrative. Millet's paintings, for example, habitually depict the worker in the midst of a gesture or action, whether it is the broad sweep of the arm of *The Sower* or the delicate dance of the fingers in the *Seated Goat Girl in Auvergne Spinning*. The motion of her fingers seems to radiate through her entire body and lift her from the ground. In each instance what we seem to watch is not arrested motion but perpetual activity. (Scarry 1994, p. 68)

Detached sufficiently to look out from a different centre, we see things from a different angle, ourselves in a new light and have a new perspective on the world, as we are changed in the development of a new gestalt of our own identity. So in a recent psychological work by one of Scarry's colleagues we find: 'The flexibility of the human mind – its ability to flip frames, shift gestalts, or reconstrue events – is a wondrous talent' (Pinker 2007, p. 51).

Rudolph Arnheim[2] employed Gestalt concepts to elucidate cognitive processes in the making and appreciation of literary and visual images (Arnheim 1969, 1971, 1974, 1982, 1996). His analysis of how images are formed not only in physical media but also in the mind provides some useful conceptual tools for understanding cognitive motivation, particularly in regard to images of identity. He elaborated the gestalt principle of simplicity in regard to balance, shape, form, growth, movement, etc., to provide a rationale for seeking completeness. He described, in opposition to this tendency to move towards the simplest configuration, a dynamic constructive tendency that creates tension: 'We envisage the human mind as an interplay of tension-heightening and tension-reducing strivings' (Arnheim 1974, p. 411).

Arnheim saw the simplicity principle as operating unopposed in a closed system, tending to equilibrium and the simplest shape possible,

[2] Arnheim was a student and colleague of Wertheimer and Köhler, and professor of the psychology of art at Harvard, to whom Scarry dedicated her Yale lectures on beauty and justice cited earlier here (Scarry 1999).

but he argued that living organisms are not controlled by this tendency alone because they are *open* systems. Being open systems, they must cope with new inputs that create tensions in a structure that resists simplification, even sometimes making jagged structural resistance to the smoothing influence of forces for simplicity. The general principles of dynamic interplay between distinctive structure and the simplifying tendency were examined in Arnheim's book *Art and Entropy: An Essay on Order and Disorder* (Arnheim 1971), in which he envisaged living organisms shedding entropy on the environment and creating islands of distinctive identity. These are principles inherent in the creation and resolution of incomplete gestalts, whether in visual perception, verbal reflection or forms of personal identity.

The distinction between iconic and narrative images is found in Arnheim's description of 'Two sources of cognition' (Arnheim 1996) in 'things seen and things read or heard' (p. 17). He related the hearing source of cognition to narrative accounts, and he drew a contrast between paintings and stories. For example, he compared Caravaggio's painting *Judith and Holofernes*, with its horrific image of the determined young woman, caught in the moment, beheading the Assyrian commander, in contrast with the extended biblical narrative, in the Apocrypha, of Judith's adventure, setting out from her own community accompanied by her maid, entering the enemy camp, forming a relationship with the principal enemy of her people, and returning triumphant with his head in her bag – a story with deep cultural meanings. Narrative forms of identity also integrate the rich ingredients of life experience.

On the other hand, in reference to iconic forms of integration, Arnheim wrote of the dynamic qualities of the centre of an image that is not the geometric centre, and of an image of multiple centres being resolved in an overall balance of competing aspirations. A centre is not defined by location alone: 'When we speak of a center we shall mean mostly the center of a field of forces, a focus from which forces issue and towards which forces converge' (Arnheim 1982, p. 2). These forces represent diverse meanings, so that 'the richness of formal structure reflects a corresponding profusion of meaning' (p. 41). As with Scarry's and Weil's idea of our being capable of restructuring what we see when we do not see ourselves as standing at the centre of our world, so Arnheim said, 'When the self looks at the world with some mature objectivity it can claim in only rare instances that it is the center of its environment' (p. 4). From varied perspectives, people experience a coherent view of the world and themselves with a subjective centre that is not fixed but dynamic in the iconic form of personal identity.

In Gestalt theory it is a basic principle that a whole image is directly perceived and not inferred, but the perception of it is nevertheless the result of a process extended over time. Verstegen expounded the idea of 'perceptual microgenesis' in reference to Arnheim's saying 'perception takes time' (Arnheim 1969) and his description of 'three stages' (Verstegen 2005, p. 105). Arnheim's model was applied to all kinds of artistic perception, as a general form of thought processes, to explain 'perception but also expression in pictorial, sculptural and architectural form (the "visual arts"), the pantomimic arts (film, dance, theater), musical form and poetic form'. It was applied from short-term microgenesis to life-long individual artistic development, 'Putting both the spatial and temporal insights of Gestalt Theory together' (pp. 149–150). These developmental processes will be recurring themes in what follows here.

The Flip of Agency

Self-understanding coheres in a meaningful way in part because of the future orientation of the images of identity in a prospective future narrative. The feeling of being personally behind movement towards chosen goals is inherent in their purposeful character. One way in which this sense of agency may be evident is in the phenomenon of gestalt shift.

Pinker presented a case of gestalt shift in conceptions of agency from his research in psycholinguistics. As in visual perception, in examples of ambiguous figures like Necker's cube, the black/white Maltese cross or the duck/rabbit illusion, we see the same stimulus pattern first one way and then the other, so in the use of language, perception can flip from one gestalt to another. Are we putting the hay into the cart or loading the cart with hay? Which, the hay or the cart, is having something done to it (Pinker 2007)? So, in regard to self-perception, we can construe the same events to see ourselves as hero or victim, as agent or object; each alternative makes sense within the form of a particular gestalt, and each can have its motivational effects. We have the capacity to reconstruct the way we see things and thereby to experience a gestalt flip, making sense of the same set of information according to a different dominant theme or in a different perspective. Pinker saw this ability as 'a wondrous talent'. In the same way we can see *ourselves* in another perspective, or from a different centre. Some views can, indeed, be quite *ec*centric. Pinker gave an example from Woody Allen: 'I snapped my chin down on some guy's fist and hit another one on the knee with my nose' (Pinker 2007, p. 52). In their very eccentricity, as in the case of visual illusions, such perceptions make sense even in nonsense. Pinker's investigations of the gestalt shift suggested that, in seeking to make sense of ourselves, we can be forced to consider a deeper layer of meaning and 'decide which of the cognitively available roles – agent, thing that moves, thing that changes – should be applied in construing *this* kind of event' (p. 56).

The executive function of the self that is experienced in the sense of agency is described by many scholars in contemporary psychology and by most traditional observers of human nature. It is perhaps most easily seen in narrative images, but in the iconic frame, too, we can picture ourselves acting, as the subject doing things to objects – pushing, pulling, lifting, lowering, physically or metaphorically.

When we regard our deliberate actions, we are not, as Dennett suggested in reference to the intentional stance, asking what a person's intentions are in order to know how to plan our responses 'as if' they had intentions (Dennett 1971, 1987). There are no 'as ifs' in subjective regard. As Dennett was told by programmers in the early days of computer programming that they asked, 'How does it know that?', I remember how we thought about the computer 'as if' it were an intentional conscious being, to help work out what the program was doing. In fact, we were reversing the processes that had been involved in designing a computer in which people like Turing, imagining such machines, first analysed how *people* think. But it would be a schizophrenic kind of detachment to regard oneself in the same way, to deny in effect the iconic gestalt of oneself as an active agent for whom the present situation and the self click into place when we take a new position in self-understanding. Of course we can be mistaken, as Wegner claims, but we can also be right.[3]

Integrating Different Perspectives on the Self

It is explicit in the understanding represented by Scarry in literary theory, and in some recent psychological theorists of the self (Neisser, for example), that there is no fixed centre from which we see ourselves and our world. Our changing perspectives are linked together in the continuing narrative of our experience. At the same time, the subjective centre from which we see things is a continuing point of reference in the changing patterns of a personal narrative. Iconic and narrative images of the self together represent both continuity and change.

Some people are more fixed than others in the position from which they see themselves and the world in general – indeed, we noted in Chapter 6 how Dweck and others have developed a theory of self-theories in which

[3] See the discussion of Wegner's position on the illusion of conscious will in Chapters 6 and 10.

people differ characteristically in their propensity to believe in fixed rather than malleable qualities in a person (Dweck 1999; Dweck and Molden 2005; Dweck 2006).

Personal identity depends upon processes of integration. Integration of self-images can be understood in terms of the central gestalt concept of 'Prägnanz' introduced by Wertheimer, the principles of which were enumerated in Chapter 9. 'Given a particular stimulus configuration, we tend to see the most clearcut, pithy, organization possible' (Verstegen 2005, p. 16). Applying this idea to a person, we might think of it as the 'essence' or 'character' of a person – 'character' in the ancient Greek sense of what a person is stamped with, or in more Platonic terms as the 'form' or the 'idea' of the person in the generative sense in which Coleridge used the term 'idea' (Coleridge and Coleridge 1852) or Newman in 'The idea of a university,' which Rothblatt elaborated in his history of Newman's contribution to higher education as a formative influence, in 'The idea of the idea of a university' (Rothblatt 1989, 1997). 'Prägnanz' refers to the most general law that was enunciated by Gestalt theorists, in which it is proposed that perceptual or cognitive organisation will form as 'good' a whole image or gestalt as the prevailing conditions allow (Koffka 1935, p. 151). Contemporary psychologists such as Pinker have retained these basic gestalt concepts.

These are high-level concepts, abstract and complex in some respects, and in that way appropriate for the identity of the human person with all its complexity and diversity, yet as a unified whole it is at the same time equally appropriate in the simplicity and goodness of form one expects to mark a distinct identity. In this sense of movement towards an ideal, I am reminded of some words attributed to Iris Murdoch in the film of her life, *Iris*. It is the sad story of a once brilliant mind falling apart with Alzheimer's disease before she died in 1999. These words, spoken in the film in a BBC radio interview, come at a point in her life when she is beginning to show symptoms of disintegration, poignantly contrasted with the Platonic imagery of holistic aspiration for which she was known in philosophy at Oxford, and as a creative writer, but not expressed in terms we would readily use in psychology today:

> Every human soul has seen, perhaps even before their birth, pure forms such as justice, temperance, beauty, and all the great moral qualities which we hold in honour. We are moved towards what is good by the faint memory of these forms, simple and calm and blessed, which we saw once in a pure, clear light, being pure ourselves.

Murdoch was unusually distinctive in her lifetime as a practicing Platonist among philosophers in Britain, although there is a sense in which she did not belong with them, her work as a creative writer taking precedence. (See the contrasting biographies of her: Bayley 1998; Conradi 2001; Wilson 2003). The assumption in this quote about innate ideas, as given forms providing a pattern of goodness in various senses, appears nevertheless to be characteristic of her philosophy. Like Scarry later (cited earlier here), she aligned beauty with justice – see *The Sovereignty of Good over Other Concepts* (Murdoch 1967). In *Metaphysics as a Guide to Morals* she spoke of universal forms, or 'ideas,' as formative patterns to which people may be drawn (Murdoch 1992). It is far removed from the evolutionary and developmental psychology of today, and from the physicalism that I have advocated in preference to the traps of dualism. Those were dangers that do not seem to have frightened her, but the sense of there being given qualities of good form in the human mind, which are somehow built into the way the brain works, and towards which people move in their thinking and acting, is a common experience.

That is not to say that I would postulate mysterious natural tendencies in 'how the mind works' with inbuilt patterns for specific qualities such as justice and beauty, but rather that when a scholar in aesthetics such as Scarry links justice with beauty (Scarry 1999), she is picking up implications of the movement towards wholeness in Wertheimer's principle of Pragnanz. Processes of integration have been studied recently as the neural correlates of consciousness (see Chapter 7). These are the processes which I suggest underlie the macro model of cognitive motivation in which people act to make sense of what they do in the iconic and narrative images they have of themselves as a whole unit, and so prepare to act purposefully in accord with their sense of identity.

An Experimental Demonstration of Gestalt Principles in Person Perception

How the perception of a person is affected by the tendency to form whole images, or gestalts, was demonstrated in an early series of experiments by Solomon Asch (1946a). In an investigation of the perception of persons, he distinguished an overall integrative response to a range of individually separate stimuli from any simple summative function of responses to each stimulus element individually. The whole was different from the sum of its parts.

> We form an impression of the entire person. We see a person as consisting not of these and those independent traits (or of the sum of mutually modified traits), but we try to get at the root of the personality. This would involve that the traits are perceived in relation to each other, in their proper place within the given personality. (Asch 1946a, p. 259)

In his conclusion Asch cited Allport 'in his comprehensive discussion of the question' (Allport 1937a, 533 ff.), saying he 'has equally stressed the importance of direct perception of a given structure in others, of our capacity for perceiving in others dynamic tendencies' (p. 290). That is the pre-eminent claim in Gestalt theory: that we do not infer, but directly perceive, an organised whole figure, in this case in the image of a personality. So with iconic and narrative forms of identity it is primarily the gestalt of a person that we perceive, in ourselves as in others.

The Imperative to Connect Reflexively

Most of us, most of the time, are conscious of ourselves as purposeful agents with a meaningful sense of who we are and where we are heading. The integrative processes of consciousness (see Chapter 7) can be applied to personal identity, aiming to make sense of our lives. Emerson had a phrase for it: 'We love whatever affirms, connects, preserves; and dislike what scatters or pulls down' (Emerson 1850/1890, from chapter 4, 'Montaigne: or, the sceptic'). I will come later to his image of a thread of meaning that runs through all things. We see it in ourselves, loving what connects and gives meaning. There is nothing more characteristic of human beings than reflexive consciousness.

It needs to be acknowledged, however, that the integrative function of cognitive motivation is not all there is to identity. Membership of reference groups can be highly significant. Identity has a base in cultural history; it varies throughout the life cycle; it has to do with how we cope with developmental challenges; it is sensitive to changes in social circumstances; it is directly experienced by conscious minds; and it can be recognized by others. There is a difference between an individual Western sense of identity and an organic community type of identity often found in African, Asian and Pacific cultures. I cannot deal with all these aspects here, but perhaps the best overall summary is the observation by Baumeister (1998): across a very large number of studies, three conceptions of the self account for most of the variation in different theories. These are: reflexive consciousness, interpersonal being and executive function. There is not room in this work for discussion of all these. Because of its theoretical relevance to cognitive motivation, I want to concentrate on the capacity to connect reflexively in narrative and iconic images of identity.

Narrative Identity

Dan McAdams has advanced a narrative understanding of personality through an extensive study of identity evident in personal life stories (McAdams 1985, 1990, 1995, 1996a, 1996b, 2000, 2006, 2008; McAdams and Olson 2010; McAdams 2015; McAdams and Guo 2015). He conceived personal narratives rather than traits or motives as important frameworks for personality organisation, decision-making and psychotherapy. His review with Olson of continuity and change in personality provides a summary of narrative identity with reference to its integrative meaning and both its past and future orientations:

> Layered on top of dispositional traits and characteristic adaptations is an internalized and evolving story of the self – a narrative identity – that aims to provide a person's life with some semblance of unity, purpose, and meaning (McLean, Pasupathi and Pals 2007, McAdams 2008). Narrative identity is the storied understanding that a person develops regarding how he or she came to be and where he or she is going in life. It is a narrative reconstruction of the autobiographical past and imagined rendering of the anticipated future … (McAdams 1985, Conway and Pleydell-Pearce 2000). (McAdams and Olson 2010, p. 527)

In order to know a person, McAdams proposed, we should have access to information from three levels or domains of personality, briefly summarized as traits, concerns and life stories (McAdams 1995, 1996a). Level 1 was conceived as dispositional properties, evident in consistent individual differences such as the Big Five taxonomy of personality traits (Goldberg 1990, 1999); Level 2 is comprised of goals, values, personal strivings and other developmental, motivational and strategic concerns that depend upon a person's context in place, time and social role; and Level 3 is a reflexively created unified view of the person evident in personal narratives of the past, present and future. McAdams recognized a distinction that had been made by William James between self-as-subject (the 'I' or the ego) and self-as-object (the 'me' or self-concept), which McAdams employed in the rationale for his theory of integration in narrative views of the self. In the reflexive nature of the self, the 'I' functions to create a perception of the 'me', with attributes that appear at Levels 1 and 2 through the narrative functions of the subjective self at Level 3.

There is a somewhat different but similar three-layered conception of personality in McAdams's recent book, *The Art and Science of Personality Development* (McAdams 2015) and related articles (Manczak, Zapata-Gietl and McAdams 2014; McAdams and Guo 2015) which came out when this book was nearing completion. I cannot give this later work the attention it deserves, but it is compatible with the earlier construction. It is more informative of developmental phenomena. It has more emphasis on personal agency and on the interaction between unique personal perspectives and the general laws of psychological science. It makes many of the same emphases as are made in cognitive motivation theory.

McAdams saw the self-conscious reflexive construction of the self-concept as a product of the culture of modernity, which has increased in its urgency to some extent in recent times in a struggle with postmodern alienation. Modernity has been characterized by a reaction against traditional sources of authority and by belief in reason, objectivity and progress through science, technology and political development, but as the certainty of these themes has been called into question, McAdams suggests that 'a new quality of consciousness about the individual self' has developed (McAdams 1996a, p. 297). A person's continuing identity and a unique definition of the self both required attention in the face of external pressures and uncertainties in changing circumstances.

A sense of self no longer being given or conferred, a modern person needs to fashion a self through reflexive self-engagement (McAdams 1996a). In this understanding of the person, work on oneself is done in the everyday life of family, employment situations and community without reference to external authorities. The modern self is multilayered, possessing an inner depth, with people being keenly aware of the distinction between public and private selves, and the inner self becomes the primary source of moral authority. Long-term development of the self is expected as people move through many stages of life in which a person, expecting a long life, anticipates self-improvement, self-actualization, self-fulfilment and the various humanistic ideals of the self. Anticipating change, the self needs to develop a coherent sense of identity through time, which is best achieved by a capacity *to keep a particular narrative going* (Giddens 1991). Finally, McAdams has suggested that, in the absence of clear externally defined roles and prescribed self-understandings, modern selves are dependent upon private intimate support in what he called 'the pure relationship' in which, to use Martin Buber's terms (Buber 1937), the *I* and the *Thou* meet each other as more or less free, independent and well-defined agents as they find life-meaning in a narrative that binds them together.

Some commentators have questioned the ability of contemporary Westerners to find unity and purpose in their lives amid the constant change and multiple global influences of postmodern life (Gergen 1992), and some psychologists have argued from deconstructionism that psychologists must develop a new conception of the person as a 'location' of impersonal intersecting forces (Sampson 1989a, 1989b). McAdams has defended a view of the self as agent. He wondered 'how many contemporary people actually see themselves as mere locations in space and time rather than as embodied actors with internalized intentions and plans'; still, he admitted that 'the postmodern take on self-hood underscores the difficulty contemporary adults are likely to experience in crafting the reflexive project of the self' (McAdams 1996a, p. 299). It is not surprising that other significant authors have taken up the theme of narrative identity.

Among contemporary philosophers who have contributed to the psychology of a personal sense of identity, Alasdair MacIntyre has emphasized a narrative concept of the self as agent: 'I am the *subject* of a history that is my own and no one else's, that has its own peculiar meaning' (MacIntyre 1984, pp. 216–217). When a person feels that his or her life is meaningless and is contemplating suicide, MacIntyre says that typically the complaint is that 'the narrative of their life has become unintelligible to them, that it lacks any point, any movement towards a climax or a *telos*' (pp. 217–218). We will come back to this purposive sense of meaning in the next chapter.

Daniel Dennett, who writes as a philosopher of psychology, has taken the view that consciousness should be understood as consisting of narrations, produced by the brain, the point of which is to interpret objects and events in some coherent way (Dennett 1991). In his understanding, the brain is assumed to have an inbuilt capacity to make stories, to integrate disparate experiences. In this he is close to Gazzaniga's view of the capacity of the 'left hemisphere interpreter' to construct consciously integrating narratives. As noted in the previous chapter, Dennett refers to 'the self as a center of narrative gravity' (Dennett 2003, p. 253). Unity joins continuity at this point in Dennett's account of consciousness.

Jerome Bruner, long after his significant early work as a cognitive psychologist in the 1950s and 1960s, and who continued publishing into his nineties, has in his later work (Bruner 1990, 2003) given attention to how people use narratives as a way of making sense of disparate elements of experience in an integrated and meaningful life. In *Acts of Meaning* Bruner took the example of children learning a language and developing a reflexive self-understanding at an early age (Bruner 1990). In more recent work Bruner has written of storytelling as a means of constructing personal identity (Bruner 2003).

A narrative approach remains a persuasive model, but we have seen that there are other ways of understanding personal identity, and that consciousness is strongly associated with cognitive integration (see Chapter 7). Consciousness has contemporaneous as well as cumulative modes of operation, and it is useful to note some ways in which a narrative account in limited.

Limitations to the Narrative Understanding of Identity

While it has sometimes been presented as a sufficient theoretical framework for understanding the unified character of a personality, two objections can be made to an overreliance on narrative integration. One is that it ignores other possible dynamics for integration even in the three-level model of personality that McAdams proposed. At his Level 2, some theorists have proposed that systems of meaning that are not in narrative form but attend to goals and strivings can make the *organisation of goals* a means of living a coherent life. Emmons construed his understanding of 'personal strivings' as a means of personality organisation through the management of goal systems. Karoly defined goals as 'an imagined or envisaged state condition toward which a person aspires and which drives voluntary activity' (Karoly 1993, p. 274). According to Emmons, goal systems are managed to facilitate these purposeful integrated strivings (Emmons 1989; Karoly 1993; Emmons, Colby and Kaiser 1998; Emmons 1999a). Austin and Vancouver (1996) describe many ways in which theorists have proposed structures for the hierarchical organisation of goals, with top-down or bottom-up control systems. A top-down system, for example, might be one like that of Royce and Powell's individuality theory (Royce and Powell 1983), in which the highest-level goal is to 'optimize personal meaning'.

The other objection to reliance upon narrative integration is that the exclusively narrative conception ignores the *iconic* form of identity which includes continuing qualities of the person that are definitive and around which the personality is organised. In addition to the structural organisation of goals, a comprehensive version of the iconic type of identity envisages an organisation of cognitive elements representing aspects of the self that are interrelated in a dynamic image in which the subject, or an observer, has expectations in an implicit personality theory about how one part is related to and modifies another.

McAdams favoured Henry Murray's *personology* and his narrative understanding of the person. An interesting sidelight on this approach was recalled to my mind by McAdams when he said that Murray was not interested in prediction (McAdams 1995, p. 370). My reservation in the light of Murray's more complex understanding of personality has quite fundamental implications for a theory in which a narrative view of integration is considered sufficient. One might, indeed, suppose that with an individual case-study approach Murray would have been satisfied with a narrative description of a personality. Yet, in my experience of his teaching, there was more to his thinking. He would ask his students to make predictions about individual cases. Murray would give out thick wads of paper containing case notes on a particular individual he had worked with in the Harvard Psychological Clinic, and the following week after we had studied this material, he would ask us to predict what that person had done in a particular situation that had arisen subsequently. It was a task I found extraordinarily difficult, perhaps because I tend to think that prediction of the individual case in a complex system is inherently impossible. I tended to favour Gordon Allport's view of the uniqueness of the individual, which suggests, even if it does not require it absolutely, that we can assume a singularity in every person, but Murray's understanding of science was the medical model in which he had been trained. The general laws of nature would guide treatment of the individual. The narrative in that sense not only has a future, but one that is in principle predicable.

Murray's class exercise helped to demonstrate his understanding of personality dynamics which employed general principles from psychoanalytic theory, understood as scientific laws in terms of which predictions could be made. It was necessary to give attention to a wider range of individual needs than Freud had acknowledged, and to recognize environmental presses that were evident in the history of the individual, but these were still continuing characteristics. Murray included continuing properties of the individual together with the narrative of change. A personal story makes sense to some degree because we can refer to abiding qualities of central importance. Allport saw these in 'the proprium', all that we regard as peculiarly ours, 'all aspects of personality that make for an inward unity' (Allport 1955, p. 40).

The Conceptual Self and Iconic Identity

An iconic form of identity with a pictorial image of the self describes a more or less well-defined centre and circumference. Most of us see ourselves and our acquaintances as complex personalities with diverse traits that do not always hold well together, yet we experience people as unitary whole beings, distinct entities organised in a more or less coherent whole despite modern and postmodern pressures to disbelieve our sense of personal integrity. We hold traits together, sometimes in tension, in ways that make sense. The self is seen as a figure with some structure, as an iconic form that stands out from a background in our cognitive maps. In this discussion it is sufficient to see that these perceptions of persons are not mere collections of separate items of information. These patterns of organisation define identities, with a kind of personal constancy, even if they may be perceived differently from different viewpoints, or at different times.

We may have cognitive schemas representing our emotionality, intelligence, social preferences, values and life style, indeed a very wide range of attributes. We may think of some as typical, central and perhaps essential to understanding who we are (as Asch and Allport argued). These schemas will be organised into a meaningful pattern in the perception of ourselves and others. In this cognitive organisation we have a conceptual self, a picture of who we are, with a centre and a circumference, as the poet said, but not a fixed centre or a permanently secure boundary. As Arnheim said, we are open systems, but the conceptual self tends to take an iconic form, while at the same time we have a dynamic self-image organised in narrative form that changes as it develops. It is the same self seen in different ways, or in images taking different forms. The common two, iconic and narrative forms, together with some other inputs such as awareness of the body, give us our contemporaneous unity and continuity of personal identity through time.

Making Sense of Ourselves

Gazzaniga quotes the American writer John Updike (1989) musing upon the subject of consciousness as a means of personal integration:

> 'Consciousness is a disease,' Unamuno says. Religion would relieve the symptoms. Religion construed, of course, broadly ... in the form of any private system, be it adoration of Elvis Presley or hatred of nuclear weapons ... Falling in love – its mythologization of the beloved and everything that touches her or him is an invented religion, and religious also is our persistence, against all the powerful post-Copernican, post-Darwinian evidence that we are insignificant accidents within a vast uncaused churning, in feeling that our life is a story, with a pattern and a moral and an inevitability – that as Emerson said, 'a thread runs through all things: all worlds are strung on it, as beads: and men, and events, and life come to us, only because of that thread.' That our subjectivity, in other words, dominates, through secret channels, outer reality, and the universe has a personal structure. (Gazzaniga 1997, pp 69–70)

Updike gives expression here to the 'last passion' aspect of curiosity extolled by Samuel Johnson, and to curiosity as wonder. Whether its cultural expression is in science, the arts, politics or religion, there is the potential for great inspiration and insight, or the cognitive processes employed for making sense can also make nonsense. Man is a dreamer. The imperative to make sense, to complete the incomplete gestalt, can be so urgently demanding that we can make sense of almost anything, rightly or wrongly.

On the 'disease' of consciousness, with a similar regard for its potential for good or ill as an evolutionary development, Damasio quotes F. Scott Fitzgerald saying, 'His was a great sin who first invented consciousness' (Damasio 2010, p. 30). Damasio saw both the positive and negative consequences, saying of Fitzgerald's cryptic comment:

> I can understand why he said so, but his condemnation is only half the story, appropriate for moments of discouragement with the imperfections of nature

that conscious minds expose so nakedly. The other half of the story should be occupied with praise for such an invention as the enabler of all the creations and discoveries that trade loss and grief for joy and celebration. The emergence of consciousness opened the way to a life worth living. Understanding how it comes about can only strengthen that worth. (Damasio 2010, p. 30)

A genie was let loose when reflexive consciousness set people free from the control of automatic modular processing – for good or ill. That is, as Gazzaniga said, 'the system that takes the vast output of our thousands upon thousands of specialized systems and ties them into our subjectivity' (Gazzaniga 1997, p. 70).

Baumeister and Masicampo suggested a verbal function as an alternative to Gazzaniga's general cognitive integrating function. They noted the suggestion of Tomasello and colleagues in regard to intentions (Tomasello et al. 2005), in which they proposed 'two crucial changes from ape mind to human: the understanding of others' inner states and the drive to express one's own states' (Baumeister and Masicampo 2010, p. 951). As an alternative to Gazzaniga's proposal of the left-brain interpreter producing an inner narrative of one's life, 'an autobiographic coherence and sense of self (Gazzaniga 2000, Gazzaniga 2008),' Baumeister and Masicampo proposed that it might have a different function, 'to render one's activities and experiences in language so that they can be readily shared with others. Hence, we suspect that the left brain interpreter emerged to serve a social function rather than an intrapsychic one' (Baumeister and Masicampo 2010, p. 951). It is conceivable that the development of social and personal processes of integration were symbiotically related, as George Mead long ago suggested when he related the reflexive nature of the self to the experience of social interaction (Mead 1934). Indeed Dennett has suggested that it is likely that there was interactive co-development of language and this reflective capacity (Dennett 2003).

Our conclusion here must be limited, but it appears that language, intelligent behaviour, personal and social problem solving and voluntary behaviour are associated with conscious integration in such a way that we not only have a sequential understanding of what has happened but we also have a coherent orientation to the future. Despite the fact that we can also be mistaken in our self-perceptions, we who have a continuing sense of our own identity can consciously decide upon a future course of action by commitment to a sequential image of action that extends from the past into the future. Our sense of agency is thus part of cognitive motivation as we see it operating in consciously guided intelligent purposive behaviour, even if unconscious processes also contribute to deliberately chosen actions.

Updike, in his mode of being a creative writer rather than a literary critic, gives us a positive point or two on art, life and order at the edge of chaos, where human creativity brings into being what did not exist before. At the end of one of his novels, he gave his character *Bech* the privilege of delivering a Nobel lecture when receiving the prize for literature. Like the real-life Heaney quoted at the beginning of this chapter, Bech credited art with an eye or an ear for connectedness. It appeared as a human act of love rising above our inclination to discontent and separation in an imperfect world. In this Updike set cynicism aside, at least for the moment:

> Is art, as the ancients proposed, an imitation of life, or is it, as the moderns suggest, everything that life is not – order instead of disorder, resolution rather than inconclusiveness, peace and harmony in preference to our insatiable discontent and, at the bottom of our souls, as Kierkegaard and Strindberg and Munch teach us, our terror? Our dread – dread at being here, on this planet that appears lonelier and more negligible with each new revelation from astronomy. Or is art *both* duplication and escape – life tweaked, as it were, into something slightly higher, brighter, other? We feel it to be so, as it is engendered at the end of a pencil point or on a computer screen. Art is somehow *good*, if only for the artist. (Updike 1998, p. 239)

Like Heaney's 'fluid and restorative relationship', this therapeutic and creative product of identity development can only appear with a sense of agency. If we are ever so dispossessed of personal power as to lose all control over our destinies, we become so far alienated from life that our sense of self tends to disappear. I referred in Chapter 2 to reports of this phenomenon of fatal disintegration observed by Frankl in a concentration camp. Research on intrinsic motivation has pointed in many ways to the critical importance of this sense of agency (see Chapter 3). Similar findings come from studies of attribution processes and self-efficacy (Chapter 6) and recent work on personal development: 'Human agency suggests intention, volition, will, purpose, and some modicum of personal control in life ... A belief in personal agency (even if some philosophers consider it to be a belief in an illusion or myth) seems to be a good thing for most people, most of the time' (McAdams 2015, p. 142). The purpose and meaning aspect of identity that is inherent in an agentic perspective is the subject of the next chapter.

Summary

This chapter is concerned with how images of our identity are formed and how they function in cognitive motivation. These images commonly, but not exclusively, take either iconic (picture/visual/contemporaneous) or narrative (melody/verbal/sequential) forms; and in this theory they function according to gestalt principles. They are often experienced as incomplete, and the fundamental process of cognitive motivation is to move towards their completion with a purposive orientation to the future which includes a sense of agency. Meaning and purpose are the subject of the next chapter, but relevant also to the study of identity.

Narrative (or verbal) and iconic (or visual) types of image formation and appreciation are found in the psychology of art understood in gestalt terms. It is seen also in the gestalt flip of agency in language and social perception, and in literary applications of the idea of 'decentering' which is described by contemporary authors in literary criticism. The same principles were applied to person perception and they also serve as a model of self-understanding. In these gestalt processes people do not infer, but directly perceive, an organised whole figure in the image of a person.

A narrative understanding of personality has been advanced from the extensive study of identity evident in personal life stories. Narrative integration has been described from a cognitive theoretical base and in neurophysiological accounts of how people make sense of diverse experiences. Besides narrative integration, we may also have iconic images of people by way of cognitive schemas with a centre and a circumference that function as organised whole figures representing our emotionality, intelligence, social preferences, values and life style, integrating a wide range of attributes; and we can have different self-theories about their permanence or malleability.

There is an imperative to connect reflexively, both with other people and within ourselves. We reflect upon ourselves through central processes that integrate information from many separate sources. Consciousness plays an important part in these processes of integration that may hold together different perspectives in which we see ourselves from different centres with different meanings. The resultant image of a person's identity is a therapeutic and creative product of the cognitive motivational processes of identity development that can only appear with a sense of agency.

12 Purpose and Meaning

> Every state of the person is pointed in the direction of future possibilities.
> – Allport 1955

> There is nothing in the world, I venture to say, that would so effectively help one to survive even the worst conditions, as the knowledge that there is a meaning in his life
> – Frankl 1962

Introduction

Purpose and meaning are mutually interdependent. A meaningful life is a purposeful life, and a purposeful life is a meaningful life. As we move now from identity, understood in the theory of cognitive motivation in Chapter 11 principally in terms of iconic and narrative images representing integrated forms of self-perception, we look more closely at how meaningful organisation is shaped by a purposeful orientation to the future. An iconic organisation giving a meaningful picture of the person in the way one experiences oneself is combined with a narrative image of the person becoming who they have the potential to be with a sense of purposeful striving. This purposeful orientation is the most mature application of basic underlying processes in cognitive motivation: i.e., the processes of conscious integration in working memory (Chapter 7), the signalling function of emotions (Chapter 8), the gestalt properties of goals and the conscious agency of intentions (Chapters 9 and 10), together with the integrative functions evident in iconic and narrative images of identity (Chapter 11). I want now to spell out some of the theoretical implications of those basic processes for a sense of purpose and meaning in one's life.

Completion of Images

Cognitive motivation is concerned with the completion of incomplete images. When such an image is a picture or story of ourselves, its completion is a process of personal integration incorporating new information, and an expression of our own identity typically in the iconic or narrative forms described in the previous chapter. 'The self comprises all beliefs related to oneself, which is to say that the expected relations which unite oneself both across time (diachronically) and across roles and contexts (synchronically)' (Heine et al. 2006, p. 90). The process of completing or uniting oneself takes place during purposeful movement into a desired future that is represented by the incomplete image of a future self in relation to a goal in comparison with the present situation.

Purposeful Living

'What a life means is what that life purposes' (Klinger 1998, p. 28). Whether we are referring to the meaning of an action, a life or a sign, there are two thrusts to the meaning of 'meaning': one is what it intends in terms of an aim, and the other is what it signifies in its associations. As Klinger pointed out, etymologically, these two thrusts of meaning have a common root, meaning 'to have in mind'. In terms of the discussion of identity in Chapter 11, both narrative and iconic forms of integration are implied. Cognitive elements from memory and perception are brought together to make sense in patterns of meaning that are expressions of identity. They may be sequential in the narrative form of integration or contemporary in the iconic form, and often both. In the big picture, 'the meaning(s) of life' require(s) sequential narrative patterns that hold together around matters of central concern that are iconic expressions of identity. One of the important processes relating various iconic and narrative forms of identity images is the integrative function of a future orientation.

The Future Self

That we can reflect upon ourselves is a fundamental and universal attribute of human consciousness. Understanding our identities in reflexive self-consciousness includes the sense of being an original actor. We see ourselves doing things, not merely having things done to us. Within the limits of our own resources and circumstances, we construct our future lives. We are behind what we do. This is the sense of agency that we have discussed in the previous chapter in reference to the gestalt flip of agency and purposeful integration in a unique identity, in Chapter 3 in regard to self-determination, in Chapter 6 in reference to self-efficacy and in Chapter 10 where the possibility of a truly voluntary act is considered. At this point I wish to relate agency especially to a sense of 'becoming'. Accepting the reality of agency as characteristic of humanity, and dismissing Wegner's argument (Wegner 2002; Wegner and Commentators 2004) that it is an illusion (see Chapter 10), implies that we are all responsible to a significant degree for our own future development. An incomplete gestalt of the future self can offer a challenge and a promise of a renewed identity.

'Every state of the person is pointed in the direction of future possibilities' (Allport 1955, p. 12). The same orientation is found in the discussion of McAdams's work on narrative integration in the previous chapter. Knowledge of how we have acted in the past as responsible agents has helped to form our identities, but our sense of identity does not depend only on memory. I know myself to be the person who made this or that choice, who deliberately acted in a certain way, but deliberate acts are only possible for one who anticipates a future and can act intentionally (see Chapter 10).

As an intentional agent I know myself as the existential self that gains personal meaning from deliberate responsible actions. This principle of existential philosophy was enunciated from extreme experience in wartime by Victor Frankl in *From Death Camp to Existentialism* (Frankl 1959), later published as *Man's Search for Meaning* (Frankl 1962). For him it was the source of meaning in life. It is a belief also advanced in that period by Jean-Paul Sartre, although with less hopefulness (Sartre and Mairet 1948), and a century earlier by Søren Kierkegaard out of his struggle with what we today would probably call depression (Kierkegaard 1986). Our sense of self is intimately related to the deliberate commitments we have made, more than to progress in the normal unstressed course of life, but it does not depend entirely on the memory of commitments. Our sense of identity and the view of ourselves as acting intentionally in the world at large are formed from the experience of becoming who we are more than it is from remembering who we were. That sense of continuity in personal identity goes on into our conception of the future, so that who we are is dependent on whom we see ourselves becoming and are not yet. There is a future aspect to self-consciousness that is essential for purposeful behaviour and central to the sense of agency.

To understand what a person is, it is necessary always to refer to what he or she may be in the future. Every living person is a work in progress. 'Personality is less a finished product than a transitive process' (Allport 1955, p. 19). That is part of what it means to be alive and to be human. Purposive behaviour, in a global personal sense, is intimately tied up with a sense of identity which has a future as well as a past and a present.

Future-oriented knowledge of ourselves gives rise to a range of possible strategies. We learn how to manage our own growth and development with purposive behaviour which constructs new possibilities out of formerly unintegrated shards of experience. The motivation for doing so is found in the integrative functions of cognitive motivation in which an incomplete gestalt of a future possibility is an image conceived as something towards which we can move as we imagine steps towards its completion. We tend to construct new transformations of the person, not simply by anticipating possible new states of being that we might attain, although we might have some specific aims of that kind, but we conceive of ways of moving towards new possibilities which are consistent with who we are and who we are becoming without knowing precisely what the outcome will be. The outcome of developmental processes is often unpredictable. If the task of self-management is well done, and not over-done, the result may well be a surprise, even a cause for wonder, associated with a sense of health, wholeness and well-being.

But there is a qualification to this hopeful outlook for the autonomous person acting responsibly. The necessary unpredictability of the completion of incomplete gestalts in general (see Chapter 3) applies to the gestalt of the self. One's prospect for shaping a meaningful life is likely to be limited not only by external constraints but also by the way that an incomplete gestalt is resolved. It should not be surprising that we cannot fully anticipate the resolution of challenges that result in personal growth. When we have reached a point in our life's journey where we have never been before, a new direction cannot be set exclusively on the basis of what we have done in the past. When the combination of new information with a previously formed cognitive structure requires a significant degree of accommodation in the existing cognitive map for integration to be completed, the outcome will be unpredictable. As there has never before existed exactly the same state of affairs, neither the person concerned nor an objective observer can know in advance how the new gestalt of the personality will manifest itself. For this reason, the notion of self-determination, much loved of popular psychologists and some respected theoreticians such as Deci and Ryan (Deci 1980; Ryan and Deci 2000c; Deci and Ryan 2002a), must be somewhat misleading. As I have argued in Chapter 3, 'determination' is the wrong idea, even if it is self-determination. It implies a degree of control and foreknowledge that we do not possess. The wonder of a new creation, even in oneself, or one's child, or another loved one, is enjoyed in part because the result is a surprise. It is the kind of surprise in which we delight and which is intrinsically rewarding. With such motivation, we are delighted to engage in it for its own sake without knowing exactly what it will be like. At least for our own good and the welfare of others, that is how we *should* feel – if we are not obsessively concerned with maintaining control.

This conception of the self as becoming what it has the potential to be through conscious striving is more dynamic and less restrictive than the theory of self-determination. It is more open to the future and offers better hope for satisfying and purposeful integration of experience than do the more self-centred theories. I discuss the positive value of less self-centred conceptions in terms of personal well-being in the section on meaning, spirituality and religion and again briefly in relation to the development of positive psychology later in this chapter. To the extent that self-centred conceptions imply a view of self which assumes that identity is fixed or given, so that people seek to discover who they are and to maintain that understanding of themselves, there are limitations to personal development (Dweck 1999, 2006). A different and more satisfying outcome is likely if, instead, we understand our identities as always in the process of 'becoming' as Allport had it, or, in Dweck's theory, if we believe in a person's potential for growth and change.

The self is a project not yet completed. Accepting the not-yet-completed character of one's identity means that we are much more likely to learn constructively from experiences which do not fit well with present conceptions of who we are. A new order is developed out of the old through acceptance of new experiences which are inconsistent with the old self. This is the same process at the level of the organisation of the whole person as the cognitive processes of curiosity at the task level when a strange, unexpected or novel event disturbs one's cognitive map (Beswick 1964, 1971, 2004). The same things happen in the understanding of ourselves. We are, after all, probably the most interesting objects of our own curiosity. And there is the same sense of wonder.

We see ourselves as moving with purpose and meaning into a future that is, in part, of our own choosing and our own making, and which we strive to bring about as active agents who are the origin of acts which help to define who we are and through which we are becoming what we have the potential to be.

Propriate Striving

Allport construed integration of the personality with a purposeful orientation in reference to central attributes of the person that he called 'the proprium' (Allport 1955). He described the proprium as all those aspects of personality that we regard as peculiarly ours, the centre around which the whole personality is organised, 'all aspects of personality that make for an inward unity' (p. 40). He listed eight aspects or functions of the proprium: bodily sense or *coensthesis*, self-identity, ego-enhancement, ego-extension, rational agent, self-image, propriate striving and the self as the knower. In his concept of 'propriate striving' that makes for inward unity, Allport advocated a view of motivation which retains its intentional or consciously purposeful character. It is forward looking and different from any notion of motivation being driven from behind. 'Striving, it is apparent, always has a future reference. As a matter of fact, a great many states of mind are adequately described only in terms of their futurity' (Allport 1955, p. 51). This emphasis on future strivings as an organising principle has been applied by Emmons who was inspired not by Gordon Allport but his brother Floyd and his theory of *teleonomic* trends (Allport 1937): 'Each person can be characterized by a unique set of personal strivings' (Emmons 1986, p. 1059).

MacIntyre's emphasis on meaningfulness in one's life being a matter of personal history with a purpose was discussed in Chapter 11. Cavalier, in a book on *Personal Motivation*, cited MacIntyre's claim that what is good for a person is what contributes to the completion of his or her life story, and he related it to McAdams's narrative forms of integration (McAdams 1985, 2000; Cavalier 2002) that I have discussed in Chapter 11. Referring to McAdams, Cavalier endorsed Murray's idea of *personology*, particularly with reference to 'a *purposeful* sequence of actions. Time is the defining feature of the person ... One must never forget [Murray's dictum – DB] that "the history of the organism is the organism"' (Cavalier 2002, p. 2).

As I have argued in the previous chapter, however, and as suggested by Klinger's two thrusts to the meaning of meaning, narration alone is not sufficient for meaningful integration. Meaning is given by relationship to a larger unified whole image or schema, which represents contemporaneously the current features of a person's life as well as a personal history. Cognitive motivation sets up conditions which move a person towards completion of a gestalt that gives meaning and purpose to life as a whole. The primary source of that motivation is a sense of incompleteness in the face of a partially perceived prospect of completion. For it to work, one must feel the pull of the potential for completion in an incomplete gestalt – that is, the prospect of completing a new whole figure imperfectly imaged in the incomplete gestalt. I suggest going beyond Klinger's second thrust to the meaning of meaning in the reference to cognitive associations and then paying attention to the attraction of a gestalt in which associated elements are combined in a *meaningful* way. It requires both contemporary and historical awareness.

The iconic and narrative forms of integration are brought together in the growth of personality with its orientation to the future. In the processes of becoming there are central concerns which help to guide development:

> The first thing an adequate psychology of growth should do is draw a distinction between what are matters of *importance* to the individual and what are, as Whitehead would say, merely matters of *fact* to him; that is between what he feels to be vital and central in becoming and what belongs to the periphery of his being. (Allport 1955, p. 39)

One's becoming then depends upon what Allport called the proprium, those central aspects of personality which we regard as peculiarly ours and that make for an inward unity. It is essential for the growth of a coherent personality that the iconic form of integration gives meaning to change in the person in terms of the relationship of new developments to matters of central importance. It gives point and purpose to one's personal story. There is then interaction between iconic and narrative forms of meaning which contribute jointly to the purposeful development of an identity. The iconic centre, the source of propriate strivings, provides a continuing point of reference in goals for the narrative to proceed in a meaningful way.

Meaningful Integration

Seeking to understand why people find it important to search for meaning in life, Baumeister (1991) acknowledged something common to theories of development – a need for openness, a need for stimulation apparent in information seeking in general, and commonly aligned with curiosity. That is, human brains are complex and restless, requiring input that can be incorporated and ordered, much as we saw from several sources in the treatment of specific epistemic curiosity in Chapter 2, and in other forms of positive as opposed to deficit motivations. Baumeister saw that there are also pragmatic reasons for being able to abstract and systematise knowledge to predict future events and control adaptations to them. Such pragmatic reasons, however, are not sufficient reason to seek meaning in life:

> Meaning is imposed everywhere, even if there is no practical advantage. … Even simple curiosity may reflect this pattern, for human curiosity nearly always seeks to find out things and formulate them in meaningful terms. More generally, the myths of completeness and consistency reflect the fundamental human tendency to expect everything to make sense. (Baumeister 1991, p. 358)

This expecting 'everything to make sense' illustrates the macro model of curiosity as cognitive motivation at the level of the whole person. Gazzaniga postulated a similar need in the capacity of the 'left-hemisphere interpreter' to weave diverse elements of experience into a coherent narrative that makes sense to and of the person. He pointed out how this need to make sense of whatever happens can lead to serious errors of perception as well as objective and satisfying insights (see the discussion of narrative integration in Chapter 11). Many others have made similar proposals for a basic process of meaning making.

As we have noted in Chapters 1, 3 and 4, the meaning maintenance model of Heine, Proulx and Vohs also describes a cognitive process for meaning making (Heine et al. 2006, Proulx and Heine 2006, 2010). In their investigation of 'a need for meaning' they propose that 'humans possess an innate capacity to identify and construct mental representations of expected relationships between people, places, objects, and ideas' (Heine et al. 2006, p. 90), and they suggest that humans have a unique capacity to reflect upon these representations. Relations between mental representations of objects and events constitute meaning, and when the structure of these relations is disrupted, an effort will be made to re-establish meaning. In a particular application of this general principle they propose a mechanism of compensatory reaffirmation in which loss of meaning in one domain can lead to meaning maintenance by affirmation of meaning in another domain, thus reinforcing the general need for meaning.

Needs for Meaning

Baumeister suggested four *needs for meaning* which are satisfied by this tendency to try to make sense of whatever happens. Before considering these proposed needs, it is important to note the caution in his discussion of 'the myth of higher meaning', that 'people have unrealistic ideas about how much the world will make sense. There is a fair chance that the world is not as orderly, lawful, and sensible as people are inclined to think' (Baumeister 1991, p. 59). Our inability in some situations to make sense of our experience, in the face of a felt imperative to do so, leads not only to much puzzlement but to a good deal of nonsense arising from the belief Updike cited from Emerson that there is a thread of meaning that runs through everything. It is suggested by a number of authors that the prevalence such strivings indicates that there must be very strong needs underlying the effort to find meaning in life.

In his major work on this subject Baumeister suggested 'Four needs for meaning: An existential shopping list' (Baumeister 1991; see his chapter 3). He acknowledged that people might not feel as much today as educated people did in an earlier generation that it was necessary to have a well-worked-out philosophy of life, but he made the basic assumption 'that people have a need for life to make sense in certain ways' (p. 29). I have made a similar assumption for the macro model of cognitive motivation, but I would take a slightly different view of what he calls 'needs for meaning'. He proposed that the motivation for life to make sense could be described as *needs for meaning*, and that '[f]our basic needs for meaning can be suggested: purpose, value, efficacy and self-worth' (p. 29). As to why there should be exactly four basic needs for meaning, he said that the number was somewhat arbitrary and irrelevant, but that 'what matters is the total conceptual space that they cover' (p. 32).

In regard to the basic need for *purpose*, Baumeister singled out the previous work of Klinger (1977) dealing with life's meanings, *Meaning and Void: Inner Experience and the Incentives in People's Lives*, in which a primary place is given to purposes as means of providing incentives for action and understanding. The vital thing is to interpret one's current activities in relation to future possible states. It is not merely a matter of behaving in a goal directed way, which can be automatic, without conscious direction. As Baumeister puts it, human beings can think; they conceptualize possible outcomes of their actions and can be guided by ideas about goals. So, as a need for meaning, 'purpose' involves at least three things: a goal or state is imagined, current behaviour options are analysed and evaluated in reference to possible goal attainment, and the person makes choices of action plans to achieve a goal (Baumeister 1991). Baumeister described a 'myth of fulfilment,' which may well be an illusion but nevertheless gives meaning and purpose to peoples' lives: 'It is an *idea* of a possible future state, often associated with some idealized goal attainment, and it helps people to interpret and structure their present activities' (p. 35). It is what I have referred to as Coleridge's generative idea of an idea, and Iris Murdoch's idea of Platonic forms (discussed in Chapter 11). What matters in Baumeister's understanding of purpose as a need for meaning is that the person's current activities derive meaning from the ideas of intended future events, that is, from purposes.

Baumeister' second category of needs for meaning is *value*, for which he cited initially Victor Frankl's essays on the search for meaning which placed first emphasis on values (Frankl 1959, 1962; Frankl and Batthyány 2010). As with purpose, he says there is little doubt that people are strongly motivated to find sources of value and to justify their actions in reference to them (Baumeister 1991, p. 36). People wanting to do what is good and avoid what is bad makes value a source of motivation. Its power goes beyond determining behavioural choices. After a chosen action has taken place, even when self-interested motives take precedence over higher moral values, people still feel a need to find some justification. They tend to make an interpretation of the action, or the rules, which maintains or restores consistency, thus confirming the power of a value system as a meaning system.

In his exposition of *efficacy* as a third need for meaning, Baumeister says that 'having a meaningful life is more than having goals and values; you must feel that you have some capability to achieve these goals and these values' (p. 41). That is quite consistent with Bandura's theory of self-efficacy (see Chapter 6), but there is a difference of emphasis in regard to subjective feelings. Where Bandura appears to rely more upon cognitive processes of evaluation to form beliefs about self-efficacy, in Baumeister's theory a meaningful life is one in which a person *feels* effective. This reference to feeling effective is closer to Robert White's concept of a need for efficacy (see Chapter 3). Baumeister emphasised efficacy rather than control because he saw the *subjective* perception of effective actions as most important in achieving a meaningful life. He allowed for delusions in satisfying this efficacy need for meaning, so that it might be satisfied without a person actually having any control over the environment. He cited a study by Ellen Langer (1975), for example, in which people showed an irrational preference for lottery tickets they had chosen for themselves. Where control is theoretically possible, in a theory of *interpretative control*, merely by understanding something, meaning can be achieved by changing oneself rather than changing the world (Rothbaum, Weisz and Snyder 1982). Two explanations were offered for the desire to have illusionary control: (1) that the internal mechanism for control motivation is the desire for a *feeling* of control, so that in the desire to feel efficacious, the feeling is sufficient; and (2) it may be that illusory control may have important benefits for affect regulation.

Self-worth is the fourth and final need for meaning proposed by Baumeister. 'People need to make sense of their lives in ways that enable them to feel they have positive value' (Baumeister 1991, p. 44). Making 'sense of their lives' is what we expect from cognitive motivation theory, but, I believe mistakenly, Baumeister allowed the need for self-worth to be expressed principally in comparative terms: '[T]his need usually takes the form of finding some way to feel superior to others.' Baumeister did not offer the obvious alternatives to social comparison, but it is a well-established fact that family and peer group love and acceptance, and a feeling of well-being in one's personal integrity and self-acceptance, can contribute mightily to feelings of self-worth. What Carl Rogers called 'unconditional positive regard', which includes love without regard for comparative esteem, has therapeutic and developmental value (Rogers 1961; Cooper, O'Hara, Schmid and Wyatt 2007; Panksepp and Biven 2012). But however it is done, 'the need is to find some basis for positive self-worth' so that people can 'regard themselves and convince others to regard them positively' (Baumeister 1991, p. 44).

Towards a General Theory of Needs for Meaning

Cognitive motivation theory suggests that Baumeister's several needs for meaning can be accounted for as functions of a general system of cognitive evaluation and commitment. Klinger has argued that it would be preferable to view Baumeister's four needs as dimensions of a single process (Klinger 1998). He proposed that they are all related aspects of goal striving. In Chapter 3 I have proposed a similar rationale from cognitive motivation theory for Deci and Ryan's list of three basic needs: autonomy, competence and relatedness (Deci and Ryan 1985, 1991; Ryan 1995; Deci and Ryan 2000). That small list is relevant to the search for meaning in its relationship to well-being. It was taken up by Sheldon and Elliot in their treatment of goal striving, need-satisfaction and well-being, and by Sheldon again with Ryan, Deci and Kasser in the effect of both goal contents and motives on well-being (Sheldon and Elliot 1999; Sheldon et al. 2004).

There are many lists of what might be called cognitive needs relevant to personal meaning. Maddi, on the search for meaning, in his presentation of existential psychological theory offered a different set of psychological (mental or cognitive) needs which he said 'set humans apart' (Maddi 1998, p. 5; see also Maddi 1970). Maddi's 'symbolization, imagination, and judgment' seen as cognitive needs can also be interpreted as aspects or stages in the same process of goal striving. The various examples of cognitive motivation, such as curiosity, cognitive dissonance and achievement motivation, discussed in the early chapters of this book can also be seen to illustrate ways of satisfying needs for meaning. We might then consider the nature of cognitive need satisfaction, across a variously mapped range of needs for meaning, in reference to Klinger's suggestion of a single process (Klinger 1998).

Klinger suggested that Baumeister's need for *purpose* can be related to the need for *value* by considering how purposes vary in value, noting that goals of low value contribute to meaninglessness (Joske 1981). He referred to *efficacy* as self-perceived aptness with which people pursue their gaols. He argued that as goal striving is futile without at least a modicum of efficacy, it is reasonable to consider it as yet one more dimension of goal-striving, just as seeking *self-worth* in a social context may be viewed as one kind of purpose rather than as something essentially different from purpose as a need for meaning. That is, Klinger integrated Baumeister's needs for meaning by telling a story of their interrelationships as aspects of a single ongoing process of goal striving.

He then argued that goal striving cannot happen without an elaborate system for relating to the outside world, which must manage feedback about the degree to which behaviour is on track to achieve its goals. In such feedback, his view was that emotion provides an evaluative component of motivation. Here he points to the role of emotion in guiding action systems along the same lines as I considered the function of emotions in cognitive motivation in Chapter 8.

> Whereas the sensorium relays the objective state of affairs, emotion relays its significance for the future, whether good or bad, desirable or abhorrent … In this view, emotion is the indispensable evaluative component of a motivational system. (Klinger 1998, p. 37)

Baumeister referred frequently to feelings as criteria for identification and satisfaction of needs for meaning. I suggest that Baumeister's needs for meaning, whether four or some other number as he allowed, can be accounted for in a cognitive motivation theory as instances of a common process in which emotions are signs of the relationship between a goal and present conditions. I have discussed this process as a function of an incomplete gestalt in which incomplete schemas can vary in their feeling tone in many ways with different contents. The relevant contents do not fall into any particular number of categories. The incomplete gestalt can move towards completion in a great variety of different ways, specifying different action schemas and potential outcomes. Some of these routes to completion are quite common, and others are not. For those that are common, we can group the signs of progress towards their goals under labels such as seeking value, or efficacy, or competence, or autonomy, or consistency with the self-concept, or achievement, or social affiliation, or power, and in many other ways that name specific types of cognitive motivation. There have been many classifications of goals for a range of different motives, some common, some uncommon, each signifying a somewhat different route to completion of an incomplete gestalt with different contents. As Elliott has demonstrated in his hierarchical theory of achievement motivation, it can be useful to distinguish between goal concepts and motive concepts (Elliot 2005, 2006). Not only do feelings not necessarily specify particular motives, but neither do motives specify particular goals. The range of possible variations in the signs of motivated activity and in the underlying needs or motives is increased by these uncertainties.

Common routes to completion have names like 'achievement' and 'relatedness' that serve a social function of shared meanings and assist people with their self-understanding and social co-ordination. There are also less common routes to completion, some of which may be unique to the individual or to the particular emotion or need. However it is done, people seek a meaningful resolution of an incomplete gestalt, and they may use quite common signs or subtle differences in feelings to guide them towards satisfying solutions. Many ways of stringing the beads on Emerson's thread of meaning are common to most of us, but theoretically we can map and slice up the spectrum of possible variations in the meaning of purposeful activity – in Baumeister's terms 'the total conceptual space that they cover' – in an *infinite* number of ways.

One useful classification of personal goals that is discussed further below (Ford and Nichols 1987; Ford 1992), and has been recommended by reviewers in this field (Austin and Vancouver 1996), allows specifically for an infinite number of variations. After describing the categories of goals in Ford and Nichols Taxonomy of Human Goals, Ford says, 'As the preceding descriptions illustrate, goal content can be usefully classified into a finite number of categories. However, it is important to keep in mind that the personalized and contextualized nature of goals produces an infinite number of variations on any particular goal theme' (Ford 1992, p. 96).

In Baumeister's conception of needs for meaning, discrimination between needs requires the evidence of differentiated feelings. Differentiation within the range of possible emotions across his conceptual space of needs for meaning should include fine distinctions between feelings as well as common groupings within an infinite range of emotions. The concept of fine feelings is not as commonly employed today as it was in the time of David Hume (1711–1776), Jane Austen (1775–1817) or George Eliot (1819–1880), for whom such discernment was an accomplishment likely to be found in a cultured person's appreciation of aesthetic objects, personalities and social situations. Amongst other things it implied fine discrimination between objects of interest and between the various subjective responses to them. To employ only a few simple categories of emotional response in those days would have been considered quite gross and socially insensitive.[1]

In his essay on standards in aesthetics, Hume argued for a natural relation between form and feeling in which universal principles of beauty could be recognised by people well trained in matters of taste. He saw failure to recognise such relations as a result of personal defects, the first of which was 'the want of that *delicacy* of imagination which is requisite to convey a sensibility of finer emotions' (Hume 1997, p. 83). Hume

[1] Two passages from George Eliot that provide literary examples of the complexity and subtly of emotions experienced by a person capable of fine discrimination between feelings are included in Chapter 9.

believed that an ability to recognise examples of beauty and universal principles in their appreciation could be developed with practice, especially in making comparisons between aesthetic objects. In this view then, a high degree of cognitive development is necessary for 'finer emotions' which were thought to guide discernment of universal and lasting aesthetic principles. Whether Hume's argument for objectivity in the discernment of universal principles can be sustained is another matter. It has been a matter of considerable debate, and the argument for objectivity in aesthetic judgements may be rejected (Beswick 2012), but the capacity for aesthetic judgement is an intellectual type of achievement in which 'intellectual emotions' play a part (Averill 1991; Roberts and Wood 2006). The resolution of an incomplete gestalt in cognitive motivation depends upon a similar capacity to appreciate 'form qualities'. It requires sufficient richness and flexibility of imagination to perceive insightful differences between feelings and to envisage a great variety of possible futures and means of their attainment, many of which will be common, but in particular cases may be idiosyncratic or even unique.

This great variety suggests that any system of classification is likely to have limited application. However, the fact that there are common as well as peculiar ways of making sense of greatly varied purposive behaviour probably means that the ways in which we group cognitive motivational phenomena in 'the total conceptual space that they cover' is not arbitrary. It could be due to experience with common tasks and/or reflect some more universal qualities derived from specific brain functions such as the basic affective systems described by Panksepp (1998, 2005), which are nevertheless subject to modification with experience. As far as high-level social cognitive needs, motives and feelings are concerned, it does not mean that it is necessary to posit a set of particular needs or motives as universal substantive entities which may be discovered in human nature. One way to provide a rationale for such groupings as might indicate a common quality is to examine the kinds of feedback which guide behaviour. In so far as this guidance is a function of emotions, we need to recognise both common and uncommon feelings and take account of the great variety and subtlety of emotions guiding behaviour in pursuit of high-level cognitive goals. These feelings might be called 'intellectual emotions' (see Chapter 9).

Common needs that could be a function of common experience are not the same as *basic* needs that have been proposed as universal products of brain properties. The case for *basic* emotions has been presented by Ekman, Izard, Panksepp and others whose work is discussed in Chapter 8. Panksepp has described, in addition to a set of seven basic affective systems, a larger secondary learned group of emotions, and a further great range of tertiary emotions, varying on many dimensions at the social or cognitive level. While there may be common dimensions in tertiary emotions, due largely to common experiences, many emotional signals will vary between individuals and situations reflecting subtle differences in the ways people can experience separation from and approaches to their goals. Furthermore, even the goals themselves may be idiographic but nevertheless share something of human character in general, which may be represented on dimensions with a useful degree of commonality.

Baumeister's needs for meaning function in a similar way to another list of basic needs proposed by Kasser (2002) in his work on the effects of materialism in personal strivings, which covers a wide range of purposive strivings relevant to meaning and purpose. He contrasted materialistic with spiritual values. In cognitive motivation theory, Kasser's instrument can be regarded as one way of grouping an *infinite array* of cognitive needs rather than designating a limited set of substantive motivational predispositions. He designated four sets divided into a total of 24 categories of need, saying, 'I have come to conclude that at least four sets of needs are basic to the motivation, functioning, and well-being of all humans' (Kasser 2002, p. 24).

I suggest that his categories of needs, like the lists others have proposed, are unlikely to be universal effects. They are conceptual groupings likely to have arisen from common tasks and a great variety of experiences that do not easily fall into common categories. Nevertheless, Kasser's groups of needs have been related to the effects of materialism and spirituality on well-being. In Chapter 3 I have presented the case for needs of this kind being psychogenic, cognitive and capable of subtle variation from experience, rather than being innate and universal. They are, nevertheless, substantial in having effects that are theoretically predictable and socially valued aspects of a culture.

We do not know how much differentiation of commonly recognised motives depends upon hardwired differences in the physiological components of emotional responses, but they are at least facilitated by specific neural structures. For example, where fear plays a part, the amygdala has an important role (LeDoux 2000; Lawrence and Calder 2004), and the critical involvement of prefrontal and parietal cortices is seen in the processing of novel stimuli (Shallice and Burgess 1998), although it is also true that the relevant structures are dispersed networks rather than discrete brain locations. However, while feelings as the subjective side of emotions may depend in part upon specific brain functions, they can be shaped by experience, and they will often be affected by several different neural networks. (See also the discussion of Panksepp's theory of basic emotions below and in Chapter 9.)

Certain examples of what I have described as psychogenic needs or motives are seen by some theorists to be closer to the hardwired type of motivation than others are. For example, it has been claimed that '[c]uriosity is hardwired in the brain, and its specific function is to urge us to explore, discover, and grow. It is the engine of our evolving self' (Kashdan 2009, p. 6). Similarly, Berlyne (1960) in his early work on curiosity allowed for some such possibility in his reference to the brain having needs for stimulation that has information value. Much of what Kashdan says about the nature and function of curiosity agrees with what I have been saying, but I see curiosity taking a variety of forms as a consequence of many complex brain properties interacting with experience. These many forms of curiosity are part of the domain of cognitive motivation which can be divided in a great variety of ways. Indeed, in his notes Kashan says, 'Curiosity is not an only child; it is part of a family of terms used by writers, scientists, and everyday people making conversation to capture the essence of recognising, seeking out, and showing a preference for the new' (p. 290). He then describes the 'siblings' of curiosity as interest, flow, intrinsic motivation, novelty seeking, openness to experience and search for meaning – terms I have used to refer to various aspects of it as one part of the wide domain of cognitive motivation within which boundary lines are difficult to draw.

An Infinite Range of Needs and Feelings

Does it make sense to ask how many needs for meaning there are? Why could there not be at least as many as there are meaningful goals? All depend on emotional feedback, but if we ask how many even 'common' needs could be identified from different emotions in feedback from purposeful activity, we have no certain answer. What Panksepp called secondary and tertiary emotions, formed by experience, appear in great variety (see Chapter 8). When we come to the complex multifaceted character of human feelings associated with needs for meaning, social and personal evaluations and purposive strivings, there is a strong case for expecting an infinite variety of both needs and feelings. To this we can add the further complexity that, despite Baumeister's associating feelings with needs, there is no direct link of particular needs with particular feelings – it is possible to feel anxious about the satisfaction of quite different needs.

In reference to anthropological and experimental studies, we can safely say that there are many emotions which can serve as signs for cognitive goals. Particularly in regard to intellectual pursuits, we can agree with Averill's description of emotions as 'many splendored things' (Averill 1994). Commonality in the expression and satisfaction of needs in cognitive motivation, signified by emotions with some degree of similarity that are commonly recognised and named, comes largely from experience in common tasks, although they may well be built upon a foundation of evolutionarily defined and experientially refined basic affective systems. That conception of needs and emotions does not point to any innate or built-in propensities to seek particular goals or types of goals at the higher level of social and cognitive development.

As both Damasio (2010) and Panksepp (2011b; Panksepp and Biven 2012) have claimed in their recent work, there is increasing diversity and complexity of emotions as one moves up from common basic mammalian affective systems 'in the basement of the mind' to the tertiary level of cognitive-emotional systems in the cortex in interaction with lower brain regions. Damasio, put it succinctly in *Self Comes to Mind*: 'All feelings of emotion are complex musical variations on primordial feelings' (Damasio 2010, p. 21). It is not far from these ideas of experiential refinement and numerous combinations of core emotions to a position of *infinitely varied* shades of emotion with some common points of emphasis. The evidence points in that direction. It is the same for goals as for emotions. Elliot conceived 'an essentially limitless, idiographic array of focal endpoints' (Elliot 2006, p. 113). The notion of refined feelings, even if developed from common evolved systems, is appealing when we come to think of the subtle feelings that we should expect to be associated with needs for meaning. The model of a single system of diverse needs for meaning with an infinite variety of feelings associated with an infinite range of cognitive needs might have points of emphasis on common needs and feelings, but no fixed categories of needs or feelings.

A general theory of needs for meaning based on the principles of cognitive motivation predicts an infinite range of needs from possible variations in the incomplete gestalts that may be formed when questions of meaning arise. At the same time, there is an infinite range of emotions that can provide feedback in high-level cognitive structures of purpose and meaning.

Systems of Meaning

Meaningful integration of challenging experiences can take place in a great variety of ways. These systems of meaning might be personal and idiographic or they might correspond to publically recognised belief systems. Some are characteristic of spirituality and religion as a particular kind of expression of the more general construction of purpose and meaning. Both personal and public forms of belief systems are derived from the propensity of people to try to make sense of things – to make sense of what happens to them and in the world around them, whatever it is. We do so in wondrous and varied ways. There may be a deep and meaningful insight, to us personally even a glorious epiphany, and yet perhaps nonsense to another. It depends upon and contributes to our individual sense of identity. It is both a product of wonder and an object of wonder, personally felt, whether it arises from primitive curiosity in the moment or a life-long search for purpose and meaning.

I have discussed this general human striving to discern a pattern of meaning in whatever happens, and how it varies between people, at many points in this work. In the previous chapter, I referred, for example, to Gazzaniga's idea of a 'left hemisphere interpreter' which makes narrative sense of discrete events. He quoted the literary and philosophical reflections of Emerson and Updike, and I took note of their making sense in artistic and religious ways of thinking. Here I want to deal specifically with spiritual and religious strivings for purpose and meaning.

It is not the task of psychology to attempt to settle ontological questions about man, the universe and everything, although it is not uncommon in recent years for authors of major works in psychology, such as Pinker and Koch, to offer their own views on these things (Pinker 1997; Koch 2012). They are often negative in their attitude to religion. For most of the 20th century, psychologists tended to avoid religion. As Bloom said in a recent review, 'psychologists typically ignore religion' – it is like 'sex to a Victorian or dreams to a behaviorist – an awkward and embarrassing phenomenon best not talked about' (Bloom 2012, p. 180). Emmons quotes Gordon Allport's introduction to his classic of a previous generation, *The Individual and His Religion*, saying in 1950 that 'the persistence of religion appears as an embarrassment to the scholars of today' (Allport 1950, p. 1), and Emmons comments that little has changed in that regard (Emmons 1999b). But despite such attitudes, religious or spiritual behaviour and experience have been more readily acknowledged in the mainstream of psychological research in recent years.

The human tendency to favour structure and clarity over ambiguity and randomness has been noted as a foundation for systems of meaning (Kruglanski 1989; Heine et al. 2006; Kay, Laurin, Fitzsimons and Landau 2014). Sometimes this is presented as a compensating mechanism when meaning is asserted as a response to disorder, or belief in God serves to fill gaps in knowledge. At other points it can be seen to operate positively rather than merely to fill gaps, as people reach for new experiences of wholeness and find meaning in a comprehensive belief system that makes sense of experience and is open to new developments. In this chapter I have emphasised a future orientation as a condition for personal integration, but Kay et al. (2014, p. 486) have reported empirical support for causation in the reverse direction in the hypothesis 'that perceiving structure facilitates willingness to take goal-directed action'. This combination of purpose and meaning, which may well be reflexive and mutually reinforcing, is both a cultural and an individual phenomenon, found in public belief systems and in personal religious or spiritual experience.

Systems of Belief and Patterns of Meaning

In the general theory of cognitive motivation, a common propensity for pattern-making leads us to seek a new cognitive organisation at whatever level of organisation incompleteness is apparent. At the macro level, in big-picture visions of life as a whole, people try to make sense of challenging events like death and injustice. They might do so in terms of a general philosophy of life and make long-term commitments in accord with a system of beliefs. People can make some sort of sense of almost anything, discovering new truths, concocting fanciful theories, healing psychological and even physical wounds and enjoying a new wholeness of being. Comprehensive systems of meaning that range from daily life to cosmic theories are the natural domain of human beings, for better or worse. Some such systems of meaning are called religions, while a similar capacity for wonder in aesthetic experience and insightful thought, particularly when accompanied by a new feeling of wholeness, might sometimes be called spirituality.

These are important and universal human qualities that have been neglected in scientific psychology, although there has been more attention to them in the past 20 years than there was for most of the 20th century. It is a large subject, and there is room here for only a few recent developments in the psychological study of spirituality and religion that can be understood in terms of the general theory of cognitive motivation.

The goals of religious activity and spiritual strivings operate in the same way as other goals for which cognitive processes create motivation. Recent reviewers refer to a number of theorists who suggest that 'religious beliefs emerge from ordinary cognitive processes (Guthrie 1993, Boyer 2003)' (Laurin, Kay and Moscovitch 2008, p. 1559). Depending upon their attitudes, beliefs and commitments, people interested in religion may find this claim for universal application of common psychological methods and theories disturbingly false or blindingly obvious. As Pargament (2002a) observed, when psychologists take a pragmatic view and evaluate religions in terms of effects such as self-esteem and happiness, even if the effects are positive, people committed to a religion may be inclined to object that psychologists have stripped religion of spiritual value, elevating the profane over the sacred, and have thus engaged in idolatry. Others are keen to exclude any exceptional character and see religion as 'a natural phenomenon' (Dennett 2006) capable of being reduced to common cognitive, affective and social processes.

In this discussion I take the view that religion is indeed a natural phenomenon that can be understood within the normal range of psychological theory and observation. Emmons and Paloutzian in their general review of progress in the psychology of religion aimed 'to illustrate how all of the topics within the psychology of religion are extensions of and feed back to the overall body of theory and the database from general psychology' (Emmons and Paloutzian 2003, p. 378). When we see that spiritual and religious systems of meaning can function in the same way as systems of meaning in general, it is important to recognise that this can be done without making any implied judgement on the truth or falsity of religious beliefs. They are facts of life available for study at the level of cognitive organisation at which they appear. When a cognitive theory of the processes described in this chapter for purpose and meaning in general is applied to religion and spirituality, we assume that the same common operations as apply generally are performed on unique contents.

Whether and in what way, if any, religion is unique in its motivation has been a subject of discussion in the psychology of religion. In one sense the religion or spirituality of every individual is unique because every person is unique. 'The subjective religious attitude of every individual is in both its essential and nonessential features, unlike that of any other individual' (Allport 1950, p. 26). Because it involves what Allport called the proprium, those central aspects of personality which we regard as peculiarly ours, and that make for an inward unity, religion is of central importance to believers. That alone is not to claim that religion in general is unique among human characteristics and processes. Frankl went a little further in that direction when he introduced a specific class of psychic processes that he said were unique to humans as beings capable of transcending, objectifying and even opposing themselves: '[M]an must have an aim towards which he can constantly direct his life … he must realize the unique meaning which each of us must fulfil' (Frankl 1959 p. 100; Frankl 1962). Others have seen the uniqueness of religion in terms of its concern with the sacred: religion being 'a search for significance in ways related to the sacred' (Pargament 1997, p. 32).

'What sets religion apart from other phenomena is the involvement of the sacred' (Pargament 2002a, p. 169). That often means it will be concerned with God, but not necessarily that a different set of concepts will be needed for the psychology of religion. Some theorists have seen no need for 'special concepts, theories or methods tailored to religious life' (Pargament, Magyar-Russell and Murray-Swank 2005, p. 666). Others have argued against what is apparently a reductionist perspective on the grounds that the ultimate point of reference for religion, God or the divine cannot be reduced to common human terms (Richards and Bergin 1997). Paul Johnson seems to have suggested this when he wrote in one of the most widely used textbooks on the psychology of religion in a previous generation, 'It is the ultimate Thou whom the religious person seeks most of all' (Johnson 1959, p. 70). It implies a relationship which extends beyond the material realm of human life. The general scientific psychological consensus at present is that this seeking of 'the sacred' can be described in the normal language of psychology, but that does not mean that it has no unique qualities.

Wong quotes William James, from a still earlier period, defining religion as 'the feelings, acts, and experiences of individual men [and women] in their solitude, so far as they apprehend themselves to stand in relation to whatever they may consider divine (James 1902, p. 81)' (Wong 1998c, p. 362). Wong referred also to the theologian Paul Tillich's regarding an ultimate concern as a kind of personal encounter: 'Religion is the state of being grasped by an ultimate concern which qualifies all other concerns as preliminary and which itself contains the answer to the question of the meaning of life' (Tillich 1963, p. 4). It is an open question how well common psychological concepts like those of cognitive motivation can be applied. Unique content could require some new shape for theoretical constructs, but I would argue for understanding spirituality and religions principally in terms of meaning and purpose as it is found in the general processes of cognitive integration. That hope can only be fulfilled if the unique content of religion is recognised and not re-interpreted to fit some other ideology.

Baumeister concluded in a discussion of papers by Pargament and others on whether the study of religion could be subsumed under other headings that whether religion is unique is an intriguing empirical question, and whether it is or not, it can be 'an enormously fertile source of insights and observations that can be used to develop and refine psychological theories' (Baumeister 2002, p. 167). That would suggest that it may well have qualities not found elsewhere. Baumeister drew theoretical implications which indicated particular mechanisms for the influence of religion when he concluded with Tierney that 'religion affects two central mechanisms for self-control: building willpower and improving monitoring' (Baumeister and Tierney 2011, p. 180). The association of religion with self-regulation has been proposed as the basis for the positive effect of religiosity on health and well-being. In their review, McCullough and Willoughby (2009) found good evidence for the proposition 'that religion's ability to promote self-control or self-regulation can explain some of religion's associations with health, well-being, and social behavior' (p. 87). It is similar with other variables in cognitive motivation – unique contents can have common effects.

There is another important qualification to the claim that religion has unique qualities because of its concern with 'the sacred', and that is that people are capable of making almost anything sacred. This is an observation as old as the record of religious thought: in the Hebrew Scriptures we have the law against idolatry, in which natural powers were personified, being directly linked with the primary affirmation of belief in one God. The appreciative sense of awe and wonder which can be found in responses to the natural world is similar to that in religious devotion. So also in regard to living our daily lives with a sense of well-being, one can find supposedly secular and religious expressions of the same principles, as Baumeister and Tierney said,

> The devotion to God seems to give way to a reverence for nature's beauty and transcendence. Environmentalists' exhortations to reduce consumption and waste are teaching children some of the same self-control lessons offered in religious sermons and Victorian primers. Secular greens seem to be instinctively replacing one form of self-discipline with another, and one kind of rules with another: organic instead of kosher, sustainability instead of salvation. (Baumeister and Tierney 2011, p. 183)

This type of reverence is similar to that view of nature implied in the broad operational definitions of spirituality by Emmons and Seligman (Emmons 1999a, 2005; Seligman 2011). The *re*sacralization of nature is an interesting phenomenon. In recent years it has given rise, for example, to religious passions both in opposition to and support for scientists who contribute to public policy on environmental questions. Ideological environmentalism, as a type of secular religion, reverses the desacralization of nature which is claimed to have been one of the contributing factors to the rise of modern science out of the culture of medieval Christendom (Turner 1998; see also Butterfield 1949; Jaki 1986; Kaiser 1991). The same cognitive and affective processes are found in alternative forms of spirituality as in traditional religions. The general theory of cognitive motivation applies to both as people seek to make sense of the world and themselves and make commitments in the light of those beliefs.

A theory of religion as a meaning system has been presented by Israela Silberman in terms very similar to the functioning of a cognitive map at the macro level of organisation in cognitive motivation theory. She described a meaning system as a set of beliefs and theories: 'These beliefs or theories form idiosyncratic meaning systems that allow individuals to give meaning to the world around them and to their experiences, as well as to set goals, plan activities, and order their behavior' (Silberman 2005, p. 644). She cited a number of other authors who have presented similar conceptions (Kelly 1955; Bowlby 1969; Dweck 1999; Higgins 2000). Meaning systems in Silberman's theory contain both descriptive and motivational or prescriptive beliefs: descriptive in regard to the person, the nature of the world and relations between them; and motivational in regard to major prescriptive postulates which are broad generalizations about how to behave in the future (Epstein 1985; Higgins 2000). In the cognitive motivation theory I would put it a little differently and include those prescriptive postulates as dispositional properties within the description of the person and see motivational arousal and direction as processes arising from the pattern of interaction between the person and the situation.

Two major characteristics of religions as meaning systems were proposed by Silberman to account for the extensive influence of religion on both private and public affairs, for different ends, and through many channels: (1) the *comprehensiveness* and (2) the *uniqueness* of religious meaning systems. Religion has been described as a multifaceted construct which is unique in its concerns being both comprehensive and central to a person's life, as well as its being psychologically complex and diverse in different individuals (Batson, Schoenrade and Ventis 1992).

Some Effects of Spirituality and Religion

At the heart of the psychology of well-being in the effects of spirituality and religion is the integration of beliefs and practices with the whole person, so that religion or spirituality is not a limited, external or partial interest, but internalized and intrinsically motivated. As Emmons said in reference to 'Spiritual strivings as ultimate concerns', when he quoted Fowler as follows, we need not see faith as a separate faculty nor understand it in dualistic terms:

> Faith, classically understood, is not a separate dimension of life, a compartmentalized specialty. Faith is an orientation of the total person, giving purpose and goal to one's hopes and strivings, thoughts and actions ... as such, faith is an integral part of one's character or personality – (Fowler 1981, pp. 14, 92). (Emmons 1999a, p. 89)

As Emmons has demonstrated in his empirical research and reviews (Emmons 1989; Emmons and Paloutzian 2003; Emmons 2005), spiritual strivings evident in a person's goals can be examined in the same way as other motivational concepts. While many studies of the effects of religion have been concerned with traditional religions, a broader view of spirituality is also taken. Emmons made provision for this broader, more humanistic view within a general description of spirituality in his measurement of personal strivings which may 'reflect concern for an integration of the person with larger and more complex units: with humanity, nature, with the cosmos ("to achieve union with the totality of existence," "to immerse myself in nature and be part of it," "to live my life at all times for God," "to approach life with mystery and awe") ... spiritual strivings contain both conventional religious themes as well as more personalized expressions of spiritual concern' (Emmons 2005, p. 736).

This broad operational definition of spirituality was employed in the work of Kasser and others on the effects of spirituality and materialism. In their first study Kasser and Ryan (1993) found that those subjects who considered financial success a relatively more central value than self-acceptance, affiliation and community feeling reported lower levels of self-actualization and vitality as well as significantly higher levels of depression and anxiety. This was in a study of American college students. Their second study brought together the prominent goals of a consumer society in a broad-based community sample covering all age ranges and socio-economic levels. The findings were similar to those obtained with college students in the first study. Adults who focused on money, image and fame reported less self-actualization and vitality and more depression and anxiety. They also reported more headaches, sore throats and other symptoms of physical distress. Regardless of age or wealth, people with highly central materialistic values reported lower levels of well-being. Similar results were obtained when diaries recording daily lives were used in addition to questionnaires. The same effects of placing a central value on financial success were found for students in other countries as well as the United States (Kasser and Ryan 1996).

The same effects as those on well-being have been demonstrated for the effects of religion on mortality. McCullough and his colleagues found an association of religious activity with lower rates of mortality from all causes (McCullough, Hoyt, Larson, Koenig and Thoresen 2000). In a large-scale meta-analysis of 42 independent samples with a total of 125,826 participants, the rate of survival from initial to follow-up studies at various later intervals of time was 29% higher in those rated as having greater than average religious participation. When the effects of moderator variables such as sex and general health were taken out, the strong effect of religion remained.

Emmons found a positive effect of spiritual strivings on well-being in a study of motivational factors that contribute to improvement in the quality of life of people suffering from neuromuscular disease (NMD), treated as an example of health effects in general (Emmons 2005). A goal-based measure of integration in Emmons's Personal Strivings Assessment Package was the strongest predictor of overall levels of well-being in a composite measure of life satisfaction, positive affect, and vitality. He defined personal strivings as 'consciously accessible and personally meaningful objectives that people pursue in their daily lives (see Emmons 1999a, for a review). Personal strivings refer to the typical goals that a person characteristically is trying to accomplish' (Emmons 2005, p. 732).

In Emmons's conception of the function of spiritual strivings, goals are ordered and reconciled in such a way as to facilitate an integrated response to challenges and opportunities. In that study, as goals increased in meaningfulness and attainability, persons with NMD felt more satisfied with their lives. Using a goal-based measure of spirituality based on the concept of sanctification (Pargament et al. 2005), it was found, when the effects of different goals were compared, that 'self-ratings of the degree to which the goal brings the person closer to God were positively associated with life satisfaction and positive affect' (Emmons 2005, p. 741; see also Sheldon, Kashdan and Steger 2011).

In the personal strivings approach to motivation we are concerned with relatively high-level goals that are central aspects of a person's identity, not merely what a person is trying to *do*, but also concerned with what a person is trying to *be*. These goals are highly personal, reflecting subjective experience, values and commitments uniquely defined by the person; and personal growth is expected. Emmons says of personal strivings that 'they represent potentialities rather than actualities in that they are never fully satisfied' (Emmons 2005, p. 732). And reminiscent of our discussion of intrinsic motivation (Chapters 2 and 3), he says, 'To strive also implies that meaning comes from the "journey" and not just arriving at the "destination"' (p. 732).

A number of studies have demonstrated that intrinsic satisfaction, giving meaning while on the journey, can profoundly influence subjective personal well-being. It is in purposive striving that goals give meaning in life – not just in the attainment of a goal but in striving for it. So Emmons argues that the goals construct has given 'form and substance to the amorphous concept of "meaning in life."' (p. 734). As noted in the introduction to the section on 'Purposeful living', in Klinger's words, 'What a life means is what that life purposes.' The findings of empirical studies are that individuals who are engaged with personally meaningful goals possess greater emotional well-being and better physical health than do those who lack goal direction (Emmons 1999a). The general conclusion is that meaning matters, and specifically, that '[t]he explanations that a person offers concerning ultimate issues – the nature of life and death, the meaning of suffering and pain, of what really matters in life – have profound implications for individual well-being' (Emmons 2005, pp. 734–735).

Kashdan (2009) lists religion and spirituality, together with 'work as a "calling"', among personally meaningful activities that he describes as venues in which we are most likely to see purpose in action. Much along the same lines as the narrative form of identity discussed in Chapter 11, he says that a person's identity is expressed and developed in the meaning given to life by a guiding purpose, and that it can contribute significantly to one's well-being. He made finding a purpose in life a matter of deliberate self-guided development, achieved by learning from others, responding to life-altering events and intentional seeking.

In his introductory reference to this theme, Kashdan declared a particular position on a matter of faith. He said that, '[c]ontrary to popular belief, there is no evidence to suggest that we have a preordained purpose in life' (Kashdan 2009, p. 15). In some traditions it would be regarded as an important matter of faith whether people in general have a prescribed purpose in life, and that one might or might not find and follow one's calling. In this there may be different understandings of whether in a person's vocation he or she is responding to a call of God, or some purpose greater than oneself whatever its origin, or whether one is simply acting in accord with an individual's inclinations and abilities when fulfilling a purpose in life. And then there is the question of whether these are distinct practical alternatives or different ways of seeing the same thing. With whatever understanding of purpose in life they might have, many psychologists endorse the value of deliberately espoused meaning and purpose. This is one of the emphases made in positive psychology in which Kashdan and others have acknowledged an empirical foundation for the claim that religious practices that are intrinsically rewarding are beneficial in terms of personal well-being – more so than those practices oriented to social control and extrinsic reward (Kashdan 2004; Kashdan et al. 2004; Kashdan and Breen 2007; Kashdan and Steger 2011; Sheldon et al. 2011; Kashdan and Ciarrochi 2013; Kashdan, Young and Machell 2015). The close relationship of cognitive motivation to positive psychology is introduced in the following section.

The Cognitive Motivational Basis of Positive Psychology

Positive psychology was born with the promise of an old idea made new in a spirit of hopefulness and generosity. Human nature was virtually reconceived in a call to a fundamental change of attitude among psychologists.

'A science of positive subjective experience, positive individual traits, and positive institutions promises to improve quality of life and prevent the pathologies that arise when life is barren and meaningless.' With these words of hope and inspiration Martin Seligman and Mihaly Csikszentmihalyi began the article that introduced the special issue of the *American Psychologist* (Seligman and Csikszentmihalyi 2000, p. 5) that kicked off the 'positive psychology' movement (Kashdan and Steger 2011). Although implicit in previous work by many psychologists over the previous 50 years, the basic idea for positive psychology had been explicitly conceived when Seligman wondered whether his extensive research on learned helplessness, in which pessimism was inculcated by repeated shocks, might be transformed to show how a predisposition for optimism could be learned from the experience of frequent positive rewards (Seligman 1998; see also Seligman 1975). Positive psychology was an idea whose time had come. It was not so much a spontaneous development inspired by a new intellectual paradigm as it was a movement led from the top by elders of the tribe with a scientifically designed bottom-up strategy for creative change (Csikszentmihalyi 1988), a strategy that quickly encouraged new leadership from rising young stars.

Csikszentmihalyi, well known for his concept of 'flow' in the 'psychology of optimal experience' (Csikszentmihalyi 1990), tells the story of how during a brief winter break in Hawaii he met 'a hearty fellow' on the beach who introduced himself as Marty Seligman (Csikszentmihalyi and Nakamura 2011). They knew each other's work, of course, but had not previously had the chance to talk. Seligman was at that time preparing to take over the presidency of the American Psychological Association (APA), and they talked at length over the next few days about the direction they would like to see psychology take and the sort of mark Seligman would like to leave. They asked themselves what they could do 'to bring back into the discourse of psychology some of the concepts we found were so important to understand for a life worth living, yet were so rarely addressed by psychology, such as courage, generosity, creativity, joy, and gratitude' (Seligman 2006, p. 4). It was an action-oriented question, and positive psychology has been much concerned with the development of effective interventions with both individuals and organisations.

In seeking to change psychology from a deficit-orientation to a strength-orientation (Peterson and Seligman 2004), Seligman believed that there was much work for psychologists to do. 'One common feeling is that positive psychology is the scientific effort to improve people's lives. Research on a variety of desirable human qualities has proliferated under the banner of positive psychology, and few would argue that learning how to instil meaning, curiosity, hope, and motivation fails to work toward this goal' (Kashdan and Steger 2011, p. 9). In this book I have been concerned with the same kind of re-orientation, but I have focused less on professional applications and more on understanding the relevant motivation in depth.

Seligman and Csikszentmihalyi recognised that some of these ideas had previously been advanced by writers such as Maslow, Antonovsky and Rogers, whose work I have also cited, but they saw them as having been eclipsed 'under the hegemony first of behaviorism and psychoanalytic thought, and later of cognitive psychology' (Seligman and Csikszentmihalyi 2000, p. 6). They sought now to foster a self-conscious movement to bring the eclipsed material into the full light of day. I want to comment on the perceived negative impact of cognitive psychology, but first a little more on the growth of the movement.

Jeanne Nakamura, Csikszentmihaly's co-author, recalled more than 10 years later the excitement with which as a graduate student she had 'watched the first stirrings of positive psychology with avid interest. I recall seeing listeners moved to tears during Martin Seligman's presidential call to arms at the 1998 American Psychological Association meeting in San Francisco. I remember seeing them rise to applaud at its conclusion' (Csikszentmihalyi and Nakamura 2011, pp. 6–7). The hoped-for self-conscious identity was soon established among those who began to call themselves positive psychologists. It was not long before both research programs and applications expanded, and there were hundreds of 'life coaches' implementing and propagating the message. They even compared the movement with the rise of Christianity and, by analogy, sought ways to avoid institutional ossification defeating their original purpose; they also tried to limit the influence of charlatans and false prophets. A new identity was reinforced by distinction from humanistic psychology, which might be seen as a forerunner of positive psychology but which had been marked by calling into question the appropriateness of scientific method for psychology. Positive psychologists did not wish to abandon the scientific approach, but to enrich it. Csikszentmihaly and Nakamura envisaged several possible futures: (1) a fully fleshed out and scientifically grounded psychology of well-being; (2) a positive perspective ultimately integrated with the rest of the sub-disciplines, such as social and clinical psychology, with neither a universal theory nor a separate positive psychology; and (3) a less directed future, 'from rallying around a shared purpose and a shared set of questions or problems and letting the domain evolve organically' (Csikszentmihalyi and Nakamura 2011, p. 7).

They thought it likely that 'the majority of positive psychologists will continue to hold "dual citizenship," belonging to the positive psychology community and to the community of (for example) cognitive psychologists, personality psychologists, or developmental psychologists' (p. 7). Dual citizenship with cognitive psychologists could, hopefully, accommodate those interested in cognitive motivation without suffering ill effects from the hegemony of a restrictive form of cognitive psychology to which Csikszentmihaly and Nakamura had referred in their historical perspective. Much of what positive psychology has sought to achieve in turning from a deficit-orientation to a strength-orientation was already embraced in the cognitive revolution of the late 1950s. It certainly was when motivation theorists like Harlow, White, McReynolds and Hunt laid foundations for the theory of cognitive motivation as they sought to replace a tension reduction model, but the new cognitive alternative was soon under threat from a type of cognitive psychology in which mechanistic information processing displaced conceptions of cognition as concerned with meaning.

As I noted in Chapter 1, Bruner, one of the founders of cognitive studies at the time of the cognitive revolution, complained in his later book *Acts of Meaning* (Bruner 1990) that as cognitive psychology developed, there was an early shift from the construction of meaning to the processing of information. Baars reported a comment by Maltzman that cognitive psychologists were 'worse than Hull', while Deci and Ryan separated a motivational approach from a cognitive approach, seeing a cognitive approach as mechanistic (see also Chapter 3), and Bandura warned against slippage from computational models being approximations of cognitive processes to a view of cognition as 'nothing but' the computations (see Chapter 7).

The theory of cognitive motivation I have been developing should avoid those traps. In many respects it supports positive psychology, particularly in its emphasis on personal agency and openness to the future. It provides a theoretical account of the motivational basis of positive psychology without relying upon a shortcut to innate basic needs. As argued in Chapter 3, Deci's and Ryan's preference for a set of three basic innate needs (i.e. needs for autonomy, competence and relatedness) that some positive psychologists have endorsed (Kashdan and Steger 2011) is unnecessary, simplistic and a distraction. Rather than speculating upon innate needs, I suggest that it is necessary to understand the cognitive motivational basis for positive psychology in such a way as to explicate the underlying processes. It is necessary to go into detail on the role of conscious integration in working memory (Chapter 7), how emotions function as feedback in goal-directed behaviour (Chapter 8), how goals and intentions appear in a cognitive map (Chapters 9 and 10), how personal identity is enhanced as people make sense of diverse experience (Chapter 11) and above all how the resolution of an incomplete gestalt of the person moves people in a meaningful way towards their own fulfilment, as argued in this chapter.

In their introductory article Seligman and Csikszentmihalyi (2000) called for a turn away from negative qualities that had marked much of psychology and towards more positive qualities: 'Hope, wisdom, creativity, future mindedness, courage, spirituality, responsibility, and perseverance are ignored or explained as transformations of more authentic negative impulses' (p. 5). They described the alternative of positive psychology as follows:

> The field of positive psychology at the subjective level is about valued subjective experiences: well-being, contentment, and satisfaction (in the past); hope and optimism (for the future); and flow and happiness (in the present). At the individual level, it is about positive individual traits: the capacity for love and vocation, courage, interpersonal skill, aesthetic sensibility, perseverance, forgiveness, originality, future mindedness, spirituality, high talent, and wisdom. At the group level, it is about the civic virtues and the institutions that move individuals toward better citizenship: responsibility, nurturance, altruism, civility, moderation, tolerance, and work ethic. (Seligman and Csikszentmihalyi 2000, p. 5)

Much good work was done subsequently in research and professional practice to promote ways of making positive feelings more likely to occur in daily life and in education, business and psychotherapy, especially following the publication of Seligman's *Authentic Happiness* (Seligman 2002) and major handbooks like the APA publications on positive psychology – *Flourishing: Positive Psychology and the Life Well-Lived* (Keyes and Haidt 2003) and *Character Strengths and Virtues* (Peterson and Seligman 2004). The original statement by Seligman and Csikszentmihalyi envisaged a much wider range of virtuous outcomes than happiness alone, but such was the strength of the happiness industry that, in reaction against it, and for more direct theoretical reasons, the question was raised of whether seeking happiness as an end in itself might be self-defeating. It was suggested that there was a 'happiness trap' (Harris 2007; Kashdan and Steger 2011; Kashdan and Ciarrochi 2013), so, for example, acceptance and commitment therapy, with its appeal to mindfulness and its emphasis on personal meaning, might be more effective, at least for some people than, say, a form of cognitive behaviour therapy which concentrated upon identifying and changing negative thoughts and feelings.

Many scientists and lay people agree that 'happiness is primarily a cognitive evaluation that one's life is satisfying', that it is going in the right direction (Diener, Suh, Lucas and Smith 1999). 'The problem with happiness arises when people ascribe it to be the primary objective of their life (which reflects the vast majority of people (Oishi, Diener and Lucas 2007))' (Kashdan and Steger 2011, p. 10). 'Other dimensions in this broad, matrix approach include meaning and purpose in life, mindfulness/achievement, life balance and flexibility, and psychological needs for belonging, competence, and autonomy, among others (King, Hicks, Krull and Baker 2006)' (Kashdan and Steger 2011, p. 11).

In his application of research on curiosity, Kashdan prefers strategies that enhance a sense of meaning in life rather than making a direct pursuit of happiness (Kashdan 2009). At various points in this work I have referred to emotions as signals that guide purposive behaviour, so as Kashdan and Steger say of happiness, 'it is a simple barometer that life is moving in a desired direction' Kashdan and Steger 2011, p. 10). In cognitive motivation theory, positive affect does not stand alone as something sought for its own sake. Emotions in general are signs of relationships between goals and the situations in which people see themselves; that is, emotions have a function and are therefore not ends in themselves. From an evolutionary perspective, emotions have survived as properties of organisms because they are useful. If a positive emotion is directly sought, there is the 'happiness trap' (Harris 2007). Kashdan discussed the inadequacy of directly pursuing happiness rather than engaging in meaningful behaviour of which happiness may be a sign and a consequence (Kashdan 2009). Wong has distinguished between meaning-orientation and happiness-orientation as two different visions of the good life with profound practical implications that have emerged in recent developments of what he has called Positive Psychology 2.0 (Wong 2011).

A Common Root in the Cognitive Revolution

When Seligman changed his basic theory of positive psychology from an account of authentic happiness to one of well-being (Seligman 2002, 2011), he added a fourth and a fifth fundamental element to the three he had previously advocated: that is, to positive feeling, engagement and meaning, he added accomplishment and relatedness. The fourth element, accomplishment or achievement sought for its own sake, was derived from one of the primary historical inspirations for positive psychology. For Seligman, this idea was a long time in the making. His account of its origin confirms my impression that the extraordinary 'flourishing' of positive psychology in the first decade or so of the 21st century is a rediscovery and working out of the insights and commitments some of us experienced at the time of the cognitive revolution and the beginning of serious work on curiosity and intrinsic motivation about 50 years before Seligman made his recollection. This is his account:

> I added accomplishment pursued for its own sake because of one of the most formative articles I ever read. In the early 1960s, I was working in psychology professor Byron Campbell's rat lab at Princeton University, and at that time

the umbrella theory of motivation was 'drive-reduction' theory: the notion that animals acted only to satisfy their biological needs. In 1959 Robert White had published a heretical article, 'Motivation Reconsidered: The Concept of Competence,' which threw cold water on the entire drive-reduction enterprise by arguing that rats and people often acted simply to exert mastery over the environment. We pooh-poohed it as soft-headed then, but White, I discovered on my own long and winding road, was right on target. (Seligman 2011, pp 19–20)

Robert White was my adviser for the final writing of my thesis on curiosity, when my principal adviser David McClelland was away on sabbatical leave. My interest in what White called effectance motivation goes back to a lecture on competence he gave to graduate students in clinical and social psychology at Harvard in November 1958. I discussed the article (White 1959) with him when it was published the following year, and, like countless others, have referred to it many times since. It is considered in detail in Chapter 7, where a comparison is made of effectance motivation with self-efficacy, to a lesser extent in Chapter 2 in relation to curiosity, and in Chapters 5 and 6 on achievement motivation and attribution theory.

My own 'long and winding road' since those early days at Harvard has, I imagine, been even more circuitous than Seligman's since he was at Princeton. I must at least have spent more time in the wilderness if, apart from being on the other side of the world most of the time, my many years of ministry in the church and of applied research and development work in education are seen to be apart from the mainstream of psychological research. I have ranged far and wide in these later years within the more or less conventional boundaries of the psychology of cognition and motivation, and can see how an attempt could be made to give a comprehensive treatment of the burgeoning field of positive psychology in terms of cognitive motivation. But that would take more time and energy than I am likely to be able to muster at this late stage of life. I have given some of the basics in this work. How good a fit there is depends upon the kind of emphasis that is made in positive psychology. My theory is much closer to an approach such as Kashdan's than to some others, especially in regard to the seeking of purpose and meaning. Seligman's later formulation is closer than his original version. It will be sufficient if the fruits of my labour on cognitive motivation, across the range from curiosity to identity, purpose and meaning, contribute in some small way to the future development of this important field that is so much more positive than the general tone of psychology was when I began to travel that long road.

Summary

Much of what has been considered in the general theory of cognitive motivation is illustrated at the macro level in research on purpose and meaning in human life.

An orientation to the future, with an image of the future self, is one of the means by which meaningful integration is achieved. This is one of the ways in which Allport's concept of propriate strivings produces a coherent sense of self by seeking the fulfilment of those aims that are most central and definitive in our understanding of ourselves as unique individuals. In discussing this process Baumeister's understanding of needs for meaning is extended from a limited set of four needs to allow an infinite range of cognitive needs and an infinite range of feelings which guide their satisfaction.

The general function of purpose and meaning in human life is explored in the specific case of religion and spirituality. Religion that is intrinsically motivated is considered as one integrating factor in a purposeful and meaningful life. Some results of research on the effects of religion and spirituality on well-being are discussed as examples of the effects of meaningful integration in the functioning of cognitive motivation.

Finally, we review the cognitive motivational basis for positive psychology with reference to a common origin in the cognitive revolution of the late 1950s. It is suggested that the motivation underlying the positive psychology of well-being is typically cognitive motivation, but the fit of positive psychology with cognitive motivation theory is best when the search for meaning is given more emphasis than the pursuit of happiness.

References

Abelson, R. P., E. Aronson, W. J. McGuire, T. M. Newcombe, M. J. Rosenberg and P. H. Tannenbaum, Eds. (1968). *Theories of cognitive consistency: A source book*. Chicago, Rand McNally.

Adolphs, R. (2009). 'The social brain: Neural basis of social knowledge.' *Annual Review of Psychology* 60: 693–716.

Adorno, T. W., E. Frenkel-Brunswick, D. J. Levinson and R. N. Sanford (1950). *The authoritarian personality*. New York, Harper & Row.

Ainley, M. D. (1987). 'The factor structure of curiosity measures: Breadth and depth of interest curiosity styles.' *Australian Journal of Psychology* 39: 53–59.

Ainley, M. (2006). 'Connecting with learning: Motivation, affect and cognition in interest processes.' *Educational Psychology Review* 18: 391–405.

Ainley, M., S. Hidi and D. Berndorff (2002). 'Interest, learning and the psychological processes that mediate their relationship.' *Journal of Educational Psychology* 94(3): 545–561.

Alkire, M. T., A. G. Hudetz and G. Tononi (2008). 'Consciousness and anesthesia.' *Science* 322(5903): 876–880.

Allport, A. (1988). What concept of consciousness? In A. J. Marcel and E. Brisiach (Eds.), *Consciousness in contemporary science* (pp. 159–182). New York, Oxford University Press.

Allport, F. H. (1937). 'Teleonomic description in the study of personality.' *Character and Personality* 5: 202–214.

Allport, G. W. (1937a). *Personality: A psychological interpretation*. London, Constable.

(1937b). 'The functional autonomy of motives.' *American Journal of Psychology*, 50: 141–156.

(1943). 'The ego in contemporary psychology.' *Psychological Review* 50: 451–478.

(1950). *The individual and his religion: A psychological interpretation*. New York, MacMillan Publishing Company.

(1955). *Becoming: Basic considerations in the psychology of personality*. New Haven, Yale University Press.

(1961b). *Pattern and growth in personality*. New York, Holt Rinehart and Winston.

Amabile, T. M. (1983a). *The social psychology of creativity*. New York, Springer-Verlag.

(1993). 'Motivational synergy: Towards new conceptions of intrinsic and extrinsic motivation in the workplace.' *Human Resource Management Review* 3: 185–201.

(1996). *Creativity in context.* Boulder, Westview Press.

(1998). 'How to kill creativity.' *Harvard Business Review* 76(5): 76–87.

Amabile, T. M. and S. J. Kramer (2010). 'What really motivates workers.' *Harvard Business Review* 88(1): 44–45.

Ames, C. (1984). Competitive, cooperative, and individualistic goal structures: A cognitive-motivational analysis. In R. Ames and C. Ames (Eds.), *Research on motivation in education, Vol 1: Student motivation* (pp. 177–207). New York, Academic.

(1992). 'Classrooms: Goals, structures, and student motivation.' *Journal of Educational Psychology* 84: 261–271.

Anselme, P. (2010). 'The uncertainty processing theory of motivation.' *Behavioural Brain Research* 208(2): 291–310.

Antonovsky, A. (1987). *Unravelling the mystery of health: How people manage stress and stay well.* San Francisco, Jossey-Bass.

(1998). The sense of coherence: An historical and future perspective. In H. I. McCubbin, E. A. Thompson, A. I. Thompson and J. E. From (Eds.), *Stress, coping and health in families: Sense of coherence and resiliency* (pp. 3–20). Thousand Oaks, CA: Sage Publications.

Apperly, I. A. and S. A. Butterfill (2009). 'Do humans have two systems to track beliefs and belief-like states?' *Psychological Review* 116(4): 953–970.

Apperly, I. A., D. Samson and G. W. Humphreys (2009). 'Studies of adults can inform accounts of theory of mind development.' *Developmental Psychology* 45: 190–201.

Appley, M. H. (1991). Motivation, equilibrium, and stress. In R. Dienster (Ed.), *Nebraska Symposium on Motivation 1990* (Vol. 38, pp. 1–67). Lincoln and London, University of Nebraska Press.

Arnheim, R. (1969). *Visual thinking.* Berkeley and Los Angeles, University of California Press.

(1971). *Entropy and art: An essay on disorder and order.* Berkeley, University of California Press.

(1974). *Art and visual perception: A psychology of the creative eye.* Berkeley, University of California Press.

(1982). *The power of the center: A study of composition in the visual arts.* Berkeley, University of California Press.

(1996). *The split and the structure: Twenty-eight essays.* Berkeley, University of California Press.

(1998). 'Wolfgang Köhler and Gestalt theory: An English translation of Köhler's introduction to *Diephysischen Gestalten* for philosophers and biologists.' *History of Psychology* 1: 21–26.

Aronoff, J. (1962). 'Freud's conception of the origin of curiosity.' *The Journal of Psychology* 54: 39–45.

Aronson, E. (1958). The need for achievement as measured by graphic expression. In J. W. Atkinson (Ed.), *Motives in fantasy, action, and society: A method of assessment and study* (pp. 249–265). Princeton, NJ, Van Nostrand.

(1968). Dissonance theory: Progress and problems. In R. P. Abelson, E. Aronson, W. J. McGuire et al. (Eds.), *Theories of cognitive consistency: A source book* (pp. 5–27). Chicago, Rand McNally.

(1992). 'The return of the repressed: Dissonance theory makes a comeback.' *Psychological Inquiry* 3: 303–311.

(1999). Dissonance, hypocracy and self-concept. In E. Harmon-Jones and J. Mills (Eds.), *Cognitive dissonance: Progress on a pivotal theory in social psychology* (pp. 103–126). Washington, DC, APA Books.

Aronson, E. and J. M. Carlsmith (1962). 'Performance expectancy as a determinant of actual performance.' *Journal of Abnormal and Social Psychology* 65: 178–182.

(1963). 'Effect of severity of threat on devaluation of forbidden behavior.' *Journal of Abnormal and Social Psychology* 66: 584–588.

Aronson, E., C. Fried and J. Stone (1991). 'Overcoming denial and increasing the intention to use condoms through the induction of hypocrisy.' *American Journal of Public Health* 81: 1636–1638.

Aronson, E. and J. Mills (1959). 'The effect of severity of initiation on liking for a group.' *Journal of Abnormal and Social Psychology* 59: 177–181.

Aronson, J., G. Cohen and P. R. Nail (1999). Self-affirmation theory: An update and appraisal. In E. Harmon-Jones and J. Mills (Eds.), *Cognitive dissonance: Progress on a pivotal theory in social psychology* (pp. 127–145). Washington, DC, APA Books.

Asch, S. E. (1946a). 'Forming impressions of personality.' *Journal of Abnormal and Social Psychology* 41(3): 258–290.

(1946b). 'Max Wertheimer's contribution to psychology.' *Social Research* 13: 81–102.

Ash, M. (1995). *Gestalt psychology in German culture, 1890–1967: Holism and the quest for objectivity*. Cambridge and New York, Cambridge University Press.

Atkinson, J. W. (1953). 'The achievement motive and the recall of interrupted and completed tasks.' *Journal of Experimental Psychology* 46: 381–390.

(1957). 'Motivational determinants of risktaking behavior.' *Psychological Review* 64: 359–372.

(Ed.) (1958a). *Motives in fantasy, action, and society: A method of assessment and study*. Princeton, NJ, Van Nostrand.

(1958b). Towards experimental analysis of human motivation in terms of motives, expectancies, and incentives. In J. W. E. Atkinson (Ed.), *Motives in fantasy action and society* (pp. 288–305). Princeton, NJ, Van Nostrand.

(1964). *An introduction to motivation*. New York, Van Nostrand Reinhold.

(1982). Old and new conceptions of how expected consequences influence actions. In N. T. Feather (Ed.), *Expectations and actions* (pp. 395–420). Hillsdale, NJ, Lawrence Erlbaum Associates.

Atkinson, J. W., J. R. Bastian, R. W. Earl and G. H. Litwin (1960). 'The achievement motive, goalsetting, and probability preferences.' *Journal of Abnormal and Social Psychology* 60: 27–36.

Atkinson, J. W. and D. Birch (1970). *The dynamics of action*. New York, Wiley.

(1974). The dynamics of achievement-oriented activity. In J. W. Atkinson and J. O. Raynor (Eds.), *Motivation and achievement* (pp. 271–325). Washington, DC, Winston.

Atkinson, J. W. and N. T. Feather (1966a). *A theory of achievement motivation*. New York, Wiley.

(1966b). Review and appraisal. In J. W. Atkinson and N. T. Feather (Eds.), *A theory of achievement motivation* (pp. 327–370). New York, Wiley.

Atkinson, J. W. and G. H. Litwin (1960). 'Achievement motive and test anxiety conceived as motive to approach success and motive to avoid failure.' *Journal of Abnormal and Social Psychology* 60: 52–63.

Atkinson, J. W. and D. C. McClelland (1948). 'The projective expression of needs: II. The effect of different intensities of the hunger drive on thematic apperception.' *Journal of Experimental Psychology* 38: 643–658.

Atkinson, R. C. and R. M. Shiffrin (1968). Human memory: A proposed system and its control processes. In K. W. Spence and J. T. Spence (Eds.), *The psychology of learning and motivation* (Vol. 2, pp. 98–195). New York, Academic Press.

Austin, J. T. and J. B. Vancouver (1996). 'Goal constructs in psychology: Structure, process, and content.' *Psychological Bulletin* 120(3): 338–375.

Averill, J. R. (1991). Intellectual emotions. In C. D. Spielberger and I. G. Sarason (Eds.), *Stress and emotion: Anxiety, anger and curiosity* (Vol. 14, pp. 3–16). New York, Hemisphere Publishing.

(1994). Emotions are many splendored things. In P. Ekman and R. J. Davidson (Eds.), *The nature of emotions: Fundamental questions* (pp. 99–102). New York and Oxford, Oxford University Press.

Baars, B. J. (1986). *The cognitive revolution in psychology*. New York, Guilford Press.

(1988). *A cognitive theory of consciousness*. Cambridge and New York, Cambridge University Press.

(1997). *In the theater of consciousness: The workspace of the mind*. New York, Oxford University Press.

(2002a). 'The conscious access hypothesis: Origins and recent evidence.' *Trends in Cognitive Science* 6(1): 47–52.

(2002b). 'Behaviorism redux: Review of *The illusion of conscious will* by Daniel M. Wegner, MIT Press 2002.' *Trends in Cognitive Science* 6(6): 268–269.

(2003). Working memory requires conscious processes, not vice versa: A global workspace account. In N. Osaka (Ed.), *Neural basis of consciousness* (pp. 11–26). Amsterdam, John Benjamins.

(2005a). 'Global workspace theory of consciousness: Toward a cognitive neuroscience of human experience.' *Progress in Brain Research* 150 (Boundaries of Consciousness: Neurobiology and Neurolopathology): 45–53.

(2005b). 'Subjective experience is probably not limited to humans: The evidence from neurobiology and behavior.' *Consciousness & Cognition* 14(1): 7–21.

Baars, B. J. and N. M. Gage (2007). *Cognition, brain, and consciousness: Introduction to cognitive neuroscience*. Amsterdam and London, Academic.

Baars, B. J., T. Z. Ramsøy and S. Laureys (2003). 'Brain, conscious experience and the observing self.' *Trends in Neurosciences* 26(12): 671–675.

Baddeley, A. D. (1986). *Working memory*. Oxford and New York, Clarendon Press and Oxford University Press.

(1996). 'Exploring the central executive.' *Quarterly Journal of Experimental Psychology* 49: 5–28.

(2000). 'The episodic buffer: A new component of working memory.' *Trends in Cognitive Science* 4(11): 417–423.

(2007). *Working memory, thought, and action*. Oxford and New York, Oxford University Press.

(2012). 'Working memory: Theories, models, and controversies.' *Annual Review of Psychology* 63: 1–29.

Baddeley, A. D. and S. Della Sala (1998). Working memory and executive control. In A. C. Roberts, T. W. Robbins and L. E. Weiskrantz (Eds.), *The prefrontal cortex: Executive and cognitive functions: Royal Society (Great Britain). Discussion Meeting* (pp. 9–21). New York and Oxford, Oxford University Press.

Baddeley, A. D. and G. Hitch (1974). Working memory. In G. H. Bower (Ed.), *The psychology of learning and motivation* (Vol. 8). New York, Academic.

Baddeley, A. D. and R. H. Logie (1999). Working memory: The multiple component model. In A. Miyake and P. Shah (Eds.), *Models of working memory: Mechanisms of active maintenance and executive control* (pp. 28–61). Cambridge, Cambridge University Press.

Bandura, A. (1969). *Principles of behavior modification*. New York, Holt, Rinehart & Winston.

(1977a). 'Self-efficacy: Toward a unifying theory of behavioral change.' *Psychological Review* 84: 191–215.

(1977b). *Social learning theory*. Englewood Cliffs, NJ, Prentice Hall.

(1982). 'Self-efficacy mechanism in human agency.' *American Psychologist* 37(2): 122–147.

(1986). *Social foundations of thought and action: A social cognitive theory*. Englewood Cliffs, NJ, Prentice-Hall.

(1989a). 'Human agency in social cognitive theory.' *American Psychologist* 44: 1175–1184.

(1989b). Self-regulation of motivation and action through internal standards and goal systems. In L. A. Pervin (Ed.), *Goal concepts in personality and social psychology* (pp. 19–88). Hillsdale, NJ, Lawrence Erlbaum.

(1991). Self-regulation of motivation through anticipatory and self-reactive mechanisms. In R. Diestbier (Ed.), *Nebraska symposium on motivation 1990: Perspectives on motivation* (Vol. 38, pp. 69–164). Lincoln and London, University of Nebraska.

(1997). *Self-efficacy: The exercise of control*. New York, W. H. Freeman.

(1999). A social cognitive theory of personality. In L. Pervin and O. John (Eds.), *Handbook of personality* (2nd ed., pp. 154–196). New York, Guilford.

(2001). 'Social cognitive theory: An agentic perspective.' *Annual Review of Psychology* 52: 1–26.

(2008). Reconstrual of 'free will' from the agentic perspective or social cognitive. In J. Baer, J. C. Kaufman and R. F. Baumeister (Eds.), *Are we free? Psychology and free will* (pp. 86–123). Oxford and New York, Oxford University Press.

Bandura, A. and R. H. Walters (1959). *Adolescent aggression*. New York, Ronald Press.

Barnett, S. A. (1958). 'Exploratory behavior.' *British Journal of Psychology* 9: 289–310.

Barrett, L. F. (2006a). 'Emotions as natural kinds?' *Perspectives on Psychological Science* 1: 28–58.

(2006b). 'Solving the emotion paradox: Categorization and the experience of emotion.' *Personality and Social Psychology Review* 10: 20–46.

(2012). 'Emotions are real.' *Emotion* 12(3): 413–429.

Barrett, L. F., K. A. Lindquist, E. Bliss-Moreau, S. Duncan, M. Gendron, J. Mize and L. Brennan (2007). 'Of mice and men: Natural kinds of emotions in the mammalian brain? A response to Panksepp and Izard.' *Perspectives on Psychological Science* 2: 297–312.

Barsalou, L. W., P. M. Niedenthal, A. K. Barbey and J. A. Ruppert (2003). Social embodiment. In B. Ross (Ed.), *The psychology of learning and motivation.* (Vol. 43, pp. 43–92). New York, Academic Press.

Bartels, J. M., S. Magun-Jackson and J. J. Ryan (2010). 'Dispositional approach-avoidance achievement motivation and cognitive self-regulated learning: The mediation of achievement goals.' *Individual Differences Research* 8(2): 97–110.

Batson, C. D., P. Schoenrade and W. L. Ventis (1992). *Religion and the individual: A social-psychological perspective.* New York, Oxford University Press.

Batthyany, A. (2009). Reclaiming conscious agency: Mental causation after Libet. In A. Batthyany and A. Elitzur (Eds.), *Irreducibly conscious: Selected papers on consciousness* (pp. 1–27). Heidelberg, Winter.

Baumeister, R. F. (1991). *Meanings of life.* New York, Guilford Press.

(1998). The self. In D. T. Gilbert, Fiske, Susan T., and Lindzey, Gardener (Eds.), *The handbook of social psychology* (Vol. 1, pp. 680–740). Boston, McGraw-Hill.

(2002). 'Religion and psychology: Introduction to the special issue.' *Psychological Inquiry* 13(3): 165–167.

(2005). *The cultural animal: Human nature, meaning, and social life.* Oxford and New York, Oxford University Press.

(2008). Free will, consciousness, and cultural animals. In J. Baer, J. C. Kaufman and R. F. Baumeister (Eds.), *Are we free? Psychology and free will* (pp. 3–9). Oxford and New York, Oxford University Press.

(2016). 'Toward a general theory of motivation: Problems, challenges, opportunities, and the big picture.' *Motivation and Emotion* 40: 1–10.

Baumeister, R. F., E. Bratslavsky, M. Muraven and D. M. Tice (1998). 'Ego depletion: Is the active self a limited resource?' *Journal of Personality and Social Psychology* 74: 1252–1265.

Baumeister, R. F. and E. J. Masicampo (2010). 'Conscious thought is for facilitating social and cultural interactions: How mental simulations serve the animal-culture interface.' *Psychological Review* 117(3): 945–971.

Baumeister, R. F., E. J. Masicampo and K. D. Vohs (2011). 'Do conscious thoughts cause behavior?' *Annual Review of Psychology* 62: 331–361.

Baumeister, R. F., A. R. Mele and K. D. Vohs, Eds. (2010). *Free will and consciousness: How might they work?* New York, Oxford University Press.

Baumeister, R. F. and A. E. Monroe (2014). 'Recent research on free will: Conceptualizations, beliefs, and processes.' *Advances in Experimental Social Psychology* 50: 1–52.

Baumeister, R. F. and J. Tierney (2011). *Willpower: Rediscovering the greatest human strength*. New York, Penguin Press.

Baumeister, R. F. and K. D. Vohs, Eds. (2004). *Handbook of self-regulation: Research, theory, and applications*. New York, Guilford.

Baumeister, R. F., K. D. Vohs, C. N. DeWall and L. Zhang (2007). 'How emotion shapes behavior: Feedback, anticipation, and reflection, rather than direct causation.' *Personality and Social Psychology Review* 11: 167–203.

Bayley, J. (1998). *Iris: A memoir of Iris Murdoch*. London, Duckworth.

Beauvois, J.-L. and R.-V. Joule (1996). *A radical dissonance theory*. London, Taylor & Francis.

(1999). A radical point of view on dissonance theory. In E. Harmon-Jones and J. Mills (Eds.), *Cognitive dissonance: Progress on a pivotal theory in social psychology* (pp. 43–70). Washington, DC, APA Books.

Bechara, A., A. R. Damasio, H. Damasio and S. Anderson (1994). 'Insensitivity to future consequences following damage to human prefrontal cortex.' *Cognition* 50: 7–15.

Bechara, A., H. Damasio, D. Tranel and A. R. Damasio (1997). 'Deciding advantageously before knowing the advantageous strategy.' *Science* 275: 1293–1295.

(2005). 'The Iowa Gambling Task and the somatic marker hypothesis: Some questions and answers.' *Trends in Cognitive Sciences* 9: 159–162.

Bennett, M. R., D. C. Dennett, P. Hacker and J. Searle (2007). *Neuroscience and philosophy: Brain, mind, and language*. New York, Columbia University Press.

Bennett, M. R. and P. M. S. Hacker (2003). *Philosophical foundations of neuroscience*. Malden, MA, Blackwell Publishers.

Berlyne, D. E. (1949). 'Interest as a psychological concept.' *British Journal of Psychology* 39: 184–185.

(1950). 'Novelty and curiosity as determinants of exploratory behavior.' *British Journal of Psychology* 41: 68–80.

(1954). 'A theory of human curiosity.' *British Journal of Psychology* 45: 180–191.

(1955). 'The arousal and satiation of perceptual curiosity in the rat.' *Journal of Comparative and Physiological Psychology* 45: 180–191.

(1957). 'Conflict and information theory variables as determinants of human perceptual curiosity.' *Journal of Experimental Psychology* 53: 399–404.

(1958). 'The influence of complexity and novelty in visual figures on orienting responses.' *Journal of Experimental Psychology* 55: 289–296.

(1960). *Conflict, arousal, and curiosity*. New York, McGraw-Hill.

(1963). Motivational problems raised by exploratory and epistemic behavior. In S. Koch (Ed.), *Psychology: The study of a science* (Vol. 5, pp. 284–364). New York, McGraw-Hill.

(1965). *Structure and direction in thinking*. New York, Wiley.

(1966). 'Curiosity and exploration.' *Science* 153(July): 25–33.

(1971a). What next? Concluding summary. In H. I. Day, D. E. Berlyne and D. E. E. Hunt (Eds.), *Intrinsic motivation: A new direction in education* (pp. 186–196). Toronto, Holt, Rinehart and Winston of Canada.

(1975). 'Behaviourism? Cognitive theory? Humanistic psychology? – To Hull with them all.' *Canadian Psychological Review* 16: 69–80.

(1978). 'Curiosity and learning.' *Motivation and Emotion* 2(2): 97–175.

Berridge, K. C. (1996). 'Food reward: Brain substrates of wanting and liking.' *Neuroscience and Biobehavioral Review* 20: 1–25.

(1999). Pleasure, pain, desire, and dread: Hidden core processes of emotion. In D. Kahneman, E. Diener and N. Schwarz (Eds.), *Well-being: Foundations of hedonic psychology* (pp. 527–559). New York, Russell Sage Foundation.

Berridge, K. C. and T. E. Robinson (1998). 'The role of dopamine in reward: Hedonics, learning, or incentive salience?' *Brain Research Reviews* 28: 308–367.

Beswick, B. (2012). A solution to the paradox of taste. PhD dissertation. School of Historical and Philosophical studies. The University of Melbourne.

Beswick, D. G. (1964). Theory and measurement of human curiosity. PhD dissertation. Social Relations (Social Psychology). Harvard University, Cambridge, MA. Available at http://www.beswick.info/psychres/BeswickCuriosity1964.html.

(1971). Cognitive process theory of individual differences in curiosity. In H. I. Day, D. E. Berlyne and D. E. Hunt (Eds.), *Intrinsic Motivation: A new direction in education* (pp. 156–170). Toronto, Holt, Rinehart and Winston.

(1974). 'Intrinsic motivation in senior secondary school students.' *Education Research and Perspectives* 1: 15–25.

(1983). 'The changing student population in Australia from the seventies to the eighties.' *Journal of Tertiary Educational Administration*: 5–19.

(2004). 'From curiosity to identity: Wonder, curiosity, purpose, and identity; the function of identity in the psychology of intrinsic motivation.' Available at http://www.beswick.info/psychres/CuriosityIdentity.htm.

(2009). Management implications of the interaction between intrinsic motivation and extrinsic rewards. In R. Raj (Ed.), *Intrinsic motivation* (pp. 130–159). Punagutta, Hyderabad, India, Icfai University Press.

Beswick, D. G. and J. Boreham (1986). Development of scientific interests and competence, Research Working Paper 86.1. From a paper presented at the 53rd ANZAAS Congress, Perth, May 1983. Melbourne, Centre for the Study of Higher Education, University of Melbourne.

Beswick, D. G. and P. Ramsden (1987). 'Curiosity and learning with understanding.' *Journal of Higher Education (India)* 13: 26–43.

Beswick, D. G. and G. K. Tallmadge (1971). 'Re-examination of two learning style experiments in the light of the cognitive process theory of curiosity.' *Journal of Educational Psychology* 62: 456–462.

Birch, D., J. W. Atkinson and K. Bongard (1974). Cognitive control of action. In B. Weiner (Ed.), *Cognitive views of human motivation* (pp. 71–84). New York, Academic Press.

Bless, H. (2002). 'Where has the feeling gone? The signal function of affective states.' *Psychological Inquiry* 13(1): 29–31.

Bloom, P. (2012). 'Religion, morality, evolution.' *Annual Review of Psychology* 63: 179–199.

Bolles, R. C. (1972). 'Reinforcement, expectancy, and learning.' *Psychological Review* 79(5): 394–409.

(1974). Cognition and motivation: Some historic trends. In B. Weiner (Ed.), *Cognitive views of human motivation.* (pp. 1–20). New York, Academic Press.

(1975). *Theory of motivation* (2nd ed.). New York, Harper and Row.
Bowlby, J. (1969). *Attachment and loss, Vol. 1: Attachment.* New York, Basic Books.
(1979). *The making and breaking of affectional bonds.* London, Tavistock.
Boyer, P. (2003). 'Religious thought and behaviour as by-products of brain function.' *Trends in Cognitive Sciences* 7: 119–124.
Brass, M. and P. Haggard (2007). 'To do or not to do: The neural signature of self-control.' *Journal of Neuroscience* 27: 9141–9145.
Bratman, M. E. (1999). *Faces of intention: Selected essays on intention and agency.* New York, Cambridge University Press.
Brehm, J. (1956). 'Post-decision changes in the desirability of alternatives.' *Journal of Abnormal and Social Psychology* 52: 384–389.
Brehm, J. W. (1962). Motivation effects of cognitive dissonance. In M. R. Jones (Ed.), *Nebraska symposium on motivation* (pp. 51–77). Lincoln, University of Nebraska Press.
Brehm, J. W. and A. R. Cohen (1962). *Explorations in cognitive dissonance.* New York, Wiley.
Broadbent, D. E. (1954). 'The role of auditory localization in attention and memory span.' *Journal of Experimental Psychology* 47: 191–196.
(1958). *Perception and communication.* New York, Pergamon Press.
Bruner, J. S. (1957). 'On perceptual readiness.' *Psychological Review* 64: 123–152.
(1962). *On knowing; essays for the left hand.* Cambridge, MA, Belknap Press of Harvard University Press.
(1966). *Toward a theory of instruction.* Cambridge, MA, Belknap Press of Harvard University Press.
(1990). *Acts of meaning.* Cambridge, MA, Harvard University Press.
(1996). *The culture of education.* Cambridge, MA, Harvard University Press.
(2003). *Making stories: Law, literature, life.* Cambridge, MA and London, Harvard University Press.
Buber, M. (1937). *I and thou.* New York, Scribner.
Buck, R. (1985). 'Prime theory: An integrated view of motivation and emotion.' *Psychological Review* 92(3): 389–413.
Burkart, J. M. (2009). Socio-cognitive abilities in cooperative breeding. In L. S. Roska-Hardy and E. M. Neumann (Eds.), *Learning from animals? Examining the nature of human uniqueness* (pp. 123–141). New York, Psychology Press.
Butler, R. A. (1957). 'The effect of deprivation of visual incentives on visual exploration motivation in monkeys.' *Journal of Comparative and Physiological Psychology* 48: 247–249.
(1958). 'Exploratory and related behavior: A new trend in animal research.' *Journal of Individual Psychology* 14: 111–120.
Butterfield, H. (1949). *The origins of modern science.* London, G. Bell.
Byman, R. (2005). 'Curiosity and sensation seeking: A conceptual and empirical examination.' *Personality and Individual Differences* 38: 1365–1379.
Cacioppo, J. T., R. E. Petty, J. Feinstein, A. and W. B. G. Jarvis (1996). 'Dispositional differences in cognitive motivation: The life and times of individuals varying in need for cognition.' *American Psychologist* 119(2): 197–253.
Cacioppo, J. T., R. E. Petty and C. F. Kao (1984). 'The efficient assessment of need for cognition.' *Journal of Personality Assessment* 48: 306–307.

Call, J. and M. Tomasello (1998). 'Distinguishing intentional from accidental actions in orangutans (*Pongo pygmaeus*), chimpanzees (*Pan troglodytes*) and human children (*Homo sapiens*).' *Journal of Comparative Psychology* 112: 192–206.

(1999). 'A nonverbal false belief task: The performance of children and great apes.' *Child Development* 70: 381–395.

(2008). 'Does the chimpanzee have a theory of mind? 30 years later.' *Trends in Cognitive Sciences* 12: 187–192.

Camazine, S. (2003). 'Patterns in nature.' *Natural History* 112(5): 34–41.

Camazine, S., S.-L. Deneubourg, N. Franks, J. Sneyd, G. Theraulag and E. Banabeau (2001). *Self-organization in biological systems*. Princeton, NJ, Princeton University Press.

Cameron, J. and W. D. Pierce (1994). 'Reinforcement, reward, and intrinsic motivation. A meta-analysis.' *Review of Educational Research* 64: 363–423.

Cannon, W. B. (1927). 'The James-Lange theory of emotions: A critical examination and an alternative theory.' *American Journal of Psychology* 39: 106–124.

(1929). *Bodily changes in pain, hunger, fear and rage*. New York, Appleton.

Carbonneau, N., Vallerand, R. J. and Lafrenière, M. K. (2012). 'Towards a tripartite model of intrinsic motivation.' *Journal of Personality* 80, 1147–1178.

Carson, R., N. Kelsh and C. Pratt (1998/1964). *The sense of wonder*. New York, HarperCollins.

Cartwright, D. and F. Harary (1956). 'Structural balance: A generalization of Heider's theory.' *Psychological Review* 63: 277–293.

Carver, C. S. and M. F. Scheier (1990). 'Origins and functions of positive and negative affect: A control-process view.' *Psychological Review* 97: 19–35.

(1998). *On the self-regulation of behavior*. New York, Cambridge University Press.

(2000). On the structure of behavioral self-regulation. In M. Boekaerts, P. R. Pintrich and M. H. Zeidner (Eds.), *Handbook of self-regulation* (pp. 42–62). San Diego, CA, Academic Press.

(2009). Action, affect, multitasking, and layers of control. In J. P. Forgas, R. Baumeister and D. M. Tice (Eds.), *Psychology of self-regulation* (pp. 109–126). New York, London, Psychology Press.

Cavalier, R. J. (2002). *Personal motivation: A model for decision making*. Westport, Praeger.

Cave, K. R. and J. M. Wolfe (1990). 'Modeling the role of parallel processing in visual search.' *Cognitive Psychology* 22: 225–271.

Chan, R. C. K., D. Shum, T. Toulopoulou and E. Y. H. Chen (2008). 'Assessment of executive functions: Review of instruments and identification of critical issues.' *Archives of Clinical Neuropsychology* 23(2): 201–216.

Chaucer, G. (1387/1969). *The Prologue and Three Tales: Edited with notes and commentary by Francis King and Bruce Steele*. Melbourne, Cheshire.

Cherry, C. (1956). *Information theory: Papers read at a symposium on information theory held at the Royal Institution, London, September 12th to 16th, 1955*. London, Butterworths Scientific Publications.

(1957). *On human communication: A review, a survey, and a criticism*. Cambridge, MA, Technology Press of Massachusetts Institute of Technology.

Cherry, E. C. (1953). 'Some experiments on the recognition of speech, with one and with two ears.' *Journal of the Acoustical Society of America* 25: 975–979.

Chomsky, N. (1959). 'A review of B. F. Skinner's "Verbal Behavior".' *Language* 35(1): 26–58.

(1965). *Aspects of the theory of syntax.* Cambridge, MA, MIT Press.

Church, R. M. (1963). 'The varied effects of punishment.' *Psychological Review* 70: 369–402.

Clore, G. (1992). Cognitive phenomenology: Feelings and the construction of judgement. In L. L. Martin and A. Tesser (Eds.), *The construction of social judgments* (pp. 133–163). Hillsdale, NJ, Lawrence Erlbaum Associates.

Clore, G. and A. Ortony (2000). Cognition in emotion: Always, sometimes, or never? In R. D. Lane and L. Nadel (Eds.), *Cognitive neuroscience of emotion* (pp. 24–61). New York, Oxford University Press.

Clore, G. L. (1994). Why emotions are felt. In P. Ekman and R. J. Davidson (Eds.), *The nature of emotion: Fundamental questions* (pp. 103–111). New York and Oxford, Oxford University Press.

Clore, G. L., A. Ortony and M. A. Foss 1987. 'The psychological foundations of the affective lexicon'. *Journal of Personality and Social Psychology*, 53(4), 751–766.

Clore, G. L., R. S. Wyer, B. Dienes, K. Gasper, C. Gohm and L. Isbell (2001). Affective feelings as feedback: Some cognitive consequences. In L. L. Martin and G. L. Clore (Eds.), *Theories of mood and cognition: A user's handbook* (pp. 27–62). Mahwah, NJ, Erlbaum.

Coleridge, S. T. (1825). *Aids to reflection in the formation of a manly character on the several grounds of prudence, morality, and religion: illustrated by select passages from our elder divines, especially from Archbishop Leighton.* London, Printed for Taylor and Hessey.

Coleridge, S. T. and H. N. Coleridge (1852). *On the constitution of the church and state according to the idea of each.* London, Edward Moxon.

Collins, R. P., J. A. Litman and C. D. Spielberger (2004). 'The measurement of perceptual curiosity.' *Personality and Individual Differences* 36: 1127–1141.

Conradi, P. J. (2001). *Iris Murdoch: A life.* London, Harper Collins.

Conway, M. A. and C. W. Pleydell-Pearce (2000). 'The construction of autobiographical memories in the self memory system.' *Psychological Review* 107: 261–288.

Cooper, J. (1999). Unwanted consequences and the self: In search of the motivation for dissonance reduction. In E. Harmon-Jones and J. Mills (Eds.), *Cognitive dissonance: Progress on a pivotal theory in social psychology* (pp. 149–173). Washington, DC, APA Books.

(2010). Riding the D train with Elliot: The Aronsonian legacy of cognitive dissonance. In M. H. Gonzales, C. Tarvis and J. Aronson (Eds.), *The scientist and the humanist: A festschrift in honor of Elliot Aronson* (pp. 159–174). New York, Psychology Press.

Cooper, J. and R. H. Fazio (1984). A new look at dissonance theory. In L. Berkowitz (Ed.), *Advances in experimental social psychology* (pp. 229–266). Orlando, FL, Academic Press.

Cooper, M., M. O'Hara, P. Schmid and G. Wyatt (2007). *The handbook of person-centered psychotherapy and counseling.* London, Palgrave MacMillan.

Corballis, M. C. (2004). 'The origins of modernity: Was autonomous speech the critical factor?' *Psychological Review* 111: 543–552.

(2009). 'The evolution of language.' *Annals of the New York Academy of Sciences* 1156: 19–43.

Corlis, C. and J. Wiess (1973). *Curiosity and openness: Empirical testing of a basic assumption.* New Orleans, Annual Conference of the American Psychological Association.

Cornwell, J. F. M. and E. T. Higgins (2016). 'Eager feelings and vigilant reasons: Regulatory focus differences in judging moral wrongs.' *Journal of Experimental Psychology: General* 145(3): 338–355.

Corteen, R. S. and B. Wood (1972). 'Autonomic responses to shockassociated words in an unattended channel.' *Journal of Experimental Psychology* 94: 308–313.

Couch, A. and K. Keniston (1960). 'Yeasayers and naysayers: Agreeing response set as a personality variable.' *Journal of Abnormal and Social Psychology* 60: 151–174.

Cowan, N. (1988). 'Evolving conceptions of memory storage, selective attention, and their mutual constraints within the human information processing system.' *Psychological Bulletin* 104: 163–191.

(1993). 'Activation, attention and short term memory.' *Memory & Cognition* 21: 162–167.

(1995). *Attention and memory: An integrated framework.* Oxford, Oxford University Press.

(1999). An embedded processes model of working memory. In A. Miyake and P. Shah (Eds.), *Models of working memory: Mechanisms of active maintenance and executive control* (pp. 62–101). Cambridge, Cambridge University Press.

(2005). *Working memory capacity.* Hove, Psychology Press.

Crane, R. (2009). *Mindfulness based cognitive therapy: Distinctive features.* New York, Routledge.

Crick, F. (1984). 'Function of the thalamic reticular complex: The searchlight hypothesis.' *Proceedings of the National Academy of Sciences* 81: 4586–4590.

Crick, F. and C. Koch (1990). 'Towards a neurobiological theory of consciousness.' *Seminars in Neurosciences* 2: 263–275.

(1995). 'Are we aware of neural activity in primary visual cortex?' *Nature* 375: 121–123.

(2003). 'A framework for consciousness.' *Nature: Neuroscience* 6: 119–126.

Csikszentmihalyi, M. (1988). Society, culture, and person: A systems view of creativity. In R. J. Sternberg (Ed.), *The nature of creativity* (pp. 325–339). Cambridge, Cambridge University Press.

(1990). *Flow: The psychology of optimal experience.* New York, Harper & Row.

Csikszentmihalyi, M. and J. Nakamura (2011). Positive psychology: Where did it come from, where is it going? In K. M. Sheldon, T. B. Kashdan and M. F. Steger (Eds.), *Designing positive psychology* (pp. 3–8). Oxford and New York, Oxford University Press.

Dalgleish, T. and M. J. Power (1999). *Handbook of cognition and emotion.* Chichester, New York, Weinheim, Brisbane, Singapore and Toronto, John Wiley & Sons.

Damasio, A. R. (1994). *Descartes' error: Emotion, reason, and the human brain.* New York, G. P. Putnam.

(1996). 'The somatic marker hypothesis and the possible functions of the prefrontal cortex.' *Philosophical Transactions of the Royal Society of London (series B)* 351: 1413–1420.

(1999). *The feeling of what happens: Body and emotion in the making of consciousness*. New York, Harcourt Brace.

(2000a). A second chance for emotion. In R. D. Lane and L. Nadel (Eds.), *Cognitive neuroscience of emotion* (pp. 12–23). New York, Oxford University Press.

(2000b). *The feeling of what happens: Body and emotion in the making of consciousness*. New York, Harcourt Brace.

(2003). *Looking for Spinoza: Joy, sorrow, and the feeling brain*. New York, Harcourt.

(2004). William James and the modern neurobiology of emotion. In D. Evans and P. Cruse (Eds.), *Emotion, evolution and rationality* (pp. 3–14). Oxford, Oxford University Press.

(2010). *Self comes to mind*. New York, Pantheon Books.

Damasio, A. R. and S. W. Anderson (2003). The frontal lobes. In K. M. Heilman and E. Valenstein (Eds.), *Clinical neuropsychology* (4th ed., pp. 404–446). New York, Oxford University Press.

Damasio, A. R., D. Tranel and H. Damasio (1990). 'Individuals with sociopathic behavior caused by frontal damage fail to respond autonomically to social stimuli.' *Behavioural Brain Research* 41: 81–94.

(1991). Somatic markers and the guidance of behaviour: Theory and preliminary testing. In H. S. Levin, H. M. Eisenberg and A. L. Benton (Eds.), *Frontal lobe function and dysfunction* (pp. 217–229). New York, Oxford University Press.

Damasio, H., T. Grabowski, R. Frank, A. M. Galaburda and A. R. Damasio (1994). 'The return of Phineas Gage: Clues about the brain from the skull of a famous patient.' *Science* 264: 1102–1105.

Darwin, C. (1872/1998). *Expression of the emotions in man and animals*. Chicago, University of Chicago Press.

(1988). *Beagle diary*, edited by R. D. Keynes. London, Cambridge University Press.

Darwin, C. and N. Barlow (1958). *The autobiography of Charles Darwin, 1809–1882: With original omissions restored*. London, Collins.

Darwin, C., P. Ekman and P. Prodger (1998). *The expression of the emotions in man and animals*. London, HarperCollins Publishers.

Darwin, C. R. (1876–1882). Recollections of the development of my mind & character: Autobiography [1876-4.1882] CUL-DAR26.1–121 Transcribed by Kees Rookmaaker. Darwin Online. Available at http://darwin-online.org.uk/.

Davies, P. (1999a). *The fifth miracle: The search for the origin and meaning of life*. New, London, Simon and Schuster.

Dawkins, R. (1989). *The selfish gene* (2nd ed.). Oxford, Oxford University Press.

Day, H. (1969). *An instrument for the measurement of intrinsic motivation: An interim report to the Department of Manpower and Immigration*. Toronto, Canada, Ontario Institute for Studies in Education.

(1971). The measure of specific curiosity. In H. Day, D. E. Berlyne and D. E. Hunt (Eds.), *Intrinsic motivation: A new direction in education* (pp. 99–112). Toronto, Holt, Rinehart & Winston of Canada.

Day, H. I. (1968). 'The role of specific curiosity in school achievement.' *Journal of Educational Psychology* 59: 37–43.

Day, H. I., D. E. Berlyne and D. E. Hunt, Eds. (1971). *Intrinsic motivation: A new direction in education.* Toronto, Holt, Rinehart and Winston.

deCharms, R. (1968). *Personal causation: The internal affective determinants of behavior.* New York, Academic Press.

(1987). Personal causation, agency, and the self. In P. Young-Eisendrath and J. A. E. Hall (Eds.), *The book of the self* (pp. 77-41). New York, New York University Press.

(1992). Personal causation and the origin concept. In C. P. E. Smith (Ed.), *Motivation and personality: Handbook of thematic content analysis* (pp. 325–333). Cambridge, Cambridge University Press.

deCharms, R. and F. Plimpton (1992). The origin scoring system. In C. P. E. Smith (Ed.), *Motivation and personality: Handbook of thematic content analysis* (pp. 334–375). Cambridge, Cambridge University Press.

Deci, E. L. (1971). 'Effects of externally mediated rewards on intrinsic motivation.' *Journal of Personality and Social Psychology* 18: 105–155.

(1972). 'The effects of contingent and non-contingent rewards and controls on intrinsic motivation.' *Organizational Behavior and Human Performance* 8: 217–229.

(1975). *Intrinsic motivation.* New York, Plenum Press.

(1980). *The psychology of self-determination.* Lexington, MA, Lexington Books.

Deci, E. L. and R. Flaste (1995). *Why we do what we do: The dynamics of personal autonomy.* New York, Putnam's Sons.

Deci, E. L., L. R. Koestner and R. M. Ryan (1999a). 'The undermining effect is a reality after all – extrinsic rewards, task interest, and self-determination: Reply to Eisenberger, Pierce and Cameron (1999) and Lepper, Henderlong, and Griingras (1999).' *Psychological Bulletin* 125, 692–700.

Deci, E. L., R. Koestner and R. M. Ryan (1999b). 'A meta-analytic review of experiments examining the effects of extrinsic rewards on intrinsic motivation.' *Psychological Bulletin* 125: 627–668.

(2001). 'Extrinsic rewards and intrinsic motivation in education: Reconsidered once again.' *Review of Educational Research* 71(1): 1–27.

Deci, E. L. and A. C. Moller (2005). The concept of competence: A starting place for understanding intrinsic motivation and self-determined extrinsic motivation. In A. J. Elliot and C. S. Dweck (Eds.), *Handbook of competence and motivation* (pp. 579–597). New York, Guilford.

Deci, E. L. and R. M. Ryan (1985). *Intrinsic motivation and self-determination in human behavior.* New York, Plenum Press.

(1987). 'The support of autonomy and the control of behavior.' *Journal of Personality and Social Psychology* 53: 1024–1037.

(1991). 'A motivational approach to self: Integration in personality.' *Nebraska Symposium on Motivation* 1990: 237–288.

(2000). 'The 'what' and 'why' of goal pursuits: Human needs and the self-determination of behavior.' *Psychological Inquiry* 11: 227–268.

(2002a). *Handbook of self-determination research*. Rochester, NY, University of Rochester Press.

(2002b). Overview of self-determination theory: An organismic-dialectical perspective. In E. L. Deci and R. M. Ryan (Eds.), *Handbook of self-determination research* (pp. 3–33). Rochester, NY, University of Rochester Press.

Dehaene, S., J.-R. Duhamel, M. D. Hauser and G. Rizzolatti, Eds. (2005). *From monkey brain to human brain*. Cambridge, MA, MIT Press.

Dehaene, S., M. Kerszberg and J. P. Changeux (1998). 'A neuronal model of a global workspace in effortful cognitive tasks.' *Proceedings of the National Academy of Sciences USA* 95: 14529–14534.

Dehaene, S. and L. Naccache (2001). 'Towards a cognitive neuroscience of consciousness: Basic evidence and a workspace framework.' *Cognition* 79: 1–37.

Dehaene, S., L. Naccache, L. Cohen, D. Le Bilan, J.-R. Mangin, J.-B. Poline and D. Rivire (2001). 'Cerebral mechanisms of word masking and unconscious repetition priming.' *Nature Neuroscience* 4 (678–680): 1–37.

Dember, W. N. and R. W. Earl (1957). 'Analysis of exploratory, manipulatory, and curiosity behaviors.' *Psychological Review* 64: 91–96.

Dembo, T. (1931). 'Der Arger als dynamisches problem. (Untersuchungen zur Handlungs-und Affektpsychologie. X. Ed. by Kurt Lewin.) *Psychologiche Forschung* 15: 1–144.

Dennett, D. C. (1971). 'Intentional systems.' *Journal of Philosophy* 8: 87–106.

(1978). *Brainstorms: Philosophical essays on mind and psychology*. Montgomery, VT, Bradford.

(1984). *Elbow room: The varieties of free will worth wanting*. Oxford and New York, Clarendon Press and Oxford University Press.

(1987). *The intentional stance*. Cambridge, MA, MIT Press.

(1991). *Consciousness explained*. Boston, Little Brown and Co.

(1996). *Kinds of minds: Toward an understanding of consciousness*. New York, Basic Books.

(1998). *Brainchildren: Essays on designing minds*. Cambridge, MA, MIT Press.

(2001). 'Are we explaining consciousness yet?' *Cognition* 79: 221–237.

(2003). *Freedom evolves*. New York, Viking.

(2004). 'Calling in the Cartesian loans: Commentary on Wegner's *The illusion of conscious will*.' *Behavioral and Brain Sciences* 27: 661.

(2006). *Breaking the spell: Religion as a natural phenomenon*. New York, Viking.

Desmond, A. and J. Moore (2010). *Darwin's sacred cause: Race, slavery and the quest for human origins*. London, Penguin.

Desmond, A. J. and J. R. Moore (1991). *Darwin*. London, Michael Joseph.

Deutsch, J. A. and D. Deutsch (1963). 'Attention: Some theoretical considerations.' *Psychological Review* 70: 80–90.

DeWall, C. N., R. F. Baumeister and E. J. Masicampo (2008). 'Evidence that logical reasoning depends on conscious processing.' *Consciousness and Cognition* 17: 628–645.

Diamond, M. C. (1988). *Enriching heredity*. New York, Free Press.

Dickerson, C. A., R. Thibodeau, E. Aronson and D. Miller (1992). 'Using cognitive dissonace to encourage water conservation.' *Journal of Applied Social Psychology* 22: 841–854.

Diener, E., E. M. Suh, R. E. Lucas and H. L. Smith (1999). 'Subjective well-being: Three decades of progress.' *Psychological Bulletin* 125: 276–302.

Digman, J. M. (1990). 'Personality structure: Emergence of the Five-Factor Model.' *Annual Review of Psychology* 41: 417–440.

Dijksterhuis, A., T. L. Chartrand and H. Aarts (2007). Effects of priming and perception on social behavior and goal pursuit. In J. A. Bargh (Ed.), *Social psychology and the unconscious: The automaticity of higher mental processes* (pp. 51–132). Philadelphia, Psychology Press.

Dolan, R. J. (2002). 'Emotion, cognition, and behavior.' *Science* 298: 1191–1194.

Dollard, L. and N. E. Miller (1950). *Personality and psychotherapy*. New York, McGraw-Hill.

Dweck, C. S. (1985). Intrinsic motivation, perceived control, and self-evaluation maintenance: An achievement goal analysis. In R. Ames and C. Ames (Eds.), *Research on motivation in education* (Vol. II, pp. 289–305). New York, Academic Press.

(1996). 'Capturing the dynamic nature of personality.' *Journal of Research in Personality* 30: 348–362.

(1999). *Self-theories: Their role in motivation, personality, and development*. Philadelphia, Psychology Press.

(2006). *Mindset: The new psychology of success*. New York, Random House.

Dweck, C. S. and E. S. Elliott (1983). Achievement motivation. In P. Mussen and E. M. Hetherington (Eds.), *Handbook of child psychology*. Vol. IV. Social and personality development (pp. 643–691). New York, Wiley.

Dweck, C. S. and E. S. Leggett (1988). 'A social-cognitive approach to motivation and personality.' *Psychological Review* 95: 256–273.

Dweck, C. S. and D. C. Molden (2005). Self theories: Their impact on competence motivation and acquisition. In A. J. Elliot and C. S. Dweck (Eds.), *Handbook of competence and motivation* (pp. 122–140). New York and London, The Guildford Press.

Eco, U. (1999). *Kant and the platypus: Essays on language and cognition*. London, Secker & Warburg.

Edwards, J. A., A. L. Wichman and G. Weary (2009). 'Causal uncertainty as a chronically accessible construct.' *European Journal of Social Psychology* 39: 694–706.

Ehrlich, D., I. Guttman, P. Schoenbach and J. Mills (1957). 'Postdecision exposure to relevant information.' *Journal of Abnormal and Social Psychology* 54: 98–102.

Eisenberger, R. and J. Cameron (1996). 'Detrimental effects of reward: Reality or myth?' *American Psychologist* 51(11): 1153–1166.

Eisenberger, R. and M. Selbst (1994). 'Does reward increase or decrease creativity?' *Journal of Personality and Social Psychology* 66: 1116–1127.

Ekman, P. (1972). Universals and cultural differences in facial expressions of emotion. In J. Cole (Ed.), *Nebraska symposium on motivation 1971* (pp. 207–283). Lincoln, University of Nebraska Press.

(1973). *Darwin and facial expression: A century of research in review*. New York, Academic Press.

(1977). Biological and cultural contributions to body and facial movement. In J. Blacking (Ed.), *A. S. A. Monograph 15, The anthropology of the body* (pp. 39–84). London, Academic Press.

(1992a). 'Are there basic emotions.' *Psychological Review* 99(3): 550–553.

(1992b). 'Facial expressions of emotions: New findings, new questions.' *Psychological Science* 3: 34–38.

(1992c). 'An argument for basic emotions.' *Cognition and Emotion* 6: 169–200.

(1994a). All emotions are basic. In P. Ekman and R. J. Davidson (Eds.), *The nature of emotion: Fundamental questions* (pp. 15–19). New York, Oxford University Press.

(1994b). 'Strong evidence for universals in facial expressions: A reply to Russell's mistaken critique.' *Psychological Bulletin* 115: 268–287.

(1998). Afterword: Universality of emotional expression? A personal history of the dispute. In C. Darwin and P. Ekman (Eds.), *The expression of emotions in man and animals* (pp. 363–393). London, HarperCollins.

(1999b). Facial expressions. In T. Dalgleish and M. J. Power (Eds.), *Handbook of cognition and emotion* (pp. 301–320). New York, John Wiley & Sons Ltd.

Ekman, P. and W. V. Friesen (1971). 'Constants across cultures in the face and emotion.' *Journal of Personality and Social Psychology* 17: 124–129.

Ekman, P., E. R. Sorenson and W. V. Friesen (1969). 'Pan-cultural elements in facial displays of emotions.' *Science*, 164: 86–88.

Eliot, G. (1965). *Middlemarch*. Harmondsworth, UK, Penguin.

Elliot, A. J. (1994). Approach and avoidance achievement goals: An intrinsic motivation analysis. PhD dissertation, University of Wisconsin, Madison.

(1997). Integrating 'classic' and 'contemporary' approaches to achievement motivation: A hierarchical model of approach and avoidance achievement motivation. In P. Pintrich and M. Maehr (Eds.), *Advances in motivation and achievement* (Vol. 10, pp. 143–179). Greenwich, CT, JAI Press.

(1999). 'Approach and avoidance motivation and achievement goals.' *Educational Psychologist* 34: 169–189.

(2005). A conceptual history of the achievement goal construct. In A. J. Elliot and C. S. Dweck (Eds.), *Handbook of competence and motivation* (pp. 52–72). New York and London, The Guilford Press.

(2006). 'The hierarchical model of approach-avoidance motivation.' *Motivation and Emotion* 30(2 Special Issue: Approach/Avoidance): 111–116.

(2008). Approach and avoidance motivation. In A. J. Elliot (Ed.), *Handbook of approach and avoidance motivation* (pp. 3–14). New York, Psychology Press.

Elliot, A. J. and M. Church (1997). 'A hierarchical model of approach and avoidance achievement motivation.' *Journal of Personality and Social Psychology* 72: 218–232.

Elliot, A. J. and M. V. Covington (2001). 'Approach and avoidance motivation.' *Educational Psychology Review* 13(2): 73–92.

Elliot, A. J. and C. S. Dweck, Eds. (2005a). *Handbook of competence and motivation*. New York and London, The Guilford Press.

Elliot, A. J. and C. S. Dweck (2005b). Competence and motivation: Competence as the core of achievement motivation. In A. J. Elliot and C. S. Dweck (Eds.), *Handbook of competence and motivation* (pp. 3–12). New York and London, The Guilford Press.

Elliot, A. J. and J. M. Harackiewicz (1994). 'Goal setting, achievement orientation, and intrinsic motivation: A mediational analysis.' *Journal of Personality and Social Psychology* 66: 968–980.

(1996). 'Approach and avoidance achievement goals and intrinsic motivation: A mediational analysis.' *Journal of Personality and Social Psychology* 70: 461–475.

Elliot, A. J. and H. A. McGregor (2001). 'A 2 X 2 achievement goal framework.' *Journal of Personality and Social Psychology* 80(3): 501–519.

Elliot, A. J. and H. T. Reis (2003). 'Attachment and adult exploration.' *Journal of Personality and Social Psychology* 85: 317–331.

Elliott, E. S. and C. S. Dweck (1988). 'Goals: An approach to motivation and achievement.' *Journal of Personality and Social Psychology* 54: 5–12.

Ellsworth, P. C. (1994). Some reasons to expect universal antecedents of emotion. In P. Ekman and R. J. Davidson (Eds.), *The nature of emotion: Fundamental questions* (pp. 150–154). New York and Oxford, Oxford University Press.

Emerson, R. W. (1850/1890). *Representative men; seven lectures*. New York and Boston, Thomas Y. Crowell.

Emmons, R. (1997). Motives and life goals. In R. Hogan, J. Johnson and S. Briggs (Eds.), *Handbook of personality psychology* (pp. 485–512). San Diego, CA, Academic Press.

Emmons, R. A. (1986). 'Personal strivings: An approach to personality and subjective well-being.' *Journal of Personality and Social Psychology* 51(5): 1058–1068.

(1989). The personal striving approach to personality. In L. A. Pervin (Ed.), *Goal concepts in personality and social psychology* (pp. 87–126). Hillsdale, NJ, Erlbaum.

(1999a). *The psychology of ultimate concerns: Motivation and spirituality in personality*, New York, The Guilford Press.

(1999b). 'Religion in the psychology of personality: An introduction.' *Journal of Personality* 67(6): 873–888.

(2005). 'Striving for the sacred: Personal goals, life meaning, and religion.' *Journal of Social Issues* 61(4): 731–745.

Emmons, R. A., P. M. Colby and H. A. Kaiser (1998). Personal goals and the recovery of meaning. In P. T. P. Wong and P. S. Fry (Eds.), *The human quest for meaning: A handbook of psychological applications* (pp. 163–178). Mahwah, NJ and London, Lawrence Erlbaum and Associates.

Emmons, R. A. and R. F. Paloutzian (2003). 'The psychology of religion.' *Annual Review of Psychology* 54: 377–402.

Epstein, S. (1985). 'The implications of cognitive-experiential self theory for research in social psychology and personality.' *Journal of the Theory of Social Behavior* 15(3): 283–310.

Escalona, S. K. (1940). 'The effect of success and failure upon the level of aspiration and behavior in manic-depressive psychoses.' *University of Iowa studies in child welfare* 16(199–302).

Evans, D. (2004). The search hypothesis of emotion. In D. Evans and D. Cruse (Eds.), *Emotion, evolution and rationality* (pp. 179–191). Oxford, Oxford University Press.

Feather, N. T. (1959). 'Subjective probability and decision under uncertainty.' *Psychological Review* 66: 150–164.

(1961). 'The relationship of persistence at a task to expectation of success and achievement related motives.' *Journal of Abnormal and Social Psychology* 63: 552–561.

(1962). 'The study of persistence.' *Psychological Bulletin* 59: 94–115.

(1963). 'Persistence at a difficult task with alternative task of intermediate difficulty.' *Journal of Abnormal and Social Psychology* 66: 604–609.

(1967). 'Valence of outcome and expectation of success in relation to task difficulty and perceived locus of control.' *Journal of Personality and Social Psychology* 7: 372–386.

(1971). 'Organization and discrepancy in cognitive structures.' *Psychological Review* 78(5): 355–379.

Feather, N. T., Ed. (1982a). *Expectations and actions*. Hillsdale, NJ, Lawrence Erlbaum Associates.

Feather, N. T. (1982b). Expectancy-value approaches: Present and future directions. In N. T. Feather (Ed.), *Expectations and actions* (pp. 395–420). Hillsdale, NJ, Lawrence Erlbaum Associates.

Feist, G. J. (1994). 'Affective consequences of insight in art and science students.' *Cognition and Emotion* 8: 489–502.

Festinger, L. (1942). 'A theoretical interpretation of shifts in level of aspiration.' *Psychological Review* 49: 335–350.

(1957). *A theory of cognitive dissonance*. Stanford, CA, Stanford University Press.

(1964). *Conflict, decision, and dissonance*. Stanford, CA, Stanford University Press.

(1987/1999). Reflections on cognitive dissonance: 30 years later. In E. Harmon-Jones and J. Mills (Eds.), *Cognitive dissonance: Progress on a pivotal theory in social psychology* (pp. 381–385). Washington, DC, APA Books.

Festinger, L. and J. M. Carlsmith (1959). 'Cognitive consequences of forced compliance.' *Journal of Abnormal and Social Psychology* 58: 203–210.

Fisher, P. (1998). *Wonder, the rainbow, and the aesthetics of rare experiences*. Cambridge, MA: Harvard University Press.

Fitzgerald, E. T. (1966). 'Measurement of openness to experience: A study of regression in the service of the ego.' *Journal of Personality and Social Psychology* 4: 655–663.

Fleming, J. and M. S. Horner (1992). The motive to avoid success. In C. P. Smith (Ed.), *Motivation and personality: Handbook of thematic content analysis* (pp. 179–189). Cambridge, Cambridge University Press.

Fodor, J. A. (1983). *The modularity of mind: An essay on faculty psychology*. Cambridge, MA, MIT Press.

(1987). Modules, frames, fridgeons, sleeping dogs, and the music of the spheres. In Z. W. Phylyshyn (Ed.), *The robot's dilemma: The frame problem in artificial intelligence* (pp. 139–149). Cambridge, MA and London, MIT Press.

(2000). *The mind doesn't work that way: The scope and limits of computational psychology*. Cambridge, MA, MIT Press.

(2005). 'Reply to Steven Pinker "So how *does* the mind work?".' *Mind and Language* 20(1): 25–32.

(2006). 'How the mind works; what we still don't know.' *Daedalus* 135: 86–94.

Fonagy, P., G. Gergely, E. Jurist and M. Target (2002). *Affect regulation, mentalization, and the development of self*. New York, Other Press.

Ford, M. E. (1992). *Motivating humans: Goals, emotions, and personal agency beliefs*. Newbury Park, CA, Sage Publications.

Ford, M. E. and C. W. Nichols (1987). A taxonomy of human goals and some possible applications. In M. E. Ford and D. H. Ford (Eds.), *Humans as self-constructing systems: Putting the framework to work* (pp. 289–311). Hillsdale, NJ, Erlbaum.

Forgas, J. P., R. Baumeister and D. M. Tice, Eds. (2009). *Psychology of self-regulation*. New York and London, Psychology Press.

Forsyth, D. T. (1980). 'The function of attributions.' *Social Psychology Quarterly* 43: 184–189.

Fowler, H. (1965). *Curiosity and exploratory behavior*. New York, Macmillan.

Fowler, J. W. (1981). *Stages of faith: The psychology of human development and the quest for meaning*. New York, HarperCollins.

Fox, M. D. and M. E. Raichle (2007). 'Spontaneous fluctuations in brain activity observed with functional magnetic resonance imaging.' *Nature Reviews Neuroscience* 8: 700–711.

Frank, J. D. (1941). 'Recent studies of the level of aspiration.' *Psychological Bulletin* 38: 218–225.

Frankl, V. E. (1959). *From death camp to existentialism*. Boston, Beacon Press.

(1962). *Man's search for meaning: An introduction to logotherapy: A newly revised and enlarged edition of from death-camp to existentialism*. New York, Simon and Schuster.

Frankl, V. E. and A. Batthyány (2010). *The feeling of meaninglessness: A challenge to psychotherapy and philosophy*. Milwaukee, WI, Marquette University Press.

Frenkel-Brunswick, E. (1949). Intolerance of ambiguity as an emotional and perceptual personality variable. In J. S. Bruner and D. Krech (Eds.), *Perception and personality: A symposium* (pp. 108–143). Durham, NC, Duke University Press.

Freud, S. (1923/1962). *The ego and the id*. New York, Norton.

(1936). *The outline of psychoanalysis*. London, Hogarth.

Frijda, N. (1994). Emotions are functional, most of the time. In P. Ekman and R. J. Davidson (Eds.), *The nature of emotion: Fundamental questions* (pp. 112–122). New York and Oxford, Oxford University Press.

Frijda, N. H. (1986). *The emotions*. Cambridge, New York and Paris, Cambridge University Press and Editions de la Maison des sciences de l'homme.

Frijda, N. H., A. S. R. Manstead and S. Bem (2000). *Emotions and beliefs: How feelings influence thoughts*. Cambridge, Cambridge University Press.

Frijda, N. H., A. Ortony, Clore. J. Sonnemans and G. L. Clore (1992). The complexity of intensity: Issues concerning the structure of emotion intensity. In M. Clark (Ed.), *Emotion: Review of personality and social psychology* (pp. 60–89). Newbury Park, CA, Sage.

Frith, C. D. and U. Frith (2012). 'Mechanisms of social cognition.' *Annual Review of Psychology* 63: 287–313.

Frost, R. (1931/2007). 'Education by poetry.' *Amherst Graduates' Quarterly* (February). In Richardson, M. (Ed.), *The Collected Prose of Robert Frost* (pp. 102–111). Cambridge, MA, The Belnap Press of Harvard University Press.

Fu, G. and K. Lee (2007). 'Social grooming in the kindergarten: The emergence of flattery behavior.' *Developmental Science* 10: 255–265.

Gailliot, M. T., R. F. Baumeister, C. N. DeWall, J. K. Maner, E. A. Plant, D. M. Tice, Brewer, L. E.; Schmeichel, B. J (2007). 'Self-control relies on glucose

as a limited energy source: Willpower is more than a metaphor.' *Journal of Personality and Social Psychology* 92: 325–336.
Galton, F. (1894). 'Arithmetic by smell.' *Psychological Review* 1(1): 61–62.
Gardner, H. (1985). *The mind's new science: A history of the cognitive revolution.* New York, Basic Books.
Gardner, J. W. (1940). 'The use of the term "level of aspiration".' *Psychological Review* 47: 59–68.
Gazzaniga, M. S. (1970). *The bisected brain.* New York, Appleton-Century-Crofts.
(1995). 'Principles of human brain organization derived from split-brain studies.' *Neuron* 14: 217–228.
(1997). Why can't I control my brain? Aspects of conscious experience. In M. Ito, Y. Miyashita and E. E. Rolls (Eds.), *Cognition, computation and consciousness* (pp. 69–79). Oxford, New York and Tokyo, Oxford University Press.
(1998). *The mind's past.* Berkeley, University of California Press.
(2000). 'Cerebral specialization and interhemispheric communication: Does the corpus callosum enable the human condition?' *Brain* 123: 1293–1326.
(2005). *The ethical brain.* New York, Dana Press.
(2008). *Human: The science behind what makes your brain unique.* New York, HarperCollins.
Gazzaniga, M. S. and J. E. Ledoux (1978). *The integrated mind.* New York, Plenum Press.
Gergen, K. J. (1992). *The saturated self: Dilemmas of identity in modern life.* New York, Basic Books.
Giddens, A. (1991). *Modernity and self-identity: Self and society in the late modern age.* Stanford, CA, Stanford University Press.
Goldberg, I. I., M. Harel and R. Malach (2006). 'When the brain loses its self: Prefrontal inactivation during sensorimotor processing.' *Neuron* 50: 329–339.
Goldberg, L. R. (1990). 'An alternative "description of personality": The Big-Five factor structure.' *Journal of Personality and Social Psychology* 59: 1216–1229.
(1999). A broad-bandwidth, public domain, personality inventory measuring the lower-level facets of several five-factor models. In I. Mervielde, I. Deary, F. De Fruyt and F. Ostendorf (Eds.), *Personality psychology in Europe* (Vol. 7, pp. 7–28). Tilburg, The Netherlands, Tilburg University Press.
Gollwitzer, P. M. (1999). 'Implementation intentions: Strong effects of simple plans.' *American Psychologist* 54(7): 493–503.
Gollwitzer, P. M., K. Fujita and G. Oettingen (2004). Planning and the implementation of goals. In R. F. Baumeister and K. D. Vohs (Eds.), *Hanbbook of self-regulation* (pp. 211–228). New York and London, Guilford.
Gollwitzer, P. M., R. A. Wicklund and J. L. Hilton (1982). 'Admission of failure and symbolic self-completion: Extending Lewinian theory.' *Journal of Personality and Social Psychology* 43(2): 358–371.
Gomes, G. (1999). Volition and the readiness potential. Journal of Consciousness Studies, 6, pp. 59–76.
Gonzales, M. H., C. Tarvis and J. Aronson, Eds. (2010). *The scientist and the humanist: A festschrift in honor of Elliot Aronson.* New York, Psychology Press.

Gould, S. J. (1991). *Bully for brontosaurus: reflections in natural history*. London: Hutchinson Radius.

Gray, J. A. (2004). *Consciousness: Creeping up on the hard problem*. Oxford, Oxford University Press.

Gray, J. R., A. Schaeffer and S. T. Braver (2005). Affect and the resolution of cognitive control dilemmas. In L. F. Barrett, P. M. Niedenthal and P. Winkielman (Eds.), *Emotion and consciousness* (pp. 67–94). New York and London, The Guilford Press.

Gruber, M. J., B. D. Gelman and C. Ranganath (2014). "States of curiosity modulate hippocampus-dependent learning via the dopaminergic circuit." *Neuron* 84: 486–496.

Guthrie, S. E. (1993). *Faces in the clouds: A new theory of religion*. New York, Oxford University Press.

Haggard, P. (2005). 'Conscious intention and motor cognition.' *Trends in Cognitive Science* 9: 290–295.

(2008). 'Human volition: Towards a neuroscience of will.' *Nature Reviews Neuroscience* 9: 934–946.

Haggard, P. and M. Eimer (1999). 'On the relation between brain potentials and the awareness of voluntary movements.' *Experimental Brain Research* 126: 128–133.

Haggard, P. and E. Magno (1999). 'Localizing awareness of action with transcranial magnetic stimulation.' *Experimental Brain Research* 127: 102–107.

Hagger, M. S., C. Wood, C. Stiff and N. L. D. Chatzisarantis (2010). 'Ego depletion and the strength model of self-control: A meta-analysis.' *Psychological Bulletin* 136: 495–525.

Haier, R. J., B. V. Siegel, A. MacLachlan, E. Soderling, S. Lottenberg and M. S. Buchsbaum (1992). 'Regional glucose metabolic changes after learning a complex visuospatial motor task: A positron emission tomographic study.' *Brain Research* 570(1–2): 134–143.

Harackiewicz, J. M. (2004). *Optimal motivation in education: The importance of students' goals and interests. Supporting Student Wellbeing*, Adelaide, South Australia, ACER.

Harackiewicz, J. M. and C. Sansone (1991). Goals and intrinsic motivation: You can't get there from here. In M. L. Maehr and P. R. Pintrich (Eds.), *Advances in motivation and achievement* (pp. 21–49). Greenwich, Cambridge University Press.

(2000). Rewarding competence: The importance of goals in the study of intrinsic motivation. In C. a. J. M. Sansone and J. M. Harackiewicz (Eds.), *Intrinsic and extrinsic motivation: The search for optimal motivation and perform* (pp. 79–103). San Diego, CA and London, Academic Press.

Harlow, H. F. (1950). 'Learning and satiation of response in intrinsically motivated complex puzzle performance by monkeys.' *Journal of Comparative and Physiological Psychology* 43: 289–294.

(1953a). Motivation as a factor in the acquisition of new responses. In M. R. Jones (Ed.), *Current theory and research in motivation, symposium* (pp. 24–49). Lincoln, University of Nebraska Press.

(1953b). 'Mice, monkeys, men, and motives.' *Psychological Review* 60: 23–32.

(1954). Learning theory, personality theory, and clinical research. In *Kentucky symposium* (Vol. 9, pp. 36–53). Oxford, Wiley.

Harmon-Jones, E. (1999). Towards an understanding of the motivation underlying dissonance effects: Is the production of aversive consequences necessary? In E. Harmon-Jones and J. Mills (Eds.), *Cognitive dissonance: Progress on a pivotal theory in social psychology* (pp. 71–99). Washington, DC, APA Books.

Harmon-Jones, E., J.W. Brehm, J. Greenberg, L. Simon and D. E. Nelson (1996). 'Evidence that the production of aversive consequences is not necessary to create cognitive dissonance.' *Journal of Personality and Social Psychology* 70: 5–16.

Harmon-Jones, E. and J. Mills, Eds. (1999). *Cognitive dissonance: Progress on a pivotal theory in social psychology*. Washington, DC, APA Books.

Harris, P. (2000). *The work of the imagination*. Oxford, Blackwell.

Harris, R. (2007). *The happiness trap: Stop struggling, start living*. Wollombi, N.S.W, Exisle Publishing.

Hauser, M. D. (2009). 'The possibility of impossible cultures.' *Nature* 460: 190–196.

Hauser, M. D., N. W. Chomsky and T. Fitch (2002). 'The faculty of language: What is it, who has it, and how did it evolve?' *Science* 298: 1569–1579.

Hayes-Roth, B. (1985). 'A blackboard architecture for control.' *Artificial Intelligence* 26: 251–321.

Heaney, S. (2006). Crediting poetry, 1995 Nobel Lecture. In *Nobel lectures: from the literature laureates, 1986 to 2005. Nobelstiftelsen*. Carlton, Victoria, Melbourne University Publishing.

Hebb, D. O. (1949). *The organization of behavior: A neuropsychological theory*. New York, Wiley.

(1955). 'Drives and the C.N.S. (conceptual nervous system).' *Psychological Review* 62: 243–254.

(1958). 'The motivating effects of exteroceptive stimulation.' *American Psychologist* 13: 109–113.

Heckhausen, H. (1977). 'Achievement motivation and its constructs: A cognitive model.' *Motivation and Emotion* 1: 283–329.

(1991). *Motivation and action*. Berlin, Springer-Verlag.

Heider, F. (1944). 'Social perception and phenomenal causality.' *Psychological Review* 51: 358–374.

(1946). 'Attitudes and cognitive organization.' *Journal of Psychology* 21: 107–112.

(1958). *The psychology of interpersonal relations*. New York, Wiley.

(1960). 'The Gestalt theory of motivation.' *Nebraska Symposium on Motivation* 8: 145–172.

Heider, K. G. (1991). *Landscapes of emotion: Mapping three cultures of emotion in Indonesia*. Cambridge, New York and Paris, Cambridge University Press and Editions de la maison des sciences de l'homme.

Heine, S. J. and D. R. Lehman (1997). 'Culture, dissonance and self-affirmation.' *Personality and Social Psychology Bulletin* 23: 389–400.

Heine, S. J., T. Proulx and K. D. Vohs (2006). 'The meaning maintenance model: On the coherence of social motivations.' *Personality and Social Psychology Review* 10: 88–110.

Henderlong, J. and M. R. Lepper (2002). 'The effects of praise on children's intrinsic motivation: A review and synthesis.' *Psychological Bulletin* 128: 774–795.

Hendrick, I. (1942). 'Instinct and the ego during infancy.' *Psychoanalitic Quarterly* 11: 33–58.

Henle, M. (1955). 'Some effects of motivational processes on cognition.' *Psychological Review* 62: 423–432.

Hennessey, B. A. and T. M. Amabile (1998). 'Reward, intrinsic motivation, and creativity.' *American Psychologist* 53(6): 674–675.

Herrmann, E., J. Call, M. V. Hernandez-Lloreda, B. Hare and M. Tomasello (2007). 'Humans have evolved specialized skills of social cognition: The cultural intelligence hypothesis.' *Science* 317(September 7): 1360–1366.

Hidi, S. (2000). An interest researcher's perspective: The effects of extrinsic and intrinsic factors on motivation. In C. Sansone and J. M. Harackiewicz (Eds.), *Intrinsic and extrinsic motivation: The search for optimal motivation and performance* (pp. 309–339). San Diego, CA and London, Academic Press.

Hidi, S., M. Ainley, D. Berndorff and L. Del Favero (2007). The role of interest and self-efficacy in science-related expository writing. In S. H. P. Boscolo (Ed.), *Motivation and interest in writing* (pp. 203–217). Oxford, Elsevier.

Hidi, S. and D. Berndorff (1998). Situational interest and learning. In L. Hoffmann, A. Krapp, K. A. Renninger and J. Baunert (Eds.), *Interest and learning: Proceedings of the Seeon Conference on Interest and Gender.* (pp. 74–90). Kiel, Germany, IPN.

Hidi, S. and J. M. Harackiewicz (2000). 'Motivating the academically unmotivated: A critical issue for the 21st century.' *Review of Educational Research* 70: 151–179.

Higgins, E. T. (1987). 'Self-discrepancy: A theory of relating self and affect.' *Psychological Review* 94: 319–340.

(1997). 'Beyond pleasure and pain.' *American Psychologist* 52(12): 1280–1300.

(1998). 'Promotion and prevention: Regulatory focus as a motivational principle.' *Advances in Experimental Social Psychology* 30: 1–46.

(2000). 'Social cognition: Learning about what matters in the social world.' *European Journal of Social Psychology* 30: 3–39.

(2001). Promotion and prevention experiences: Relating emotions to nonemotional motivational states. In J. P. Forgas (Ed.), *Handbook of affect and social cognition* (pp. 186–211). Mahwah, NJ, Erlbaum.

Higgins, E. T., R. Klein and T. Strauman (1985). 'Self-concept discrepancy theory: A psychological model for distinguishing among different aspects of depression and anxiety.' *Social Cognition* 3: 51–76.

Higgins, E. T., C. Roney, E. Crowe and C. Hymes (1994). 'Ideal versus ought predilections for approach and avoidance: Distinct self-regulatory systems.' *Journal of Personality and Social Psychology* 66: 276–286.

Higgins, E. T., J. Shah and R. Friedman (1997). 'Emotional responses to goal attainment: Strength of regulatory focus as moderator.' *Journal of Personality and Social Psychology* 72: 515–525.

Holmes, R. (2008). *The age of wonder: How the romantic generation discovered the beauty and terror of science.* London, Harper Press.

Hoppe, F. (1930). 'Erfolg und Misserfolg (Untersuchaungen zur Handlungs – und affekpsychologie IV).' *Psychologiche Forschung* 14: 1–62.

Horner, M. S. (1968). Sex differences in achievement motivation and performance in competitive and noncompetitive situations. PhD dissertation, *Psychology*. University of Michigan, Ann Arbor, Michigan.

(1971). The psychological significance of success in competitive achievement situations: A threat as well as a promise. In H. I. Day, D. E. Berlyne and D.

E. Hunt (Eds.), *Intrinsic motivation: A new direction in education* (pp. 46–60). Toronto, Holt, Rinehart and Winston.

(1972). 'Towards an understanding of achievement-related conflicts in women.' *Journal of Social Issues* 28: 157–175.

(1974). The measurement and behavioral implications of fear of success in women. In J. W. Atkinson and J. Raynor (Eds.), *Motivation and achievement* (pp. 91–120). Washington, DC, V. W. Winston.

Horner, M. S. and J. Fleming (1992). A revised scoring manual for the motive to avoid success. In C. P. Smith (Ed.), *Motivation and personality: Handbook of thematic content analysis* (pp. 190–204). Cambridge, Cambridge University Press.

Hrdy, S. B. (2009). *Mothers and others: The evolutionary origins of mutual understanding*. Cambridge, MA, The Belknap Press of Harvard University Press.

Hull, C. L. (1943a). *Principles of behavior: An introduction to behavior theory*. New York and London, D. Appleton-Century Company, Inc.

(1943b). 'The problem of intervening variables in molar behavior theory.' *Psychological Review* 50(3): 273–291.

(1951/1964). *A behavior system: An introduction to behavior theory concerning the individual organism*. New York, Wiley.

Hull, R., R. C. Martin, M. E. Beier, D. Lane and A. C. Hamilton (2008). 'Executive function in older adults: A structural equation modeling approach.' *Neuropsychology* 22(4): 508–522.

Hume, D. (1997). Of the standard of taste. In D. Cooper (Ed.), *Aesthetics: The classical readings* (pp. 76–94). Oxford, Blackwell

Hunt, J. M. (1960). 'Experience and the development of motivation: Some reinterpretations.' *Child Development* 31: 489–504.

(1963). Motivation inherent in information processing and action. In O. J. Harvey (Ed.), *Motivation and social interaction* (pp. 35–94). New York, Ronald Press.

(1965). 'Intrinsic motivation and its role in psychological development.' *Nebraska Symposium on Motivation* 13: 189–282.

(1971). Towards a history of intrinsic motivation. In H. I. Day, D. E. Berlyne and D. E. Hunt (Eds.), *Intrinsic motivation: A new direction in education* (pp. 1–32). Toronto, Holt, Rinehart and Winston.

Izard, C. E. (1971). *The face of emotion*. New York, Meredity.

(1977). *Human emotions*. New York, Plenum.

(1993). 'Four systems for emotion activation: Cognitive and non-cognitive processes.' *Psychological Review* 100: 69–90.

(2000). 'Reinforcement, emotion, and consciousness.' *Behavioral and Brain Sciences* 23(2): 202–204.

(2007). 'Basic emotions, natural kinds, emotion schemas, and a new paradigm.' *Perspectives on Psychological Science* 2(3): 260–280.

Jack, A. I. and T. Shallice (2001). 'Introspective physicalism as an approach to the science of consciousness.' *Cognition* 79(1–2): 161–196.

Jackendoff, R. (2008). *Language, consciousness, culture: Essays on mental structure*. Cambridge, MA, MIT Press.

Jackson, H. (1976). *An assessment of long term effects of personal causation training*. St. Louis, MO, Washington University Press.

Jaki, S. L. (1986). *Science and creation*. Edinburgh, Scottish Academic Press.

James, W. (1884). 'What is an emotion?' *Mind* 4: 188–204.
(1890). *The principles of psychology*. New York, Holt.
(1902). *The varieties of religious experience*. London, Longmans, Green.
Johnson, P. E. (1959). *Psychology of religion*. Nashville, TN, Abingdon.
Johnson, S. (1751/1969). *The Yale edition of the works of Samuel Johnson Vol V*. New Haven, CT, Yale University Press.
Johnson-Laird, P. N. and K. Oatley (1989). 'The language of emotions: An analysis of a semantic field.' *Cognition and Emotion* 3: 81–123.
Jones, D. M. (1993). Objects, streams and threads of auditory attention. In A. D. Baddeley and L. Weiskrantz (Eds.), *Attention: Selection, awareness and control* (pp. 87–104). Oxford, Clarendon Press.
Jones, D. M., R. W. Hughes and W. J. Macken (2006). 'Perceptual organization masquerading as phonological storage: Further support for a perceptual-gestural view of short-term memory.' *Journal of Memory and Language* 54: 265–281.
Jones, D. M., W. J. Macken and A. P. Nicholls (2004). 'The phonological store of working memory: Is it phonological and is it a store?' *Journal of Experimental Psychology: Learning, Memory and Cognition* 30(3): 656–674.
Jonides, J. (1998). 'The role of parietal cortex in verbal working memory.' *Journal of Neuroscience* 18(13): 5026–5034.
Joske, W. D. (1981). Philosophy and the meaning of life. In E. D. Klemke (Eds.), *The meaning of life* (pp. 248–261). New York, Oxford University Press.
Judd, C. H. (1908). 'The relation of special training to general intelligence.' *Educational Review* 36: 28–42.
Jung, C. G. (1951/1959). *Collected works*. New York, Pantheon.
Kagan, J. (1972). 'Motives and development.' *Journal of Personality and Social Psychology* 22(1): 51–66.
Kahneman, D. and S. Frederick (2002). Representativeness revisited: Attribute substitution in intuitive judgment. In D. G. T Gilovich and D Kahneman (Eds.), *Heuristics and biases* (pp. 49–81). New York, Cambridge University Press.
Kaiser, C. B. (1991). *Creation and the history of science*. Grand Rapids, MI, Eerdmans.
Kang, M. J., M. Hsu, I. M. Krajbich, G. Loewenstein, S. M. McClure, J. T. Wang et al. (2009). 'The wick in the candle of learning: Epistemic curiosity activates reward circuitry and enhances memory.' *Psychological Science* 20(8): 963–973.
Karoly, P. (1993). 'Goal systems: An organizational framework for clinical assessment and treatment planning.' *Psychological Assessment* 3: 273–280.
Kashdan, T. (2009). *Curious? Discover the missing ingredient to a fulfilling life*. New York, William Morrow; Harper.
Kashdan, T. and J. Ciarrochi, Eds. (2013). *Mindfulness, acceptance, and positive psychology: The seven foundations of well-being*. Oakland, CA, Context Press.
Kashdan, T. B. (2004). Curiosity. In C. Peterson and M. Seligman (Eds.), *Character strengths and virtues* (pp. 125–141). Washington and New York, American Psychological Association and Oxford University Press.

Kashdan, T. B. and W. E. Breen (2007). 'Materialism and diminished well-being: Experiential avoidance as a mediating mechanism.' *Journal of Social and Clinical Psychology* 26: 521–539.

Kashdan, T. B., C. N. Dewal, R. S. Pond, P. J. Silvia, N. M Lambert, F. D. Fincham, et al. (2013a). 'Curiosity protects against interpersonal aggression: Cross-sectional, daily process, and behavioral evidence.' *Journal of Personality* 81: 87–102.

Kashdan, T. B., M. W. Gallagher, P. J. Silvia, B. P. Winterstein, W. E. Breen, D. Terhar, et al. (2009). 'The Curiosity and Exploration Inventory-II: Development, factor structure, and initial psychometrics.' *Journal of Research in Personality* 43: 987–998.

Kashdan, T. B., P. E. McKnight, P. P. Fincham and P. Rose (2011). 'When curiosity breeds intimacy: Taking advantage of intimacy opportunities and transforming boring conversations.' *Journal of Personality* 79: 1369–1401.

Kashdan, T. B., P. Rose and F. D. Fincham (2004). 'Curiosity and exploration: Facilitating positive subjective experiences and personal growth opportunities.' *Journal of Personality Assessment* 82(3): 291–305.

Kashdan, T. B., R. A. Sherman, J. Yarbro and D. C. Funder (2013b). 'How are curious people viewed and how do they behave in social situations? From the perspectives of self, friends, parents, and unacquainted observers.' *Journal of Personality* 81: 142–154.

Kashdan, T. B. and P. J. Silvia (2009). Curiosity and interest: The benefits of thriving on novelty and challenge. In S. J. S. Lopez (Ed.), *Oxford handbook of positive psychology* (2nd ed., pp. 367–374). New York, Oxford University Press.

Kashdan, T. B. and M. F. Steger (2011). Challenges, pitfalls, and aspirations for positive psychology. In K. M. Sheldon, T. B. Kashdan and M. F. Steger (Eds.), *Designing positive psychology* (pp. 9–21). Oxford and New York, Oxford University Press.

Kashdan, T. B., K. C. Young and K. A. Machell (2015). 'Positive emotion regulation: Addressing two myths.' *Current Opinion in Psychology* 3: 117–121.

Kashdan, T. B. and M. Yuen (2007). 'Whether highly curious students thrive academically depends on the learning environment of their school: A study of Hong Kong adolescents.' *Motivation and Emotion* 31: 260–270.

Kasser, T. (2002). *The high price of materialism.* Cambridge, MA, MIT Press.

Kasser, T. and R. M. Ryan (1993). 'A dark side of the American dream: Correlates of financial success as a central life aspiration.' *Journal of Personality and Social Psychology* 65: 410–422.

(1996). 'Further examining the American dream: Differential correlates of intrinsic and extrinsic goals.' *Personality and Social Psychology Bulletin* 22: 280–287.

Katz, L. D. (2000). 'Emotion, representation, and consciousness.' *Behavioral and Brain Sciences* 23(2): 204–205.

Kauffman, S. A. (1993). *The origins of order: Self-organization and selection in evolution.* New York, Oxford University Press.

(2008). *Reinventing the sacred: A new view of science, reason and religion.* New York, Basic Books.

Kay, A., C., K. Laurin, G. M. Fitzsimons and M. J. Landau (2014). 'A functional basis for structure-seeking: Exposure to structure promotes willingness to engage in motivated action.' *Journal of Experimental Psychology* 143(2): 486–491.

Kelly, G. (1955). *The psychology of personal constructs*. New York, Norton.

Kelly, H. H. (1967). Attribution theory in social psychology. In D. E. Levine (Ed.), *Nebraska symposium on motivation* (Vol. 15, pp. 192–240). Lincoln, University of Nebraska Press.

(1971). *Attributions in social interactions*. Morristown, NJ, General Learning Press.

(1973). 'The processes of causal attribution.' *American Psychologist* 28: 107–128.

Keyes, C. L. M. and J. Haidt, Eds. (2003). *Flourishing: Positive psychology and the life well-lived*. Washington, DC, American Psychological Association.

Kidd, C. and B.Y. Hayden (2015). 'The psychology and neuroscience of curiosity.' *Neuron* 88(3): 449–460.

Kierkegaard, S. (1986). *Either/or*. New York, Perennial Library.

Kiesler, C. A. (1971). *The psychology of commitment*. New York, Academic Press.

Kimble, G. A., M. Wertheimer and C. L. White (1991). *Portraits of Pioneers in Psychology*. Washington, DC, American Psychological Association.

King, L. A., J. A. Hicks, J. Krull and A. G. Baker (2006). 'Positive affect and the experience of meaning in life.' *Journal of Personality and Social Psychology* 90: 179–196.

Kirsch, A. (2014). 'Extracting the Woodchuck: Robert Frost's "doubleness," revealed in his letters – and poems.' *Harvard Magazine*, 116(3 January–February), 44–48.

Kjaer, T.W., M. Nowak, K.W. Kjaer, A. R. Lou and H. C. Lou (2001). 'Precuneus prefrontal activity during awareness of visual verbal stimuli.' *Consciousness and Cognition* 10(3): 356–365.

Klauer, K. C. and Z. M. Zhao (2004). 'Double dissociations in visual and spatial short-term memory.' *Journal of Educational Psychology – General* 133(3): 355–381.

Klinger, E. (1977). *Meaning and void: Inner experience and the incentives in people's lives*. Minneapolis, University of Minnesota Press.

(1998). The search for meaning in evolutionary perspective and its clinical implications. In P. T. P. Wong and P. S. Fry (Eds.), *The human quest for meaning: A handbook of psychological applications* (pp. 27–50). Mahwah, NJ and London, Lawrence Erlbaum and Associates.

Koch, C. (2004). *The quest for consciousness: A neurobiological approach*. Denver, CO, Roberts and Co.

(2012). *Consciousness: Confessions of a romantic reductionist*. Cambridge, MA, MIT Press.

Koch, C. and N. Tsuchiya (2007). 'Attention and consciousness: Two distinct brain processes.' *Trends in Cognitive Science* 11: 16–22.

Koffka, K. (1935). *Principles of gestalt psychology*. London Routledge & K. Paul.

Köhler, W. (1920/1924). *Die physischen Gestalten in Ruhe und im stanionaren Zustand*. Erlangen, Germany, Verlag der Philosophischen Akademie.

(1929/1947). *Gestalt psychology: An introduction to new concepts in modern psychology*. New York, New American Library.

(1938). *The place of value in a world of facts*. New York, Liveright.
Kolb, B. and I. Q. Whishaw (1998). 'Brain plasticity and behavior.' *Annual Review of Psychology* 49: 43–64.
Kornhuber, H. H. and L. Deecke (1965). 'Hirnpotentialanderungen bei Wilkurbewegungen und passiven Bewegungen des Menschen: Bereitschaf tspotential und reafferente Potentiale.' *Pflügers Archiv: European Journal of Physiology* 284: 1–17.
Korotkov, D. (1998). The sense of coherence: Making sense out of chaos. In P. T. P. Wong and P. S. Fry (Eds.), *The human quest for meaning: A handbook of psychological research and clinical applications* (pp. 51–70). Mahwah, NJ and London, Lawrence Erlbaum Associates.
Korsgaard, C. (1983). The normativity of instrumental reasoning. In G. Cullity and B. Gaut (Eds.), *Ethics and practical reason* (pp. 215–254). Oxford, Oxford University Press.
Krapp, A., S. Hidi and K. A. Renninger (1992). Interest, learning and develop ment. In K. A. Renninger, S. Hidi and A. Krapp (Eds.), *The role of interest in learning and development* (pp. 3–25). Hillsdale, NJ, Erlbaum.
Kross, E. and W. Mischel (2010). From stimulus control to self-control: Towards an integrative understanding of the processes underlying willpower. In R. Hassin, K. Ochsner and Y. Trope (Eds.), *Self control in society, mind, and brain* (pp. 428–446). New York, Oxford University Press.
Kruglanski, A. W. (1989). *Lay epistemics and human knowledge: Cognitive and motivational bases*. New York, Plenum Press.
(2004). *The psychology of closed mindedness*. New York, Psychology Press.
Kruglanski, A. W., I. Friedman and G. Zeevi (1971). 'The effects of extrinsic incentives on some qualitative aspects of task performance.' *Journal of Personality* 39: 606–617.
Kruglanski, A. W. and D. M. Webster (1996). 'Motivated closing of the mind: "Seizing" and "freezing"' *Psychological Review* 103: 263–283.
Lane, R. D. and L. Nadel, Eds. (2000). *Cognitive neuroscience of emotion*. Series in affective science. New York and Oxford, Oxford University Press.
Langer, E. J. (1975). 'The illusion of control.' *Journal of Personality and Social Psychology* 32: 311–328.
Langevin, R. (1971). 'Is curiosity a unitary construct?' *Canadian Journal of Psychology* 25: 361–374.
Lashley, K., K. Chow and J. Semmes (1951). 'An examination of the electric field theory of cerebral integration.' *Psychological Review* 58: 123–136.
Laurin, K., A. Kay and D. A. Moscovitch (2008). 'On the belief in God: Towards an understanding of the emotional substrates of compensatory control.' *Journal of Experimental Social Psychology* 44: 1559–1562.
Lauriola, M., J. A. Litman, P. Mussel, R. De Santis, H. M. Crowson and R. R. Hoffman (2015). 'Epistemic curiosity and self-regulation.' *Personality and Individual Differences* 83: 202–207.
Lawrence, A. D. and A. J. Calder (2004). Homologizing human emotions. In D. Evans and P. Cruse (Eds.), *Emotion, evolution and rationality* (pp. 15–47). Oxford, Oxford University Pres.
Lazarus, R. (1984). 'On the primacy of cognition.' *American Psychologist* 39: 124–126.

Lazarus, R. S. (1974). Cognition and coping processes in emotion. In B. Weiner (Ed.), *Cognitive views of human motivation* (pp. 21–32). New York, Academic Press.

(1991). *Emotion and adaptation*. New York, Oxford University Press.

(1994a). Universal antecedents of the emotions. In P. Ekman and R. J. Davidson (Eds.), *The nature of emotion: Fundamental questions* (pp. 163–171). New York, Oxford University Press.

(1994b). The stable and the unstable in emotion. In P. Ekman and R. J. Davidson (Eds.), *The nature of emotion: Fundamental questions* (pp. 79–85). New York, Oxford University Press.

(1999). The cognition-emotion debate: A bit of history. In T. Dalgleish and M. J. Power (Eds.), *Handbook of cognition and motivation* (pp. 3–19). Chichester and New York, Wiley.

LeDoux, J. E., Ed. (1996). *The emotional brain*. New York, Simon & Schuster.

LeDoux, J. E. (2000). 'Emotion circuits in the brain.' *Annual Review of Neuroscience* 23: 155–184.

Lepper, M. R. (1998). 'A whole much less than the sum of its parts.' *American Psychologist* 53(6): 675–676.

Lepper, M. R., D. Greene and R. E. Nisbett (1973). 'Undermining children's intrinsic interest with extrinsic rewards: A test of the "overjustification" hypothesis.' *Journal of Personality and Social Psychology* 28: 129–137.

Leslie, A. M. (2005). 'Developmental parallels in understanding minds and bodies.' *Trends in Cognitive Science* 9: 459–462.

Lewin, K. (1926). 'Vorsatz, Wille, und Bedürfnis.' *Psychologische Forschung (Psychological Research)* 7: 330–385.

(1935). *A dynamic theory of personality*. New York and London, McGraw-Hill.

(1938). *The conceptual representation and the measurement of psychological forces*. Durham, NC, Duke University Press.

(1951). *Field theory in social science*. New York, Harper.

Lewin, K., T. Dembo, L. Festinger and P. S. Sears (1944). Level of aspiration. In J. McV Hunt (Ed.), *Personality and the behavior disorders* (pp. 333–378). New York, The Ronald Press.

Lewin, K., F. Heider and G. M. Heider (1936). *Principles of topological psychology*. New York and London, McGraw-Hill.

Libet, B. (1965). 'Cortical activation in conscious and unconscious experience.' *Perspectives in Biology and Medicine* 9: 77–86.

(1985). 'Unconscious cerebral initiative and the role of conscious will in voluntary action.' *Behavioral and Brain Sciences* 8: 529–566.

(1999). 'Do we have free will?' *Journal of Consciousness Studies* 6(8–9): 47–57.

(2004). *Mind time: The temporal factor in consciousness*. Cambridge, MA, Harvard University Press.

Libet, B., C. A. Gleason, T. Wright and D. K. Pearl (1983). 'Time of conscious intention to act in relation to onset of cerebral activity (readiness-potential): The unconscious initiation of a freely voluntary act.' *Brain* 106: 623–642.

Libet, B., E. W. J. Wright, B. Feinstein and D. K. Pearl (1979). 'Subjective referral of the timing for a conscious sensory experience: A functional role for the somatosensory specific projection system in man.' *Brain* 102: 193–224.

Libet, B., E. W. Wright Jr. and C. A. Gleason (1982). 'Readiness-potentials preceding unrestricted "spontaneous" vs pre-planned voluntary acts.' *Electroencephalography and Clinical Neurophysiology* 54: 322–335.

Litman, J. A. (2005). 'Curiosity and the pleasure of learning: Wanting and liking new information.' *Cognition and Emotion* 19(6): 793–814.

(2008). 'Interest and deprivation factors of epistemic curiosity.' *Personality and Individual Differences* 44: 1585–1595.

(2010). 'Relationships between measures of I- and D-type curiosity, ambiguity tolerance, and need for closure: An initial test of the wanting-liking model of information seeking.' *Personality and Individual Differences* 48: 397–402.

Litman, J. A., R. P. Collins and C. D. Spielberger (2005). 'The nature and measurement of sensory curiosity.' *Personality and Individual Differences* 39: 1123–1133.

Litman, J. A., T. L. Hutchins and R. K. Russon (2005). 'Epistemic curiosity, feeling-of-knowing, and exploratory behavior.' *Cognition and Emotion* 19(4): 559–582.

Litman, J. A. and T. L. Jimerson (2004). 'The measurement of curiosity as a feeling of deprivation.' *Journal of Personality Assessment* 82(2): 147–157.

Litman, J. A. and P. Mussel (2013). 'Validity of the interest-and deprivation-type epistemic curiosity model in Germany.' *Journal of Individual Differences* 34(2): 59–68.

Litman, J. A. and P. J. Silvia (2006). 'The latent structure of trait curiosity: Evidence of interest and deprivation curiosity dimensions.' *Journal of Personality Assessment* 86(3): 318–328.

Litman, J. A. and C. D. Spielberger (2003). 'Measuring epistemic curiosity and its diversive and specific components.' *Journal of Personality Assessment* 80: 75–86.

Litwin, G. H. and R. A. Stringer (1968). *Motivation and organizational climate.* Boston, Graduate School of Business Administration, Harvard University.

Locke, E. A. and G. P. Latham (1990). *A theory of goal setting & task performance.* Englewood Cliffs, NJ, Prentice Hall.

Loewenstein, G. (1994). 'The psychology of curiosity: A review and reinterpretation.' *Psychological Bulletin* 116(1): 75–98.

Loewenstein, G., D. Adler, D. Behrens and J. Gillis (1992). *Why Pandora opened the box: Cuiosity as a desire for missing information.* Pittsburgh, PA, Department of Social and Decision Sciences, Carnegie Mellon University.

MacDonald, A. P. (1970). 'Revised scale for ambiguity tolerance: Reliability and validity.' *Psychological Reports* 26: 791–798.

Mach, E. (1886). *Beiträge zur Analyse der Empfindungen.* Jena, Fischer.

(1897). *Contributions to the analysis of sensations, with new additions by the author.* Translated by C. M. Williams. Chicago, The Open Court Publishing Company.

MacIntyre, A. C. (1984). *After virtue: A study in moral theory.* South Bend, IN, University of Notre Dame Press.

Maddi, S. R. (1970). The search for meaning. In M. Page (Ed.), *Nebraska symposium on motivation* (pp. 137–186). Lincoln, University of Nebraska Press.

(1971). Comments on Nunnally's and Suchman's papers. In H. I. Day, D. E. Berlyne and D. E. E. Hunt (Eds.), *Intrinsic motivation: A new direction in education* (pp. 83–90). Toronto, Holt, Rinehart and Winston.

(1998). Creating meaning through making decisions. In P. T. P. Wong and P. S. Fry (Eds.), *The human quest for meaning: A handbook of psychological applications* (pp. 3–26). Mahwah, NJ and London, Lawrence Erlbaum Associates.

Maehr, M. (1974). 'Culture and achievement motivation.' *American Psychologist* 29: 887–896.

Maehr, M. L. (1983). On doing well in science: Why Jonny no longer excels; why Sarah never did. In S. G. Paris, G. M. Olson and H. W. Stevenson (Eds.), *Learning and motivation in the classroom* (pp. 179–210). Hillsdale, NJ, Erlbaum.

(1989). Thoughts about motivation. In C. Ames and R. Ames (Eds.), *Research on motivation in education, Vol. 3: Goals and cognitions* (pp. 299–315). New York, Academic.

Maehr, M. L. and H. A. Meyer (1997). 'Understanding motivation and schooling: Where we've been, where we are, and where we need to go.' *Educational Psychology Review* 9: 371–409.

Maehr, M. L. and A. P. Nicholls (1980). Culture and achievement motivation: A second look. In N. Warren (Ed.), *Studies in cross-cultural psychology.* (Vol. 2, pp. 221–267). New York, Academic.

Maia, T. V. and J. L. McClelland (2004). 'A reexamination of the evidence for the somatic marker hypothesis: What participants really know in the Iowa gambling task.' *Proceedings of the National Academy of Sciences* 101(45): 16075–16080.

Manczak, E., C. Zapata-Gietl and D. P. McAdams (2014). 'Regulatory focus in the life story: Prevention and promotion as expressed in three layers of personality.' *Journal of Personality and Social Psychology* 106: 169–181.

Mandler, G. (1975). *Mind and emotion.* New York, Wiley.

(1984). *Mind and body.* New York, Norton.

(1985). *Cognitive psychology: An essay in cognitive science.* Hillsdale, NJ, Lawrence Erlbaum Associates.

(1997). *Human nature explored.* New York, Oxford University Press.

(2002). *Consciousness recovered: Psychological functions and origins of conscious thought.* Amsterdam and Philadelphia, John Benjamins Pub.

(2004). 'Free will for everyone – with flaws.' *Behavioral and Brain Sciences* 27: 669.

(2007). *A history of modern experimental psychology: From James and Wundt to cognitive science.* Cambridge, MA, MIT Press.

Mandler, G. and J. E. Cowen (1958). 'Test anxiety questionnaires.' *Journal of Consulting Psychology* 22: 228–229.

Mandler, G. and S. B. Sarason (1952). 'A study of anxiety and learning.' *Journal of Abnormal and Social Psychology* 47: 166–173.

Mandler, J. M. and G. Mandler (1964). *Thinking: From association to gestalt.* New York, Wiley.

Maslow, A. H. (1954). 'The instinctoid nature of basic needs.' *Journal of Personality* 22(3): 326–347.

(1954). *Motivation and personality.* New York, Harper.

Maw, W. H. (1971). Difference in the personality of children differing in curiosity. In H. I. Day, D. E. Berlyne and D. E. Hunt (Eds.), *Intrinsic motivation: A new direction in education* (pp. 91–98). Toronto, Holt Rinehart and Winston of Canada.

Maw, W. H. and E. W. Maw (1964). *Differences between children with high and low curiosity: A summary*. Moravia, NY, Chronicle Guidance Publications.

(1968). 'Self appraisal of curiosity.' *The Journal of Educational Research* 61: 462–465.

McAdams, D. P. (1985). *Power, intimacy, and the life story: Personological inquiries into identity*. Homewood, IL, Dorsey Press.

(1990). *The person: An introduction to personality psychology*. New York, Harcourt Brace Jovanovich.

(1995). 'What do we know when we know a person?' *Journal of Personality* 63: 365–396.

(1996a). 'Personality, modernity, and the storied self: A contemporary framework for studying persons.' *Psychological Inquiry* 7(4): 295–321.

(1996b). *The stories we live by: Personal myths and the making of the self*. New York, Guilford Press.

(2000). *The person: An integrated introduction to personality psychology*. Fort Worth, TX, Harcourt College Publishers.

(2006). *The redemptive self: Stories Americans live by*. Oxford and New York, Oxford University Press.

(2008). Personal narratives and the life story. In O. P. John, R. W. Robins and L. A. Pervin (Eds.), *Handbook of personality: Theory and research* (3rd ed., pp. 241–261). New York, Guilford.

(2015). *The art and science of personality development*. New York, Guilford Press.

McAdams, D. P. and J. Guo (2015). 'Narrating the generative life.' *Psychological Science* 26: 475–483.

McAdams, D. P. and B. D. Olson (2010). 'Personality development: Continuity and change over the life course.' *Annual Review of Psychology* 61: 517–542.

McClelland, D. C. (1958a). Methods of measuring human motivation. In J. W Atkinson (Ed.), *Motives in fantasy, action, and society: A method of assessment and study* (pp. 7–42). Princeton, NJ, Van Nostrand.

(1958b). Risk-taking in children with high and low need for achievement. In J. W. Atkinson (Ed.), *Motives in fantasy, action, and society: A method of assessment and study* (pp. 306–321). Princeton, NJ, Van Nostrand.

(1958c). The importance of early learning in the formation of motives. In J. W. Atkinson (Ed.), *Motives in fantasy, action, and society: A method of assessment and study* (pp. 437–452). Princeton, NJ, Van Nostrand.

(1961). *The achieving society*. Princeton, NJ, Van Nostrand.

(1965a). 'Toward a theory of motive acquisition.' *American Psychologist* 20: 321–333.

(1965b). "Achievement and entrepreneurship: A longitudinal study." *Journal of Personality and Social Psychology* 1: 389–392.

(1976). *The achieving society: With a new introduction*. New York, Irvington Publishers: distributed by Halsted Press.

(1978). 'Managing motivation to expand human freedom.' *American Psychologist* 33: 201–210.

(1984). *Motives, personality, and society: Selected papers*. New York, Praeger.
(1985). *Human motivation*. Glenview, IL, Scott, Foresman.
(1989). 'Motivational factors in health and disease.' *American Psychologist* 44: 675–683.
McClelland, D. C., J. W. Atkinson, R. A. Clark and E. L. Lowell (1953). *The achievement motive*. New York, Appleton Century Crofts.
McClelland, D. C. and R. E. Boyatzis (1982). 'The leadership motive pattern and long-term success in management.' *Journal of Applied Psychology* 67: 737–743.
McClelland, D. C., R. A. Clark, T. B. Roby and J. W. Atkinson (1949). 'The projective expression of needs: IV. The effect of the need for achievement on thematic apperception.' *Journal of Experimental Psychology* 39: 242–255.
McClelland, D. C., R. Koestner and J. Weinberger (1989). 'How do self-attributed and implicit motives differ?' *Psychological Review* 96: 690–702.
McClelland, D. C., S. Rhindlisbacher and R. deCharms (1955). Religious and other sources of parental attitudes towards independence training. In D. C. McClelland (Ed.), *Studies in motivation* (pp. 389–397). New York, Appleton-Century-Crofts.
McClelland, D. C. and D. G. Winter (1969). *Motivating economic achievement*. New York, The Free Press.
McClure, S. M., N. D. Daw and P. R. Montague (2003). 'A computational substrate for incentive salience.' *Trends in Neurosciences* 26: 423–428.
McCullough, M. E., W. T. Hoyt, D. B. Larson, H. G. Koenig and C. E. Thoresen (2000). 'Religious involvement and mortality: A meta-analytic review.' *Health Psychology* 19: 211–222.
McCullough, M. E. and B. L. B. Willoughby (2009). 'Religion, self-regulation, and self-control: Associations, explanations, and implications.' *Psychological Bulletin* 135: 69–93.
McDougall, W. (1908). *An introduction to social psychology*. London, Methuen.
(1920). 'Motives in the light of recent discussion.' *Mind* 29: 277–293.
(1923). *Outline of psychology*. New York, Scribner.
(1945). *An introduction to social psychology*. London, Methuen.
McGeogh, J. A. (1932). 'Forgetting and the law of disuse.' *Psychological Review* 39: 352–370.
McGeogh, J. A. and A. L. Irion (1952). *The psychology of human learning*. New York, Longmans.
McLean, K. C., M. Pasupathi and J. L. Pals (2007). 'Selves creating stories creating selves: A process model of selfdevelopment.' *Personality and Social Psychology Review* 11: 262–278.
McReynolds, P. (1962). 'Exploratory behavior: A theoretical interpretation.' *Psychological Reports* 11(2): 311–318.
(1971). The three faces of cognitive motivation. In H. I. Day, D. E. Berlyne and D. E. E. Hunt (Eds.), *Intrinsic motivation: A new direction in education* (pp. 33–45). Toronto, Holt, Rinehart and Winston.
(1987). Self-theory, anxiety and intrapsychic conflicts. In N. Cheshire and H. Thomas (Eds.), *Self, symptoms and psychotherapy* (pp. 197–223). New York, Wiley.
Mead, G. H. (1934). *Mind, self & society from the standpoint of a social behaviorist*. Ed. by Charles W. Morris. Chicago, University of Chicago press.

Mead, M. (1975). 'Review of *Darwin and Facial Expression.*' *Journal of Communication* 25: 210.

Mele, A. R. (2010). Conscious deciding and the science of free will. In R. F. Baumeister, A. R. Mele and K. D. Vohs (Eds.), *Free will and consciousness: How might they work?* (pp. 43–65). New York, Oxford University Press.

Metcalfe, J. (2008). Evolution of metacognition. In J. Dunlosky and R. Bjork (Eds.), *Handbook of metamemory and memory* (pp. 29–46). New York, Psychology Press.

Miller, G. A. (1956). 'The magic number seven, plus or minus two: Some limits on our capacity for processing information.' *Psychological Review* 63: 81–97.

(1962). *Psychology: The science of mental life.* London, Hutchinson.

Miller, G. A., E. Galanter and K. Pribram (1960). *Plans and the structure of behavior.* New York, Holt.

Miller, N. E. (1951). Learnable drives and rewards. In S. S. Stevens (Ed.), *Handbook of experimental psychology* (pp. 436–472). New York, Wiley.

Miller, N. E. and J. Dollard (1941). *Social learning and imitation.* New Haven, CT, Yale University Press.

Mills, J. (1999). Improving the 1957 version of dissonance theory. In E. Harmon-Jones and J. Mills (Eds.), *Cognitive dissonance: Progress on a pivotal theory in social psychology* (pp. 25–42). Washington, DC, APA Books.

Mischel, W. (1968). *Personality and assessment.* New York, Wiley.

(1973). 'Towards a cognitive social learning reconceptualization of personality.' *Psychological Review* 80: 252–283.

(1974). Cognitive appraisals and transformations in self-control. In B. Weiner (Ed.), *Cognitive views of human motivation* (pp. 33–49). New York, Academic Press.

(1996). From good intentions to willpower. In P. M. Gollwitzer and J. A. Bargh (Eds.), *The psychology of action: Linking cognition and motivation to behavior* (pp. 197–218). New York, Guilford Press.

(2004). 'Toward an integrative science of the person (prefatory chapter).' *Annual Review of Psychology* 55: 1–22.

(2009). 'From *Personality and Assessment* (1968) to personality science, 2009.' *Journal of Research in Personality (Special Issue: Personality and Assessment 40 years later)* 43: 282–290.

(2012). Self-control theory. In P. A. M. van Lange, A. Kruglanski and E. T. Higgins (Eds.), *Handbook of theories of social psychology* (Vol. 2, pp. 1–22). Washington, DC, Sage.

Mischel, W. and O. Ayduk (2002). 'Self-regulation in a cognitive-affective personality system: Attentional control in the service of the self.' *Self and Identity* 1: 113–120.

(2004). Willpower in a cognitive-affective processing system: The dynamics of delay of gratification. In R. F. Baumeister and K. D. Vohs (Eds.), *Handbook of self-regulation: Research, Theory, and Applications* (pp. 99–129). New York, Guilford.

(2010). Willpower in a cognitive-affective processing system: The dynamics of delay of gratification. In K. D. Vohs and R. F. Baumeister (Eds.), *Handbook of self-regulation: Research, theory, and applications* (2nd ed., pp. 83–105). New York, Guilford.

Mischel, W. and R. Metzner (1962). 'Preference for delayed reward as a function of age, intelligence, and length of delay interval.' *Journal of Abnormal and Social Psychology* 64: 425–431.

Mischel, W. and Y. Shoda (1995). 'A cognitive-affective system theory of personality: Reconceptualizing situations, dispositions, dynamics, and invariance in personality structure.' *Psychological Review* 102: 246–268.

(2008). Toward a unified theory of personality: Integrating dispositions and processing dynamics within the Cognitive-Affective Processing System (CAPS). In O. P. John, R. W. Robins and L. A. Pervin (Eds.), *Handbook of personality* (3rd ed., pp. 208–241). New York, Guilford.

Miyake, A., N. P. Friedman, M. J. Emerson, A. H. Witzki, A. Howerter and T. D. Wager (2000). 'The unity and diversity of executive functions and their contributions to complex "frontal lobe" tasks: A latent variable analysis.' *Cognitive Psychology* 41: 49–100.

Miyake, A. and P. Shah (1999a). *Models of working memory: Mechanisms of active maintenance and executive control.* Cambridge, Cambridge University Press.

Moller, A. C., E. L. Deci and R. M. Ryan (2006). 'Choice and ego-depletion: The moderating role of autonomy.' *Personality and Social Psychology Bulletin* 32: 1024–1036.

Montgomery, K. C. (1954). 'The role of exploratory drive in learning.' *Journal of Comparative and Physiological Psychology* 47: 60–64.

Montgomery, K. C. and M. Segall (1955). 'Discrimination learning based upon the exploratory drive.' *Journal Comparative and Physiological Psychology* 48: 225–228.

Moray, N. (1959). 'Attention in dichotic listening: Affective cues and the influence of instructions.' *Quarterly Journal of Experimental Psychology* 11: 56–60.

Morsella, E. (2005). 'The function of phenomenal states: Supramodular interaction theory.' *Psychological Review* 112: 1000–1021.

Mowrer, O. H. (1960). *Learning theory and behavior.* New York, Wiley.

(1961). *The crisis in psychiatry and religion.* Princeton, NJ, Van Nostrand.

Muraven, M., D. Shmueli and E. Burkley (2006). 'Conserving self-control strength.' *Journal of Personality and Social Psychology* 91: 524–537.

Murdoch, I. (1967). *The sovereignty of good over other concepts: The Leslie Stephen Lecture.* Cambridge, Cambridge University Press.

(1992). *Metaphysics as a guide to morals.* London, Chatto & Windus.

Murphy, N. (2007a). Introduction. In N. C. Murphy and W. R. Stoeger (Eds.), *Evolution and emergence: Systems, organisms, persons* (pp. 1–15). Oxford and New York, Oxford University Press.

(2007b). Reductionism: How did we fall into it? And can we emerge from it? In N. C. Murphy and W. R. Stoeger (Eds.), *Evolution and emergence: Systems, organisms, person* (pp. 24–39). Oxford and New York, Oxford University Press.

Murphy, N. C. and W. R. Stoeger, Eds. (2007). *Evolution and emergence: Systems, organisms, persons.* Oxford and New York, Oxford University Press.

Murphy, P. K. and P. A. Alexander (2000). 'A motivated exploration of motivation terminology.' *Contemporary Educational Psychology* 25(1): 3–53.

Murray, D. J. (1995). *Gestalt psychology and the cognitive revolution.* Hemel Hempstead, Harvester Wheatsheaf.

Murray, H. A. (1936). 'Facts which support the concept of need or drive.' *Journal of Personality* 3: 27–42.

(1938). *Explorations in personality: A clinical and experimental study of fifty men of college age*. New York and London, Oxford University Press.

(1953). *Thematic Apperception Test manual*. Cambridge, MA, Harvard University Press.

Mussel, P. (2010). 'Epistemic curiosity and related constructs: Lacking evidence of discriminant validity.' *Personality and Individual Differences* 49: 506–510.

Nairne, J. S. (2002). 'Remembering over the short-term: The case against the standard model.' *Annual Review of Psychology* 53: 53–81.

Neisser, U. (2002). 'Wolfgang Köhler.' *National Academy of Sciences of the United States of America, Biographical Memoirs, Volume 81*. Retrieved 22 February 2016 from http://www.nap.edu/readingroom.php?book=biomems&page=wkohler.html

Nelson, K. and J. S. Bruner (2006). *Narratives from the crib*. Cambridge, MA and London, Harvard University Press.

Newcombe, T. M. (1968a). Interpersonal balance. In R. P. Abelson, E. Aronson, W. J. McGuire et al. (Eds.), *Theories of cognitive consistency: A source book* (pp. 28–51). Chicago, Rand McNally.

(1968b). Introduction. In R. P. Abelson, E. Aronson, W. J. McGuire et al. (Eds.), *Theories of cognitive consistency: A source book* (pp. xv–xvii). Chicago, Rand McNally.

Newell, A. (1990). *Unified theories of cognition*. Cambridge, MA, Harvard University Press.

Newell, A., J. Laird and P. S. Rosenbloom (1993). *The Soar papers: Research on integrated intelligence*. Cambridge, MA, MIT Press.

Newell, A. and H. A. Simon (1972). *Human problem solving*. Englewood Cliffs, NJ, Prentice-Hall.

Nicholls, J. G. (1984). 'Achievement motivation: Conceptions of ability, subjective experience, task choice, and performance.' *Psychological Review* 91: 328–346.

(1989). *The competitive ethos and democratic education*. Cambridge, MA, Harvard University Press.

Norman, D. A. (1968). 'Towards a theory of memory and attention.' *Psychological Review* 75: 522–536.

Norman, D. A. and T. Shallice (1986). Attention to action: Willed and automatic control of behavior. In R. J. Davidson, E. Schwartz and D. Shapiro (Eds.), *Consciousness and self-regulation* (pp. 1–18). New York, Plenum Press.

Norretranders, T. (1999). *The user illusion, cutting consciousness down to size*. Harmondsworth, Penguin.

Oatley, K. and P. N. Johnson-Laird (1987). 'Towards a cognitive theory of emotions.' *Cognition and Emotion* 1: 29–50.

(1996). The communicative theory of emotions: Empirical tests, mental models, and implications for social interaction. In L. Martin and A. Tesser (Eds.), *Striving and feeling: Interactions among goals, affect, and self-regulation* (pp. 363–393). Mahwah, NJ, Erlbaum Associates.

Oatley, K., D. Keltner and J. M. Jenkins (2006). *Understanding emotions*. Malden, MA, Blackwell Pub.

Oatley, K. (1987). 'Cognitive science and the understanding of emotion.' *Cognition and Emotion* 1, 209–216.

Oettingen, G. and P. M. Gollwitzer (2009). Making goal pursuit effective: Expectancy-dependent goal setting and planned goal striving. In J. P. Forgas, R. Baumeister and D. M. Tice (Eds.), *Psychology of self-regulation* (pp. 127–146). New York and London, Psychology Press.

Oishi, S., E. Diener and R. Lucas (2007). 'The optimum level of well-being: Can people be too happy?' *Perspectives on Psychological Science* 2: 346–360.

Onishi, K. H. and R. Baillargeon (2005). 'Do 15-month-old infants understand false beliefs?' *Science* 308: 255–258.

Ortony, A., G. L. Clore and A. Collins (1988). *The cognitive structure of emotions*. New York, Cambridge University Press.

Oster, J. (1991). *Toward Robert Frost: The reader and the poet*. Athens and London, University of Georgia.

Ovsiankina, M. (1928). 'Die Wiederanfnahme unterbrochener Handlugen.' *Psychologische Forschung* 11: 302–379.

Panksepp, J. (1998). *Affective neuroscience: The foundations of human and animal emotions*. New York, Oxford University Press.

(2000). The neurodynamics of emotions: An evolutionary-neurodevelopmental view. In M. D. Lewis and I. Granic (Eds.), *Emotion, development, and self-organization: Dynamic systems approaches to emotional development* (pp. 236–264). Cambridge, Cambridge University Press.

(2005). 'Affective consciousness: Core emotional feelings in animals and humans.' *Consciousness and Cognition* 14: 30–80.

(2007). 'Neurologizing the psychology of affects: How appraisal-based constructivism and basic emotion theory can coexist.' *Perspectives on Psychological Science* 2(3): 281–296.

(2011a). The primary process affects in human development, happiness, and thriving. In K. M. Sheldon, T. B. Kashdan and M. F. Steger (Eds.), *Designing positive psychology* (pp. 51–85). Oxford and New York, Oxford University Press.

(2011b). 'Toward a cross-species neuroscientific understanding of the affective mind: Do animals have emotional feelings?' *American Journal of Primatology* 73(6): 545–561.

Panksepp, J. and L. Biven (2012). *The archaeology of mind: Neuroevolutionary origins of human emotions*. New York, W. W. Norton & Co.

Pargament, K. I. (1997). *The psychology of religion and coping: Theory, research, practice*. New York, Guilford Press.

(2002a). 'The bitter and the sweet: An evaluation of the costs and benefits of religiousness.' *Psychological Inquiry* 13(3): 168–181.

Pargament, K. I., G. M. Magyar-Russell and N. A. Murray-Swank (2005). 'The sacred and the search for significance: Religion as a unique process.' *Journal of Social Issues* 61(4): 665–687.

Parr, A. (2010). Emotion and social cognition in primates. In M. D. M. Breed (Ed.), *Encyclopedia of animal behavior* (pp. 621–627). Janice, Elsevier.

Pashler, H. E. (1998). *The psychology of attention*. Cambridge, MA, MIT Press.
Patmore, C. (1856). *The angel in the house, book II*. London, J. W. Parker.
Patnoe, S. (1988). *A narrative history of experimental social psychology*. New York, Springer.
Paulesu, E., C. D. Frith and R. S. J. Franckowiak (1993). 'The neural correlates of the verbal components of working memory.' *Nature* 362(6418): 342–345.
Peacocke, A. (2007). Emergent realities with causal efficacy: Some philosophical and theological applications. In N. C. Murphy and W. R. Stoeger (Eds.), *Evolution and emergence: Systems, organisms, persons* (pp. 267–283). Oxford and New York, Oxford University Press.
Penfield, W. (1958). *The excitable cortex in conscious man*. Liverpool, Liverpool University Press.
(1975). *The mystery of the mind: A critical study of consciousness and the human brain*. Princeton, NJ, Princeton University Press.
Peplau, L. A. (1976). 'Impact of fear of success and sex-role attitudes on women's competitive achievement.' *Journal of Personality and Social Psychology* 34(4): 561–568.
Perls, F. S. (1951/1972). *Gestalt therapy: Excitement and growth in the human personality*. London, Souvenir Press.
(1976). *The Gestalt approach: An eye witness to therapy*. New York, Bantam Books.
Perls, F. S., R. F. Hefferline and P. Goodman (1951). *Gestalt therapy: Excitement and growth in the human personality*. New York, Dell.
Perner, J. and T. Ruffman (2005). 'Infant's insight into the mind: How deep?' *Science* 308: 214–216.
Perner, J., T. Ruffman and S. R. Leekam (1994). 'Theory of mind is contagious: You catch it from your sibs.' *Child Development* 65: 1228–1235.
Pervin, L. A. (1983). The stasis and flow of behavior: Towards a general theory of goals. In M. M. Page (Ed.), *Nebraska symposium on motivation: Vol. 30 Personality: Current theory and research* (pp. 1–53). Lincoln, University of Nebraska Press.
Pervin, L. A., Ed. (1989). *Goal concepts in personality and social psychology*. Hillsdale, NJ, Erlbaum.
Peters, R. A. (1978). 'Effects of anxiety, curiosity, and perceived-instructor threat on student verbal behavior in the college classroom.' *Journal of Educational Psychology* 70: 388–395.
Peterson, C. and M. E. P. Seligman, Eds. (2004). *Character strengths and virtues: A handbook and classification*. New York, Oxford University Press.
Petri, H. L. and J. M. Govern (2004). *Motivation: Theory, research and applications* (5th ed.). Belmont, CA, Thomson/Wadsworth.
(2013). *Motivation: Theory, research and applications* (6th ed.). Belmont, CA, Wadsworth, Cengage Learning.
Piaget, J. (1950). *The psychology of intelligence*. London, Routledge & Kegan Paul.
(1953). *The origin of intelligence in the child*. London, Routledge & Kegan Paul.
(1971). *Biology and knowledge*. Chicago, University of Chicago Press.

Piaget, J., C. Gattegno and F. M. Hodgson (1951). *Play, dreams and imitation in childhood.* Melbourne, Heinemann in association with the New Education Fellowship.

Pinker, S. (1997). *How the mind works.* New York, Norton.

(2005a). 'So how *does* the mind work?' *Mind and Language* 20: 1–24.

(2005b). 'A reply to Jerry Fodor on how the mind works.' *Mind and Language* 20(1): 33–38.

(2007). *The stuff of thought: Language as a window into human nature.* New York, Viking.

Pintrich, P. R. (2000b). 'An achievement goal theory perspective on issues in motivation terminology, theory, and research.' *Contemporary Educational Psychology* 25: 92–104.

Pintrich, P. R., A. M. Conley and T. M. Kempler (2003). 'Current issues in achievement goal theory and research.' *International Journal of Educational Research* 39: 319–337.

Piotrowski, J. T., J. A. Litman and P. Valkenburg (2014). 'Measuring epistemic curiosity in young children.' *Infant and Child Development* 23: 542–553.

Polger, T. W. (2001). 'Review of Dennett, Daniel C. Brainchildren: Essays on designing minds.' *Philosophical Psychology* 14: 245–250.

Pomerantz, E. M., W. S. Grolnick and C. E. Price (2005). The role of parents in how children approach achievement In A. J. Elliot and C. S. Dweck (Eds.), *Handbook of competence and motivation* (pp. 259–278). New York and London, The Guilford Press.

Posner, M. I. (1978). *Chronometric explorations of mind.* Hillsdale, NJ, Erlbaum.

(1994). 'Attention: The mechanisms of consciousness.' *Proceedings of the National Academy of Sciences USA* 91: 7398–7403.

Posner, M. I. and S. Dehaene (1994). 'Attentional networks.' *Trends in Neurosciences* 17: 75–79.

Posner, M. I. and M. E. Raichle (1994). *Images of mind.* New York, Scientific American Library.

Powers, W. T. (1973). *Behavior: The control of perception.* Chicago, Aldine.

Powers, W. T., R. Clark and R. McFarland (1960). 'A general feedback theory of human behavior: Part 2.' *Perceptual and Motor Skills Monograph* 11(3, Serial No. 7).

Premack, D. and G. Woodruff (1978). 'Does the chimpanzee have a theory of mind?' *Behavioral and Brain Sciences* 1(4): 515–526.

Pribram, K. (1971). *Languages of the brain.* Englewood Cliffs, NJ, Prentice Hall.

(1984). 'What is iso and what is morphic in isomorphism?' *Psychological Research* 46: 329–332.

Prinz, J. (2004). Which emotions are basic? In D. Evans and P. Cruse (Eds.), *Emotion, evolution and rationality* (pp. 69–87). Oxford, Oxford University Press.

Prinzmetal, W., R. Ha and A. Khani (2010). 'The mechanisms of involuntary attention.' *Journal of Experimental Psychology: Human Perception and Performance* 36(2): 255–267.

Proulx, T. and S. J. Heine (2006). 'Death and black diamonds: Meaning, mortality, and the meaning maintenance model.' *Psychological Inquiry* 17(4): 309–318.

(2010). 'The frog in Kierkegaard's beer: Finding meaning in the threat-compensation literature.' *Social and Personality Psychology Compass* 4(10): 889–890.

Ramsden, P., D. Beswick and J. A. Bowden (1986). 'Effects of learning skills interventions on first year students' learning.' *Human Learning* 5(3): 151–164.

Rausch, E. (1966). Das Eigenschaftsproblem in der Gestalttheorie der Wahrnehmung. In W. Metzger and H. Erke (Eds.), *Handbuch der Psychologie. Bd 1/1. Wahrnehmung und Bewußstein* (pp. 866–953). Göttingen, Hogrefe.

Raynor, J. (1969). 'Future orientation and motivation of immediate activity: An elaboration of the theory of achievement motivation.' *Psychological Review* 76: 606–610.

(1970). 'Relationships between achievement-related motives, future orientation, and academic performance.' *Journal of Personality and Social Psychology* 15: 28–33.

(1974a). Future orientation: The cognitive elaboration of a theory of achievement motivation. In J. W. Atkinson and J. Raynor (Eds.), *Motivation and achievement* (pp. 121–154). Washington, DC, V. W. Winston.

Raynor, J. O. (1974b). Motivation and career striving. In J. W. Atkinson and J. O. Raynor (Eds.), *Motivation and achievement* (pp. 369–387). Washington, DC, V. W. Winston.

(1981). Self-possession of attributes, self-evaluation, and future orientation: A theory of adult competence motivation. In J. O. Raynor and E. E. Entin (Eds.), *Motivation, career striving, and aging* (pp. 207–226). Washington DC, Hemisphere Publishing Corporation.

(1982). Future orientation, self-evaluation, and achievement motivation: Use of an expectancy x value theory of personality and change. In N. T. Feather (Ed.), *Expectations and actions* (pp. 97–124). Hillsdale, NJ, Lawrence Erlbaum and Associates.

Renninger, A. (1992). Individual interest and development: Implications for theory and practice. In A. Renninger, S. Hidi and A. Krapp (Eds.), *The role of interest in learning and development* (pp. 361–395). Hillsdale, NJ, Erlbaum.

Renninger, K. A., S. Hidi and A. Krapp (1992). *The role of interest in learning and development*. Hillsdale, NJ, Lawrence Erlbaum Associates.

Richards, J. B., J. A. Litman and Roberts, D. H. (2013). 'Performance characteristics of measurement instruments of epistemic curiosity in third-year medical students.' *Medical Science Educator* 23: 355–363.

Richards, P. S. and A. E. Bergin (1997). *A spiritual strategy for counseling and psychotherapy*. Washington, DC, APA Press.

Riesman, D. (1950). *The lonely crowd: A study of the changing American character*. New Haven, CT, Yale University Press.

Roberts, B. W. and R. W. Robins (2000). 'Broad dispositions, broad aspirations: The intersection of the Big Five dimensions and major life goals.' *Personality and Social Psychology Bulletin*, 26: 1284–1296.

Roberts, R. C. and W. J. Wood (2006). *Intellectual virtues: An essay in regulative epistemology*. Oxford and New York, Oxford University Press.

Rodin, J., K. Rennert and S. K. Solomon (1980). Intrinsic motivation for control: Fact or fiction. In A. Baum and J. E. Singer (Eds.), *Advances in environmental psychology* (Vol. 2, pp. 131–148). Hillsdale, NJ: Taylor and Francis.

Rogers, C. (1963). The actualizing tendency in relation to 'motives' and to consciousness. In M. R. Jones (Ed.), *Nebraska symposium on motivation* (Vol. 11, pp. 1–24). Lincoln, University of Nebraska Press.

Rogers, C. R. (1961). *On becoming a person: A therapist's view of psychotherapy.* Boston, Houghton Mifflin.

Rolls, E. T. (1999). *The brain and emotion.* Oxford and New York, Oxford University Press.

(2005). *Emotion explained.* Oxford and New York, Oxford University Press.

(2008). *Memory, attention, and decision-making: a unifying computational neuroscience approach.* Oxford, Oxford University Press.

Rosen, B. C. (1959). 'Race, ethnicity and the achievement syndrome.' *American Sociological Review* 24: 47–60.

Rosen, B. C. and R. G. D'Andrade (1959). 'The psychosocial origins of achievement motivation.' *Sociometry* 22(3): 185–218.

Rosenthal, D. (1990). A theory of consciousness: ZIF Report 40/1990. Bielefeld, Zentrumflir Interdisziplinaire Forschung (Reprinted in Block, N., O. Flanagan and G. Guzeldere (1997). *The Nature of Consciousness: Philosophical Debates*).

(1993). Thinking as one thinks. In M. Davies and G. W. Humphrey (Eds.), *Consciousness* (pp. 197–223). Oxford, Blackwell.

(1997). A theory of consciousness. In N. Block, O. Flanagan and G. Guzeldere (Eds.), *The nature of consciousness: Philosophical debates* (pp. 729–853). Cambridge MA, MIT Press.

Rothbaum, F., J. R. Weisz and S. S. Snyder (1982). 'Changing the world and changing the self: A two process model perceived control.' *Journal of Personality and Social Psychology* 42: 5–37.

Rothblatt, S. (1989). The idea of a university and its antithesis. *Conversazione.* Bundoora, La Trobe University.

(1997). *The modern university and its discontents: The fate of Newman's legacies in Britain and America.* Cambridge and New York, Cambridge University Press.

Rotter, J. B. (1954). *Social learning and clinical psychology.* New York, Prentice-Hall.

(1966). 'Generalized expectancies for internal versus external control of reinforcement.' *Psychological Monographs* 80: 809.

Royce, J. R. and A. Powell (1983). *Theory of personality and individual differences: Factors, systems, processes.* Englewood Cliffs, NJ, Prentice-Hall.

Russell, J. A. (1994). 'Is there universal recognition of emotion from facial expressions? A review of cross-cultural studies.' *Psychological Bulletin* 115: 102–141.

(2003). 'Core affect and the psychological construction of emotions.' *Psychological Review* 110: 145–172.

(2009). 'Emotion, core affect, and psychological construction.' *Cognition and Emotion* 23: 1259–1283.

Ryan, R. M. (1993). Agency and organization: Intrinsic motivation, autonomy and the self in psychological development. In J. Jacobs (Ed.), *Nebraska symposium on motivation: Developmental perspectives on motivation* (Vol. 40, pp. 1–56). Lincoln, University of Nebraska Press.

(1995). 'Psychological needs and the facilitation of integrative processes.' *Journal of Personality* 63: 397–427.

Ryan, R. M. and E. L. Deci (2000a). When rewards compete with nature: The undermining of intrinsic motivation and self-regulation. In C. Sansone and J. M. Harackiewicz (Eds.), *Intrinsic and extrinsic motivation* (pp. 13–54). San Diego, Academic Press.

(2000b). 'Intrinsic and extrinsic motivations: Classic definitions and new directions.' *Contemporary Educational Psychology* 25: 54–67.

(2000c). 'Self-determination theory and the facilitation of intrinsic motivation, social development, and well-being.' *American Psychologist* 55(1): 68–78.

(2017). *Self-determination theory: basic psychological needs, in motivation, development, and wellness.* New York and London, The Guilford Press.

Ryan, R. M., J. Kuhl and E. L. Deci (1997). 'Nature and autonomy: Organizational view of social and neurological aspects of self-regulation in behavior and development.' *Development and Psychopathology* 9: 701–728.

Ryan, R. M., K. M. Sheldon, T. Kasser and E. L. Deci (1996). All goals are not created equal: An organismic perspective on the nature of goals and their regulations. In J. A. Bargh and P. M. Gollwitzer (Eds.), *The psychology of action: Linking cognition and motivation to behavior* (pp. 7–26). New York, Guilford Press.

Ryle, G. (1949). *The concept of mind.* London, Hutchinson's University Library.

Sampson, R. E. (1989a). 'The challenge of social change for psychology: Globalization and psychology's theory of the person.' *American Psychologist* 44: 914–921.

(1989b). The deconstruction of the self. In J. Shotter and K. J. Gergen (Eds.), *Texts of identity* (pp. 1–19). London, Sage.

Sansone, C. and J. M. Harackiewicz (1996). 'I don't feel like it': The function of interest in self-regulation. In L. L. Martin and A. E. Tesser (Eds.), *Striving and feeling: Interactions among goals, affects, and self regulation* (pp. 203–228). Hillsdale, NJ, Erlbaum.

(1998). '"Reality" is complicated.' *American Psychologist* 53: 673–674.

(Ed.) (2000a). *Intrinsic and extrinsic motivation: The search for optimal motivation and performance.* San Diego, CA and London, Academic Press.

(2000b). Looking beyond rewards: The problem and promise of intrinsic rewards. In C. Sansone and J. M. Harackiewicz (Eds.), *Intrinsic and extrinsic motivation: The search for optimal motivation and performance.* San Diego, CA and London, Academic Press.

(2000c). Controversies and new directions – Is it déjà vu all over again! In C. Sansone and J. M. Harackiewicz (Eds.), *Intrinsic and extrinsic motivation: The search for optimal motivation and performance* (pp. 443–453). San Diego, CA and London, Academic Press.

Sansone, C. and C. Morgan (1992). 'Intrinsic motivation and education: Competence in context.' *Motivation and Emotion* 16: 249–270.

Sartre, J.-P. and P. Mairet (1948). *Existentialism and humanism.* London, Methuen.

Saver, J. L. and A. R. Damasio (1991). 'Preserved access and processing of social knowledge in a patient with acquired sociopathy due to ventromedial frontal damage.' *Neuropsychologia* 29: 1241–1249.

Scarry, E. (1994). *Resisting representation.* New York, Oxford University Press.
(1999). *On beauty and being just.* Princeton, NJ, Princeton University Press.
Schank, R. C. (1990). *Tell me a story: A new look at real and artificial memory.* New York, Scribner.
Schank, R. C. and R. P. Abelson (1977). *Scripts, plans, goals, and understanding: An inquiry into human knowledge structures.* Hillsdale, NJ and New York, L. Erlbaum Associates; distributed by the Halsted Press Division of John Wiley and Sons.
Schank, R. C. and R. C. Schank (1999). *Dynamic memory revisited.* Cambridge and New York, Cambridge University Press.
Schiefele, U., A. Krapp and A. Winteler (1992). Interest as a predictor of academic achievement: A meta-analysis of research. In K. A. Renninger, S. Hidi and A. Krapp (Eds.), *The role of interest in learning and development* (pp. 188–212). Hillsdale, NJ, Erlbaum.
Schrödinger, E. (1944). *What is life?* Cambridge, Cambridge University Press.
(2000). *What is life? With mind and matter and autobiographical sketches.* Cambridge, Cambridge University Press.
Schwarz, N. (1990). Feelings as information: Informational and motivational functions of affective states. In R. M. Sorrentino and E. T. Higgins (Eds.), *Handbook of motivation and cognition: Foundations of social behavior.* (Vol. 2, pp. 527–561). New York, Guilford.
Scott, S. and G. Kelly (1762/1995). *A description of Millenium Hall.* Peterborough, ON, Broadview Press.
Searle, J. (1992). *The rediscovery of the mind.* Cambridge, MA and London, MIT Press.
(2010). Consciousness and the problem of free will. In R. F. Baumeister, A. R. Mele and K. D. Vohs (Eds.), *Free will and consciousness: How might they work?* (pp. 121–134). New York, Oxford University Press.
Searle, J. R. (1983). *Intentionality: An essay in the philosophy of mind.* Cambridge and New York, Cambridge University Press.
Sears, R. R. (1974). Discussion. In B. Weiner (Ed.), *Cognitive views of human motivation* (pp. 86–90). New York, Academic Press.
Seligman, M. E. P. (1975). *Helplessness: On depression, development, and death.* San Francisco and New York, W. H. Freeman (trade distributor, Scribner).
(1998). *Learned optimism.* New York, Pocket Books (Simon and Schuster).
(2002). *Authentic happiness: Using the new positive psychology to realize your potential for lasting fulfillment.* New York, Free Press.
(2006). *Learned optimism: How to change your mind and your life.* New York, Vintage Books.
(2011). *Flourish: A visionary new understanding of happiness and well-being.* New York, Free Press.
Seligman, M. E. P. and M. Csikszentmihalyi (2000). 'Positive psychology: An introduction.' *American Psychologist* 55 (1), 5–14.
Shallice, T. (1988). *From neuropsychology to mental structure.* Cambridge and New York, Cambridge University Press.
Shallice, T. and P. Burgess (1998). The domain of supervisory processes and the temporal organisation of behaviour. In A. C. Roberts, T. W. Robbins and

L. Weiskrantz (Eds.), *The prefrontal cortex: Executive and cognitive functions. Royal Society (Great Britain). Discussion Meeting* (pp. 22–35). New York and Oxford, Oxford University Press.

Sheldon, K. M. and A. J. Elliot (1999). 'Goal striving, need-satisfaction, and longitudinal well-being: The self-concordance model.' *Journal of Personality and Social Psychology* 76: 482–497.

Sheldon, K. M., T. B. Kashdan and M. F. Steger, Eds. (2011). *Designing positive psychology*. Oxford and New York, Oxford University Press.

Sheldon, K. M., R. M. Ryan, E. L. Deci and T. Kasser (2004). 'The independent effects of goal contents and motives on well-being: It's both what you pursue and why you pursue it.' *Personality and Social Psychology Bulletin* 30: 475–486.

Silberman, I. (2005). 'Religion as a meaning system: Implications for the new millennium.' *Journal of Social Issues* 61(4): 641–663.

Simon, D., C. J. Snow and S. J. Read (2004). 'The redux of cognitive consistency theories: Evidence judgments by constraint satisfaction.' *Journal of Personality and Social Psychology* 86(6): 814–837.

Simon, H. A. (1967). 'Motivational and emotional controls of cognition.' *Psychological Review* 74: 29–39.

Sirigu, A., E. Daprati, S. Ciancia, P. Giraux, N. Nighoghossian, A. Posada and P. Haggard (2003). 'Altered awareness of voluntary action after damage to the parietal cortex.' *Nature Neuroscience* 7: 80–84.

Skår, J. (2003). 'Self-organization as an actual theme.' *Philosophical Transactions: Mathematical, Physical and Engineering Sciences: No. 1807, Self-Organization: The Quest for the Origin and Evolution of Structure* 361(1807): 1049–1056.

Skinner, B. F. (1957). *Verbal behavior*. New York, Appleton-Century-Crofts.

Smith, B. (1988). Gestalt theory: An essay in philosophy. In B. Smith and C. Ehrenfels (Eds.), *Foundations of Gestalt theory* (pp. 11–81). München, Philosophia Verlag.

Smith, B. and C. Ehrenfels (1988). *Foundations of Gestalt theory*. München, Philosophia Verlag.

Smith, C. P., Ed. (1992). *Motivation and personality: Handbook of thematic content analysis*. Cambridge and New York, Cambridge University Press.

Sokolov, E. N. (2002). *The orienting response in information processing*. Mahwah, NJ, Lawrence Erlbaum Associates.

Sokolov, E. N. and O. S. Vinogradova (1975). *Neuronal mechanisms of the orienting reflex*. Hillsdale, NJ and New York, Lawrence Erlbaum Associates; distributed by the Halsted Press Division of Wiley.

Sommerhoff, G. (2002). *Understanding consciousness: Its function and brain processes*. London, Sage Publications.

Soon, C. S., M. Brass, H.-J. Heinze and J.-D. Haynes (2008). 'Unconscious determinants of free decisions in the human brain.' *Nature: Neuroscience* 11: 543–545.

Sorrentino, R. M., C. J. R. Roney and S. E. Hanna (1992). Uncertainty orientation. In C. P. Smith (Ed.), *Motivation and personality: Handbook of thematic content analysis* (pp. 419–427). Cambridge, Cambridge University Press.

Spence, K. W. (1956). *Behavior theory and conditioning*. New Haven, CT, Yale University Press.

Sperry, R., N. Miner and R. Myers (1955). 'Visual pattern perception following subpail slicing and tantalum wire implantations in the visual cortex.' *Journal of Comparative and Physiological Psychology* 48: 50–58.

Spielberger, C. D. and L. M. Starr (1994). Curiosity and exploratory behavior. In H. F. J. O'Neil and M. Drillings (Eds.), *Motivation: Theory and research*. (pp. 221–243). Hillsdale, NJ, Erlbaum.

Starr, L. M. (1992). *Assessment of curiosity as a multifaceted construct*, Tampa, University Press of South Florida.

Steele, C. M. (1988). The psychology of self-affirmation: Sustaining the integrity of the self. In L. Berkowitz (Ed.), *Advances in experimental social psychology* (Vol. 21, pp. 261–302). San Diego, CA, Academic Press.

Steele, C. M. and T. J. Liu (1983). 'Dissonance processes as self-affirmation.' *Journal of Personality and Social Psychology* 45(1): 5–19.

Steele, C. M., S. J. Spencer and M. Lynch (1993). 'Self-image resilience and dissonance: The role of affirmational resources.' *Journal of Personality and Social Psychology* 64: 885–896.

Stone, J., E. Aronson, A. L. Crain, M. P. Winslow and C. B. Fried (1994). 'Inducing hypocrisy as a means of encouraging young adults to use condoms.' *Personality and Social Psychology Bulletin* 1: 116–128.

Stringer, C. and R. McKie (1996). *African exodus: The origins of modern humanity*. London, Jonathon Cape.

Surian, L., S. Caldi and D. Sperber (2007). 'Attribution of beliefs by 13-month-old infants.' *Psychological Science* 18: 580–586.

Swartz, H. and G. L. Clore (1983). 'Mood, missattribution, and judgments of well-being: Informative and directive functions of affective states.' *Journal of Personality and Social Psychology* 45: 513–523.

Tawney, R. H. (1938). *Religion and the rise of capitalism: A historical study*. Harmondsworth, Penguin.

Taylor, S. E. (1989). *Positive illusions: Creative self-deception and the healthy mind*. New York, Basic Books.

Thagard, P. N. (2002). 'Emotional gestalts: Appraisal, change, and the dynamics of affect.' *Personality and Social Psychology Review* 6(4): 274–282.

Thibodeau, R. and E. Aronson (1992). 'Taking a closer look: Reasserting the role of self-concept in dissonance theory.' *Personality and Social Psychology Bulletin* 18: 591–602.

Thomas, E. J. and A. Zander (1959). 'The relationship of goal structure to motivation under extreme conditions.' *Journal of Individual Psychology* 15: 121–127.

Thorndike, E. L. (1911). *Animal intelligence: Experimental studies*. New York, The Macmillan Company.

(1913). *The psychology of learning*. New York, Teachers College, Columbia University.

(1935). *The psychology of wants, interests and attitudes*. New York, D. Appleton-Century.

Thrash, T. M. and A. J. Elliot (2001). Delimiting and integrating achievement motive and goal constructs. In A. Efflides, J. Kuhl and R. M. Sorrentino

(Eds.), *Trends and prospects in motivation research* (pp. 3–21). Dordrecht, Boston and London, Kluwer Academic Publishers.

Tice, D. M. (2009). How emotions affect self-regulation. In J. P. Forgas, R. Baumeister and D. M. Tice (Eds.), *Psychology of self-regulation* (pp. 201–215). New York and London, Psychology Press.

Tillich, P. (1963). *Christianity and the encounter of the world religions*. New York, Columbia University Press.

Todt, E. and S. Schreiber (1998). Development of interests. In L. Hoffmann, A. Krapp, K. A. Renninger and J. Baunert (Eds.), *Interest and learning: Proceedings of the Seeon Conference on Interest and Gender* (pp. 25–40). Keil, Germany, IPN.

Tolman, E. C. (1925). 'Purpose and cognition: The determiners of animal learning.' *Psychological Review* 32: 285–297.

(1926). 'A behavioristic theory of ideas.' *Psychological Review* 33: 352–369.

(1927). 'A behaviorist's definition of consciousness.' *Psychological Review* 34: 433–439.

(1932/1949). *Purposive behavior in animals and men*. Berkeley, University of California Press.

(1948). 'Cognitive maps in rats and men.' *Psychological Review* 55: 189–208.

Tomasello, M. (1999). *The cultural origins of human cognition*. Cambridge, MA, Harvard University Press.

Tomasello, M. and J. Call (1997). *Primate cognition*. New York and Oxford, Oxford University Press.

Tomasello, M., M. Carpenter, J. Call, T. Behne and H. Moll (2005). 'Understanding and sharing intentions: The origins of cultural cognition.' *Behavioral and Brain Sciences* 28: 675–691.

Tomasello, M., A. Kruger and H. Ratner (1993). 'Cultural learning.' *Behavioral and Brain Sciences* 16: 495–552.

Tomkins, S. S. (1962–1963). *Affect, imagery, consciousness* (Vols. 1 and 2). New York, Springer.

Tononi, G. (2004). 'An information integration theory of consciousness.' *BMC Neuroscience* 5(42)22 pages.

(2005). 'Consciousness, information integration, and the brain.' *Progress in Brain Research* 150 (The Boundaries of Consciousness: Neurobiology and Neuropathology): 109–126.

Tononi, G. and G. M. Edelman (1998). 'Consciousness and complexity.' *Science* 282(5395): 1846–1851.

Tononi, G. and C. Koch (2008). 'The neural correlates of consciousness: An update.' *Annals of the New York Academy of Sciences* 1124: 239–261.

Treisman, A. and G. Gelade (1980). 'A feature-integration theory of attention.' *Cognitive Psychology* 12: 97–136.

Treisman, A. M. (1960). 'Contextual cues in selective listening.' *Quarterly Journal of Experimental Psychology* 12: 242–248.

Tulving, E. (1983). *Elements of episodic memory*. New York, Oxford University Press.

Turing, A. (1952). 'The chemical basis for morphogenesis.' *Philosophical transactions of the Royal Society* 237: 37–72.

Turner, H. (1998). *The Roots of Science: An Investigative Journey through the World's Religions*. Auckland, The Deepsight Trust.

Tweney, R. D. (1997). 'Jonathan Edwards and determinism.' *Journal for the History of the Behavioral Sciences* 33: 365.

Tweney, R. D. and A. B. Wachholtz (2004). 'Wegner's "illusion" anticipated: Jonathan Edwards on the will.' *Behavioral and Brain Sciences* 27(5): 676.

Updike, J. (1989). *Self-consciousness: Memoirs*. New York, Knopf.

(1998). *Bech at Bay*. London, Hamish Hamilton.

Van Gulick, R. R. (2007). Who's in charge here? And who's doing all the work? In N. C. Murphy and W. R. Stoeger (Eds.), *Evolution and emergence: Systems, organisms, persons* (pp. 74–87). Oxford and New York, Oxford University Press.

Van Yperen, N. W. (2006). 'A novel approach to assessing achievement goals in the context of the 2X2 framework: Identifying distinct profiles of individuals with different dominant achievement goals.' *Personality and Social Psychology Bulletin* 32: 1432–1445.

Van Yperen, N. W., A. J. Elliot and F. Ansell (2009). 'The influence of mastery-avoidance goals on performance improvement.' *European Journal of Social Psychology* 39: 932–943.

Vansteenkiste, M., J. Simons, W. Lens, B. Soenens, L. Matos and M. Lacan (2004). 'Less is sometimes more: Goal content matters.' *Journal of Educational Psychology* 96(4): 755–764.

Velmans, P. H. (2000). *Understanding consciousness*. London, Routledge.

(2003). 'Preconscious free will.' *Journal of Consciousness Studies* 10(12): 42–61.

Veroff, J. (1969). 'Social comparison and the development of achievement motivation.' In C. Smith (Ed.), *Achievement related motives in children* (pp. 46–100).

Verstegen, I. (2005). *Arnheim, Gestalt and art: A psychological theory*. Wien and New York, Springer.

Vittersø, J., Y. Søholt, A. Hetland, I. A. Thoresen and E. Røysamb (2010). 'Was Hercules happy? Some answers from a functional model of human well-being.' *Social Indicators Research* 95: 1–18.

Vohs, K. D. and R. F. Baumeister, Eds. (2010). *Handbook of self-regulation: Research, theory, and applications* (2nd ed). New York, Guilford.

Vohs, K. D., R. F. Baumeister, B. J. Schmeichel, J. M. Twenge, N. M. Nelson and D. M. Tice (2008). 'Making choices impairs subsequent self-control: A limited-resource account of decision making, self-regulation, and active initiative.' *Journal of Personality and Social Psychology* 94: 883–898.

von Ehrenfels, C. (1890). 'Über Gestaltqualtitaten.' *Vierteljahrsschriftfur wissenschaftliche (Philosophical Psychology)*: 249–292.

(1890/1988). On "gestalt qualities". In B. Smith (Eds.), *Foundations of Gestalt theory* (pp. 82–117). Munchen, Wien, Philosopia Verlag.

(1916/1988). Gestalt level and gestalt purity. In B. Smith (Eds.), *Foundations of Gestalt theory* (pp. 118–120). Munchen, Wien, Philosopia Verlag.

(1937). 'On gestalt-qualities.' *Psychological Review* 44(6): 521–524.

Vytal, K. and S. Hamann (2010). 'Neuroimaging support for discrete neural correlates of basic emotions: A Voxel-based meta-analysis.' *Journal of Cognitive Neuroscience* 22(12): 2864–2885.

Watson, J. B. (1913). 'Psychology as the behaviorist views it.' *Psychological Review* 20: 158–177.

Weary, G. and J. A. Edwards (1994). 'Individual differences in causal uncertainty.' *Journal of Personality and Social Psychology* 67: 308–318.

(1996). Causal uncertainty beliefs and related goal structures. In R. Sorrentino and E. T. Higgins (Eds.), *Handbook of motivation and cognition: The interpersonal context* (Vol. 3, pp. 148–181). New York, Guilford Press.

Weary, G., L. A. Vaughn, B. D. Stewart and Edwards, John A. (2006). 'Adjusting for the correspondence bias: Effects of causal uncertainty, cognitive busyness, and causal strength of situational information.' *Journal of Experimental Social Psychology* 42: 87–94.

Weber, M., T. Parsons and R. H. Tawney (1930). *The Protestant ethic and the spirit of capitalism.* London, G. Allen & Unwin, Ltd.

Webster, D. M. and A. W. Kruglanski (1994). 'Individual differences in need for cognitive closure.' *Journal of Personality & Social Psychology* 67: 1049–1062.

Wegner, D. M. (2002). *The illusion of conscious will.* Cambridge, MA and London, MIT Press.

Wegner, D. M. and commentators (2004). 'Precis of *The illusion of conscious will* with open peer commentary.' *Behavioral and Brain Sciences* 27: 649–694.

Weil, S. (1951/1979). *Waiting on God.* London, Routledge and Kegan Paul.

Weiner, B. (1972). *Theories of motivation: From mechanism to cognition.* Chicago, Markham Pub. Co.

Weiner, B., Ed. (1974a). *Achievement motivation and attribution theory.* Morristown, NJ, General Learning Press.

Ed. (1974b). *Cognitive views of human motivation.* New York, Academic Press.

(1974c). An attributional interpretation of expectacy-value theory. In B. Weiner (Ed.), *Cognitive views of human motivation* (pp. 51–70). New York, Academic Press.

(1979). 'A theory of motivation for some classroom experience.' *Journal of Educational Psychology* 71: 3–25.

(1985a). 'An attributional theory of achievement motivation and emotion.' *Psychological Review* 92: 548–573.

(1985b). '"Spontaneous" causal search.' *Psychological Bulletin* 97(74–84).

(1986). *An attributional theory of motivation and emotion.* New York, Springer-Verlag.

(1995). *Judgements of responsibility: A foundation for a theory of social conduct.* New York, Guilford Press.

(2005). Motivation from an attribution perspective and the social psychology of perceived competence. In A. J. Elliot and C. S. Dweck (Eds.), *Handbook of competence and motivation* (pp. 73–84). New York and London, The Guildford Press.

(2010). 'The development of an attribution-based theory of motivation: A history of ideas.' *Educational Psychologist* 45(1): 28–36.

Weiner, B., I. Frieze, A. Kukla, L. Reed, R. Stanley and R. M. Rosenbaum (1971). Perceiving the causes of success and failure. In E. E. Jones, D. E. Kanouse, H. H. Kelly et al. (Eds.), *Attribution: Perceiving the causes of behaviour* (pp. 95–120). Morristown, NJ, General Learning Press.

Weiner, B. and A. Kukla (1970). 'An attributional analysis of achievement motivation.' *Journal of Personality and Social Psychology* 15: 1–20.

Weiner, B., D. Russell and D. Lerman (1978). Affective consequences of causal ascriptions. In J. H. Harvey, W. Ickes and R. F. Kidd (Eds.), *New directions in attribution research* (Vol. 2, pp. 59–90). Hillsdale, NJ, Lawrence Erlbaum Associates.

Werner, H. (1948). *Comparative psychology of mental development.* New York, International Universities Press.

Wertheimer, M. (1912). 'Experimentelle Studien uber das Sehen von Bewegung.' *Zeitschrift fur Psychologie* 61: 161–265.

(1922/1938). The general theoretical situation. In W. D. Ellis (Ed.), *A source book of Gestalt psychology* (pp. 12–16). New York, Humanities Press.

(1923/1938). Laws of organization in perceptual forms. In W. D. Ellis (Ed.), *A source book of Gestalt psychology* (pp. 71–88). London, Routledge and Kegan Paul.

(1945). *Productive thinking.* New York, Harper.

Wesley, J. and C. Wesley (1747). *Hymns and sacred poems.* Dublin, Samuel Powell.

West, R., H. Schwarb and B. N. Johnson (2010). 'The influence of age and individual differences in executive function on stimulus processing in the oddball task.' *Cortex*: 46(4 Special issue: The Cognitive Neuroscience of Aging): 550–563.

White, G., F. Greenoak and R. Mabey (1986). *The journals of Gilbert White.* London, Century.

White, R. W. (1959). 'Motivation reconsidered: The concept of competence.' *Psychological Review* 66: 297–333.

(1960). Competence and the psychosexual stages of development. In M. R. Jones (Ed.), *Nebraska symposium on motivation* (pp. 97–140). Lincoln, University of Nebraska Press.

(1972). *The enterprise of living: Growth and organization in personality.* New York, Holt, Rinehart and Winston.

Wicklund, R. A. and P. M. Gollwitzer (1982). *Symbolic self-completion.* Hillsdale, NJ, Lawrence Erlbaum Associates.

Wilson, A. N. (2003). *Iris Murdoch, as I knew her.* London, Hutchinson.

Wilson, T. D., Centerbar, D. B., Kermer, D. A., & Gilbert, D. T. (2005). 'The pleasures of uncertainty: Prolonging positive moods in ways people do not anticipate.' *Journal of Personality and Social Psychology* 88: 5–21.

Winter, D. G. (1973). *The power motive.* New York, Free Press.

(1992a). Power motivation revisited. In C. P. E. Smith (Ed.), *Motivation and personality: Handbook of thematic content analysis* (pp. 301–310). Cambridge, Cambridge University Press.

(1992b). Responsibility. In C. P. Smith (Ed.), *Motivation and personality: Handbook of thematic content analysis* (pp. 500–505). Cambridge, Cambridge University Press.

Winterbottom, M. R. (1958). The relation of need for achievement to learning experiences in independence and mastery. In J. W. Atkinson (Ed.), *Motives and fantasy, action and society* (pp. 453–478). Princeton, NJ, Nan Nostrand.

Wolfe, J. M. (1994b). 'Guided search II: A revised model of visual search.' *Psychonomic Bulletin and Review* 1: 202–238.

(1998). Visual search. In H. Pashler (Ed.), *Attention* (pp. 13–73). Hove, East Sussex, Psychology Press.

Wolfe, J. M., K. R. Cave and S. L. Franzel (1989). 'Guided search: An alternative to the feature integration model for visual search.' *Journal of Experimental Psychology: Human Perception and Performance* 15: 419–433.

Wolford, G., M. B. Miller and M. S. Gazzaniga (2004). Split decisions. In M. S. Gazzaniga (Ed.), *The cogntive neurosciences III* (pp. 1189–1200). Cambridge, MA, MIT Press.

Wolpert, D. and R. Miall (1996). 'Forward models for physiological motor control.' *Neural Networks* 9: 1265–1279.

Wong, P. T. P. (1998c). Spirituality, meaning, and successful aging. In P. T. P. Wong and P. S. Fry (Eds.), *The human quest for meaning: A handbook of psychological research and clinical applications* (pp. 359–394). Mahwah, NJ and London, Lawrence Erlbaum Associates.

(2011). 'Positive psychology 2.0: Towards a balanced interactive model of the good life.' *Canadian Psychology* 52(2): 69–81

Wong, P. T. P. and P. S. Fry, Eds. (1998). *The human quest for meaning: A handbook of psychological research and clinical applications.* Mahwah, NJ and London, Lawrence Erlbaum Associates.

Wood, N. and N. Cowan (1995). 'The cocktail party phenomenon revisited: How frequent are attention shifts to one's name in an irrelevant auditory channel?' *Journal of Experimental Psychology: Learning, Memory, and Cognition* 21(1): 255–260.

Woodworth, R. S. (1918). *Dynamic psychology.* New York, Columbia University Press.

(1921). *Psychology: A study of mental life.* New York, Henry Holt.

(1932). *Psychology: A study of mental life.* London, Methuen.

(1958). *Dynamics of behavior.* New York, Holt.

Wordsworth, W. (1977). *The Poems.* Harmondsworth, Penguin Classics.

Young, P. T. (1949). 'Food-seeking drive, affective process, and learning.' *Psychological Review* 56: 98–121.

Zachar, P. and R. Ellis, Eds. (2012). *Emotional theories of Jaak Panksepp and Jim Russell.* Amsterdam, John Benjamin.

Zajonc, R. B. (1968). Cognitive theories in social psychology. In G. Lindzey and E. Aronson (Eds.), *Handbook of social psychology* (2nd ed., Vol. 1, pp. 320–411). Reading, MA, Addison-Wesley.

(1980). 'Feeling and thinking: Preferences need no inferences.' *American Psychologist* 35: 151–175.

(1984). 'On the primacy of affect.' *American Psychologist* 39: 117–123.

(1990). 'Leon Festinger (1919–1989).' *American Psychologist* 45: 661–662.

(1998). Emotions. In D. Gilbert, S. T. Fiske and G. Lindzey (Eds.), *Handbook of social psychology* (pp. 591–632). New York, McGraw-Hill.

Zanna, M. P. and J. Cooper (1974). 'Dissonance and the pill: An attributional approach to studying the arousal properties of dissonance.' *Journal of Personality and Social Psychology* 29: 703–709.

(1976). Dissonance and the attribution process. In J. H. Harvey, W. J. Ickes and R. F. Kidd (Eds.), *New directions in attribution research* (Vol. 1, pp. 199–217). Hillsdale, NJ, Erlbaum.

Zanna, M. P., E. T. Higgins and P. A. Taves (1975). Dissonance and the phenomenology of arousal: A test of the aversive nature of dissonance arousal. Unpublished manuscript, Princeton University.

Zeigarnik, B. (1927). 'Das Behalten erledigten und unerledigten Handlungen.' *Psychologische Forschung* 9: 1–85.

Zuckerman, M. (1994). *Behavioral expressions and biosocial bases of sensation seeking*. Cambridge and New York, Cambridge University Press.

Index